The Story
of the Last
Thought

EDGAR HILSENRATH

The Story
of the Last
Thought

TRANSLATED BY NIVENE RAAFAT

OWL OF MINERVA

Author's website:
www.hilsenrath.de

Publisher's website:
www.owlofminerva.net

Website for this work:

The Story of the Last Thought
http://doi.org/10.4444/10.6

Copyright © 1989 Freundeskreis Edgar Hilsenrath e.V.

English translation by Nivene Raafat.

English translation © 2015 Freundeskreis Edgar Hilsenrath e.V.

 Owl of Minerva Press
First edition
Berlin 2017

doi: 10.4444/10.6
ISBN 978-3-943334-26-5

Prologue

"I am the storyteller inside your mind. You can call me Meddah.[1]

Hush now, Thovma Khatisian. Don't make a sound. Not long left now. Soon it will be time. And then … as your light gradually begins to fade … I will tell you a story."

"What kind of story, Meddah?"

"The Story of the Last Thought. I will start by saying, 'Once upon a time there was a Last Thought. It lay inside a cry of fear where it had concealed itself – "

"Why, Meddah?"

"Well, why do you think, Thovma Khatisian? What sort of a question is that? Are you out of your mind? It's obvious why. The thought concealed itself there so it could break free together with the final cry of fear … through your gaping mouth."

"Where to, Meddah?"

"To Hayastan."

---

1 A detailed glossary can be found at the end of this book.

"So it's going to Hayastan?"

"Yes, Thovma Khatisian."

"To the land of my forebears? The land that lies at the foot of Mount Ararat?"

"That's right."

"Precisely there?"

"Where else should it go, Thovma?"

"To the Holy Land of the Armenians, desecrated by the Turks?"

"Desecrated, Thovma. Desecrated by the Turks."

"To the place where Christ was crucified – for the second time?"

"You've got it."

"Perhaps for the last time? For good!"

"No one knows."

"Tell me, Meddah, what actually happened?"

"What do you mean, Thovma?"

"Where are the Armenians from Hayastan?"

"They disappeared, Thovma."

"But that's not true, Meddah."

"And why isn't it true?"

"Because I know that they are still there. Their desecrated bodies are rotting deep beneath the holy soil."

"You're right, Thovma. Indeed, you are not as stupid as you look. You seem to know a great deal."

"I know quite a lot, Meddah."

"So why are you asking me?"

"No reason, Meddah."

"Do you take me for a fool?"

"No, Meddah."

"Tell me, Meddah …"

"What is it now?"

"When my Last Thought escapes to freedom … will it be able to find Hayastan?"

"Oh, Thovma Khatisian. What a silly question. Of course it will find it."

"Are you sure?"

"I'd bet my life on it."

"Tell it to go to the place where the sunflowers stretch right up to heaven."

"Right up to heaven?"

"Or to the gates of paradise."

"But, Thovma Khatisian, that is nothing but a wild exaggeration."

"You think so?"

"Absolutely."

"Hayastan … where the watermelons are rounder and bigger and juicier than the ass of the fattest girl alive?"

"That's Hayastan."

"Where bulgur is mixed with honey? And where the juice of ripe mulberries dries in rooftop gardens?"

"Yes, Thovma Khatisian."

"Where milk is shaken inside goatskin pouches until it turns into butter?"

"That's it. That's Hayastan."

"Or in crock butter churns like my grandmother used to have? She used to rock it on her lap just like she used to rock my father. And at the same time she would sing the butter song: '*Garak geschinem* … I'm making butter … making butter for Hagob … making butter'?"

"That's right."

"Where the women have beautiful, taut breasts. So pearly and juicy … like fresh pomegranates covered in early morning dew?"

"Only when they are young and sweaty."

"Well, that's irrelevant."

"Irrelevant, Thovma Khatisian."

"Where men of all ages tiptoe around the village well when the women are fetching water to watch as they bend right over the edge of the wall, farther than any other women bend anywhere else in the world?"

"Yes."

"Hayastan? Where the mountains reach up and touch the clouds. Where strong men take hold of the *kutan,* that large, Armenian plow – right there on their pitiful fields – to race the oxen up and down the rows. Where my great-grandfather would thresh the corn and throw the chaff into the air, which the Armenian wind would simply carry away – up to the mountains or down to the sea. Where there were fat-tailed sheep and mutton and yogurt. Do you remember? The yogurt that Grandmother used to call *madsun?*"

"*Madsun.* I remember it well."

"Tell me, Meddah. How do I look?"

"You look hideous, Thovma Khatisian. No woman could love you except your mother. Your eyes are slightly askew and both fixed on the floor. Pungent saliva is trickling out of the half-open mouth that you will soon wrench open to release the Last Thought, which – as I already told you – will fly off into the air with your final cry of fear."

"And my hands? Tell me, Meddah. How do they look?"

"They have stopped sweating. You're as good as dead."

"And my feet?"

"The same."

"You know, Thovma Khatisian, you really aren't that old. Born in 1915 – that makes you 73. You're just a little, snotty-nosed kid who should still be furiously pissing into the wind. What on earth's happened to you?"

"I don't know, Meddah."

"Your forebears were quite different, Thovma Khatisian. Particularly one: your grandfather's great-grandfather. He was cut from a completely different cloth. He even lived to be over 100."

"Yes, Meddah."

"It's true, Thovma Khatisian. These Armenians from Hayastan live to a grand old age because of all the fucking they do and because they drink pail-loads of the yoghurt that they call *madsun*."

"Yes, Meddah."

"They only die young when the Turks or the Kurds cut their heads off."

"Yes, Meddah."

"Or kill them some other way, with a curved butcher's knife, say."

"Yes, Meddah."

"You see, Thovma Khatisian. This one particular forebear, by that I mean your grandfather's great-grandfather, he was cut from a completely different cloth. Even at the age of ninety-seven he was still able to have it off twice a day: once before he went to sleep and once early in the morning."

"How did he manage it, Meddah?"

"Well, before he went to sleep he would do it with your grandfather's great-grandmother because, like all Armenians, he was smart. Everyone knows Armenians are smarter than even the Jews or the Greeks. Your grandfather's great-grandfather would say to himself, 'If I don't give her one tonight, tomorrow instead of honey she'll stir some dried cow shit into my bulgur, and I'd rather not risk that, even though my gut is still in fine fettle and I can still break wind like a young whippersnapper of seventy-three.'"

"Is that true?"

"It is."

"And what about early in the morning?"

"While your grandfather's great-grandmother was still sleeping, your forebear would sneak out to the stable where he would have it off with a young Kurdish girl. She was nine and had a hole the size of a dove's egg. That's right, Thovma Khatisian, that's the kind of man your forebear was. But one time the little Kurdish girl refused and stood defiantly against the back stable wall."

"And then what happened?"

"Your forebear, full of rage, ran toward her with his stiff member. But the little minx quickly jumped out of the way, and so your forebear ended up ramming a cock-sized hole in the stable wall. That's the kind of man he was."

"Was the stable wall made of wood?"

"No, it was made of clay and the dried cow dung, which the people in that region called *tezek.*"

"Enough, Meddah. Tell me again how I look."

"But I've already told you. You look like a man whom only his mother could love; in a mother's eyes, even a dirty old codger like you is still the sweetest little angel. Your mother doesn't see your bulging eyes or smell your malodorous saliva. Can you feel it, Thovma Khatisian? Your mother is with you now. She's stroking your hands, your hands that are no longer able to perspire. And she's stroking your cold feet. She's stroking your bald, ugly head, and she's kissing your half-dead eyes."

"Where is she?"

"She's already gone, Thovma Khatisian."

"Tell me, Meddah, how did I come into this world? I never knew my mother."

"Hayastan gave birth to you, Thovma Khatisian, as did the wind from the mountains of Kurdistan. The dust gave birth to you, and the blazing sun that shone on the country road that day."

"So I never had a mother?"

"You never had a mother."

"Is that the truth?"

"That is the truth.

And yet that cannot be the truth, Thovma Khatisian, as even our Savior Jesus Christ was born of a woman. Or do you believe that the Spirit of God planted his seed in the rays of the sun? Or in the wind ushered down from the mountains of Kurdistan? Or in the dust on a miserable country road on that day in Hayastan?"

"No, Meddah."

"You see, Thovma Khatisian, a woman gave birth to you, and yet you never had a mother. At least, not one that sang you lullabies, or breastfed you or rocked you to sleep."

"And yet someone must have breastfed me."

"Of course someone breastfed you. But it was not your biological mother."

"Who was it?"

"A Turkish woman. She was the one who found you on that dusty country road and took you with her. She was the one who breastfed you and rocked you to sleep. And she sang you many lullabies."

"Armenian lullabies?"

"No. Turkish ones."

"Are they just as tender as Armenian lullabies?"

"They are just as sweet.

This is how I imagine it, Thovma Khatisian: I think that you, Thovma Khatisian, were born via caesarian."

"How can you say such nonsense, Meddah? Who would be able to perform a caesarian on a miserable country road?"

"A Turkish man, Thovma Khatisian. They were experts in caesarians. I can picture it now: It's a hot day in August 1915. Thousands of starving Armenians are staggering along a country road towards Mesopotamia, still in the Armenian highlands close to the Kurdistan Mountains, being lashed by the whips of the Turkish gendarmes. Your mother is among them. Yes, your mother. She's nine months pregnant. She starts to feel contractions. It's around midday."

"Don't stop, Meddah."

"I don't know exactly how many Armenians were on the country road that day, but there must have been a few thousand. They had been walking for weeks because the *saptiehs* – as the Turkish gendarmes were called – were deliberately marching them in one large circle. These Armenians came from all over: from Erzurum and Moush, from Mersivan and Kharput, from cities, villages and market towns, some large, some small. Hundreds of thousands of them had been captured, perhaps even millions, but there were not very many on that day. As I said, perhaps a few thousand, for this was just a single country road."

"Speak, storyteller. Tell me, my Meddah, can you also see my father? Is he there?"

"No, Thovma Khatisian. Your father was not in this transport as the saptiehs had shot dead all the Armenian men; well, any man who could still just about stand up straight, was not yet gray-haired or who still had teeth."

"So they shot my father?"

"No, Thovma Khatisian. You father was an exception."

"Why?"

"I'll tell you later."

"Later?"

"Yes. Later.

So there was your mother. She was larger than most of the other women in the transport."

"Did she have a pretty face?"

"She had no face at all. All she had left were eyes."

"What kind of eyes?"

"The reflective eyes of a pregnant woman. Large, window-like eyes through which you can see the child she's carrying inside. And at the heart of those two windows lay the small, unborn Thovma Khatisian, waving."

"Was it time?"

"It was time.

It was around midday, Thovma Khatisian. Through your mother's eyes you could see the long line of women, children and old men, and you thought to yourself, 'Where are all these strange people going? Why is the sun shining if no one is laughing? Why is it so hot? And why is everyone marching barefoot? Why isn't there any water, and why are the saptiehs lashing out at the marchers when they aren't even trying to put up a fight? Aren't they marching fast enough already? And why do they need to march faster if they are only being forced to march in a circle? Why has mother stopped? And why has she suddenly dropped to her knees? Look out, Mother! Be careful! Don't let me disappear from sight.'

As your mother collapsed and writhed on the floor, screaming in agony, and as she finally realized that she would have to give birth in the middle of that country road, she used her last ounce of strength to rip off her shalvar trousers before lying down on her back in the dusty road, spreading her legs apart and lifting her feet up towards the sun and the sky.

Yes. That's how it happened," said the storyteller. "The guards were furious because your mother was holding up the entire transport, and one of the saptiehs jerked his horse around violently and galloped to the point on the country road where she lay, screaming in the dust, her feet stretched up towards the sky and the sun. He drew his saber from its sheath and jumped down off his horse."

"Did the saptieh cut my mother's head off?"

"No, Thovma Khatisian. Although saptiehs tend to decapitate Armenians often, they also enjoy cutting open bellies, especially those of pregnant women. They seem to take pleasure in it. But your mother, Thovma Khatisian, she was lucky. The saptieh placed the tip of his saber on her naked belly, but in more of a playful than an angry manner, and he cut her open, but not too deep. And look, can you see?"

"See what?"

"There you are, Thovma Khatisian. You simply slipped out of your mother's belly. And when the saptieh cut through the umbilical cord with his saber for the sheer joy of it, you started to cry out. You cried like the first rooster that God created to stand on the world's first ever dunghill to greet the first ever day. And the saptieh looked, laughed and re-sheathed his saber as deep down he was no more malicious than most servants of the state who obediently go about their duties.

Of course, it may have also happened differently," said the story-teller. "Perhaps your mother survived that hot day without letting go of you forever, and the transport only stopped walking in the evening as darkness gradually began to set in. By that time even the saptiehs were tired, and their horses were starting to protest. They ordered the prisoners to sit so that they could give some food and water to their steeds.

In that region," said the storyteller, "night falls quickly, as every evening the Kurds high up in the mountains hurry to pull the sun back down from the sky using their goat's-hair ropes out of fear that the devil worshippers, of which there were many in the region, might steal it. At night the Kurds hide the sun in a large tent, which is also made of black goat's hair, and only release it back into the sky when the golden eagle awakens from its slumber and lets out a cry that echoes far across the mountains and can be heard down in the chasms and valleys and pastures of

Hayastan.

Thus, night fell quickly on the transport," said the storyteller. "Your mother lay down to sleep together with the others. They all lay in the dusty road. Some managed to actually sleep, others just lay there numb. Some lay silent, others cried out for water. When night reached the depths of total darkness, your mother began to feel the contractions."

"So I was born in the middle of the night, whilst the Kurds had the sun hidden in a large, black tent?"

"That's right, Thovma Khatisian. As your mother realized that you were slowly disappearing from the glint in her eye – that you were retreating back, deep into her womb, preparing to force your way out into the world as a fully-formed being – she staggered to her feet and squatted down in a ditch along the side of the road."

"So she gave birth to me in a squatting position?"

"Many women in that region give birth in a squatting position."

"How does that work, Meddah?"

"They simply crap their children out."

"And what happened to me?"

"Well, this and that happened, Thovma Khatisian. Your mother simply crapped you out. She had no other choice. And suddenly there you were, lying there in a ditch at the side of the road, a piece of crying shit in the night. The saptiehs didn't even notice you as there were several women in the transport who had small children that cried just like you. In the morning, after the Kurds had released the sun back into the sky, and the light of dawn had crept down from the canyons and onto the country road, the pitiful horde of prisoners moved on. They simply left you behind."

"Why didn't my mother take me with her?"

"I don't know. Perhaps she was convinced that that forsaken country road was your only hope. And she was right, Thovma Khatisian, as later that day the Holy Virgin Mary came to you. She came in the shape of a Turkish Muslim who was with her husband named Yussuf. And Mary recognized you instantly; Yussuf also recognized you and said to his wife:

– Look there. That baby is the most powerless witness in the world and also the most ignorant: He doesn't even know what he has seen.

– Whether he knows it or not is of no importance, said Mary. All that matters is that one day he will bear witness to the fact that not all human beings are evil. And Mary smiled, dismounted her donkey and took you in her arms. And then later, in their bed, she allowed Yussuf, the Turk, to stroke you, and she rocked you to sleep."

Suddenly there was nothing but silence inside my head, and I was sure my time had come. My mind focused on my Last Thought which would soon take leave for the land of my forbears, to find each one that I had not known in life. But I was wrong. Suddenly I had another thought, just one, but I couldn't help but laugh, and let loose a fart.

"That was your last one," said the Meddah.

"Is it time?"

"Not quite," said the Meddah.

"Perhaps I still have time to let another one go," I said.

"Perhaps," said the Meddah. And then the Meddah asked:

"Why were you laughing just now, Thovma Khatisian?"

"Barely a moment ago, I was speaking to the Turkish Prime Minister."

"Did he say anything?"

"Yes.

I had finally managed to get hold of him, the Turkish Prime Minister. His voice sounded threatening down the phone line as he demanded, 'Who dares call here?' And there was I, on the other, safe end of the line, saying, 'I do!'

– And who are you?

– I'm your Armenian psychiatrist.

– And what do you want?

– Nothing. Nothing at all.

– So that must mean that I am the one who wants something from you?

– Precisely.

– Then I'll stop by your office tomorrow.

– Yes, please do.

I gave him my address and he actually did stop by. On time, too.

– I have been having nightmares, he said.

– All Turks have nightmares, I said.

– And why?

– Because of the Armenians.

– Because of the Armenians?

– Yes.

– What about the Armenians?

– They were exterminated by the Turks.

– I had nothing to do with that. None of today's Turks had

anything to do with that.

— I never said that you did.

— It happened a very long time ago, I said. In 1915. During the First World War. An entire people was wiped out.

— Wiped out. Just like that?

— Just like that.

— It rings a bell. I'm sure I heard someone mention something about it once, said the Turkish Prime Minister, but I always just thought they were stories made up by our enemies.

— It wasn't a story, I said.

— A genocide?

— That's right.

— A spontaneous eruption of Turkish rage?

— No.

— Then it wasn't initiated by the people?

— It started from the very top, I said. It was all carried out upon the order of the then Turkish government. It was all meticulously organized. We are talking about the first planned and systematically executed genocide of the 20th century.

— I thought that was an invention of the Germans.

— No, they didn't invent it; they copied it.

— From us Turks?

— Precisely.

— But there is nothing written about it in our history books, said the Turkish Prime Minister.

— I know.

— Is it because of the gap?

— The gap in history? Yes, I said.

– That's why I'm so afraid, said the Turkish Prime Minister. In my dreams all I see are gaps and holes.

– Take a seat, I said.
> – Where?
> – Anywhere in my office.
> – But this isn't an office. It's a Turkish history book.
> – That doesn't matter.
> – Should I actually sit?
> – Yes.
> – Or lie down?
> – Whichever you prefer.

– It would be best if you took a seat there, on that stool.
> – But I can't see any stool.
> – Then take a seat on my couch. You can also lie down if you wish.
> – But I can't see any couch.
> – Then why don't you just sit down right there on the floor.

The Turkish Prime Minister nodded before simply replying, 'But I can't see any floor.' Then he let out an almighty scream."

"No one can hear you, Thovma Khatisian," said the storyteller, "because your voice has gone. But I heard what you said."

"Did you also hear him scream – the Turkish Prime Minister – as he fell into the endless abyss?"

"Yes. I heard that, too."

"I met him another time, the Turkish Prime Minister," I began to explain to the storyteller.

"When?"

"Just a few seconds ago."

"And where?"

"In the main chamber of the United Assembly of International Conscience. The usual general assembly was taking place.

He was sitting next to the state representatives, looking unremarkable and distant. I found out that he was no longer Prime Minister, but instead was working as an archivist at the United Assembly of International Conscience. He had been officially elected by all represented nations. When he saw me, he got up and went down to the archive. I followed him:

– I'm looking for the Armenian file, I said. It's for a report on the forgotten genocide.

  – The forgotten genocide?

  – Yes.

  – And when is this 'genocide' supposed to have taken place?

  – In 1915.

  – That was a very long time ago. It's now 1988.

  – Yes, I said.

  – Let me show you, he said.

And then he led me to the filing cabinets. He said, 'Our filing cabinets do not have any doors. They are just open shelves. Anyone can come and have a look; we don't have any secrets here.'

  – Then could you show me where I might find the file on the Armenians?

  – I'm afraid I can't, he said. A file as old as the one on the Armenians will now be covered in so much dust that it will be impossible to find.

– Then why don't you call in your cleaner and get her to dust the file?

– I already tried that years ago, said the archivist, but it's more complicated than that.

– Why?

– Because all of the cleaners who work at the United Assembly of International Conscience are asthmatic and don't want to clean any old, dusty files, especially one as old and as dusty as a file on a forgotten genocide. That would stir up a great deal of dust and make them cough.

– A valid point, I said.

– The Forgotten should not be disturbed, said the archivist. It is too dangerous. And with those words, he disappeared.

Later I went back up to the main chamber. I sat in the audience and stood up several times to interrupt the Turkish speaker before security officials escorted me out.

At one point I managed to sneak back in. I stood next to the Secretary-General and gave a rousing speech. I spoke of my people – a people exterminated by the Turks – and for some time all the state representatives listened to my story, but then they started to get bored and began to leave the chamber one by one, until I was completely alone.

Then the cleaner came in. As it so happens, she was indeed asthmatic, and between coughs she said to me, 'What are you still doing here?'

– I was waiting for you.

– For me?

– Yes. You.

– Are you one of those diplomats who likes to have it off with cleaners?

– No.

– Then what do you want from me?

I said, 'I want you to bring the Forgotten to light.' She just laughed.

Whilst the cleaner was scrubbing the floor, I told her my story. 'Cleaners love to gossip,' I thought to myself. 'She'll tell others my story in the antechambers and corridors of the United Assembly of International Conscience until eventually all the state representatives will have heard it', but then I realized that the cleaner wasn't even listening. I only received the full attention of her rear as she scrubbed, and then she left the main chamber.

Then I was alone again. A little dazed, I walked past the tables of the individual states, reading each nameplate before finally coming to a halt in front of the one that read 'Secretary-General'. I stepped behind his lectern and addressed the empty chamber.

Into the silence, I told the story of the genocide. I explained to the silence just how important it was to speak openly about such things. I said, 'Everybody must be told! How else will we prevent another genocide from happening if everyone claims that they knew nothing about it and did nothing to stop it because they never imagined that such a thing could actually exist?' I spoke at length and in great detail. I demanded nothing for my people, not even punishment for their persecutors. I simply said, 'I want only to break the silence.'

Only much later did I begin to speak of myself. I told the empty chamber my story and the story of my family. I spoke of my father and my mother, my grandparents and my great-grandparents, my aunts and my uncles. I spoke of all those whom I had never met. I spoke until exhaustion came, when I paused, closed my eyes and buried my head in my hands.

When I looked up, the Secretary-General was standing beside me. He said, 'You didn't see me, but I was standing beside you the entire time.'

– Then you heard all of it?
– Every single word.

– Will you tell my story?
– No, said the Secretary-General. I will not.

We then smoked a cigarette together. The Secretary-General said, 'I thought your family's story was particularly muddled and implausible. I mean, how they lived before the great massacre and how they were exterminated. Just like that.'

I nodded and remained silent.

– I just find it strange, said the Secretary-General, that you, Mr. Khatisian, remember everything so vividly. As far as I understand it, you never actually knew any member of your family, not even your own mother. When you were born, Mr. Khatisian, in 1915, all of your family were either already dead or missing.

– My mother was with me.
– How do you know that?
– I don't, Mr. Secretary-General, and yet I am completely

sure of it.

– Just now you told the empty chamber that two Turks found you lying on a country road.

   – Yes, Mr. Secretary-General. A man and a woman.

   – And you said that later on, the two handed you over to an orphanage, just one of the many orphanages that existed back then.

   – Yes.

   – Then, shortly after the Great War, two women from the Red Cross came and took you to Switzerland? That is what you said, am I right?

   – Yes, Mr. Secretary-General.

   – That is where you remained, and you are now a Swiss citizen?

   – Yes.

   – So you are Swiss?

   – No, Mr. Secretary-General. I'm Armenian. An Armenian with a Swiss passport.

– But your family, Mr. Khatisian! You didn't even meet them! You never knew a single one. You don't even know your own family name.

   – True.

   – Eventually they gave you the name Khatisian because they thought that might have been your family name.

   – Yes, Mr. Secretary-General. Khatisian is a very common Armenian name.

The Secretary-General smiled and said, 'You don't even know where your family came from, you don't even have the name

of a city or a village to go by. You know nothing about them.
Nothing.'

– You see, Mr. Secretary-General, I said. When I was thirteen, I
started to search and for sixty long years I have done nothing but
search.
    – Did you find any trace of your family?
    – Several times, but they all led to dead-ends.
    – So it is true then. You don't know who you are?
    – No, I said. I know who I am.

For sixty long years I went in search of those who had survived
the massacre and listened to their stories, stories from Hayastan –
a place also known as Turkish-Armenia or Anatolia, call it how
you like – and I took pieces from all the many stories I heard and
started to create my own, until one day I had a genuine family
history. I knew my roots. I had a father and mother again, and
countless relatives. I also had a name steeped in heritage, one that
I could pass on to my children and grandchildren. And yes, Mr.
Secretary-General, this story may still be a little muddled in my
head, but soon it will take shape and it will be as real as the truest
story ever told.
    – When will that be?
    – Soon. It will be soon.
    – Final clarity always comes too late, said the Secretary-Gen-
eral, adding almost jokingly, it usually only comes with a man's
last thought.
    – But that isn't too late, I said. In that last thought all of this
will make sense. I can see it now. That last thought will bring
clarity to all the muddled ideas in my head, and the order it

brings will allow me to pass gently out of this life. People will say, 'Look at that man, he died like a tree.' You see, a tree can lose its leaves, but never its roots. Why should it be any different for people?"

And now here I am, back on my deathbed. The Meddah in my mind says, "You are filled with anticipation, Thovma Khatisian. You await the Last Thought like a bride awaits the arrival of her groom, who has come to reveal her true roots. But let me warn you, Thovma Khatisian, the Last Thought is brief, shorter than a fraction of a second."

"Is it possible to have just a little more time?"

"No, Thovma Khatisian."

Then the Meddah said, "What I can do is to tell you all about the Last Thought held within that final cry of fear, which will fly back in eager anticipation to your father and your mother and to all those people whom you never knew. And I can also tell you right now that that final cry of fear will change."

"What do you mean?"

"It will change into a joyful cry of anticipation."

"You mean I won't die in fear?"

"You will not die in uncertainty."

"Is that the same?"

"It is the same."

And I said to the Meddah inside my mind, "While we wait, and to prolong what little time is left, tell me about the Last Thought and all that will flash through my mind in less than a fraction of a second in that final moment? You did promise me that, after all."

"I only promised you a story."

"The Story of the Last Thought?"

"The Story of the Last Thought."

And the Meddah said, "Once I held your great-grandfather on my knee. It was on the market square of Bakir, a large city in Turkey. I began to tell him a Turkish story and said to him, '*bir varmish, bir yokmush, bir varmish*' – once there was one, once there were none, once upon a time … – as that is how all stories began in that region. It seems fitting that the story I am about to tell you should start the same way.

So, hear now, Thovma Khatisian, as I tell you my story: *bir varmish, bir yokmush, bir varmish* – once there was one, once there were none, once upon a time …"

Book One

1

Once upon a time there was a Last Thought. This Thought could travel forwards or backwards to any point in time – past, present or future – as it was immortal. So when the Last Thought flew out of the gaping mouth of a dying man, wrenched open as he let out a final cry of anticipation, it thought to itself, "Before you set off for the future, why not first pay a visit to the enormous Turkish city of Bakir, where your parents are waiting for you?"

And so it came to pass that the Last Thought travelled back in time to a spring day in the year 1915, a year of war, landing on the dome of one of the gates on the eastern side of the city called the *Bab-i-Se'adet,* the Gate of Happiness. It was a large, ironwork gate held within the thousand-year-old stone that formed Bakir's city wall. No one saw the Last Thought land on the dome of the city gate because the Thought could be neither seen nor heard, and so it spoke to the storyteller quite unabashedly:

"Where are you, Meddah?"

"I am right here with you," said the storyteller.

"But I don't have a body."

"That doesn't matter."

"Where are you exactly?"

"I'm inside you. And right now you are a part of Thovma

Khatisian, who is about to breathe his last breath."

"How long does it take to breathe a last breath?"

"Less than a fraction of a second."

"That's not a very long time."

"You're right, it isn't. Or maybe it is? Perhaps eternity is shorter than a fraction of a second, it is just measured differently."

"Tell me where I am, Meddah!"

"You are sitting on the Bab-i-Se'adet Gate, the Gate of Happiness. If you look to the southeast, you will be facing directly towards Mecca, the place where all practicing Muslims must go on a pilgrimage at least once in their lives as that is where the Prophet lived and preached. It is also where the Holy Ka'aba is."

"The Ka'aba? And Mecca? The Gate of Happiness? But I don't understand … why are there three Armenians hanging beneath this very gate? Their mouths are wrenched open as if their final cry of fear was still caught in their throats. They are dangling from a long rope, swaying gently in the evening breeze with their eyes fixed straight ahead."

"They are traitors."

"Is that true?"

"It's what the Turks claim."

"Is one of those three dead Armenians my father?"

"No. He is not among them."

"Are you going to take me to my father and mother now?"

"Not yet," said the Meddah. "Wait just a little bit longer. Haven't your dreams always told you that Bakir was the most beautiful city in the world?" said the Meddah. "The Turks call it the city of a thousand and one mosques. In summer a thousand

and one storks sit on their golden domes. At the break of day, when the sun escapes the Kurds' goat's-hair ropes and prepares to melt away the last traces of the night with its burning rays, and the first bird is warming up to deliver its dawn chorus, the storks sitting on the mosque domes can be seen bathing their white wings in the morning light, clacking their long beaks and calling forth the muezzins to come up to the minarets so that they can shout their 'Allahu Akbars' towards heaven."⁻

"But I can't see any storks."

"They are still in Mecca. They only come here when it gets warmer."

"I also can't see very many mosques. Didn't you say there were a thousand and one?"

"Yes, a thousand and one."

"I can only see eleven. I just counted them. There are eleven mosques in Bakir."

"That depends, my son. You see, the Turks like to exaggerate, just like the Jews and the Greeks and the devil worshippers and the gypsies, and everyone else in this region. In truth, there are only eleven mosques here. You're right. I've counted them, too. Eight are located in the Turkish district, two in the Kurdish district and one in the Armenian *mahalle,* although it really shouldn't be there."

"Why, Meddah?"

"Because Armenians are Christians. You know that, Thovma Khatisian. You've seen the Armenians' churches with your own eyes."

"But I haven't seen them."

"Then look around you, Thovma Khatisian. Look around. Here there are churches everywhere, especially in the Armenian *mahalle.* They are just less conspicuous."

"Why did you call me *Thovma Khatisian?*"
    "Because you are his proxy."
    "And why did you call me *my son?*"
    "It is of no importance. I could just as easily call you *my little lamb,* or *my little Pasha.* I could call you by all sorts of names, but only one is your real name."
    "Which one?"
    "Thovma Khatisian."

Soon the sun will disappear: The Kurds are already fumbling around with their goat's-hair rope, getting ready to usher in the evening. Shall I tell you what happens on an evening like this in Bakir?"
    "Yes, Meddah. But keep it brief as I am in a hurry to get to my father and mother."

And the Meddah said, "At this moment in time, there are four gentlemen sitting in the office of the mudir of Bakir, located on the top floor of the hukumet – the government's *konak* – a weatherproof building in *rue Hodja Pasha,* as the street is called by the genteel, French-speaking Turks. It is otherwise known more simply as *Hodja Pasha Sokagi.* One of these gentlemen is wearing a brown military uniform and has a fur cap on his head. He is the one-eyed mudir of Bakir, governor and commander-in-chief of the local gendarmerie. The other gentlemen are in civilian clothing and wearing only a red fez on their heads. Two of them – the kaimakam and the mutasarrif – are high-ranking officials within the complex Turkish chain of command. They control the individual districts and sub districts – the *sanjaks* and *kazas* – into which the Vilayet of Bakir is divided. The fourth gentlemen is none other than the vali himself, the provincial governor of the entire Vilayet of Bakir: a vilayet the size of the Vilayet of Erzurum or the Vilayet of Van. The gentlemen are sitting on an expensive carpet, each perched atop a colorfully-embroidered cushion stuffed with goose feathers, their legs crossed, drinking sweet coffee out of tiny copper cups and smoking *chibouk.*

– I shall order the head of this Vardan Khatisian to be chopped off first thing tomorrow morning, says the mudir. And I will place it on a spike with my own two hands and set it atop the city wall.

– Where on the wall? asks the mutasarrif.

– On the Gate of Happiness, says the mudir, just above and slightly to the left of the heads of those three Armenians I had hanged yesterday. The mudir laughs and glances expressionlessly with his glass eye at the two other men.

– I wouldn't do that if I were you, says the corpulent vali, languidly motioning with his hand. You see, we can still get a lot of information out of this Vardan Khatisian.

– The vali is right, says the mutasarrif. Vardan Khatisian can tell us a lot more alive than he can dead.

The vali once more gestures languidly with his hand and says, 'Efendiler, once I tried to extract a confession from a dead man, but he was as mute as a fish pulled straight out of Lake Van. Not even I, the vali of Bakir, could squeeze a word out of him.'"

The gentlemen fall silent, sip their sweet coffees and smoke their chibouk. Unbeknownst to them, the Last Thought of Thovma Khatisian could feel a shiver running all the way down its spine, although it was a disembodied entity and had no spine of which to speak. Their words terrified the Thought and so it asked the Meddah, "Who are they talking about?"

"They are talking about your father, my little lamb. Your father."

"Where is my father?"

"He is in prison."

"In prison?"

"Yes."

"When will you take me to him?"

"Soon, my little lamb. Soon."

"Will they cut his head off?"

"We shall find out soon enough.

And now listen, my little lamb," said the storyteller, "whilst these four men sit inside the government building discussing your father's fate, in many of the houses of Bakir the evening's first oil lamps are being lit. The traders in the bazaars are dismantling their stalls and loading their goods onto mule- or donkey-drawn carriages. Some are just stuffing them into large flour sacks which they will either carry home themselves or have dragged by a *hamal* for a few lousy paras. The hamals of Bakir are the laziest laborers in the whole of Turkey, even lazier than the laborers in the port of Constantinople, and do you know why? Let me tell you, my little lamb: because they are mostly Kurds. A Kurd is either a proud and free man, living high up in the mountains in his tent made of black goat's hair, and making a living from his sheep or through pillaging, with his own horse and gun, or he waves goodbye to his pride and his freedom – and with it, his dignity – and he goes to work as a hamal in Bakir. It's true. These

Kurdish laborers in Bakir are worth even less than donkeys."

"Why are you telling me all this, Meddah?"

"To sharpen my tongue before I tell you any more about your father who, unbeknownst to him, is waiting for you and whom you will see soon."

"When?"

"Soon."

"You don't mind if I call you Thovma," said the storyteller to the Last Thought. "Or *my little lamb* or *my son* or something like that?"

"No," said the Last Thought. "You can call me whatever you like, as long as you take me to my father."

"Don't you want to see your mother as well?"

"Of course," said the Last Thought. "Very much so. But I think that right now it is more important that I get to my father, otherwise they might chop off his head before I lay eyes on him."

"You are absolutely right," said the Meddah. "But first take a look around."

"I already have," said the Last Thought.

"And what do you see?"

"I see all the Turks at the Grand Bazaar taking down their stalls."

"They aren't Turks," said the Meddah, "they are Armenian traders. At least most of them are. For centuries they have been living together with the Turks in the same country, and most of the time you can hardly tell the two apart. Look, most of the men are wearing a red fez, and their baggy shalvar trousers are gathered at the ankles. They wear the same sleeveless jackets beneath their abayas as the Turks. Some are even parading around in western clothes, just like the new Young Turk generation, and they also wear a fur cap or a fez. Their unkempt whiskers instill a sense of awe amongst the women and are no less impressive than those of the Turks or the mountain-dwelling Kurds. They smoke the same cigarettes or pipes, such as the chibouk which the vali of Bakir and the mutasarrif and the mudir also smoke, or they smoke *nargilehs,* a hookah with a winding tube – an activity to be savored, not rushed. And when you ask an Armenian which tobacco he uses to fill his chibouk, he will always reply, '*Abu Ri'ha* Persian tobacco, the king of aromatic tobaccos', which is exactly how any self-respecting Turk would answer."

The Meddah said, "My little lamb, these things, they are all superficial. If you really want to know if a man is Armenian, you must look into his eyes.

Soon the bazaar will be almost completely deserted," said the Meddah, "and the only ones left will be the water sellers with their half-filled goatskin pouches, running after traders on their way home and shouting their final cries of '*Iyi su, soguk su, bus gibi, on para*' – good water, cold water, like ice, 10 paras. The water sellers are always the last to leave the bazaar as the Prophet said, 'Haste is from Satan', and they follow the Prophet's teachings to the letter.

Yes, my little lamb, haste is from Satan, and in this country the only ones who ever seem to be in a hurry are deaf-mutes, rushing as they do to mosque in the evening – to recite the Namaz prayer with their absent voices – because they can't hear the call to prayer of the muezzins as they stand on the balconies of the minarets, shouting their heads off."

"Where do deaf-mutes pray, Meddah?"

"Anywhere that other Muslims pray," said the Meddah, "many of them probably go to the *Hirka Sherif Djamissi* Mosque, the Mosque of the Holy Mantel, in the Turkish district in *Kuru Sebil Sokagi,* the Street of the Dry Sebil, or they go to the *Deli-Avret-Djami,* the Mosque of the Foolish Wife down in the Kurdish district. I don't know for sure, my little lamb, but I presume that most deaf-mutes go to the Muhammad Pasha the Miracle Healer Mosque, *Cherrah Muhammad Pasha Djami.*

It's a pity that you weren't here this morning," said the Meddah. "There was a group of newly recruited soldiers marching through the Armenian district. They left their barracks accompanied by Janissary music, marched past Bit Bazari – that's the 'louse' or junk market – turned into Divan Yoli, the Street of the Divan, then marched through the Armenian artisan district, along the streets where the pottery makers and silversmiths were working – they even walked past the *urbadshis,* Bakir's Armenian garment makers who once made your great-grandfather a *pamuklu,* a suit made of genuine wool, which he later passed on to your grandfather who then passed it on to your father. Guess where the recruits were marching to?"

"How should I know, Meddah?"

"They were marching to *Top Kapi,* to the Cannon Gate in the west of the city. And anyone who passes through that gate is heading straight for Erzurum."

"What's in Erzurum?"

"That's where the Turks have their Third Army stationed."

"Why, Meddah?"

"To halt the advancing Russian juggernaut that is currently

steamrolling its way across the Caucasus and heading for Constantinople, my little lamb.

Regiments marched through Bakir the entire afternoon," said the Meddah, "mainly *mustahfiz*. They are the last reservists, and amongst them I saw old men and soldiers who looked like children, and the lame and other cripples. And would you believe it, the mustahfiz were followed by wailing women. And then came the dervishes from the Rifa'i order. They suddenly appeared, crying, '*Ya Ghasi, Ya Shahid, Ya Allah, Ya Hu*' – Oh fighters, Oh martyrs, Oh Allah, Oh Lord. And on the balcony of the hukumet stood the vali and the mutasarrif, the kaimakam and the one-eyed mudir, and had they been Christians, they would have most certainly made the sign of the cross.

But now the mudir is no longer standing on the balcony. Neither is the vali nor the mutasarrif nor the kaimakam; they are still in the mudir's office discussing your father's fate."

"Have they reached a decision?"

"Not yet, my little lamb, not yet. The men have now been joined by a late arrival: a German officer, a major, who works as an instructor for the Turkish army. Now they are all sitting on that expensive carpet, each with a pillow beneath his behind, drinking coffee and smoking chibouk.

– This morning, says the German major, as I was riding into the city with my people, I saw three Armenians beneath the Gate of Happiness. They were dangling at the end of on a long rope.

– They are traitors, says the vali.

– All Armenians are traitors, says the mudir. In fact, they all deserve to be strung up.

– How many Armenians live in this area? asks the major.

– Five million, replies the vali.

– But that cannot possibly be true, says the German major. According to the statistics, there are only one point two million of these curious people living in the whole of Turkey.

– Those were the statistics used by Sultan Abdul Hamid, says the vali, and the Young Turks discredited those figures long ago.

– Are you saying that Abdul Hamid wanted to play down the presence of minorities?

– That's right, Binbashi Bey, says the vali.

– These Armenians are a dangerous people, says the vali. And they live on both sides of the border: four million on our side and one million over in Russia.

– But that's an exaggeration, says the major.

– No, Binbashi Bey, says the vali. There might even be more; these people breed like rats. The vali smiles and sips his sweet coffee. And they are all related to each other.

– What do you mean?

– What else could I mean, Binbashi Bey? Please, tell me. The Turkish Armenians have aunts and uncles on the other side of that border. Some have sons and daughters over there, parents and grandparents and other relatives. They are all related to each other.

– And if they weren't related to one another, says the mudir, – I mean officially related – then they would still be somehow related because they are a unique race that has been practicing incest for millennia. They all have the same blood.

– It's bad blood, says the vali. It comes from Satan.

– They're all in cahoots together, says the mudir, every single Armenian, on both sides of the border. And they're all siding with the Russians.

– Are you saying that the Armenians here on the Turkish side of the border are waiting for a Russian invasion, or are even supporting it? asks the major.

– You guess correctly, Binbashi Bey, says the vali. The Turkish Armenians are waiting for the Russians and their relatives, who are over there fighting for the Tsar, to invade. They all want the invasion to happen.

– Do you have any concrete evidence to support this?

– We don't need any, says the vali. We know it to be true: that's all the evidence we need.

– A dangerous position to be in, says the major.

– And so close to the front, too, says the mudir. Millions of Armenians with Turkish passports breathing down our necks. Millions that we know are siding with the enemy.

– An extremely dangerous position indeed, says the major.

– Now you understand, Binbashi Bey, says the mutasarrif, why we needed to set an example by hanging those three Armenians.

– I see why it was done, says the major.

– And the Gate of Happiness is the ideal place to do it.

– Yes, says the major.

– We strung the three of them up so that they weren't facing towards Mecca.

– Where are they facing? asks the major.

– The other way, says the mudir.

– We found a bottle of Russian liquor on one of those hanged Armenians, says the mudir. That is a serious offense here; Russia is our enemy.

– He was allegedly given the liquor by his brother-in-law, says the mutasarrif, his wife's brother who has a liquor factory over there on the wrong side of the border.

– He claimed it was a bottle of liquor he acquired before the war, says the mudir, but he had no way to prove it.

– And what crimes had the other two Armenians committed? asks the major.

– The second one had a letter on his person, says the mudir. A letter from his grandmother in Russia.

– Contact with the enemy?

– That's right, Binbashi Bey.

– And how did the letter enter Turkey?

– Well, Binbashi Bey, the letter was sent by post.

– So it was sent before the war?

– Of course, it was sent before the war.

– Was the delivery date and a Russian stamp still on the envelope?

– No. There was neither a delivery date nor a stamp on the envelope.

– There wasn't actually an envelope, says the mudir, because the mail carrier had opened the letter and thrown the envelope away.

– And why would he have done that?

– Because the Armenian owed him a tip and he intended to keep hold of the letter until he received his tip.

– Baksheesh?

– Of course. Baksheesh, a standard tip. What else? These

mail carriers are petty, underpaid clerks, open to bribery and reliant upon tips. Since the change of government, we Young Turks have been doing everything within our power to clean up corruption, but what use is it when a mail carrier like that man is still acting in the spirit of the deposed Abdul Hamid and fails to comprehend our new ethical code?

– Exactly, says the vali.

– You see, Binbashi Bey, begins the kaimakam, the mail carrier held onto the letter for two years and only delivered it last week. When we found the letter – a letter without an envelope – of course we immediately thought that it was smuggled. What else were we supposed to think? In times of war no post from over there enters this country legally. And there was no way for us to be sure that the letter was written before war broke out.

– Didn't the mail carrier say anything?

– He did, Binbashi Bey. But he only gave a statement after the Armenian had been hanged from the gate. The Gate of Happiness. Facing the wrong way: away from Mecca.

– So that's what happened, says the major.

– That's right, Binbashi Bey, says the kaimakam. With Allah as my witness.

– And what about the third traitor?

– He's an Armenian priest, says the mudir. We caught him giving a sermon.

– So, I assume you ordered informants to spy on the Christian church?

– We are at war, Binbashi Bey. At war. What else should we do?

– And what did the priest do?

– He prayed for victory together with his congregation, but

we did not know which side he was praying for.

– I'm not sure I follow you, Mudir Bey.

– At the end of the prayer he called the people to give three cheers for the sovereign leader, and then he said, and I quote, 'Long live the Padishah!' Except we didn't know which padishah he was referring to. You see, Binbashi Bey, there is a Russian padishah and a Turkish padishah. In Russia they have their Tsar and we have our new Sultan, whom Enver Pasha placed on the throne. How were we to know which padishah the priest was referring to?

– Very difficult to determine indeed, says the major.

– But we were able to establish exactly whom he meant, says the mudir triumphantly, because as he pronounced that very sentence referring to the padishah, the priest's hand moved to his cross.

– Which cross?

– The long cross hanging down to his chest. And then we were certain that he could only have meant the Russian Tsar. No one else.

– I'm not so sure about that, says the major.

– Well, we are, says the mudir.

– I was astonished that the Armenians didn't go on strike today. I even went to some of their shops to buy some food and they were all open, says the major.

– Why should they be closed?

– Well, because three of their people have been hanged.

– But, Binbashi Bey, says the mudir, these rats are far too cowardly to protest openly.

– A few weeks ago I was in Galicia, says the major, on the Austrian front. And do you know what I realized while I was there, Mudir Bey?

– No, says the mudir.

– There are far too many Jews there. And do you know how Jews behave when they barter?

– No, says the mudir.

– Just like Armenians, says the major. These two peoples are almost identical. It's staggering.

– Perhaps, says the mudir.

– Do you have a problem with Jews here?

– No, says the mudir. Here we have a problem with Armenians.

– These Armenians are worse than rats, says the mudir. Wherever they go, they infiltrate the people; eroding them and then, eventually, annihilating them.

– Exactly, says the vali.

– They take advantage of us Turks and act as if they were the masters here.

– Exactly, says the vali.

– And these Armenians are swimming in money, believe me. Their women are draped in velvet and silk and wear the most expensive jewelry. How does the saying go? 'Every Armenian is a walking jewelry shop.' The mudir laughs. And they own everything: the banks, the currency exchange offices, the craft trades and businesses. They are our doctors and lawyers, and they send their sons and daughters to good schools.

– And they are in cahoots with the enemy, says the mutasarrif.

– Yes, says the mudir. Every Armenian is a Russian in disguise.

– They are just waiting for the right moment to drive the dagger into our backs, says the vali, before adding softly, 'Something has to be done'. He leisurely sips his coffee, takes a puff of chibouk and says, 'Something absolutely has to be done'.

– And what about that spy you captured a while ago? asks the major. Is he an Armenian?

– Of course he's an Armenian. What else do you expect?

– What is his name?

– His name is Vardan Khatisian.

The major laughs and says, 'That's a typical Armenian name if ever I heard one'.

– The Armenians are an ancient people, says the German major. If I am not mistaken, they were already living in this region when Muhammad received his first revelation.

– You're right, says the vali.

– Even before that, says the major, I mean … as far back as the moment when Christ held his sermon on the mount.

– It's true, says the vali.

– And before that, says the major. They predate both our respective calendars.

– Yes, says the vali.

The vali pensively takes a puff of his chibouk and smiles. Might you be suggesting that the Armenians were here in this region before the Turks?

– I'm not suggesting anything, says the major.

– Well, that may well be the case, says the vali, but what does it mean?

– It means nothing, says the mudir. They are nothing more

than rats, and even the rats were here before the Turks.

– And now we find ourselves back on the subject of rats, says the mudir. He smiles and says, 'You see, Efendiler, not long ago I followed a rat down to my cellar. Of course, I held a club in my hand, ready to strike the creature dead.' For a brief moment the mudir closes his one eye, opens it and glances at the major with a look of innocence. 'When I reached the cellar, I suddenly saw another rat. Then another one, and another two. More and more of them started appearing. They were coming out of every crevice in the cellar. More and more of them appeared. Hundreds and thousands. Wherever I stepped, there was a rat. Suddenly there were millions of them. They ate the clothes from my body, swallowed up my club, jumped at my throat and, finally, devoured me.'

– Was it at that point that you woke up? asks the major.
   – No.
   – But surely that must just have been a dream?

Some time passes without anyone uttering a word. Only after the mudir nervously claps his hands and orders the summoned saptieh to bring some fresh coffee, does the vali awkwardly clear his throat and address the question to the major that had long been hanging over them all:
   – How are things progressing with the war, Binbashi Bey? Are the Germans set to occupy Paris?
   – It is merely a matter of time, says the major.
   – And Petersburg?
   – We shall soon be in Petersburg, too.

– And what is the situation in the Caucasus?

    – Enver Pasha's army had to temporarily pull back.

    – And yet the Turkish soldiers are the world's finest.

    – The problem is cholera, says the major. And the cold winter.

    – But hasn't winter been and gone?

    – Yes, says the major.

– Everything was going well when Enver Pasha held command over the Caucasus army, says the vali. He should have carried on marching until he met the German Kaiser in Petersburg. I cannot fathom why the front collapsed and Enver returned to Constantinople.

    – No one can, says the mudir.

    – Perhaps because of cholera, says the vali. Or because they didn't have enough winter clothing. Or because of the Armenians. The Armenian soldiers have cursed our troops. It's all their fault.

    – Yes, says the mudir."

Silence envelops me, and although I, Thovma Khatisian, am nothing more than a timeless thought, I hear a ticking sound.

"That's just time," says the Meddah, "and whether you like it or not, time is running out. Soon a decision will be made."

"What decision?"

"The provincial governor's, the vali of Bakir. Soon he will order the mudir to behead your father – or perhaps not."

"Will you take me to see my father now?"

"Soon, my little lamb, soon."

And the Meddah said, "Do you see that blind, old beggar sitting next to the Gate of Happiness?"

"Yes, I see him."

"His name is Mechmed Efendi and he is a shrewd man. He is so shrewd that people say that he has the body of a Turk and the mind of an Armenian."

"And the young boy at his feet?"

"That is his grandson, Ali."

"Two hungry mouths surely forsaken by Allah?"

"You are wrong, my little lamb. Do you see their collection cloth on the pavement, weighed down by four stones so that the wind doesn't carry it away? It contains only a few lousy paras, not a cent more. But this beggar is in fact filthy rich. You don't believe me, do you?"

"No, I don't."

"Well, you can believe what you like," said the Meddah. "But it's the truth. And this Mechmed Efendi wanted to buy your father's freedom because your father once saved his life. But I will tell you about that later."

"Did the beggar manage to buy my father's freedom?"

"No," said the Meddah.

"And why?"

"Because nobody can buy your father's freedom. The vali considers him too important."

"So it's not possible?"

"No, it isn't.

Of course, there were others who tried to buy your father's freedom. Your mother was one. In fact, the entire family tried. Every single one of them tried, but it was in vain. And they say Turkish officials are easy to bribe."

"Are they?"

"Of course they are, my little lamb. Here you can make almost anything happen with a little baksheesh, except buy your father's freedom."

"Because he is too important? In the vali's eyes?"

"Not only in his eyes. The others consider him important, too, particularly the mudir. The officials still have a lot in store for him."

"If he is so important, he must surely still be needed, and if he is still needed, then they wouldn't be so foolish as to cut off his head?"

"Precisely, my little lamb. You've got it right. That's also what I thought. Just this second, my little lamb … just now … the old, blind beggar winced. Did you see it?"

"Yes, I saw it."

"It looks as though something gave him a fright, but he is only pretending. He likes to joke around with his grandson. And can you hear what he is saying to his grandson?"

"Yes, I can hear it."

And I hear the blind beggar say to the young boy:

– Ali, my Nazar. I think death is near.

– Nonsense, Dede, says the boy. Death won't come for you until you've told me where you've hidden your money.

– You're right there, my Nazar, says the blind man. You're an intelligent boy, aren't you? You inherited that from me.

– Yes, Dede, says the boy.

The beggar then says, 'I thought it was near because I could feel something cold wrapping itself around my throat.'

– What kind of cold, Dede?

– A cold wind.

– But there is no wind, Dede.

– There is, my Nazar. A cold wind is blowing, and it's coming from the Gate of Happiness.

– From the Gate of Happiness?

– Yes, Ali, my Nazar. It's coming from there. And I bet you that death is perched atop the gate's archway.

– Death is hanging beneath the archway, Dede.

– And what does it look like?

– It looks like three dangling Armenians.

– Oh, really? That's what it looks like?

– Yes, that's what I can see.

– We need to think of a way, my Nazar, to get hold of those old clothes and shoes. And your old Dede always cooks up a good plan. Right, my Nazar? Or do you think I'm too old and that my days of cooking up plans are over?

– No, Dede. Not at all.

– Now, play close attention, my Nazar. It's best if we forget about getting the clothes: It probably won't be easy to undress those dead bodies if some dunderheaded saptieh is watching over them … and then there are all the people below waiting to plunder the hanged men. Not an easy task, my Nazar.

– Yes, Dede.

– But the shoes, now that's a different kettle of fish.

– How do you mean, Dede?

– It's just different, my Nazar.

Tell me, my Nazar. What kind of shoes do those dead men have on their feet?

— One is barefoot, Dede. He is an Armenian priest and looks like a Persian king, wearing a long cloak with a cross across his chest, but no crown.

— But Persian kings don't wear crosses, my Nazar. Not a single one wears a cross.

— Perhaps, Dede. I didn't know.

— And what kind of shoes is the second one wearing?

— He is wearing a pair of red velvet slippers.

— They probably dragged him out of bed.

— Yes, Dede.

— These Armenians go to sleep in their slippers, after the fire has gone out in their tonirs.

— Yes, Dede.

— Slippers don't sell for much, my Nazar, so let's forget about those.

— Yes, Dede.

— And what's the third one got on his feet?

— A pair of yellow goatskin leather boots.

— Yellow goatskin leather, you say?

— Yes, Dede.

— Now, listen closely, my Nazar. How high are those dead men hanging?

— Very high, Dede. The yellow boots are out of reach.

— What do you mean, my Nazar? How high is 'out of reach'?

— As high as a hop, a skip and a jump, Dede.

— Now, that is high.

— Yes, Dede.

– Now, listen closely, my Nazar. I want you to climb up the thousand and one steps, by that I mean the steps leading up to the archway: the archway of the Gate of Happiness.

– To the place where they strung up those dead men?

– Yes, my Nazar.

– To the top of the long rope?

– Yes, my Nazar.

– But I don't see a thousand and one steps.

– That doesn't matter, my Nazar.

– There are fewer, Dede.

– Even better, my Nazar.

– Now, listen closely, my Nazar. I want you to climb up there and untie the dead man, the one with the yellow boots.

– Yes, Dede.

– And then he will fall down. Right under the nose of the saptieh. And he will wonder where the dead body came from. And that dunderheaded saptieh will get an almighty scare and think that the Prophet Himself has sent the dead body down from heaven, even though he should still be down here on earth, hanging under the Gate of Happiness.

– What will the saptieh do?

– He will do nothing, my Nazar. He will scratch his head and look at the dead man.

– And what will I do?

– You will run back down the thousand and one steps as fast as you can. And you will run to the saptieh and you will speak to him.

– What should I say?

– You will address him as if he were a captain. You see, these saptiehs are simple and therefore particularly vain. You will say to him, 'Yuzbashi Bey, you cannot simply leave that dead man lying here on the street. But of course you know better than me, Yuzbashi Bey.'

And the saptieh will feel flattered and stroke your hair, and then he will say to you, 'Of course, I know better than you.'

– Then you will say, 'I know that you'll hang that dead man up again: The mudir won't stand to have three men hanged and see only two of them beneath the archway.'

– The saptieh will then say, 'That would be unacceptable, my little lamb. If the mudir ordered three hanged men, then three there must be.'

– Then let me help you string him up again.

– The saptieh will say, 'That's a good idea, but have you seen the thousand and one steps?'

– 'I have seen them,' you will say.

– That's quite a lot of steps.

– Yes, Yuzbashi Bey.

– And you really want to help me climb up all of those steps, right up to the highest archway, with this dead swine, this infidel, this uncircumcised runt whose soul, if he ever even had one, is already rotting in the depths of hell?

– 'Yes,' you will reply.

– And that's what will happen, my Nazar. As you are still small and weaker than the saptieh, you will take the lighter end of the body; you will take the man's legs.

– You mean the legs with a yellow goatskin leather boot at the end of each one?

– That's right, my Nazar. The saptieh will take the heavy end, grabbing the dead man underneath the arms, and the pair of you will drag the load up the steps, puffing and panting all the way. Then, suddenly, you stop.

– Why, Dede?

– Because you want to say something to the saptieh.

– And what do I want to say to him?

– You will say to him, 'Yuzbashi Bey, you are walking up the steps backwards. You cannot do that.'

– And the saptieh will say, 'Why not?'

– Because only a donkey walks up steps backwards; they walk backwards when their master is trying to make them go forwards – in the right direction – of course by tugging on the rope that most donkeys have around their necks.

– Then the saptieh will say, 'Do you take me for a donkey?'

– You will say, 'No, Yuzbashi Bey. A man as clever as you is surely no donkey, and a man such as yourself would never walk up steps backwards.'

– And what will happen then, Dede?

– Well, what you would expect to happen, my Nazar? The saptieh will turn around and grab the dead man from behind and start to climb up the steps like any normal man would, facing forwards: by that I mean towards the archway, looking at the place where he will string the dead man up again.

– I see, Dede.

– The saptieh will turn his back to you and will no longer be able to see you. He will puff and pant his way up with the dead man in tow, cussing and spitting. He will curse all the dead men who have ever been hanged by the Turks in all of history. And he will curse the infidels, particularly the Armenians. And he will rant on about the war and the authorities and the vali of Bakir and the mutasarrif and the mudir and the kaimakam, all the big wigs, pocketing their baksheesh while he, a saptieh, so often has to walk away empty handed or make do with their scraps. He will curse the day he was born, and he will curse all of the mothers who gave birth to people like the vali or people like the mutasarrif, the kaimakam or the mudir: people who lead a good life whilst he, a saptieh, lives no better than a common dog, with hardly any baksheesh and a monthly wage of just a few paras, which the authorities in Constantinople often forget to pay. As I said, he will curse and he will sweat, and whilst he curses and sweats and struggles up the steps, he will completely forget about the other end of the dead man, by that I mean the part dangling down: the dead man's legs, which are being held by a certain clever, young boy.

– But I will be holding the boots, right, Dede? The boots made of yellow goatskin leather?

– Correct, my Nazar. You will hold on tightly to those boots, and you will pull them off the dead man's feet without a care in the world as the saptieh won't be able to see you. Then you will leave the boots on the steps. Trust me, the saptieh won't notice a thing, and I will be walking right behind you, even though I am blind. You see, I know the thousand and one steps like the back of my hand; I've been walking them for years. I lose count of the number of times I've gone up and down those steps. So I will follow you, and I will put those beautiful boots in my sack.

– In your sack?

– Well, where else do you think, my Nazar!

"And that is exactly what took place," said the Meddah to the Last Thought. "The young boy, Ali, untied the dead man from the archway. He fell plum in front of the dunderheaded saptieh, who behaved exactly as the blind beggar Mechmed Efendi said he would: He simply scratched his head and gazed dumbfounded at the dead man. His lips seemed to whisper something, which only the last Prophet understood.

I can see that young boy, Ali," said the Meddah. "I can see him running down the thousand and one steps and making a beeline for the saptieh to talk to him. I can see them both carrying the dead man back up the thousand and one steps, the saptieh holding the heavy end, the boy holding the lighter end. It all happened precisely as planned.

The saptieh turned to face the other way because only a donkey walks backwards. He took the dead body from behind and carried him the proper way. As the saptieh cursed and sweated, the boy gently pulled the boots off the dead man's stiff feet. Before he knew it, the blind beggar appeared right behind them, and the yellow boots disappeared into his sack.

As the pair finally managed to heave the body to the top of the thousand and one steps, the saptieh turned around.

– We should really get a better rope, said the saptieh.

– Yes, said the boy.

– This rope could easily break again.

– Yes, said the boy.

– We need a rope like the goat's-hair one the Kurds use to catch the sun.

– Yes, said the boy.

– Only at this point did the saptieh notice the dead man's bare feet.

– What happened to the boots? asked the saptieh.

– I don't know, said the boy.

– Do you believe that Armenians can still cast spells, even after they're dead? asked the saptieh.

– Yes, said the boy.

– This is just like some sort of dark magic.

They laid the dead man out on the top step so that he was staring at the sky.

– I need a breather, said the saptieh, whilst wiping the sweat from his brow. Then you will help me string him back up.

– Yes, said the boy.

– But first we should turn him over so that he's not looking at the sky, said the saptieh. Otherwise he'll manage to make all of his clothes disappear.

– Yes, said the boy, helping the saptieh turn the dead man over.

– These Armenians really can perform dark magic, said the saptieh. It's true. As long as they have been on earth, they have been mysteriously vanishing money from the Turks' pockets … and when they die, their boots disappear.

– Yes, said the boy.

– They are all devil worshippers, said the saptieh, just like the Yazidis in the village of Birik next to Terbizek, the village where my late mother gave me the gift of life, with Allah as my witness.

– But the Armenians are not like the Yazidis, said the boy.

– And who told you that?

– Mechmed Efendi. He knows the Armenians. Mechmed Efendi told me that the Armenians pray to Jesus.

– And who is Jesus?

– The God of the Infidels.

– Who said that?

– Mechmed Efendi.

– Did he say anything else?

– Yes. He said that Jesus hangs nailed to a cross and that he can work magic.

– Allah, have mercy upon me, said the saptieh.

The saptieh lit himself a cigarette. The brand was *Amroian* – the cheapest cigarettes – and they were made here in Bakir by the Armenian Levon Amroian. Do you think this Jesus character was the one who made that dead man's boots vanish?

– It's possible, said the boy. Mechmed Efendi told me that Jesus could definitely make use of a pair of yellow, genuine goatskin leather boots because he hangs on his cross barefoot.

– Barefoot, you say?

– Yes, said the boy.

– Allah, have mercy upon me, said the saptieh.

And so it came to pass," said the Meddah. "Whilst the pair strung the dead man up for a second time – and that took quite a while as the saptieh was not the most skillful of men, and he had little clue as to how to tie a Turkish hangman's knot, while young Ali did not know how to firmly attach such a knot around a rusty hook, a hook purported to be as old as the Gate of Happiness itself, which was very old indeed: older than the first cry of death to come from the first man to be hanged beneath this very archway – so whilst the two struggled, especially the saptieh, who was only fulfilling his duty so that not two but three dead bodies were hanging beneath the Gate of Happiness as should be and indeed as the mudir had ordered – whilst they were doing their level best not to upset the authorities and to put everything back as it should be, and while this and that took place, night had begun its rapid descent from the Kurdish mountains down to the city. Night never crept in slowly, like a thief in the night as the saying goes. No, no, my little lamb. In Bakir night always fell suddenly because the Djinns, who live up in the canyons, were impatient fellows who eagerly awaited the moment when the Kurds would capture the sun. Once the Djinns saw that the sun had been overpowered, they came out of their canyons laughing and, in the blink of an eye, grabbed hold of the long shadow which the sun had left lying in front of the great tent and cast it over the city.

Of course, whether or not the sun shone on Bakir mattered little to the three dead men," said the Meddah. "They also didn't care much about the long shadow, which the Djinns had cast over the city of a thousand and one mosques in one fell swoop, or about the endless number of tiny little oil lamps and street lamps that were being lit one by one in the darkness of the city. They saw none of it because they could no longer see, and yet their dead eyes were looking in a particular direction."

"How can you look in a particular direction if you can no longer see?"

"The direction does not need to be seen, my little lamb."

"In which direction were they looking then, without seeing?"

"In many different directions, my little lamb. Each one of them was looking in a different direction.

The one with the red slippers was called Muschegh Inglisian. He was the wealthiest corn merchant in Bakir. Guess where his dead eyes are looking?"

"How should I know, Meddah?"

"His dead eyes are looking to *askeri ambari,* my little lamb, the military provisions warehouse. For years Muschegh Inglisian supplied the Turkish army with the best corn from this region, and it was no coincidence that the soldiers would often remark, 'This ekmek is the best bread in the world because the flour comes from the stores of that rich Armenian, Inglisian. It may be true that all Armenians are crooks, but this Muschegh Inglisian is an exception: He is an honest man'."

"But I can't see any military warehouses, Meddah."

"You just have to look properly," said the Meddah to the Last Thought. "Then you will see it. It isn't far away."

"How far away is it?"

"The time it takes to smoke four cigarettes, my little lamb. When you walk through the Armenian quarter, straight across the mahalle, first passing through the streets of the coppersmiths, pottery makers and tinkers, then through the alleyways lined with gold- and silversmiths, moneychangers and jewelers, then along the felt-makers' street, along the alleyway and through the vaulted arches – *Kemer alti Sokagi* – quickly cross the 'louse' market – the Bit Bazari – then back along the streets lined with tobacco traders, tailors and upholsterers – the *tununshis, urbadshis and saradshis* – once you have gone past all of those places in just four smokes, you will arrive in the Turkish district. Then you have to walk just two more smokes past squalid clay huts, a small number of businesses – most of which are closed down – past empty fruit and vegetable stalls and over small, rickety wooden bridges, and you will finally arrive at the barracks."

"Barracks?"

"That's right, my little lamb. The Turks call them *kishla*. And this particular kishla is impossible to miss because at this very moment there is Janissary music coming from within."

"Janissary music?"

"That's right, my little lamb," said the Meddah. "The Janissaries were once elite soldiers of the Ottoman army, but that was a very long time ago. There are no Janissaries anymore. All that remains is their marching music."

"Now I can hear it, Meddah."

"Good, my little lamb. You're now walking towards the barracks. Walk a little bit farther and then you'll see it."

"See what?"

"The military provisions warehouse. The place where the corn trader's darkened eyes are looking. It's empty, of course."

"Why is it empty?"

"Because the country is at war, my little lamb, and the Turks have no more provisions. All that was left was sent to Syria last week. To the headquarters of the Fourth Army … and then farther south, to the English-Turkish front."

"And what's happening on the Russian front?"

"You mean the front in the Caucasus?"

"Yes, that one."

"There the armies are beset by hunger and cholera. And Turkish soldiers are pillaging the Armenian villages, taking whatever they can find.

The second hanged man, the priest, is also looking toward something specific. Do you know what?"

"No, Meddah."

"He is looking towards heaven, my little lamb, as Jesus once did when he was hanging on the cross."

"And what do his dead eyes say?"

"They say, 'Father, forgive them for they know not what they do'.

And now look at the third hanging body, my little lamb. What do you see?"

"It's too dark, Meddah. I can't see anything."

"Then use your imagination: Imagine that this third dead man looks like your father."

"Is he my father?"

"Of course not, my little lamb. Your father is in prison. This man is his brother Dikran … Dikran Khatisian … your very uncle. The two have always looked very similar."

"My uncle Dikran, the very one?"

"Correct."

"The man whose yellow boots the blind beggar stole?"

"That's the one."

And the Meddah said, "Your uncle was not a rich man. He was a poor cobbler who had twelve children to feed."

"And his yellow leather boots?"

"They were his pride and joy; they were the most beautiful goatskin leather boots in the whole of Bakir."

– Listen, my Nazar, says the blind beggar, Mechmed Efendi, to the young boy, Ali. You did a very good job with these boots, very good indeed. You see, these boots are worth a fortune.

– Because they are made of real goatskin leather?

– No, my Nazar, because there is gold hidden inside them.

– How do you know?

– Every Armenian sews a nugget of gold into his boots, says the blind beggar. Sometimes even two, or more.

– How do you know?

– It's common knowledge, says the blind beggar.

– And why do the Armenians do that?

– Because they are a persecuted race, says the blind beggar, just like Jews and gypsies are in other countries. An Armenian never knows when we Turks will set fire to the roof over his head, that's why he is always ready to jump.

– What do you mean by 'jump'?

– Well, my little lamb, have you ever seen an Armenian jump?

– No, Dede.

– When an Armenian's house is on fire, he jumps out like a billy goat. I even saw one jump out of a window once.

– Can Armenians run as well?

– Of course Armenians can run. That's precisely my point. An Armenian runs away with nuggets of gold sewn into his shoe so that the gold goes with him.

– Is that really necessary?

– It is, my little lamb. You see, when the great *tebk* comes – that's the word Armenians use to describe a *rare event,* which can also mean a terrible misfortune or a massacre – an Armenian doesn't have the time to pack together his worldly goods. He doesn't even have time to bury his slain children. Or his wife. Or his parents and grandparents. All he can do is run. And eventually he will stop and retrieve the gold from his boots.

– Why, Dede?

– So he can start a new life, take a new wife and father more children.

It is only at this point that Mechmed Efendi sticks his old hands inside his old sack, which is even older than his hands. He inspects the boots with his fingers for a long while before saying, 'I know the man who owned these boots. In all of Bakir there was only one pair of boots like these.'

– How do you know?

– Because I often spoke to the man who owned these boots. Whenever he needed a good piece of advice, he would come to me. He wasn't rich, so each time he came he would only ever throw half a piaster in my collection cloth.

– Does that mean you saw his boots?

– No, my Nazar. But I felt them with my hands. Let me tell you, I know every fold of these exceptional boots.

– What was the man's name?

– Dikran Khatisian. An Armenian cobbler.

– And why did they hang him?

– Because of a bottle of Russian liquor. That's what people are saying.

– We have stolen the boots of a friend, Dede.

– Yes, my Nazar. But these boots are in safer hands in my sack than in the saddle bag of a saptieh.

– Why would they be in his saddle bag?

– You see, my Nazar, this is what will happen. Tomorrow morning they will untie the bodies. Or perhaps the day after tomorrow. Or even next week. I don't know what the authorities have decided or how long the dead bodies should hang there for. But eventually they will be untied, and that's when the saptiehs will fight each other for the dead men's clothes. The strongest one would have gotten the boots and he would undoubtedly have taken them to his horse in the stable and hidden them inside his saddle bag. But what use is a pair of expensive boots in the saddle bag of a saptieh? What a waste that would be. And then the blind beggar says, 'Tomorrow I will sell the boots, but I will remove the gold beforehand.'

– But you said this Armenian cobbler wasn't a rich man?

– True, my Nazar.

– Then perhaps there isn't even any gold in his boots?

– But there is, my Nazar. Even the poorest Armenian will manage to get hold of a nugget of gold for his boots.

– Can you feel it in there?

– I've been feeling around for it the entire time but I can't find it.

– He must have hidden it very well.

– Yes, my Nazar. Perhaps he has hidden it in the heel. And these heels are made of wood.

– Take them off.

– Not now, my Nazar. Not now.

– Tomorrow I will sell the boots, says Mechmed Efendi. Or perhaps I won't; perhaps I'll give them back instead.

– To the Armenian cobbler?

– I mean to his wife. She is entitled to them, after all.

– But you won't do that, will you, Dede? Never in your life have you given something back once it's been placed inside your sack.

– True, my Nazar. I've always been tempted by the Devil. But Allah is great. Perhaps this time it is His will that I give the boots back in return for a small corner of paradise. That would be nice, wouldn't it? And Mechmed Efendi says:

– Inshallah. Only Allah knows what my decision will be.

Then Mechmet Efendi collects the few paras lying on his cloth, places them in his pocket, shoves the cloth under his turban, retrieves his cane from the gutter and swings the old sack around his shoulders.

– You'll never guess where we're going, he says to the young boy, Ali.

As they walked through the dark city, the beggar told the young boy a story. It happened a long time ago, he said. I lay there dying beneath the Gate of Happiness. Nobody came to help me. All day long Armenian and Greek traders rode past me on their arabas on their way to the bazaars of Bakir. Most of them came from the region of Diyarbakir – the city of giant watermelons. Caravans of camels also rode past me, as well as Kurds on horseback from the mountain regions and Kurdish beggars from semi-nomadic villages, who had come to the city to make their fortune. Other people came by, too; it was a real mix. Even gypsies went past. Of course, Turks also went by, mostly saptiehs, who wore colorful trousers back then. And bashi-bazouks came by, a rabble of irregulars, most of them Circassians. It was a hot day and nobody gave me any water. However, late in the afternoon one man stopped right in front of where I was lying. He gave me water to drink, lots of it. A whole pouchful. He then loaded me onto his cart and took me with him.

– Where to, Dede?

– He took me to Yedi Su, an Armenian village a two-day ride

away from here.

— So he was an Armenian?

— Yes, my Nazar. An Armenian. He was called Vardan Khatisian and he is the brother of that hanged man.

— He saved your life?

— Yes, my Nazar. He took me to his village where he left me in the care of his kertastan, that's the word Armenians use for their extended family. There were many women and children and they nursed me back to health.

— And where is this Vardan Khatisian now?

— He is in prison, my Nazar.

— Is that where we are going now?

— Yes, it is.

— Why is he in prison?

— He is waiting: Tomorrow his head will be cut off.

— Who told you that?

— The people on the street.

— Does that mean he will die tomorrow?

— If Allah wishes it so, my Nazar.

— And if Allah doesn't?

— Well, then he won't.

In this moment, the Last Thought asked the Meddah, "Can the blind beggar do anything to help my father?"

"We shall soon find out," said the Meddah. "He will probably only snoop around the prison and try to find out from the saptiehs if there is anything that can be done. And then he will ask Allah to deliver some wise advice. We shall have to wait and see."

"Where is my father?"

"I already told you. He is in prison."

"In a cell?"

"Of course in a cell."

"What is he doing?"

"He is dangling from a long rope."

"So he is already dead?"

"No, my little lamb. He isn't dead."

2

As the Last Thought laid eyes on its father for the first time, it thought to itself, "Meddah was right. He really isn't dead, even though the Turks have strung him up. But he's hanging from his feet, not from his head, and you should be happy that he is hanging the wrong way round as legs don't have a neck that can snap – and if they do snap, at least it doesn't mean certain death."

And so the Last Thought felt relieved and said to the Meddah, "My father is alive!"

And the Meddah said, "Yes, your father is alive."

"His eyes are open!"

"Yes, my little lamb. But his eyes cannot see a thing."

"Is he blind?"

"No, my little lamb. Your father is simply unconscious, but don't worry, he will wake up soon. And then he will see the floor of his cell. That is all."

"But I don't like the look of this floor."

"Me neither, my little lamb. It's a dirty floor. One made of compacted clay and covered in shit and piss.

If it were day," said the Meddah, "and not pitch black, and if your father could see or even look through the small barred window in the top left-hand corner of his cell, he would see a large wall. This wall dates all the way back to the Seljuq Dynasty and is made from the same stone as Bakir's city wall. He would, of course, also see the prison yard and the top floors of the government building."

"Do you mean the *hukumet?*"

"That's right, my little lamb."

"Does that mean the hukumet is in the prison yard?"

"Of course not, my little lamb. It's on the other side of the yard wall. But it is so close that the mudir need only open the window of his office to hear the unmistakable cries of the Armenians in the prison's torture chambers."

"Does he enjoy the sound?"

"I don't know, my little lamb. But it stimulates his digestive tract. Not long ago he said to the vali, 'You know, Vali Bey, ever since the government decided to interrogate the Armenians, I haven't needed to take any castor oil; the screams of those infidels in the torture chambers is the most effective laxative around'.

– By Allah, said the vali. I've noticed the exact same thing.

– So you've stopped taking castor oil, too?

– No, Mudir Bey. In all these years I've swallowed enough oil for a lifetime.

– Vali Bey, do you think that Allah, in all His providence, deliberately gave the Armenians a loud scream so that it would help us Turks digest better?

– Allah moves in mysterious ways, said the vali. But your theory is certainly within the realm of possibility, Mudir Bey.

A few months earlier a German officer was being given a tour of the prison when he asked the vali, 'How can it be that there are so few Armenian prisoners here? Did you not claim just recently that all Armenians are crooks?'

– Armenians are shrewd, replied the vali, and difficult to catch.

– And what about the ones who commit murder?

– They are equally difficult to find.

– Could it be that there is no truth in it?

– What do you mean?

– That in reality there are fewer murderers and thieves and crooks amongst these people than any other group?

– Everything is possible, said the vali.

– Perhaps the Armenians are an honest and peaceful people, others just don't want to see it?

– We would have to ask Allah, said the vali. Allah knows the answer.

And it is true," said the Meddah, "that on that day, when the German was visiting the prison, there were only three Armenians inside."

"Who were the other prisoners?"

"They weren't Armenians," said the Meddah. "Most of them were Kurds, but there were also Turks, Arabs, gypsies and other groups, particularly the muhajirs, Muslim emigrants from Macedonia, Bulgaria, Greece and the Caucasus. Only Armenian prisoners were few and far between in Bakir's prison."

And the Meddah said, "It's true, my little lamb. Your people have never been a group of robbers, murderers or thieves. What is it that people say? 'If you're looking for robbers and thieves, you need look no further than the Kurds, particularly the wild mountain clans'. Any one of them would slit your throat in a heart-beat so he could steal your boots or your hat, providing it's a hat without a brim, as it is not becoming of a Muslim to wear a hat with a brim. And you wouldn't need to search long to find a thief or a crook amongst the other ethnic groups either, which shouldn't be taken to mean that there are no honest individuals among them. No, no. There are many of those, but not as many as among the Armenians. How else could you explain why there were only three Armenians sitting in this very prison just a few months ago?"

And the Meddah said, "When the first wave of arrests started, and hundreds of Armenians were dragged out of their beds to be interrogated on charges of espionage and other bogus claims, the mudir consulted with the vali and the mutasarrif and arranged to have all of the prisoners in the large prison next to the hukumet moved elsewhere."

"Where to, Meddah?"

"To the empty prison down by the river."

"Why, Meddah?"

"Well, why do you think, my little lamb? To make space, of course. The mudir had to find a place to put all those Armenians. And he wanted them to be close to the hukumet because that was where they all had their offices: the vali, the mutasarrif, the kaimakam and the mudir. And because the hukumet was just a few minutes' walk away from the large prison on the other side of the wall, which was as old as Bakir's city wall."

And the Meddah said, "The prison is now full. If they arrest any more Armenians, they will have to chain them all up and put them out in the yard."

"There isn't a third prison?"

"The only other prison is for women."

And the Meddah said, "Not all Armenians are in individual cells like your father. And not all Armenians are hanging upside down, by that I mean at the end of a long rope, attached not to their necks, but merely to their feet."

And the Meddah said, "Anyway, enough idle chitchat. I'll leave you alone with your father now."

I am alone with my father. I want to speak to him. I want to say, "*Father!*" But I don't say a word. It is pitch black inside his cell. I only know that he is still alive because I can hear him wheezing.

I do not need to count the hours; I am timeless.

At some point in the night the cell door opens. An ugly saptieh with a smirk on his horse-like face enters my father's cell, brandishing a torch. Two men follow him in: the fat vali and the one-eyed mudir.

The mudir points to the prisoner. 'Why did you hang him upside down?'

– Because you ordered us to, Mudir Bey, says the saptieh.

– And when was I supposed to have given that order?

– This morning, says the saptieh.

– And what reason was I supposed to have had for giving that order, if I did indeed do so?

– I don't know, Mudir Bey, says the saptieh. The vali says,

'Perhaps because he refused to give us the confession that we want. This Armenian is a stubborn one.'

– Perhaps, says the mudir.

– Perhaps you had him hung upside down so that all his blood would rush to his head?

– That must be it, says the mudir.

– To fill his head with blood, trigger his memory and loosen his tongue?

– Perhaps, says the mudir.

The horse-faced saptieh says, 'The prisoner won't need his memory anyway after tomorrow, when Issek Efendi, the deaf-mute, cuts his head off.'

– That's very true, says the mudir.

And the mudir says to the horse-faced saptieh, 'Can you imagine what the prisoner will look like tomorrow after Issek Efendi has cut his head off?'

– Yes, Mudir Bey, says the saptieh.

The mudir says, 'We won't be cutting his head off.'

– Why not, Mudir Bey?

– Because the vali wants to interrogate the prisoner tomorrow one more time.

– That's true, says the vali, but not entirely.

– What do you mean? asks the mudir.

– I won't be the one interrogating him again, Mudir Bey. That would be you.

The mudir paces up and down the cell deep in thought. He stops right next to the shit bucket. The saptieh comes over to him with the torch.

    – Why is the bucket empty?

    – Because Armenians traditionally shit on the floor.

    – Could it be that he wasn't able to use the bucket?

    – It's possible, Mudir Bey.

    – Because he is tied up by his feet and dangling upside down from a long rope?

    – It's possible, Mudir Bey.

The mudir then noticed the bowl lying next to the shit bucket. He leaned forward and smelt what was left of the bulgur.

    – This bulgur stinks as much as the shit on the floor.

    – It's possible, Mudir Bey, said the saptieh.

    – Could it be that this is in fact not bulgur, but a bowl of shit?

    – That's also possible, says the saptieh.

– When did he eat from this bowl? asked the vali.

    – Before I strung him up, said the saptieh.

    – Then perhaps he might have poisoned himself.

    – It's possible, said the saptieh.

– It would be wise, said the mudir, to have the prisoner throw up all that slop so that I can interrogate him tomorrow. If he dies before then, he won't be able to tell me anything.

    – True, said the saptieh.

    – Perhaps he's already thrown it all up.

    – Let me check.

The saptieh lowered his torch to light up the slimy floor beneath the prisoner's head. He returned to the mudir shaking his head.

– He hasn't been sick, Mudir Bey.

– How can that be?

– I don't know, Mudir Bey.

– That can't be right.

– Why, Mudir Bey?

– Because he is hanging upside down with his head facing the floor. That slop should have slid down and out of his mouth.

– Perhaps the slop doesn't want to come out, Mudir Bey? The mudir turned to the vali. What do you think?

– Nothing, said the vali.

– It would be wise, said the vali, to have the prisoner regurgitate his food, said the vali. Otherwise you won't be able to interrogate him tomorrow.

– Yes, said the mudir.

– Do something, Mudir Bey!

– Hajde, hajde! said the mudir to the saptieh. What are you waiting for? Do something!

– What should I do, Mudir Bey?

– Something, anything, you miscreant, said the mudir.

– I could shove a spoon down the prisoner's throat, said the saptieh, but I can't see any spoons in here.

– So how did the prisoner eat his slop?

– With his fingers.

– And where is his spoon?

– He doesn't have one.

– Can't you get hold of a spoon from somewhere?

– No, Mudir Bey. Not in the middle of the night.

– Why don't you stick your finger in his mouth?

– I could, Mudir Bey, but my fingers are very short, and we need to push something long down his throat until he starts to choke.

– How about a dagger?

– It needs to be something soft, Mudir Bey.

– Or the barrel of a gun?

– It's too hard, Mudir Bey.

– The saptieh is right, said the vali. There wouldn't be much left to interrogate tomorrow if we shove the barrel of a gun, or the butt or blade of a dagger, down his throat. They have sensitive throats these Armenians. Believe me; I speak from experience.

– You mean to say that if we do that, the prisoner won't be able to speak tomorrow?

– That is precisely what I mean, Mudir Bey, said the vali.

– Don't you have anything soft on you? the mudir asked the horse-faced saptieh. Something that's soft, but long enough to make the prisoner vomit; something that you can thrust deep into his throat without causing him any serious injury? It is crucial that we interrogate him tomorrow.

– I could fuck him in the mouth, said the saptieh.

– Do you have something to fuck with? asked the mudir.

– Yes, said the saptieh.

The saptieh gave the prisoner a gentle shove with one hand as he held the burning torch in the other. The prisoner swayed back and forth, and the scene was rather eerie, at least the mudir thought as much, as did the vali, mainly because neither the mudir nor the vali was looking at the prisoner or the saptieh with the torch in his hand: They had now turned their attention to the opposite wall.

– It's shadow puppetry, said the vali. Look, Mudir Bey. You can see a stickman on the bare wall there, swinging backwards and forwards.

– Turkish shadow puppetry, said the mudir.

– *Karagoz,* said the vali.

– Exactly. Karagoz. Traditional Turkish shadow puppetry that has forever fascinated the Europeans.

– An ancient art, said the vali.

– Yes, said the mudir.

– Shall I place the torch in the hole? asked the saptieh.

– Which hole?

– The hole in the floor with the dog's head inside.

– What dog's head?

– The one the prisoner didn't want to eat.

– Who gave him a dog's head?

– You gave it to him, Mudir Bey, said the saptieh.

– Place the torch in the hole containing the dog's head, said the mudir, whilst gazing in fascination at the shadows on the opposite wall. The vali was equally transfixed by the shape of the stickman swinging backwards and forwards on the wall.

And then suddenly there were two stickmen as the saptieh now moved so he was standing in front of the torch which had been placed inside the hole – the hole in the floor containing the dog's head.

– Look, Vali Bey, said the mudir. Can you believe all these magnificent shapes we are seeing are merely shadows on a wall?

– It's art, said the vali. Genuine art. We Turks are the best in the world when it comes to shadow puppetry.

– Karagoz, said the mudir.

– Karagoz, said the vali.

– You have to use your imagination, said the vali. You have to imagine that the second stickman is dropping his trousers.

– And the first stickman, the one hanging upside down from the ceiling, opens his mouth nice and wide.

– Precisely, said the vali.

– You have to imagine that the second stickman now produces a snake from between his thin stickman legs.

– You don't have to use your imagination, said the vali. You can actually see it.

– Yes, said the mudir. I can see the snake, too. And now the snake is turning into a stick.

– And the stick is getting longer and longer.

– And bigger.

– It's incredible.

– Karagoz!

– Karagoz.

– You see that saptieh with the imbecile horse face, Vali Bey? said the mudir. Did you know he had a famous father?

– Oh, really? Who?

– He is the son of One-Legged Hassan, a man who had a hand in the great Bulgarian massacre.

– When is that said to have taken place?

– In 1876.

– During the Bulgarian Uprising?

– Precisely.

– At that time his father still had both legs, but whilst the massacres and rapes were going on, one of the Bulgarian women brandished a revolver and shot off Hassan's leg.

– You don't say!

– Yes, Vali Bey. Shot it clean off.

– In those days the English press did their level best to stir up hatred against us Turks. The story was that our troops had burnt down entire villages. They wrote that headless bodies were found; the scorched corpses of women and children.

– And is it true?

– Of course it's true. But the Turks weren't responsible.

– Who was?

– The bashi-bazouks. Irregulars serving under the then Sultan, mainly Circassians.

– But weren't the bashi-bazouks under Turkish command?

– Of course they were under Turkish command.

– These Circassians couldn't stand the Russians, said the mudir, because Russian Cossacks had burnt down their villages.

– Makes sense, said the vali.

– They fled to Turkey from the Caucasus and many of them became bashi-bazouks. The Sultan deployed them in Bulgaria when the uprising broke out. As the Circassians couldn't stand the Russians, and because they thought that all Bulgarians were Russian, they massacred the women and children.

– Understandable, said the vali.

– During that time they caused us a lot of trouble, particularly on account of the English press.

– Yes, said the vali.

– And yet the English are no better. They want to conquer the entire world, and they also have bashi-bazouks, they just go by a different name.

– And there was Hassan, a one-legged man, who actually had both legs at the time. Did you know that he was nothing more than a run-of-the-mill chiaus? But the English papers translated the Turkish word into their infidel tongue, and so One-Legged Hassan became a sergeant in their language. A sergeant is something special over there in England, and so they mentioned his name in the papers.

– The cursed English press, said the vali.

– And that horse-faced saptieh over there, ramming the Armenian in the mouth, is his son.

– In the flesh?

– Exactly.

– He's a little bent, this son of One-Legged Hassan, said the mudir. He comes from a village called Sazan-Koy which is said to be where the most handsome boys live.

– Indeed? said the vali.

– Once he rammed a three-year-old up the rear and the child nearly died.

– Did he die?

– No, said the mudir.

– How strange, said the mudir. I see that horse face every single day and yet I had absolutely no clue that the man to whom that face belonged was in fact the son of none other than One-Legged Hassan and, on top of that, a queer who almost buggered a three-year-old to death.

They both stared at the shadow figures on the wall. The mudir's voice sounded soft, with almost a hint of delight; the vali's was brash and deep-throated. Behind them they could hear the unmistakable sounds of the prisoner vomiting, and with each gurgled heave that came from the hanging man's mouth, the mudir winced and his glass eye jolted forwards as if trying to jump onto the bare wall and the shadows moving upon it.

The Last Thought was horrified at the sight of the mudir's glass eye seemingly about to break loose from its socket, and so the storyteller soothed the Last Thought with his calming storyteller voice. He said to the Last Thought, "Don't worry. His glass eye won't jump out onto the bare wall. It's just an illusion."

"My father has glass eyes, too," said the Last Thought. "And every time the saptieh thrusts his hose deep down his throat, my father's eyes spring out of their sockets. I'm frightened that they'll fall out onto the floor and be smashed to pieces."

"It's just an illusion," said the storyteller. "Eyes don't just fall out of the holes beneath the forehead where the Lord God planted them."

"But they are glass eyes. Did the Lord God plant glass eyes into the holes beneath my father's forehead?"

"No, my little lamb. They aren't glass eyes. They are just the eyes of a man who has lost his mind."

"Where did his mind go?"

"The Turks have made it disappear. But don't worry. Tomorrow morning the Lord God will return his mind to him."

The following morning my father was no longer hanging at the end of a long rope. Just before daybreak a handful of men in uniform entered his cell, unhooked him, carried him over to the straw mat under the barred window and lay him down. For a moment they stood in front of the bed, looking at him in silence. Shortly afterwards a man in civilian clothing with a fez on his head entered. It was none other than the kaimakam. The uniformed men stood to attention and saluted.

– This Armenian stinks like ten perished lambs rotting in the midday sun, said the kaimakam. Under no circumstances can he be let into the mudir's office in this state.

– You are right, Kaimakam Bey, said one of the men in uniform.

– You see, this man is going to be interrogated. He is a dangerous spy and his confession is of the utmost importance.

– But we need to wash him first.

– All Armenians are dirty, said the kaimakam. They don't wash five times a day as the Prophet decreed. They are as impure as the pork that they eat.

– Yes, Kaimakam Bey.

– Nevertheless he needs to be washed. But he, of course, needs to wake up first.

– Yes, Kaimakam Bey.

– If he doesn't kick the bucket, said the kaimakam, and if, by some miracle, he wakes up, try and put a bit of meat on his bones. Give him a decent breakfast and a decent lunch. He must be fit for questioning by this afternoon.

– Yes, Kaimakam Bey.

– He should also be in a good mood.

– What do you mean?

– Cheer him up.

– And how should we do that?

– Give him Armenian lavash bread for breakfast. That will cheer him up.

– Are you sure?

– Absolutely.

– And what should we give him for lunch?

– The dish Armenians usually eat during their festivals, the Armenian national dish which they call Harissa. Any Armenian is sure to smile when you place that slop of overcooked meat and pearl barley under his nose.

– But, Kaimakam Bey, how are we supposed to cook the Armenian national dish here in the prison? I've heard of this dish before and I know it needs to be cooked and stirred over several days.

– True, said the kaimakam.

– Of course, we could go and order it in the Armenian mahalle, but that would be quite a bit of a hassle.

– Do what you can, said the kaimakam.

"Everything I see," the Last Thought told the storyteller, "I see through your eyes. And everything I hear, I hear through your ears. But aren't the eyes and the ears of a storyteller not just as dishonest as his tongue? And why are you telling me lies when I know that you really want to tell me the truth?"

"Because I am the storyteller," said the storyteller.

"And because I do tell the truth, I just tell it differently." And the storyteller said, "And call me Meddah."

"Tell me, Meddah. Did my father really swallow the saptieh's hose?"

"His mouth resisted, my little lamb. You saw for yourself. And his throat resisted. And his gullet. Yes, even his stomach resisted. But the hose had to be swallowed. And yet, my little lamb, your father was not aware that it was happening because he was unconscious the whole time."

"Then he won't remember it?"

"He will, my little lamb. He will have dreams about the hose. And then he will wake up and he will scream."

"And what was happening with those shadows on the wall? At first I could see two stickmen, but then I saw a bat."

"Are you sure you saw a bat?"

"Yes, Meddah."

"But it was just two stickmen coming together to form a single shadow. They became a bat, and this bat twitched uncontrollably as the saptieh's hose began to twitch and the seed of One-Legged Hassan was squirted so deep down your father's throat that he vomited again.

When they unhooked him," said the storyteller, "and laid him down on the straw mat, your father fell into a deep, relaxing sleep. It was only around midday, when he passed into a lighter sleep, that he started to dream. Still half asleep, he let out a loud scream and woke himself up."

3

"The guards dragged him out of his cell early in the afternoon. He was washed, scrubbed and given fresh clothes. They then took him to another, clean cell."

"Did they give him some breakfast?"

"Yes."

"And did he get given some lavash, that delicious Armenian bread, and then harissa, the Armenian national dish?"

"Of course not, my little lamb. They just gave him some ordinary ekmek, basic Turkish bread, but they did serve it together with a spread made of grape syrup and a generous serving of spiced tea, followed by mutton and beans.

Your father was naturally very tenacious," said the storyteller. "By late afternoon he was already fit for interrogation, and by that I mean of sound mind. They chained his feet, although he was under the watchful eye of many saptiehs and so couldn't possibly run away, and led him across the large prison yard, through the gate in the old wall."

"To the hukumet?"

"Precisely. Where the mudir's office is. My little lamb ... I have already told you about the mudir's office, and yesterday afternoon I allowed you to listen in as the men were talking, do you remember? Those men – all important people – they were smoking their chibouk and talking about this, that and the other, about whether or not they were going to chop off your father's head. Well, I didn't go into detail about the office because I didn't want to bore you. Besides, it is not important what is in a room but who. And on this occasion it contains the mudir and your father. But you should know this: the one-eyed mudir is a westernized man and a fanatical supporter of the Young Turks and their newly-formed party: *Ittihad ve Terraki,* the Committee of Union and Progress. That is why his office contains two western chairs and a wide desk, although these items are rarely found in the office of a Turkish official. As you would expect, the office also contains a divan; there are also lambskin rugs on the floor as well as a small, hand-made carpet. An old saber hangs on the wall, as does a picture of the Sultan, a handful of verses from the Qur'an and, of course, a portrait of Enver Pasha, the Minister of War. There his is: the man on horseback wearing a pristine brown military uniform and a fur cap. Enver's face is as soft as that of an innocent maiden; his slender moustache almost appears stuck to his face. His hands, which hold his horse's reins in a firm grip, appear delicate, and his long, slim fingers could just as well be those of a pianist. A likeable man, a man with sensitive hands and a sensitive face. He is the executioner of the Armenians.

The saptiehs brought your father in as ordered. They now stand opposite one another, the mudir and your father. The mudir is polite. His glass eye looks straight at your father's face. He gestures warmly with his hand and says, 'Please take a seat, efendi.'

Shortly afterwards a third man enters the office. He is the bash-khatib, the chief scribe.

You might be wondering, my little lamb, why the bash-khatib isn't wearing western clothing like most of the Young Turks' followers. He doesn't even have the customary red fez on his head as would be befitting a man of his standing. Well, as you can tell, this man is rather aged, and a little old-fashioned, and he just can't bear to part with his shalvar trousers or his clean, kaftan-esque cloak that conceals his dirty undergarments. He also won't part with his white turban with a green cord, which is customary wear for strict Muslims. The bash-khatib is carrying a small basket which holds everything he needs: a large inkwell containing the standard official purple ink, a Stambul quill, a sponge and finely-powdered flour to blot the text, and, of course, your father's file. He is also holding a square board under his arm to write on. The bash-khatib doesn't bother trying to find a third chair: Firstly, because there isn't one, and, secondly, because he is used to sitting cross-legged on the floor, which is where he takes his seat. He clamps a pillow between his rear and the floor and places another behind his back, leans against the divan, lays the square board across his knees, balances the inkwell on top – the one filled with the official purple ink – lays his Stambul quill alongside it, together with the sponge and the blotting powder and, of course, your father's file.

Your father is a man whose age is nigh on impossible to guess. But I can see, my little lamb, that the bash-khatib has written the year 1878 in his file – neatly, in purple ink – so I would assume that your father is 37 years of age. His file reads:

Vardan Khatisian, born in the year 1878 in the village of Yedi Su within the Vilayet of Bakir, accused of espionage and high treason.

Yes, my little lamb. That's what is written. Come to think of it, your father doesn't actually look that much like a spy, but who could say with absolute certainty what a genuine spy looks like? When it comes to your father, my little lamb, I would say that he looks like nothing more than a typical mountain-dwelling Armenian.

His frame is tall and gaunt, and he has dark hair and eyes, although at this very moment his face is almost yellow in color, but that comes as a result of spending several weeks inside a prison cell. His chin and aquiline nose appear as though they are trying to escape his face – to go to a place where the mountains are higher, the air cleaner; where your head would almost touch the clouds and where the wind hums a different melody than down in the valley of the Turkish feudal lords, the *derebeys*. Your father has beautiful, almost delicate hands. They stand in direct contrast to his face. Enver Pasha also has beautiful, delicate hands. But should I compare your father's hands to those of an executioner?

No, my little lamb. I won't do that. But instead I will tell you this: Although your father has sensitive hands, they are quite different to those of Enver Pasha. Your father's hands are sorrowful and tortured. You see, hands are as expressive as eyes, which brings us to your father's eyes, my little lamb. At present they are not dissimilar to the mudir's glass eye; they hold no expression whatsoever. But do not be deceived, my little lamb. You should have seen his eyes before he came to this prison.

– An Armenian's eyes are lecherous, malicious, greedy, deceitful and devious, just like those of the Jews and the Greeks. These three groups of people embody all that is evil in the world!

– Now, my little lamb, those were not my words. That's just what the vali of Bakir said. He then added, 'What I hate most are the Armenians' eyes. And if there were no other grounds to exterminate them, their eyes would be reason enough.'

I would like to have said to the vali of Bakir, 'Tell me, Vali Bey, have you ever seen an Armenian's eyes when he is caressing his child?' – And the vali would surely reply, 'No, I haven't.'

– Tell me, when do you look these people in the eye?

– Only when they are changing money for me or when my cock itches.

And I would say to the vali, 'Vali Bey, when you look an Armenian in the eye, you are looking into your own eyes.' And I would watch as the vali's cheeks grew pale. He would say, 'My own eyes?'

– And I would say, 'Yes, your own eyes.'

I see a cross, my little lamb. Except on this cross I see not the hanging body of Christ but an Armenian eye, being nailed down by a Turk.

It is late afternoon, my little lamb. The sun is peeking into the mudir's office. Its rays wink at the mudir through the window, causing him some discomfort in his glass eye. He rubs it and then blows his nose. The Sultan in his picture frame and Enver Pasha in his portrait also wink at him – mockingly, encouragingly – even the Qur'an verses above their heads laugh and wink. The mudir's one eye looks at your father, the other looks asquint at the

Qur'an verses as though just noticing the Arabic lettering for the first time. Do you hear, my little lamb, how the mudir is trying to persuade your father? It's a long monologue, and your father is listening and nodding his head. It is extraordinary how polite the mudir is being. He is asking your father if he slept well, whether the straw mat in his cell was still covered in shit and piss from all the previous occupants who pissed and shat themselves there. He explains to your father how this is a regrettable situation due to the current lack of straw and, as a consequence, straw mats. After all, they were at war and straw stocks were low because of the Turkish cavalry, which was the best in the world; Turkish soldiers may be valiant, but their horses ate straw and that's all there was to it.

The mudir enquired after his teeth, by that I mean your father's teeth. He remarked that they hadn't been pulled out, adding that, after all, prisoners here were treated humanely. And he asked how his throat was, and his gullet, and his stomach. Was he aware that they had pumped his stomach in the middle of the night? Had he noticed even the slightest thing that had taken place last night? No. Your father hadn't noticed anything as he was either lying or hanging at the end on a long rope in a state of complete unconsciousness. And the mudir asked whether your father had had any dreams involving, say, a long tube, one that was squishy and flaccid but that grew larger and larger and harder and harder, and the mudir asked whether he knew who One-Legged Hassan was or his son, the one with the horse face, who sometimes squirted the seed of One-Legged Hassan, that famous bashi-bazouk and butcher of 1876, down the throats of infidels, right down to their stomachs? But none of it made sense to your father, so he just nodded and faced forward, his eyes almost glass-like with fatigue.

Finally, the mudir said, 'We have interrogated you many times, efendi – the Vali and I – each of us in his own way, and now we are going to go through it all again. But this is your last chance.'

The mudir gave the chief scribe a wave with his left hand. In fact, the mudir raised his hand imperceptibly, but the chief scribe, who had known the mudir for many years and knew each of his gestures, recognized the signal and so picked himself up, placed his board, together with all his writing equipment, on the floor, took the mudir's nargileh, a modern hookah from Erzurum which stood next to the divan, carried it over to the desk, handed the hose with the mouthpiece over to the mudir, lit it for him, returned to his place, sat himself down on the pillow in front of the divan, took hold of the board and your father's file, the inkwell and the Stambul quill, the sponge and the finely-powdered flour used for blotting and set everything straight, including the pillows – one beneath his rear and another behind his back.

The mudir puffed silently for a moment. Then he said, 'This truly is your last chance, efendi. It's best if we start right from the beginning … as with all the previous interrogations that I, and not the vali, have led … although I admit it's boring. Always starting from the beginning, I mean. But that's how we're going to do it. So, let us start from the beginning again – right from the very beginning.'

– So your name is Vardan Khatisian? said the mudir. Is that correct?

    – That is correct, said your father.

– And you come from an Armenian village where only a single Turk lived?

– A Turkish family.

– And everyone else was Armenian?

– Yes, Mudir Bey.

– Is it true that there was also a church there?

– Yes, Mudir Bey. The Church of the Holy Sarki.

– And this church still stands?

– It's still standing.

– And the Armenians?

– They are also still there; at least, most of them are.

– And the Turkish family?

– They are also there. Not much has changed in my village.

– So you come from a small Armenian village? A village with an Armenian majority where the few Turks living there are forced to go to church?

– No, Mudir Bey. No one forces any of the Turks to go to church.

– But don't you try to convince these Turks that Allah had a son, even though it says in the Qur'an that Allah did not give birth, nor was he born?

– The Armenians don't try to convince anyone of anything, Mudir Bey. They keep to themselves and are happy when they are left in peace.

– And what about these lies? Don't the Armenians in Yedi Su tell anyone who comes their way that their village is a typical Turkish village, and that there are in fact no more Turks left in Turkey, just Armenians?

– No, Mudir Bey. Why would the Armenians in Yedi Su say

such a thing? Nobody would believe it.

– But isn't it true that they claim that this country once belonged to them?

– I don't know, Mudir Bey. Anyway it's not true. The whole country never belonged to them, just a part of it.

– So, a part of it did?

– Yes. But that's history, Mudir Bey. It was such a long time ago.

– The Armenians are a group of traders and crooks. A trusting Turk is completely at their mercy.

– My father is a farmer, Mudir Bey. Most Armenians are simple farmers and craftsmen.

– And what about the Armenian traders in the big cities?

– I don't know, Mudir Bey.

– This Turkish family in your village? Surely you tried to bully them out of the village?

– No, Mudir Bey. They are my family's neighbors and our friends.

– Friends?

– Yes, Mudir Bey. As far back as I can remember, not once have we disputed with those Turks. We have always helped one another. Once – I remember it was after a bad harvest – my father borrowed corn from them. We gave them a couple of sacks of wheat flour and preserved vegetables.

– Did you give them anything else?

– Yes, Mudir Bey. We took entire clay pots filled with tan, patat and harissa.

– What are those things, efendi?

– Tan is made from madsun, Armenian yoghurt. It's the same as Turkish *ayran* but it tastes slightly different. At least, it did where I grew up because my mother sprinkled in a few spices. I still don't know what her secret recipe was. It also tasted a bit sweet; I presume she mixed in a little bit of honey.

– So it is some kind of magical Armenian potion?

– I don't know, Mudir Bey.

– And what is patat?

– It's the same as Turkish *sarma*. Just basic cabbage or vine leaves filled with meat, rice and bulgur. There are also a few vegetables inside. We call it patat, but honestly, Mudir Bey, it is no different than your Turkish sarma.

– And what is harissa?

– That is the Armenian national dish.

– Does it contain pork?

– No, Mudir Bey. It contains mutton or chicken.

– And your Turkish neighbors ate this slop?

– It wasn't slop, Mudir Bey. It was real harissa.

– And you're sure there wasn't any pork in it?

– No, Mudir Bey. There wasn't.

The mudir discreetly gestured once more to the chief scribe. This time he simply turned his head towards the chief scribe, twitched his glass eye, and the chief scribe knew immediately what his master and commander wanted. He gave a little cough, turned the pages of the file and read, 'Vardan Khatisian, primary occupation: farmer, secondary occupation: tezek salesman and poet'.

– Is that true? asked the mudir.

– It is, said your father.

– Perhaps you could explain a bit more fully?

– I can, said your father. And for the first time your father smiled, and his glass-like eyes suddenly held an element of cheer. We children all had to help out in the fields, explained your father, and so each of us was a farmer, whether we liked it or not. It was the same for all the other jobs that had to be done: we were the ones called in to do them. We also had to milk the sheep, cows and goats.

– Did you also have a donkey?

– Yes, Mudir Bey.

– And did you milk it, too?

– Yes, Mudir Bey.

– But nobody can milk a donkey.

– True, Mudir Bey.

– Do you wish to play me for a fool?

– No, Mudir Bey.

– Then it was a jenny?

– Yes, Mudir Bey.

– And what's this business with tezek?

– It's dried cow dung. We Armenians actually call it *atar* or *schortrik,* but in our region we use the Turkish word, tezek. It's ideal for heating.

– *Tezek,* said the mudir. You think I don't know what that is? It's nothing more than plain old cow shit.

– Well, Mudir Bey, let me explain. The rich heat with wood and the poor use schortrik or atar or tezek.

– Aren't there any rich people who heat their homes with cow shit?

– Oh yes, many, Mudir Bey. The richer a man is, the more frugal he becomes. And wood is very hard to come by in this region and costs a great deal of money.

— More than tezek?

— Well, tezek doesn't cost anything at all, unless you buy it from a trader.

— From an Armenian, for example?

— Perhaps, Mudir Bey.

— Armenians who know how to turn cow shit into money?

— Yes, Mudir Bey.

— Back when I was a boy, I started selling tezek. I used to drag sacks of it to Bakir because here people pay higher prices than in neighboring villages, where the farmers usually have enough tezek and their children can collect cow pats from the fields. I sold it for a few years, then I left the country.

— You went to America?

— Yes. To America.

— It's true, said the chief scribe. I have it all here in his file. You can verify it if you wish, Mudir Bey. It's all been neatly recorded.

— Yes, said the mudir.

— Vardan Khatisian, said the chief scribe. Born in the year 1878, farmer, cow shit salesman and poet. Emigrated to America in the year 1898.

— You read it differently a few moments ago, said the mudir.

— I have written this sentence numerous times, said the chief scribe.

— As a way to perfect your style? asked the mudir.

— Yes, said the chief scribe.

– Why would a farmer, who works as a cow shit salesman on the side, become a poet? asked the mudir.

– I don't know, Mudir Bey.

– Is that one of those Armenian lies?

– No, Mudir Bey.

– So, in the year 1898 you emigrated to America?

– Yes, Mudir Bey.

– To get rich quickly, I presume? To sell the Americans shit just like you sold shit to the Turks here in Turkey?

– No, Mudir Bey.

– Why did you emigrate then?

– Because I had an uncle over there who paid for me to sail across. He's my father's brother and his name is Nahapeth. Nahapeth Khatisian to be precise.

– And I presume this Nahapeth Khatisian is a trader?

– Yes, Mudir Bey. He was indeed a trader.

– He traded in cow shit, too?

– No, Mudir Bey.

– Why not?

– The Americans don't burn tezek.

– Don't they have cows in America?

– They do; they have plenty.

– And the cows over there shit nuggets of gold, I'm guessing?

– No, Mudir Bey.

– So your uncle didn't trade in cow shit?

– Correct.

– And what did he trade in?

– In rags.

– So he was a rag seller?

– Yes.

– Are all the Armenians in America rag sellers?

– No, Mudir Bey.

– What do the Armenians do over there in America?

– I'm not entirely sure, Mudir Bey, but I believe they do the same things as anyone else. Some are tradesmen, others are craftsmen. Many of them work in factories or make something or other. I have other relatives over there: one uncle is a tailor, another is a coach driver. One of my mother's cousins is a milliner.

– You were born in 1878. In 1898 you were twenty?

– Yes, I was.

– You weren't married at that time, were you?

– No, I wasn't married.

– I know your file inside out and back to front, said the mudir, and now I've caught you out. That was a lie: you were in fact married.

The chief scribe gave a little cough and the mudir turned to look at him. Is something wrong, Bash-Khatib Agah?

– He was widowed, said the chief scribe.

– But that cannot be, said the mudir.

– He married when he was just fifteen, said the chief scribe, as is common in so many of these backward villages. His wife died during childbirth in their first year of marriage, which left him widowed at just sixteen. He emigrated four years later, at the age of twenty.

– To America?

– To America, said the chief scribe.

– And what does a twenty-year-old Armenian cow shit salesman do in America, I wonder? asked the mudir. One who is also a farmer and who claims to be a poet?

– At night I went to school to learn to speak their language and to finish my education.

– Do all Armenians go to school at night and not during the day like normal people?

– Not all of them, Mudir Bey. Only those who need to catch up on their schooling or who work during the day.

– Weren't you a little too old to still be going to school?

– There were many there who were older than me, Mudir Bey. Many of them were married with a wife and children.

– Married, you say?

– Yes, Mudir Bey.

– And not perhaps divorced or widowed?

– Many of them were, in fact, married.

– But that can't be right now, can it? How is a married American supposed to find time to give his wife one if he spends his nights at school?

– I don't know, Mudir Bey.

– And what did you do during the day?

– During the day I worked.

The mudir turned his head to the chief scribe again. Is that true?

– It's true, Mudir Bey. During the day he worked as a street sweeper on a street with no name.

– So, it's not true then, said the mudir. No street is nameless.

– Over there the streets have numbers, said Vardan Khatisian.

– Numbers? asked the mudir.

– Yes, numbers, said Vardan Khatisian.

– The streets had numbers, said your father, and we street cleaners also had numbers, although we didn't wear them on our chests or sewn onto our clothes or anything like that. We just had to keep the number in our head. And the people on the streets all looked the same, although some of them were black and some of them were white. They, too, were somehow just numbers.

– So this American city was filled with nothing but numbers?

– That was how it seemed to me, said your father, at least that's how it was during my first few months in America. After a while it became less so. You get used to everything eventually, don't you?

– What's that supposed to mean? asked the mudir.

– The longer I lived over there, the more I got used to the numbers. After some time, the numbers grew faces and then I was able to clearly tell them apart.

– You must take me for a fool.

– No, Mudir Bey.

– So the people suddenly had faces again?

– Yes, Mudir Bey.

– And the numbered streets?

– They did, too, Mudir Bey.

– An Armenian street cleaner in an American city, said the mudir. One that cheats people like all other Armenians, but who couldn't sell cow shit to the Americans because the Americans aren't Turks.

– I don't know, Mudir Bey.

– And you want me to believe that you were a street cleaner

over there for sixteen years, right up until you returned to Turkey?

– No, Mudir Bey. I took any job going. Later on I worked in factories and in restaurants, and I was also a porter.

– So you were also a laborer?

– Yes.

– Just a common hamal?

– Yes, Mudir Bey.

– And what else did you do?

– I was a night watchman.

– A night watchman?

– Yes.

– Where was that, efendi?

– In a skyscraper.

– What is a skyscraper? asks the mudir.

– It's a house that looks as though it could collapse at any moment, said your father. You see, it's not a flat building, as our buildings are here … or square. It resembles a stone monument with its plinth on the ground and its head jutting up into the clouds. Inside lifts hurtle up and down, doors spin in circles, swallowing people up and spitting them out again. And when you walk into one of these buildings, you feel as though you're walking into a bazaar.

– I'm not sure I follow you there, said the mudir.

– Behind those devilish rotating doors are lots of shops, said your father, just like a bazaar, except it's not like the bazaars here where we live.

– And what's above the bazaar?

– Offices.

– Many offices? Around five or six?

– Roughly 500.
– Such a thing can't possibly be real, said the mudir.
– It can, said your father. I assure you.

– And what does a night watchman do all night long in one of these devilish buildings?

– Not much, Mudir Bey. He can count the hours until dawn. He can read in order to pass the time. And he can also write poems.
– Poems?
– Yes, Mudir Bey.
– Did you write poems?
– Yes, Mudir Bey.

– Every Armenian poet is a conspirator, said the mudir. His mind is set on turning people against us. And so I presume that you published your poetry, most probably in one of those Armenian newspapers filled with lies that are everywhere to be found ... particularly in America ... Armenian exile newspapers that aim to stir up hatred against us and sully our name. Am I right?
– No, Mudir Bey.
– Where did you publish your poetry?
– Nowhere, Mudir Bey.
– I suppose you weren't good enough?
– I don't know, Mudir Bey.
– I imagine no one wanted to print them?
– They did, Mudir Bey.

Your father's eyes suddenly came to life. It was as though he were looking at the mudir for the very first time, and his gaze penetrated deep into his glass eye. But then your father sank back into himself, and his voice became very faint. Poetry shouldn't be published, he said to the mudir.

– And why not, efendi?

– Would you be willing to cut a hole in your chest to let all those curious eyes peer in at your heart?

– No, efendi.

– And would you cast your sacred texts before wolves?

– Never, efendi.

– Or thoughts, thoughts that don't concern anyone ... would you share those with all the tattlers and backbiters?

– I wouldn't do that either, efendi. The mudir smiled. For just a second, his one eye gazed at your father in a look of complete understanding. But then his expression changed, and it appeared as though both the mudir's eyes were made of glass. He said, 'Let's get down to business, efendi.'

But the mudir didn't seem to be in any great hurry; he stood up suddenly, like someone who was restless and needed to stretch his legs. He walked to the window and opened it. Coincidence or not, at that very moment – just as the mudir opened the window – a machine gun sounded somewhere in the distance, causing him to shiver.

– You could easily think that the Russians were already in the city, he said to the chief scribe. Although I read in the papers yesterday that the Russians had already lost the war.

– They are not in the city yet, said the chief scribe. That will have just been a Turkish soldier – perhaps one of those young recruits – firing off a few rounds to show off to some curious onlookers.

– Have you ever set eyes on one of those machine guns?

– No.

– They're German.

The mudir smiled. He stood at the window and looked down into the courtyard. The screams of a tortured prisoner could now also be heard coming from the other side of the prison wall.

The mudir closed the window. He slowly walked over to his desk, walking around the hookah and shoving it to the side a little, before sitting down opposite the prisoner and folding his hands in his lap.

– Let's get down to business, he said.

His glass eye opened up wide. He said, 'Let's get down to business, efendi.'

– You were in America for sixteen years and it just so happens that you return to Turkey right as a world war breaks out. Don't you find that a little odd?

– I wanted to see my family again, said your father, and I wanted to marry again.

– And you could think of no other time to return to this country than at the outbreak of the Great War?

– It was pure coincidence, Mudir Bey.

– What really brought you back to Turkey? And who sent you?

– No one, Mudir Bey.

– Whose orders are you following?

– No one's, Mudir Bey.

– Why are you lying, efendi?

– I'm telling the truth.

– All I really wanted was to get married, said your father. And I wanted to take a wife from the village of my birth. That was the real reason why I came back. I wanted to marry again and then to take my wife back with me to America.

– Aren't there any women in America?

– There are, Mudir Bey. There are plenty of women over there. But they are somehow different.

– In what way?

– Well, Mudir Bey, they don't obey their husbands. They believe themselves to be independent. And they show their legs to anyone and everyone.

– Like the Franks?

– Yes, Mudir Bey.

– All Franks are the same, said the mudir, whether they are German or French or Italian. All Franks are infidels and eat pork – and their women refuse to obey their husbands and show off their legs to the whole world.

– That's right, Mudir Bey.

– And it is like that in America, too?

– Over there it's even worse, Mudir Bey.

– Then it must really be awful, said the mudir.

– Yes, said your father. It's terrible.

– However, we believe that this whole story with your family and marriage is simply a pretext, said the mudir, and that you returned to your homeland on the eve of the Great War for very different reasons.

– What reasons, Mudir Bey?

– You know very well, efendi. And you know more than I do.

– Let us start with the murder of the Austrian heir to the throne, said the mudir. He and his wife were shot dead in Sarajevo on June 28, 1914: an event that triggered the Great War. The mudir smiled weakly. How did it come to be that you, efendi, were in Sarajevo on that day … that exact same day? Was it perhaps a coincidence?

– It was pure coincidence, Mudir Bey.

– So you admit that you were in Sarajevo on that day? I ask because we have your passport, which contains an Austrian visa, a two-week permit to stay, an extension of this permit, and a letter of confirmation from the Sarajevo registry office and your hotel bill dated June 28.

– I admit I was there, Mudir Bey. But it is sheer coincidence. I was in Sarajevo visiting my uncle.

– What uncle?

– My father's brother. His name is Simeon … Simeon Khatisian … he owns a coffeehouse.

– So he's a coffeehouse owner?

– Yes, Mudir Bey.

– You Armenians have uncles everywhere, don't you?

– I'm part of a large family, Mudir Bey.

– And what did you want from this uncle of yours?

– Nothing at all, Mudir Bey. My other uncle, the one living in America, he wanted to send some money to his brother, the brother living in Sarajevo … and he asked me to hand the money over in person … you know … because of the foreign exchange embargo.

– And why did you stay in a hotel?

– I only stayed there for the first few days, Mudir Bey. I didn't want to impose, but then my uncle came to fetch me from the hotel. He just arrived in a coach, sent the coach driver up to my room and had him carry out my suitcase. He didn't even ask me. You know how it is. In those situations it's impossible to refuse.

– Someone's hospitality, you mean? Or family duty? I suppose it's just common courtesy, isn't it?

– Exactly, Mudir Bey. We Armenians are hospitable people and we also carry a sense of family duty. We're like the Turks in that respect. And when a relative invites you to stay, it's impossible to say no.

– I see, said the mudir.

– And you had absolutely nothing to do with the murder of the Austrian heir to the throne?

– Nothing at all, Mudir Bey.

– It's all just a coincidence?

– Right, Mudir Bey.

– You didn't even see the heir to the throne and his wife being shot?

– No, Mudir Bey. I didn't see it happen.

– And you didn't hear any shots?

– Yes, Mudir Bey. I heard the shots.

– We were standing on the street close to the bridge on the quay, Mudir Bey. My uncle and I. Thousands of people were on the streets that day to see the royal couple. Anyone with eyes had come out to witness it; it's not something that happens every day.

– True, said the mudir. It's not something that happens every day.

– It was a major, earth-shattering event.

– Yes, said the mudir. It certainly was.

– And you claim it was a coincidence that you were there, said the mudir. And I suppose you're going to tell me that it was also a coincidence that just less than a month later – on July 25 no less – you arrived in Constantinople just as the ultimatum Austria had issued to Serbia on July 23 expired?

– It was, Mudir Bey.

– Three days before the outbreak of the Great War! A coincidence was it, efendi?

– It was all a coincidence, Mudir Bey.

– It's true that I stayed in Sarajevo for quite a long time, said your father, and that I only arrived in Constantinople on July 25. But that was because I was ill.

– What did you have?

– I don't know exactly. It looked like a venereal disease. I was convinced that I had caught it from one of the girls that sat around in my uncle's coffeehouse.

– So you got it from a prostitute?

– Yes. And you must understand, I actually only wanted to stay a few days in Sarajevo, but then I felt too scared to go home.

– You mean, you were too scared to travel back to Turkey. Back to your relatives and your bride?

– That's right, Mudir Bey. I wanted to first make sure I had recovered from this illness.

– And was it really a venereal disease?

– No, Mudir Bey. It was all just in my head.

– And when did you realize?

– A few weeks later when I finally decided to go to see a doctor … That was at the end of July. I went to see my uncle's physician, and he took a good look at me and said that it was all in my head.

– Yet another coincidence, efendi? The fact that you only arrived in Constantinople one month later, when the whole world already knew that there would be war, was nothing but plain coincidence?

– Yes.

– And I suppose it's also a coincidence that you didn't continue your journey straight away, inland, to visit your family?

– It is. Of course, I wanted to continue on my way immediately, but my clothes were dirty from such a long journey, and I couldn't arrive home with dirty and creased clothing, so I had them cleaned.

– Which, of course, took a few days?

– Correct.

– And during those days you spent waiting for your clothes, you had nothing better to do than to pass the time exploring the Bosporus. On steam boat, of course?

– I was a tourist. And I had every right to take a steam boat trip while I was there.

– And you just happened to have your camera with you?

– Yes, I took it with me.

– You also took a trip out to the Dardanelles, right up to the Gallipoli Peninsula?

– That was just the standard steamer route.

– And you took photographs there? On the eve of the outbreak of war? Out of boredom, I presume?

– Out of sheer boredom.

– Although you knew that war was imminent?

– Everybody could sense that something was coming.

— And, of course, you had no idea of the strategic importance of the Dardanelles, or the Gallipoli Peninsula?

— None whatsoever.

— Not even that our enemy intended to land there because they thought that it was a vulnerable point?

— How should I have known that?

— We found your photographs, efendi, although we cannot be certain that we have them all.

— Those photographs are completely harmless.

— You photographed the Bosporus Strait, the Golden Horn and the coastline of the Dardanelles, along with their fortifications. You even photographed the Gallipoli Peninsula.

— They are all harmless photographs, Mudir Bey. There is no malice behind them. I took several photographs during that trip: those were just some of them.

— You took them to impress your bride?

— I think so, yes.

— And your family.

— Yes, Mudir Bey.

— All of them completely harmless, correct?

— Yes, Mudir Bey.

— And what about a few days after that, efendi. What happened then?

— I packed my suitcase to continue my journey. By that time the Great War had broken out. It was at the beginning of August.

— We had not entered the war at that point, said the mudir. We were not officially at war in August, although we had mobilized our troops on August 3. We only joined the war later on.

– In November, said your father.
– In November, said the mudir.

– It's true, said the mudir. Turkey was not yet at war. And you, efendi, didn't have any difficulty travelling into the heartlands, going as far as Bakir and then farther on to the village of Yedi Su. Everything was in order with your American passport. You also wisely applied for an internal passport as well, a *teskere,* as is common practice here. And your teskere was also in order, and then, as you continued on your way … you received a stamp for each vilayet you passed. You paid the required fee, and you travelled home to your family. And you married Anahit Yeremian, a girl from your village?

– Correct, Mudir Bey.

– And then you set off to Syria on a short honeymoon where you photographed the steep Mediterranean coast?

– That is correct, Mudir Bey. All harmless photographs.

– And then later you met with Pesak Muradian?

– I met him before that. He was at my wedding. He is married to my sister Aghavni.

– So he is your brother-in-law?

– Yes.

– He is a conspirator. Did you know that?

– I don't know anything about that.

– But we know, said the mudir. Your brother-in-law has been charged with high treason.

Your father suddenly had a look of puzzlement in his eyes, and his bewilderment was reflected in the eyes of the mudir: his real eye, which now began to twitch menacingly, and in his glass eye, too.

— We have no statement from your brother-in-law, said the mudir, because he has disappeared.

— It would considerably help your case if you could tell us where he is hiding.

— I have no idea, said your father.

— Of course not, said the mudir. You were arrested before him.

— Exactly, said your father.

— And you also don't know where he might be hiding?

— How should I know that? said your father.

— So you know nothing at all?

— I am innocent, Mudir Bey.

— Tell us what you know.

— I know nothing, Mudir Bey.

— Surely you have heard of the Okhrana?

— I have never heard that name before.

— That's the name of the Russian secret service.

— I see. I didn't know.

— Members of Okhrana work behind our front lines. They are usually Russian-Armenians who have been sent over the border by the Russians and can easily blend in among the Turkish-Armenians. Many of them have lived in Turkish territory before – before they went over to the Russians. They speak Turkish and Armenian, and it is almost impossible to tell them apart from the Turkish-Armenians. They even hold valid papers. And yet, every single day we manage to nab some of them. We find them everywhere: among the Armenian traders and craftsmen – even amongst the farmers.

– I don't know anything about that, Mudir Bey.

– At first we thought that you, efendi, had been sent by the Okhrana. But then we thought to ourselves, 'The Okhrana send their people via the Turkish-Russian border. They are easy to smuggle over. Why should they go to all the trouble to use a man from America?'

– Yes, Mudir Bey.

– So they could send him straight to the Bosporus, to the Dardanelles and to the Gallipoli Peninsula?

– Yes, Mudir Bey.

– Or even to Bosnia, a former Turkish province that has been annexed by the Austrians and whose capital is Sarajevo?

– Yes, Mudir Bey.

– You see, that is why we assumed that you were working for the Americans, efendi, despite the fact that America is neutral and we weren't entirely sure why the American president would want to incite an Armenian uprising here in this country.

– I know nothing of an uprising, Mudir.

– That is why we thought to ourselves that you might be working for the English, or the French.

– What English and French?

– You know, *the* English and *the* French.

– I have no idea what you are talking about, Mudir Bey.

– It all seems very complicated, said the mudir. But the most complicated things are often the most simple.

– Yes, Mudir Bey.

– Of course, that is a cliché. What I mean to say is that surely this isn't the first time that you have heard such a phrase?

   – Yes, Mudir Bey.

   – And yet some clichés are true.

   – Perhaps, Mudir Bey.

   – There you go, efendi.

– I am an ingenious man, said the mudir. It's just that those men over in Constantinople don't know it yet.

   – I see, Mudir Bey.

– I have always been ingenious, it's just that nobody wanted to see it; nobody ever noticed.

   – Yes, Mudir Bey.

   – I have ideas.

   – Yes, Mudir Bey.

   – Do you believe me when I say that I have ideas?

   – Yes, Mudir Bey.

– Recently I said to the vali of Bakir, 'This Vardan Khatisian has nothing to do with either the Okhrana or any of the Russian secret services. He also hasn't been sent by the Americans, or the French, or the English. This Vardan Khatisian is nothing more than an agent of the Armenian global conspiracy.'

   – An Armenian global conspiracy?

   – Yes, efendi.

   – This is the first I have heard of it.

– It appears as though you've never heard anything about anything. Am I right, efendi?

– When I was still studying abroad, said the mudir, I met certain people who told me about the Protocols of the Elders of Zion.

And they also spoke of a Jewish global conspiracy. And do you know what, efendi? I laughed at those gentlemen. I said to them, 'Those Jews are harmless profiteers. I know a few from Smyrna, Stambul and Bakir. You should come to Turkey and meet our Armenians and Greeks.' – And then later, when I returned to Turkey, I often thought about those men and their arguments, and the more I thought about it, the more confident I felt about striking the Jews off my list of enemies. And, strangely enough, I also struck the Greeks off soon after. That left only one group of people who were responsible for all the misfortune in the world.

– Which people?

– The Armenians, said the mudir.

– Wherever evil is at the helm, steering the course of history, said the mudir, you will find the Armenians. Every lever and every switch is in their hands.

– I had no idea, Mudir Bey.

– And the worst part is, they want to use their powers against us Turks.

– I have no idea about that, Mudir Bey.

– There is an Armenian global conspiracy, said the mudir. They are the real masterminds behind this war. Their ultimate aim is to destroy all of humanity. But first they want to weaken us Turks. That's why they orchestrated this war. And you, efendi, are their agent.

– I'm no agent, Mudir Bey. I have no idea what you are talking about.

– What are you then, efendi?

– I was a farmer, Mudir Bey. And then later I read books

and wrote poetry, and I took any job going: I never had a proper profession.

– Tell us who sent you, efendi.

– No one sent me, Mudir Bey.

– And tell us what you know about the Armenian global conspiracy.

The Armenian global conspiracy! Upon hearing these words, the chief scribe's hand, which was holding the Stambul quill, had jerked a couple of times, so he crossed out the entire sentence and wrote it again. The mudir didn't particularly like it when his chief scribe crossed out sentences only to write them a second time, but what could he do.

A shaky sentence like that, with squiggles, loops, swerving lines and noticeable jerks, simply could not be left as it was, particularly as this report was being written in the sacred purple ink used for official purposes. The chief scribe glanced fearfully over to the mudir and suddenly felt another buzzing in his ears as had happened previously when a similar sentence about the Armenian global conspiracy was uttered. He began to feel a pain in his stomach, as if a thousand and one needles were piercing his flesh; as if every Armenian on this earth were scratching the tale of the Armenian global conspiracy into his stomach wall with a thousand and one needles. Acid rose up in his throat but he bravely swallowed it back down so as not to annoy the mudir any further. He wrote the final sentence that came from the prisoner's lips, 'I don't know anything, Mudir Bey' … then he heard nothing but the buzzing in his ears, and the stabbing and scraping sound of the story with its thousand and one needles. Luckily the interrogation was over. Allah saw to it that the mudir ran out of things to say, so that his chief scribe didn't have to listen to any further utterances that had, or needed, to be written down. And Allah, praise be His name, also made sure that the mudir clapped his hands ... thrice ... at just the right time and that three saptiehs stormed in, brandishing their bayonets as if the Armenian uprising had already begun – in the mudir's office of all places, and why not – just to make sure no harm had come to this small corner of Ottoman bureaucracy.

The saptiehs led the prisoner away again, meaning they dragged him down from this peculiar, westernized chair from Frankistan, examined the chains around his feet, made sure the prisoner couldn't run away and shoved him toward the door before finally disappearing with him into the corridor. The mudir stayed seated at his desk, examining his gnawed finger nails. He then removed a small, silver-plated nail file from his left shirt pocket and began to file them. The chief scribe collected his writing equipment together, cleared his throat and swallowed.

– Are you feeling unwell? asked the mudir, without raising his eyes.

– I have stomach cramps, said the chief scribe.

– You eat too much baklava, said the mudir.

– Yes, Mudir Bey, said the chief scribe.

– And who sells you that baklava?

– The Armenian baker, said the chief scribe.

– Those Armenian bakers put the ends of needles in their baklava so that we Turks believe it's the fault of our own stomachs if they can't assimilate foreign food.

– Yes, Mudir Bey.

– That's also part of the Armenian global conspiracy, said the mudir."

4

"After the mudir dismissed the chief scribe with a gracious hand gesture, the chief scribe made his way to the orderly room on the second floor of the hukumet, handed Vardan Khatisian's file over to Osman, the office assistant, and said, 'This contains important state secrets, lock it away carefully. I shall hold you personally responsible.' He also handed in the ink well and the Stambul quill, the blotting powder and the writing board, saying, 'If anyone needs me … I'll be in the toilet'. He did an about turn and staggered, tormented by the tremendous pain in his stomach, along the bare corridor. On his way he encountered a handful of saptiehs who were standing around idly chatting. At the end of the long corridor he spotted three men, whom he greeted submissively. One of them was actually nothing more than a pharmacist, an ordinary *eczaci,* but he was also the brother-in-law of Halil Bey, the court manager. Indeed, it was strange that this eczaci should be standing around inside the hukumet, particularly in the company of two men who were frequent visitors to the vali of Bakir's office: Defterdar Aly Bey, the Minister of Finance – a man much wooed by all officials – and the shrewd Avukat Hassan Agah, allegedly the best lawyer in the vilayet. He was a man of Armenian descent who had managed to win the trust of the vali despite the bad blood that he had inherited from his Armenian great-grandmother. What was that pharmacist doing here? And then the chief scribe realized that this eczaci's pharmacy was located inside a building that belonged to an Armenian: a house, it was claimed, that was to be confiscated and sold at auction. What was really going on here? Did Hali Bey's brother-in-law want to buy the Armenian's house at auction? Why were the three men simply standing around? And in front of the vali's office at that? The chief scribe staggered past the men. The toilet was at the end of the corridor. He tried to tear open the door but it was locked.

For a while the chief scribe stood vexed at the door, listening in an attempt to find out if the toilet was in fact occupied or if the door just happened to be stuck, but nothing seemed out of the ordinary. The door didn't have a keyhole, but it could – and this he knew from experience – be bolted from inside. The chief scribe stood hesitantly in front of the toilet door, his mood despondent. Finally, he discovered a crack in the keyhole-less door. He removed his glasses, bent forward and pressed his short-sighted eyes against the wooden slit. 'It's a pair of legs,' he thought to himself. He couldn't see any more. At any rate, the toilet was in use and there was nothing left to do but wait until the man came out.

The chief scribe paced up and down in front of the toilet door. His stomach was still aching, but somehow the pain had dulled and appeared to be slowly moving. Still, the chief scribe felt no sense of relief. He tried to look through the gap in the door once more. Now he could also make out the red fez of a man who was squatting down over the hole in the floor, his head between his knees. Just like a spider, the chief scribe thought to himself. But spiders are thin, and this man's head is fat and bulky, and his fez looks familiar. Suddenly the toilet user raised his head and stared directly at the slit in the door. Startled, the chief scribe sprang back, for the man on the toilet was none other than the provincial governor himself: the vali of Bakir.

A more foolish man would have knocked on the toilet door to signal to the vali that someone else needed to use the facilities and to kindly request that he hurry it along, but the chief scribe was far too timid to take such a risk – and to irritate such a large and powerful man. He was also not foolish enough to believe all that the Young Turks preached, namely equal rights for all Ottoman citizens. No, no. He knew exactly where his place was. His place was that of a chief scribe: He knew that the vali could have him destroyed with a single wave of his hand. And so the chief scribe simply turned around and went in search of another toilet.

Indeed, there was second toilet to be found in the hukumet of Bakir: a brand new one that had been completed just two weeks earlier. A structural achievement realized in the midst of a war, and one which even Turkey's enemies could not refute. The individual guilty of this squandering of resources in such difficult times, where savings were supposed to be being made at every available opportunity, was Haidar Efendi, an architect who, with the help of the cunning lawyer Hassan Agah – the third descendent of an Armenian great-grandmother with bad blood, and the most infamous *avukat* in the entire Vilayet of Bakir – had managed to free up some funds in Constantinople so that the powers that be in the Vilayet of Bakir could build a second toilet in their government building. An undertaking of this nature would have been impossible in November 1914, by that I mean, at the outbreak of war, but today even sceptics will tell you that there are some things in this world that beggar belief, even when you see them with your own eyes. The lawyer Hassan Agah of course had convincing reasons for this construction project – reasons which the Stambul Young Turks couldn't possibly object to without the backing, which they did not have, of the ruling triumvirate, which consisted of Enver Pasha, Talaat Bey and Djemal Bey. The reasons Hassan Agah gave were also reasonable: As the lawyer wrote, how could one possibly expect the saptiehs of Bakir, the pillars of law and order in the city, to wait in line for hours to use a single toilet simply because they had to give way to the powers that be, and that this, as the lawyer also wrote, contravened the ideas of the Committee of Union and Progress. Equally, he wrote, one could not expect those charged with keeping order to continue to be forced, due to the endless lines – as was almost always the case; or as had long been the case; or precisely because it was such an objectionable case – to go to the prison yard which lay on the other side of the hukumet wall or the prison wall – which was essentially the same wall, it purely depended on the perspective from which one looked at it – simply to answer their call of nature on a latrine that did not even have a roof. And, the lawyer's application continued, because such an unreasonable demand would not be justifiable as the saptiehs, the keepers of law and order, had to squat down over an open-air latrine that was right next to the prisoners: hordes of Armenians, who, as had now been established, were traitors. The lawyer wrote that this had a negative effect on troop morale because these Armenians were devious, had no respect for anyone, tried to pollute the mind of every Turk they met, and did not even have finger nails because they had long been wrenched out – and rightly so. They stank of dirt because they did not wash, carried infectious diseases, were covered in burn wounds, puss and lice; some of them did not even have tongues anymore, or eyes, and yet they still spoke and appeared to still be able to see because, as was common knowledge, Armenians used black magic. And besides, the report continued, this open-air latrine was not protected against the elements, which meant the saptiehs were falling ill, their uniforms were getting wet and coming apart more easily, which was costing the state money.

To cut a long story short, the vali of Bakir, who was secretly behind the very complaints levelled against him, received funds from Constantinople, a large part of which disappeared into his pockets, and with what was left, he built a second toilet for his saptiehs and lower-ranked officials. It was not a single stall, but a spacious, democratic, multi-occupant toilet, with ten holes designed for ten rears and intended to reduce queueing. The ideal solution in the age of the Young Turk revolution: a revolution that, true to the true spirit of the Committee of Union and Progress, had declared war on regression.

And that was where he was now heading: the bash-khatib or, as he was known amongst civilians, Abdul Efendi, son of Mirza Selim, a former *jassidshi,* a public scribe in the bazaars of Bakir and now chief scribe of the hukumet.

The staff in most of the hukumet's offices had finished work for the day, and so it was no surprise that the building was now heaving with people. Even the new toilet block was packed. It was the hour before evening prayers, a time when lower-ranked officials and saptiehs would generally empty their bladders and bowels before hurrying to mosque. For many, these evening ablutions were a sacred duty as they were part of the cleansing of the body that included prescribed washing rituals. As the toilet had been built in the spirit of the Committee of Union and Progress – a fact widely known – it had no door which users would have to wait in line in front of. As everyone was told, this was a democratic toilet, intended for use by every man, who could come and go as he pleased.

Just as the chief scribe reached this new toilet, he bumped into a German officer who was coming out of the block. The German rushed past him and disappeared down the long corridor of the hukumet. 'By Allah,' thought the chief scribe to himself, 'I've seen that pretty, blonde lieutenant somewhere before,' but he couldn't remember where or when. Or perhaps he could? Of course! It was yesterday in the steam baths. He was sure of it. What was this German doing here? A German officer, no less?

He tentatively set foot in the stinky, smoke-filled room. There were ten rears hovering over the ten holes in the floor. 'All occupied,' the chief scribe thought to himself. He saw a few men standing around the toilet walls waiting. 'So, not line-proof after all then,' he thought, 'although this doesn't look like much of a line.' He went over and stood between the waiting men, who all knew who he was. One of them said:

Cigarette, Bash-Khatib Agah?

– I don't smoke, replied the chief scribe.

– But surely you can smoke just one, Bash-Khatib Agah. Or do you wish to offend me?

– No, said the chief scribe. By Allah, I wish not to offend you.

The chief scribe took the cigarette and held it out to be lit. 'Everyone is so afraid of everyone else here,' he thought to himself, 'even an ordinary saptieh.' Why was he so scared to cause offense?

– So, how does that cigarette taste? asked the saptieh.

– Good, said the chief scribe.

– It's Bulgarian, said the saptieh. Those infidel pigs from Bulgaria may well be traitors to their own people and be cozying up with the Russians, but they do make some fine tobacco.

– Indeed, said the chief scribe, coughing as he smoked. He was nauseous and could feel the pain returning to his stomach: The story of the Armenian global conspiracy and its thousand and one needles began stabbing his stomach wall with even greater vigor than before.

He squatted down between a saptieh and Faruk Agah, an interpreter. Faruk Agah the interpreter also offered him a cigarette, and, once more, he didn't dare say no.

– Did you see that German? asked Faruk Agah the interpreter. He was just leaving the toilet as you came in.

– Yes, said the chief scribe.

– That fella comes here often to show off his rear.

– I see, said the chief scribe.

– He is as queer as a Greek arabadji. You know, fathered by one of their queer Greek priests and born of a bearded nun. Have you ever met a Greek arabadji?

– No, said the chief scribe. Most arabadjis in this region are Armenian. Besides, I rarely take an araba; those horse-drawn carriages are so expensive.

– So you walk everywhere?

– Yes, I always walk, said the chief scribe.

– You never go out of town?

  – Rarely.

  – And how do you travel if you never take arabas?

  – I take the Bagdad Railway that the Germans built for us.

  – And how do you get to the Bagdad Railway? As far as I am aware, there is no train that passes through the Taurus Mountains, and it takes more than a day to reach the next closest train station.

  – I go there with an araba.

  – So you do use them?

  – I suppose I do.

  – You are a strange fella.

  – What I meant is that I don't need to use arabas within the city.

  – And when you travel to the nearest train station, don't you get a Greek to take you? A Greek arabadji?

  – No, said the chief scribe. I always travel with the same arabadji, and he's Armenian.

– To go back to that German fella, said Faruk Agah the interpreter, don't you think that he's pretty? As pretty as a blonde angel?

  – I didn't really look at him that closely.

  – The saptiehs are itching to get their hands on his rear.

  – Perhaps they are, said the chief scribe.

– These Germans are a strange people, said the interpreter. Have you ever noticed that they have excessively large pockets on their uniforms, especially their trouser pockets?

  – Yes, said the chief scribe.

– And that didn't appear strange to you?
– No, said the chief scribe.
– Why not?
– I don't know, said the chief scribe.

– The Germans' uniforms look as though they've been stuffed with walnuts, except they're not walnuts.
– What is it then?
– Newspaper.
– Newspaper?
– Yes.
– By Allah! Who on earth stuffs newspaper in their pockets?
– The Germans.
– And why?
– Because they say there isn't any toilet paper here in Turkey.
– What is toilet paper?
– Paper that Europeans use to wipe their rears.
– But nobody wipes their rear end with paper!
– Right. That's what I told the Germans.

– These Germans are so afraid to use a toilet without any toilet paper that they never leave their barracks without taking some newspaper with them. And they make sure to stuff their pockets full with it.

– Yes, said the chief scribe. That sounds about right for the Germans.

– They organize everything meticulously, said Faruk Agah the interpreter. Everything they do is carefully planned in advance.

– Yes, said the chief scribe.

– Once a German said to me, 'You Turks wipe your rear ends

with your bare left hand. Of course, you pour some water from the well on it first, using the small jug that can be found in every toilet.' 'That's right,' I replied. 'And why don't you have any paper in your toilets, not even newspaper?' 'Because the Qur'an doesn't say anything about using newspaper,' I said. 'And what's written in the Qur'an?' he asked. 'I don't know exactly,' I said, 'but it says something about water and sand. That's what man should use to cleanse himself before Allah.'

– And do you know what else the German said?

– No, said the chief scribe.

– 'What you Turks have aren't really toilets,' he said.

– How could he say such a thing? asked the chief scribe. Where are we squatting then? The Sultan's divan? Does this not look like a toilet?

– Among the Franks, so this German told me, and indeed across the whole of Frankistan, people sit on a wooden or porcelain donkey with neither head nor tail. And this donkey has an enormous hole in its back.

– Are you trying to tell me that the Franks sit on a hole when they return to Allah all that they haven't digested?

– Precisely, said the interpreter.

The saptieh sitting to the right of the chief scribe now joined in, too. He laughed and said, 'The Franks sit on a hole? That's not humanly possible.'

– But that's how it is, said the interpreter.

– The customs of these infidels come from the Devil, said the saptieh. They sit down when they shit, don't wash their behinds afterwards, eat pork, don't believe in the Prophet and stuff newspapers in their pockets.

– They also invented printing ink, said the interpreter.

- What printing ink?
- To print their newspapers.
- So that they can fill their uniform pockets?
- Exactly.
- And use it to wipe their behinds?
- Correct.

The interpreter then moaned to the chief scribe about all the work he had to do, the stress, the many hours of overtime he had to work and the wages he hadn't been paid.

- Have you also been waiting three months for your wages, Bash-Khatib Agah?
- Five, Faruk Agah.
- And how are you managing to get by?
- Only Allah knows, said the chief scribe.
- Our wages vanish into the pockets of the powers that be, said the interpreter.
- There is no evidence of that, said the chief scribe warily, nervously glancing around.
- True, there isn't any, said the interpreter.
- Do they really give you so much work?
- Yes, said the interpreter.

- It's mainly the Kurds who keep me busy, said the interpreter. Those lowlifes don't speak a word of Turkish. And who has to interpret their Kurdish into Turkish? I do, of course.
- But I know Kurds who have learnt Turkish.
- There aren't many.
- And what about the other minorities?
- It's not quite as bad, said the interpreter. We rarely have

trouble with the Jews or the Greeks. Even the gypsies from Lake Urmia, who come from over the Persian border, speak a few words of Turkish. The least troublesome are the Armenians.

– What is it like with the Armenians?

– They all speak Turkish. Some of them even speak our language better than we do.

– You don't say!

– But you know that already, Bash-Khatib Agah.

– Of course I do, but each time someone brings this fact to my attention, I find myself astonished.

– But many of these Armenians really do speak better Turkish than we do, said the interpreter, and if I didn't already know that they were all traitors – infidels, pork-eaters and friends with the Russians – then I would probably say that they were the true Turks.

Still squatting, the interpreter crept along the white-tiled wall to the water jug, took it, shook a bit of water on his left hand using his right, wiped his rear, repeated the process three times, dried the wet area with his sleeve, pulled his trousers up, put the water jug back in its place, gave the chief scribe a nod, shuffled past the waiting men, who stood against the long toilet wall chatting, and disappeared out of the open entrance. Barely two seconds after he had left, a second man took his place, dropping his trousers and groaning with relief as he squatted down over the hole in the floor.

Perhaps Faruk Agah, the interpreter, was right when he claimed that it sometimes seems as though the Armenians really are the true Turks, thought the chief scribe. It was a pity, he thought to himself, that the interpreter was no longer squatting down beside him, as he would have liked to have turned to him and said, 'Do you know, Faruk Agah, there are people who even claim that the Armenians are the finest citizens of this state: true Ottomans, of whom we can be proud.' But then he realized that uttering such a sentence would be dangerous, even if the words didn't come from his mouth, and so he thought that it was probably for the best that Faruk Agah the interpreter had wasted no time washing his rear end and leaving the toilet. He then thought back to his visit to the steam bath the day before. He often went there as he had been widowed for many years, had no women in his life, detested the brothels and because there was a eunuch there, Hadshi Efendi, who would suck his cock for just a few paras.

– Well, Bash-Khatib Agah, said the eunuch, an elegant gentleman such as yourself should really be going to the Armenian hamam, the one in the Armenian mahalle. The rich Armenians who go there have a pool made of real marble.

– Yes, Hadshi Efendi, he said. That may well be true, but gone are the days when a circumcised man would sit amongst the uncircumcised.

– But there are uncircumcised men here in our hamam, said the eunuch, pointing to a German officer who was sitting not far away on one of the higher steps, huddled up against a few Turks. That man is a lieutenant. He is young and blond, and queer as well. They say he prowls the corridors of the hukumet, mainly in the new men's toilets.

– I see, said the chief scribe. I wasn't aware.

– He's not circumcised, but he's not ashamed to sit with those who are.

– Well, said the chief scribe.

– Just a few moments ago he asked me if I would suck his

cock for three piaster. Do you know what I told him, efendi?

– No.

– I said, 'Not for five lira would I suck an uncircumcised cock. How disgusting! The Shaytan can lick it. Don't you know that all kinds of dirt, including pus and piss, collect in the folds of skin on an uncircumcised cock like yours, and that all the flies in the whole of Turkey nestle quite merrily between the folds to feast on the grime as they feast on the festering eyes of a blind beggar?' – Then the German said, 'But efendi, I thought this was a hamam? A steam bath? And what is the purpose of a steam bath if not to clean off all the piss and pus and fly droppings? Anyway, I'm perfectly clean. I wash my cock five times a day, just like you Turks wash your sweaty feet before you pray. I'll even give you ten piaster.' – I said, 'No. Not for any price.'

– Was he offended?

– He'll have calmed down by now.

Later, after the eunuch had massaged him, lashed him with willow rods, thoroughly kneaded his flesh and then sucked him off, he went to sit with the same group of men with whom the German was sitting.

The German was just in the middle of telling one of the Turks that the three Armenians who had been hanged from the Gate of Happiness had changed the landscape of the city.

– True, said the Turk.

– If our current situation continues to worsen, and the front approaches even closer, you'll see more of them hanging. And not only in Bakir; Armenians will be hanging everywhere: in public squares across the land.

– Perhaps, said the Turk.

One of the other Turks said, 'We should hang them all: the entire lot.'

– That would be impractical, efendi, said the German. Surely the government couldn't have that many sets of gallows made.

– Then we shall hang them from the trees.

– That would be even more problematic, efendi, said the German. You have to remember that large parts of Turkey are relatively treeless: certain areas have no trees at all. It is as though Allah was very sparing with trees when He made these regions so that man would not sully His creation.

– What are you trying to say?

– That Allah created trees for man, said the German … just like everything else in the natural world, but He obviously didn't create them so that man could string his neighbor up from them.

– Only Allah knows the purpose for which He created trees, said the Turk.

– I'm sure He does, said the German.

The chief scribe sat silently among the men in the hamam, breathing in the steam and pricking up his ears. He had unloaded several times into the eunuch's toothless mouth and felt completely drained.

– Do you know what? said one of the Turks, joining in the conversation. Do you know what, efendiler? I just can't get my head around the whole thing.

– What don't you understand?

– Why the Armenians are being persecuted in the first place?

– There are many who fail to grasp it, efendi. But we don't need to understand everything. Do you perhaps understand why the Armenians are friends with the Russians, and why they are secretly praying for the Tsar?

    — No, I don't understand that either.

— A one-armed Turkish major, who was sat next to the German, said, 'Efendiler. You see this arm that I lost? Allah took it from me. It happened in November, during the first large-scale Russian offensive in the Caucasus. We were surrounded; it was a desperate situation. And do you know, efendiler, who Allah sent to save my life and give me back my freedom?'

    — No, efendi.

    — An Armenian.

— My Armenians were the finest soldiers, said the major. Other officers have told me the exact same thing.

    — But, Binbashi Bey. If that were the case and the Armenians actually were loyal soldiers, why were they discharged from the army? I saw it with my own eyes. They tore the epaulettes off the Armenian officers' shoulders, and many of them were shot dead.

    — I don't know, efendi.

    — But there must be a reason.

    — There is no reason.

    — Do reasons without reason exist?

    — It seems so.

    — But that's absurd.

    — It's not absurd. Allah knows all the reasons, even reasons that aren't reasons at all.

    — So it's possible that a reason without reason is in fact a reason – we just don't know what that reason is?

    — It's a possibility, efendi.

    — Could it be that not even the government knows the reason

and that they, in fact, have no clue as to why they are persecuting the Armenians?

– That'll be it, efendi.

The chief scribe remembered that he had fallen asleep from exhaustion. For a brief moment he had dreamt about the eunuch's mouth and then woken up again. The men were no longer talking and had started to doze off themselves. The one-armed major was sat slightly away from the rest, together with the young German. They were sitting on the highest and hottest step, nestled tightly against one another. When he looked more closely, through the clouds of steam, he could see that the Turk was holding the German's cock tightly in his fist, as if unable to let it go. 'By Allah,' the chief scribe thought to himself, shaking his head. It had appeared to him as though the German's cock was nothing more than an extension of the cock of the great German Kaiser.

– And we Turks hold onto it so tightly, he thought. It's true. We do it because the Kaiser gives us cannons, and without those cannons this war would be impossible to wage.

Some time ago the chief scribe asked a dervish to explain to him how the whole business with the Devil and temptation worked. And the dervish replied, 'Once you've grabbed the Devil by the cock, you'll never let him go.'

After the steam bath he took a stroll to the Gate of Happiness. There he saw three Armenians hanging at the end of a long rope. An old, blind beggar, whose face he recognized, was squatting by the side of the road. He also knew the young boy crouched down at his feet.

– How are things, Mechmed Efendi?

– Oh, it's you, Bash-Khatib Agah. Kind of you to ask. I am well. Allah has taken the light from my eyes but in turn He has given me good health.

He threw half a piaster, one riddled with holes, into the beggar's cloth and then joined the mass of onlookers. In the crowd he happened upon two Turkish dignitaries whom he had often seen in the hukumet. One was the mayor of a neighboring village, the other was a notary. They were accompanied by a German in civilian clothing, who was wearing a monocle.

– Did you know, efendiler, said the German, that Armenians are actually the original Christians?

– No, efendi.

– Well, at least politically. The Armenians were the first to confer the status of state religion to Christianity.

– Is that a fact?

– Yes, it's true. They did it even before Rome.

– Who would have thought it?

– Later on they fell into dispute with all the other churches. You see, they do not believe in the dual nature of Christ.

– What do you mean?

– They are convinced that Christ only has one nature: that he is God.

– Indeed?

– It is what they call a monophysitistic religion. The German scrawled something with a pencil on what appeared to be some kind of drawing pad, but the chief scribe couldn't quite discern what it was.

– Four thousand years ago a dolichocranic race lived in this area, said the German. But then, after some time, this dolichocranic race was forced out by the brachycephalic races.

– Forced out?

– Yes.

– And what are the Armenians?

– They are a dolichocranic race. And also Armenoids. Believed to be a Dinaric mix.

– I haven't a clue about any of that.

– One can even see it on these three hanged men: receding chin; strong, slightly aquiline nose; light-brown skin; curled, slightly frizzy hair … large, expressive, velvety eyes.

– But, efendi, the eyes of those dead men are broken!

At that very moment, one of the men in the toilet block shouted, 'Watch out! The mudir!' – The shock jolted the chief scribe out of his daydream. Indeed, there was the mudir standing at the toilet entrance, laughing, his one hand casually planted on his hip.

The chief scribe was almost paralyzed. He tried to grab for the water jug, but his body simply didn't move. He just stayed there squatting in the same position. He watched as the panicked men yanked up their trousers and left the toilet. A short while later he and the mudir were alone.

– Those pigs were in such a rush that they forgot to clean their rears, said the mudir.

– Indeed, said the chief scribe. He reached for the water jug, but the mudir bade him to stay.

– Wait, said the mudir. There is a matter I wish to discuss with you.

The toilet felt deserted. The mudir squatted down next to the chief scribe. He was smoking a Russian cigarette with a filter.

– You know, any other man would lose his head for this, said the mudir, tapping the Russian cigarette. But mine truly were acquired before the war, and my position ensures I am beyond any suspicion.

– Of course, said the chief scribe.

The mudir smiled. You were dreaming just now, Bash-Khatib Agah. I was standing at the entrance for quite some time and I observed you.

– I wasn't dreaming, Mudir Bey.

– Don't you ever dream with open eyes?

– Never, Mudir Bey. As chief scribe, I mustn't allow myself to.

– But I observed you, Bash-Khatib Agah, and let me tell you, it looked as though you were dreaming.

– Animals dream, too, said the mudir. My cat, for example. It meows in its sleep.

– Yes, Mudir Bey.

– But I don't mean daydreaming. No, no. Only humans can dream whilst they're awake.

– Do you believe so, Mudir Bey?

– Yes, Bash-Khatib Agah.

– Not that long ago, I myself was daydreaming, said the mudir. I saw a large tree. A very large tree. And it was growing in the heart of Turkey. An enormous tree. And all our fears were hanging from its branches.

– And what did those fears look like, Mudir Bey?

– They looked like Armenians. Like Armenians.

– Let's get down to business, said the mudir, turning his head towards his chief scribe, blowing smoke into his face without even the slightest concern as to whether it might bother him. The chief scribe didn't dare cough. He didn't dare even let himself think for a moment about how rude such a gesture was and that he really should object. All he could think was, 'I've heard the mudir say those words before, to a prisoner no less: the Armenian Vardan Khatisian, a man with no actual profession and who claimed to be a poet. That's exactly what the mudir said to him: Let's get down to business.'

– Let's get down to business, Bash-Khatib Agah, said the mudir.

– Yes, Mudir Bey, said the chief scribe.

– What do you think of this Vardan Khatisian?

– I think he's a stubborn fellow.

– Right, Bash-Khatib Agah.

– You will not get anything out of him, Mudir Bey. Not a thing. This man claims that he is innocent and that he knows nothing.

– Innocent or not, said the mudir, he will make a confession. That I guarantee.

– You truly believe so, Mudir Bey?

– I swear to you on my mother's head, said the mudir, the woman who gave birth to me. And I swear by Allah who, in His wisdom, gave me a tongue with which to swear my pledge. This Vardan Khatisian will confess. And that's not all. I will see to it that he is taken to Constantinople and he will make a confession there, too.

– Confess to what, Mudir Bey?

– To the existence of the Armenian global conspiracy.

– And how do you plan to make him confess, not just here but in Constantinople?

– I have ways and means, said the mudir.

– By Allah, said the chief scribe. Allah knows ways and means which will loosen the tongues of even the most obstinate men.

– And I have spoken to Allah, said the mudir, and Allah has shown me the way.

– First thing tomorrow morning I will dictate Vardan Khatisian's confession to you, said the mudir. The prisoner, as of yet, knows nothing, and his confession … hand-written in purple ink … will come as a complete surprise. All he will have to do then is sign it.

– Will he sign it?

– Of course he will.

– Will there also be witnesses who will sign?

– But of course. I will sign to confirm that I was a witness, that I have read the confession and that I was present when the prisoner made his signature. And you too will sign as a witness. And others will sign.

– Will there also be a verbal confession?

– Yes, but later. First, we need the written confession.

– And what is the process for witnesses to a verbal confession?

– It's no different.

– Who will be the witnesses?

– Myself. And you. But also the vali and the mutasarrif and the kaimakam. Perhaps also a few Turkish and German officers.

– The Christian festivities will soon be upon us, said the mudir. The next one, Ascension Day, is just around the corner, as I was told in passing by a prisoner. And do you know what, Bash-Khatib Agah, every time one of these festivals is at our door, the Christians become even more obstinate. That is why I want the confession of the Armenian Vardan Khatisian to be made this week.

– Yes, Mudir Bey. And what is Ascension Day? the chief scribe asked.

– It is the day on which that bizarre saint of theirs flew up to heaven. Similar to how our Prophet journeyed on his white steed, Al Buraq.

Both men were silent. The mudir smoked pensively and the chief scribe gazed at the toilet window that was glassless and no larger than a chimney. In fact, it was nothing more than a hole in the wall through which the pallid evening light seeped. Voices and cries from the nearby prison occasionally pierced the air of the darkened room, mingling with other voices from the hukumet's offices and corridors. Just as the mudir threw his cigarette between his feet, beneath his rear and down into the shitting hole – just at this very moment – the muezzins began singing from their minarets. One of the muezzins could be heard quite distinctly as his cawing voice resonated from the nearest mosque, the *Hirka Sherif Djamissi* Mosque, the Mosque of the Holy Mantel, in Kuru Sebil Sokagi, the Street of the Dry Sebil. *Allahu Akbar,* sang the muezzin. God is great. – And the Muezzin called all believers, including the mudir and the chief scribe. He called four times. The chief scribe closed his eyes and listened. The muezzin's cawing voice filled the room with a thousand and one crows. They circled over the mudir and the chief scribe like enormous gray butterflies, hovering over their heads, whirling around the shitting holes. The muezzin called, 'Allahu Akbar' a final time. God is the greatest. I testify that there is no god other than Allah. I testify that Muhammad is His servant and messenger. Hasten to worship! Hasten to success! Allahu Akbar. *La Ilah illa 'llah.* God is the greatest. There is no god but Allah."

5

The mudir had gone home, as had the chief scribe. And all the minor functionaries in the hukumet and other supplicants and visitors and cleaners and saptiehs – anyone who had no business being in the building at this late hour had gone home. Everyone had left. Only the night watchman was still there, and the sentry at the main entrance. It was very quiet in the hukumet. The muezzins' song had long died away. The cawing crows in the toilet had disappeared, as had the large, gray butterflies. The only voice that pierced the silence was that of the storyteller as he said, "My little lamb. As you can see, they have all gone home. Night has crept into Bakir.

Your father also heard the muezzin's call from his cell. When the muezzin called 'God is the greatest' for the third time, you father had already peacefully drifted off to sleep. But in his dreams, he could see the mudir's glass eye, telling him, 'Do you see this glass eye, Vardan Khatisian? It can see no more and no less than the eye of God. And I bet you that God, who is the greatest, didn't even see those dead Armenians hanging from the city's gates and on its squares. And He won't see the others either, those who have yet to be hanged, be they guilty or not. The government will hang many more. And many will also be shot or executed. Many will simply be beaten to death. And hear me when I say that God has glass eyes. Hear me when I say that the government will stoke up a gigantic fire and millions of corpses will be thrown upon it. And it will all take place before the glass eyes of God. And I can see a large lamb with its throat slit. And I can see that lamb screaming to the glass eye. And in that glass eye lies no response.' And when your father heard those words, he woke up and knew that he was lost.

Very little happened over the following days. Your father was treated decently. He was neither beaten nor tortured. They didn't even poison his food. The saptiehs grinned when they looked into his cell, and your father was afraid. On the third day he was brought before the mudir.

– This is your confession, said the mudir, pointing to the document that lay before him on the desk. As you can see, I have already signed it. The chief scribe also had no qualms about putting his name to it. Even the vali has signed it, and the kaimakam, and the mutasarrif. All of them have confirmed that they saw you, Vardan Khatisian, read this confession and then sign it with your own hand. Now only one signature is missing: yours.
    – But I haven't confessed to anything, said your father.
    – That doesn't matter, said the mudir.
    – Can I at least read this alleged confession of mine?
    – Of course, said the mudir.

Your father read the confession and said, 'I won't sign it'.
    – But I don't think you understand, said the mudir. The

witnesses have already confirmed that you signed the document. They saw you do it.

– But the witnesses didn't see anything, said your father. When am I supposed to have signed this confession?

– This morning, said the mudir. You can even see the exact time.

– True, said your father. The exact time is written here.

– You see? said the mudir.

– But here it is written nine twenty-two a.m. It's now the afternoon.

– Of course, we could always turn the clocks back, said the mudir. Believe me, efendi, Allah couldn't care less what time of day it is in reality, for what is reality? Do you know the answer? Do Allah's rays not always come from the same sun?

– I will not sign.

– But you have to sign, said the mudir. Otherwise the signatures of the witnesses would be false. And, after all, we are dealing here with the signatures of the vali, the mutasarrif and the kaimakam, the chief scribe and also myself. Are you suggesting that we are all liars and that we, in fact, saw nothing? We all saw you sign that document with your own hand!

– I don't want to suggest anything, said your father.

– So will you sign now?

– No, said your father.

The mudir clapped his hands irksomely. The chief scribe then stood up, opened the door and called the saptiehs in who were loitering around in front of the door and who should have responded to the mudir's clap. The mudir muttered something indiscernible to the saptiehs, which led your father to think that they would now take him away. Perhaps they would pull his fingernails out or give him a standard foot whipping. He had already heard much about it – the soles of your feet are whipped and then salt and oil are rubbed into them – but nothing of the sort took place. The saptiehs simply vanished for a moment while they went to fetch the kahvedji: the coffee seller, a man who could often be found standing around in front of the hukumet. But as they couldn't find this specific coffee seller, they went to fetch the coffee seller from the nearest coffeehouse which went by the name of Kahvehane El Rashid, Coffee of the Righteous. Soon enough, the kahvedji was on his way back with the saptiehs. He wore a dirty turban, a sleeveless jacket and shalvar trousers. His unwashed feet stank in their leather sandals. The black lines of dirt beneath his toenails were darker than the blackest coffee, which, here in Turkey, was served very black and very strong. The kahvedji brought three small cups of coffee and baklava, as well as a sweet, light-brown pudding of uncertain origin. He served the mudir and the chief scribe. He also served the prisoner. The mudir tossed a silver medshidje to the kahvedji, who was then grabbed by the saptiehs and jostled out of the room.

The mudir slurped his coffee and smacked his lips, before saying to your father, 'My advice to you would be to sign.'

– How can I sign saying that there is an Armenian global conspiracy? said your father. How can I confess to being their agent and say that I travelled to Turkey shortly before the outbreak of war to carry out a mission on behalf of these conspirators? And what do I have to do with the assassination of the Austrian heir to the throne? No, I cannot sign this.

– If you do not sign, said the mudir, we shall have you executed. But not publically as we first intended. No, no. We will simply make you disappear.

– I am an American citizen.

– That doesn't count for much, efendi.

– There will be protests!

– Nobody will protest, efendi, particularly not when one regrettably and quite unexpectedly dies of heart failure. Remember, America is neutral. We, however, are at war. The Americans will not intervene in our affairs, particularly when it concerns a case of espionage in an area so close to the front.

– And the American press?

– Who cares about the press? The press are nothing but whores that are always screaming about something.

– The offices of the consulate will protest.

– You are mistaken, efendi. The consulates will remain silent, and wisely so. We are at war, efendi. And you are a spy.

– I am no spy.

– Well, we can discuss that later.

– And what if I do sign?

– Then you are guilty.

– Will I be executed?

– No. Quite the opposite. If you admit to your guilt, we will take you to Constantinople where you will testify to everything that is written in your confession. There will be a trial. A grand trial. A public trial. The entire world will be listening. Even America and its representatives. Even the American ambassador in Constantinople … Morgenthau. A Jew. A man who, astonishingly, is foolish enough to defend the Armenians – much to our annoyance, of course. He too will be listening. And everyone will see that the Armenians are guilty.

– But they aren't guilty!

– That is a matter of opinion, efendi.

– Look here, efendi. If you are guilty, then you are of great use to us. And as long as you are of use, you will be allowed to live. The trial will last many weeks and months, and during that time we will let you live.

– And after the trial?

– After the trial, we won't, said the mudir. But I wouldn't worry about that right now if I were you. Who knows how long such a trial will last? And when it eventually comes to an end, perhaps the war will already be over. And then it wouldn't matter if you were allowed to live or die as far as we're concerned; we might decide to exchange you for one of our men that has been captured by the Russians, or the English, or the French. So you see, there is hope for you. There is, efendi. A guilty man may still hope.

– But I don't understand, Mudir Bey.

– Not everything must be understood, efendi. There are times when an innocent man must die while a guilty man is allowed to live. And in such times it is better to be guilty. You see?

– No, Mudir Bey. I don't.

– This Armenian knows absolutely nothing, the mudir said later to the chief scribe after Vardan Khatisian had been taken back down to his cell. Do you know how I know that this Armenian knows nothing, although he actually should know what every idiot knows?

– No, said the chief scribe.

– Of course, it would be easy to get him to sign, said the mudir. It would take but a matter of seconds. Let me give you an example. I could threaten him with a pistol, for instance. I could put my pistol to his head. And do you know what would happen then?

– No, said the chief scribe.

– He would sign immediately.

– Do you think so?

– I am absolutely sure of it.

– But that would be pointless, said the mudir.

– Why?

– Because we want to take him to Constantinople, said the mudir. And because once he is there, he needs to testify in front of the world and tell them exactly what is written in his confession. Don't you see?

– No, said the chief scribe.

– Well, look, said the mudir. Let me put it this way: This stubborn Armenian needs to testify in front of the world in Constantinople that there is an Armenian global conspiracy that wishes to destroy humanity: all people, all law and order, all sense of morality. But, above all, they want to destroy us.

– Turkey and the Turks?

– Correct. – And that is why we need to persuade him first; he must believe in what he is confessing to.

– And why?

– Because otherwise his signature would be meaningless, and his testimony in Constantinople wouldn't be convincing. Don't you see? He can only give a convincing testimony if he is convinced of it himself.

    – I see, said the chief scribe.

– And what is the best way to convince a man?

    – I don't know, said the chief scribe.

    – You terrify him, said the mudir.

    – Terrify him?

    – Of course. Fear.

    – The man is already completely petrified.

    – But he is not petrified enough.

    – But if you were to put a pistol to his head …

    – No, no, Bash-Khatib Agah. He would be terrified for but a number of seconds. That won't suffice for Constantinople.

    – You mean by the time he reaches Constantinople, he will have forgotten his fear?

    – Overcome. He will have overcome his fear.

    – We could threaten him with execution?

    – We have done that already. It's not enough.

    – He is a particularly obstinate man.

    – Yes, he certainly is.

– Of course, we could pull out his fingernails. Or give him a foot whipping. But believe me, it will make little difference to a fellow like that. And we couldn't do it anyway.

    – Why not?

– Because we can't send him to Constantinople without any finger nails. Or with crippled feet. Otherwise the world might think that we were barbaric. Or that we forced him to confess or who knows what. No, Bash-Khatib Agah. This man must reach Constantinople unhurt. And his testimony there has to convince everyone, even those observers from neutral states, such as the American representatives in Constantinople.

– Who do you mean exactly?

– I've told you already. That Jew Morgenthau.

– Really, him?

– Yes, him. He is an Armenian at heart. At least, he defends them.

– It's a difficult matter.

– Yes. It is rather difficult indeed.

– Have you seen that Armenian priest, the one we hanged from the Gate of Happiness?

– Yes, I have.

– We've just caught another one.

– An Armenian priest?

– Yes.

– Will you have him hanged?

– No. I have something else in mind for him.

– Right now this priest is sitting barefoot in his cell, so, I thought to myself, 'An Armenian shouldn't be walking around barefoot, not even in his cell. You see, these Armenians are a sensitive race'.

– True, Mudir Bey.

– So I thought, 'Perhaps he should be shod.'

– What do you mean exactly?

– You know, shod. Like a horse. He will have horseshoes nailed to the bare soles of his feet.

– What type of horseshoes?

– Either Anatolian ones – you know, those thin ones made

out of ordinary sheet metal; the ones with three holes – or, if I ask one of the German officers, a set from the German cavalry. German horses are shod with different shoes: They are two fingers thick and don't bend.

– But we don't have any bellows here in the prison. There aren't even any in the hukumet.

– We'll find some from somewhere. If needs be, we can always nail them onto the priest's feet cold.

– I'm sure it would work without the bellows, said the chief scribe.

– Indeed, said the mudir.

– When we have the priest shod, I'll see to it that this Vardan Khatisian watches. Perhaps that will change his mind.

– Perhaps, said the chief scribe.

– If not, I shall have to come up with something else.

– What exactly? asked the chief scribe.

– I don't know yet, said the mudir.

– Do you not think it would be possible to persuade this Vardan Khatisian with clever words? asked the chief scribe.

– No, said the mudir.

– Fear is the only way?

– Yes, said the mudir.

And the mudir said, 'A frightened man listens only to his inner voice, and that voice is the voice of fear. I will therefore speak to the frightened man in his own tongue.'

– And what if this frightened man is suddenly no longer afraid?

– That's not possible, said the mudir. Then he wouldn't be frightened. Or he would be a saint whose fear Allah has driven out of his heart.

– This Vardan Khatisian is no saint.

– Indeed, said the mudir. He certainly isn't."

And suddenly silence descended upon the mudir's office. All that could be heard was the scratching of the Stambul quill as the chief scribe began copying out a duplicate of the confession. The mudir lit his chibouk, leant his head against the headrest of his Frankish armchair, closed his one healthy eye and starred at the ceiling with the other made of glass. The only voice in the room was the voice of the storyteller, and it said, "Do you see the mudir's glass eye, my little lamb? And do you see the Stambul quill of the chief scribe? And his blotting vials, such as the one filled with finely powdered flour? When that duplicate is finished, it will be sprinkled with pounce, dried and blotted, then it will make its way to Constantinople, where it will arrive ahead of your father. And I bet you that it will land on the desk of Enver Pasha, the God of War and savior of all Turks. And did you see, my little lamb, how the chief scribe suddenly placed his Stambul quill back into the inkwell just now as if he had writer's cramp, or needed time to think? And should I tell you what he is thinking at this very moment, even though they are thoughts that the mudir's ears should never hear? Fear not: no one can hear my voice except you."

And the Meddah said, "The chief scribe is thinking about this and that. He's thinking, 'By Allah. We are all frightened. I am frightened of the mudir: in fact, of all my superiors. The mudir is frightened, too, although I am not sure of what or whom. But he is afraid. That is why he wishes to frighten others, so that their fear will drown out his own.'"

And the Meddah said, "I am the Meddah and the storyteller. They are one and the same. Let me tell you a story. Once upon a time, there were two children. They went into the woods where there stood a gingerbread house that was occupied by a witch. And the witch had a gigantic cooking pot, one that was very big indeed. And when she saw the children in the woods – not very far away from her little house – she thought to herself, 'I will lure those children into my house, and then I will put them in my gigantic cooking pot, and then I will cook them and eat them.'

You see, my little lamb, this witch lived in Frankistan and not in Anatolia. It's a completely different story here.

It's true. Here the world is a very different place – and small children are not cooked in gigantic cooking pots. And yet, for some, this part of the world is even worse and even more terrifying than a place where two small children can be cooked alive in large pots. Here fear does not rise from the steam of certain cauldrons; it hangs in the air. You have no choice but to breathe it in.

And I'll tell you another story, my little lamb: Once upon a time there was a boy who went forth to learn fear, but this boy did not go as far as Anatolia.

It was spring of 1915," said the storyteller. "Preparations were being made – preparations for the extermination of a people, and for the name of the sacrificial lamb to be wiped from the book of names. But it was not yet time. Interrogations were still being carried out, including with your father, a man who was just a common farmer. Or perhaps he wasn't that common after all, seeing as he was also a cow shit salesman and a night watchman and many other things, besides also being a poet. His time had not yet come for they were still preoccupied with him. He was led around the prison and shown a priest being shod. He was also shown other torture methods which I wish not to describe in detail, for what are a few torn out fingernails or pulled out teeth, or stomachs that have ruptured from the sheer volume of slurry being poured down the prisoners' throats? What are a few festering feet that have been whipped by Turkish guards for days on end and which end up having to be sawn off because no one could stand the stench? Your father saw everything, and he also saw the carts loaded with bodies that were hauled out of the prison yard every single day. And he heard the stray dogs outside howl as the smell of rot and decay scaled the prison walls."

And the storyteller, who called himself Meddah, said, "Your father is sitting alone in his cell. And yet he is not alone; his fear is keeping him company. Would you like me to tell you about his fear?"

"Yes," said the Last Thought.

"And his waking dreams? The ones that whisper those fearful words into his ear?"

"Yes," said the Last Thought.

"Or should I let his fear speak for itself?"

"As you wish," said the Last Thought.

And Vardan Khatisian's fear told the storyteller the story of the waking dream that Vardan Khatisian dreamt whilst in his cell. And the storyteller told this story to the Last Thought:

"One morning," said the storyteller, "the cell door sprang open and the mudir entered, flanked by two saptiehs. A third saptieh also stood outside, together with a short, bow-legged man, whom the third saptieh had held by the collar before proceeding to shove him inside. There were five of them: the mudir, three saptiehs and the short, bow-legged man. Your father was struck by a feeling of terror when he laid eyes on the bow-legged man; he resembled an angel of death that your father once saw in a childhood dream. He listened as the mudir said, 'By Allah, you wouldn't believe how long we waited for this man.' Then your father lost consciousness.

When your father came to, he noticed that even the angel of death was afraid. He was a small man with a large bald patch. And he had big, black, terrified eyes. And he had an aquiline nose, and strange bow legs. The mudir said, 'This man is a cement mason'.

The mudir jabbed one of the saptiehs in the rear with the toe of his boot. Do you know what cement is? he asked.

– No, Mudir Bey. By Allah, I do not know.

And he asked the other saptiehs, 'Do you know what cement is?' And the saptiehs said, 'No, Mudir Bey. By Allah, we do not know'

The mudir asked the angel of death, who was nothing but a small, terrified Armenian, one with bow legs and an aquiline nose and a large bald head and big, black eyes. 'Do you know what cement is?'

And the small man said, 'Of course I do. I'm a cement mason.'

– In this region there isn't any cement, the mudir explained to your father. But there is in Constantinople, and in a few other large cities. This man – and he pointed to the small, quivering Armenian – was in Smyrna, and there he worked for a foreign building contractor. He also brought a bag of the wretched stuff with him.

– I brought a bag with me, said the small man.

   – Tell this one – and the mudir pointed to your father – what cement is and what can be done with it.

– Cement is a powder that was invented in the Occident, said the small man. The birthplace of all the Devil's creations … If you mix the powder with a bit of sand and a bit of water, it eventually becomes hard. Then we call it concrete.

   – Concrete?
   – Yes, concrete.
   – How hard is concrete?
   – It is very hard, Mudir Bey.

– What would happen if someone accidently put their finger in that mush whilst mixing the cement?

   – Which mush?
   – The cement mush.

   – Nothing at all, Mudir Bey. Nothing happens if you pull your finger straight back out again.

   – And if you don't: if you leave it in there?

   – Then your finger would be stuck in the mush. You see, after a while the mush turns into concrete, exactly as I just explained.

   – So it stops being mush?

— Yes.

— And becomes a hard, solid mass?

— Correct.

— Does that mean that you would never be able to pull your finger out again?

— Yes, Mudir Bey. Never again.

— And what would happen if someone put their cock in this cement mush?

— Nothing at all, Mudir Bey. Nothing happens if you pull your cock straight back out again.

— And if you don't pull it out?

— Then the cock would stay stuck.

— And you can never pull it back out again?

— Correct.

— So that man's cock would stay jammed in there forever?

— Yes, Mudir Bey. For all eternity."

The storyteller said to the Last Thought, "Do you see how scared your father is?" And he said, "Remember what I told you? The boy who went forth to learn fear never went as far as Anatolia.

— Only the infidels could come up with such a thing, said the mudir, and those possessed by the Devil.

— Yes, said the small man. This is true. Before adding, 'I'm a cement mason.'

— This cement mason is Armenian, the mudir told the saptiehs. He belongs to a race that is devious and which conspires against humanity. The Armenians are arrogant and insubordinate, but when you show them the strap, they will come crawling to your feet. They are essentially a fearful race, and the fact that they are so fearful is linked to their fertility. This one here – he pointed once again to the small cement mason – has thirteen children. And he knows exactly what I will do to them if he doesn't do as I order him to.

– I will do anything you order me to, said the cement mason.

The mudir said, 'All Armenians see themselves as brothers and sisters. Go ahead and tell your brother what I have ordered you to do to him.'

– You ordered me to cement his openings shut.

– Which openings? Tell your brother.

– The one opening, said the cement mason, where undigested food comes out. And the other opening where his water comes out.

The mudir turned to your father with a grin on his face. Do you wish to sign your confession now?

– No, said your father. I won't sign anything.

It's not hard to imagine what is about to take place in your father's waking dream," said the storyteller, "and we two – you and I, my little lamb – need little more than the imagination of a saptieh devoid of fantasy, a simpleton if you will, to picture what comes next. The mudir has your father tied up. The saptiehs stuff sheep's wool into his rear because cotton wool is scarce and can only be obtained from the German medics. The saptiehs also stuff sheep's wool up his pisser. They don't have any tweezers, so they use matchsticks that they have sharpened with a knife.

They jam as much in as they can, making sure to push the wool down each time, and paying no regard to your father's screams or the cement mason, who has now fetched his sack along with a wooden bucket, and begins to pour the fine powder into the bucket before leaving to fetch some water and some sand. He returns with a long wooden stick, and starts to mix and stir the gray mass.

The two of us," said the storyteller to the Last Thought, "are merely observers, and I, the storyteller, can do everything that you, my little lamb, cannot. I can also read thoughts. Now, although I do not wish to read the cement mixer's thoughts, I can imagine what he is thinking. And I can tell you that there is not a single thought in his head. Why? Because he is afraid of them. Or perhaps a thought does come into his mind. Perhaps he thinks, 'That sheep's wool should be enough to block his openings. Why does the mudir want me to cover them with cement as well? I won't need much. The piss hole is tiny. The asshole is slightly bigger, but then not so big that I will need to use all of the cement. I brought an entire sack along with me.'

A short while later your father was hanging against the barred window dressed in only a prison smock. The saptiehs had hung him up by his arms and left him there, like a piece of clothing on a washing line.

– How long does that stuff take to dry? asked the mudir.

– A few hours, said the cement mason. Then it will become concrete.

– Does that mean he'll never be able to shit or piss again? asked one of the dunderheaded saptiehs.

– No. Never again, said the mudir.

– You have a few hours to consider the matter with the signature, said the mudir to your father. If you sign quickly, we can remove the cement. But you'll have to hurry, for once that stuff is dry, it will already be too late and you will never be able to shit again. Or piss. I know you are but an Armenian, but every man needs to shit and piss. – And before Allah extinguishes the light from your eyes, you will scream. You will scream so loudly that the birds will fall from the sky.

– When the sun starts shining through the barred window, said the cement mason, that stuff will dry even faster.

– It's still too early for the sun to shine into the prison yard, said the mudir.

And one of the dunderheaded saptiehs said, 'I think it's because it's still early morning. The sun doesn't shine in here until shortly before midday prayers.'

Your father hung alone in his cell. Somewhere he heard the voice of his mother. It was clear as day and it said, 'My son, why did I give birth to you?'

He was five and sat on his mother's lap.

– How did I come into the world, Mother?

– I don't know, my little pasha.

– Who does?

– Your grandmother.

– Grandmother, how did I come into the world?

– All Armenian children are somehow born.

– But how does it happen, Grandmother?

– Well, the Armenian girls are born under a fig tree.

– And the Armenian boys?

– Under a grapevine.

– But there aren't any grapevines here where we live.

– True, said his grandmother. This land is mountainous and full of nothing but pitiful fields.

– And where is my grapevine?

– Beyond the Kurdish mountains. On the other side. Where the sea lies.

– Is it far?

– No, my little pasha. It's a two-day ride with a donkey and cart.

– Beyond the mountains? Where the sea lies?

– Yes, my little pasha.

– In the land of grapevines?

– Yes. In the land of grapevines.

– When Armenian children are born, the Mother of God smiles and blesses all the fig trees and grapevines, and the angelic voices of all the birds in the land of Hayastan break into song.

– Tell me the story of how I was born.

– I'm not sure I can remember exactly, my little angel.

– And who would remember?

– Let's see, who would remember … well, the grapevine, of course! The grapevine would remember your birth.

And his parents climbed up into their cart to go and fetch him. His mother had a large belly because she was nine months pregnant. She was groaning and screaming as the contractions had already started. She said to your father, 'Hurry the donkey along. Make it walk faster. My little Vardan is lying beneath the grapevine, waiting for us to fetch him.' – And your father said, 'I shall try and hurry the creature along, but it is but a donkey. No cane, not even the finest one, will hasten its pace.'

The donkey walked through the Kurdish territory at its own leisurely pace. The mountains grew taller and taller; their peaks touched the clouds.

– A donkey is but a donkey, said your father.

– I cannot bear it any longer.

– Then pray to our Savior.

And his mother prayed to the One who died for all mankind. 'Jesus,' she whispered. 'Help me.' And she heard Jesus say, 'I shall help you. You will feel no pain.' And her pain really did vanish. The donkey continued to leisurely pull the cart through the clouds. The Kurdish mountains were so high that looking down onto the semi-nomadic villages of the Kurds, or even farther to where the Armenians lived, right down into valley, was enough to make you feel light-headed.

– The pain has gone, his mother said to his father. The Lord has heard my prayer.

– Then everything will be fine, said his father.

– Will it really take us two days to reach the grapevines?

– It will, as long as the donkey doesn't stop.

– And do you think our Vardan will wait that long for us?

– Don't worry, he'll wait.

But during the journey a great deal of milk began collecting in your mother's breasts. And her breasts swelled and grew larger and larger until they hung over the planks of the cart like two heavy sacks.

– The milk cannot wait any longer, said his mother to his

father.

– The milk is searching for the mouth of our dear little Vardan, said his father.

– But our Vardan is under the grapevine, isn't he?

– That's where he'll be, said his father.

– We should have taken a puppy along with us, said his mother. That's what the gypsies do. When they have too much milk in their breasts, they let the puppies suck on them.

– We're almost there, said his father. The milk can wait until then.

– Until when?

– Until you take our little Vardan in your arms and give him your breast.

– I'm sure his little mouth will be hungry.

– Oh yes, said your father.

But the milk couldn't wait. And the donkey began to protest, walking more and more slowly. Sometimes he simply stood still and refused to carry on. But the milk couldn't wait.

And suddenly his mother's large sacks, filled as they were with milk, burst. And entire streams of milk flowed down the side of the mountain and gushed into the Anatolian valleys. And more and more milk kept coming. The streams became rivers. And the rivers became seas. The entire world drowned in his mother's milk. Only the grapevine where little Vardan lay remained dry. And little Vardan cried and cried. He cried for his mother's milk that flowed everywhere, except to him.

Vardan Khatisian had been hung out to dry before the barred window of his cell. He needed to relieve himself, but couldn't. He cried out for his mother but the only person who came was a saptieh. He asked what the matter was.

– I can't take it anymore, Saptieh Agah.

– Shall I fetch the mudir?

– Yes.

The mudir entered the cell.

– Shall we unblock your openings?

– Yes, Mudir Bey.

– And what about the confession? Will you sign it?

– No.

– But efendi, don't you understand? Only once you have declared yourself willing to sign will we unblock your openings.

Vardan Khatisian began to cry, and the mudir let him cry for a moment.

– I'm actually doing you a favor by letting you sign, said the mudir. I'm doing you an enormous favor and, in fact, you should be begging me to do it.

– I can't take it anymore, Mudir Bey.

– Will you sign, efendi?

– Yes, Mudir Bey.

– Beg me?

– I beg you, Mudir Bey.

Vardan Khatisian was untied. The cement, which was not yet dry and also not yet set, was washed away, the sheep's wool was pulled out of his pisser and his rear. The saptieh brought him a pair of trousers and helped him put them on. But before he could even button them closed, the inevitable happened.

– He just shat himself, said the saptieh.

– Never mind, said the mudir. It was to be expected."

The Last Thought had tried to understand the fear its father was feeling, but as it had already passed into a world without fear, it felt nothing. The storyteller had moved him to the mudir's desk, and as the office was empty, and the door closed, and as the storyteller had thrown a dark storyteller's cloak over the entire hukumet and the wall – and with it the prison, with your father's cell inside – he could neither see nor imagine anything.

"Is that a true story?"

"Everything that happens inside a person's mind is true," said the storyteller, "although it takes place in a reality separate from our own, true reality: one which often seems unreal itself."

"I don't understand what you mean."

"It doesn't matter," said the storyteller. "I made it clear to you beforehand that the story I just told was a story I was simply relaying from your father's fear. It was his nightmares telling me the story of a nightmare. A nightmare of nightmares if you like."

"Why can't my father simply banish away his fear?"

"Because he has been worn down, my little lamb. Because there is no longer any strength left in his soul. Because he has seen too much in this prison and because he knows that the mudir can bring nightmares to life if he so pleases."

The storyteller waited for the Last Thought to ask the all-important question, which was, "Did my father sign? Will he confess?" But the Last Thought didn't ask anything. So the storyteller said, "Your father had seen a priest being shod, and he saw other things. Things that were even worse. And he heard the cries of the tortured. At first they came in waves, then the entire day. Eventually he could hear them all night long, too, until the entire prison consisted solely of cries. And, as I told you, your father had been worn down. Above all, he had no idea what the mudir had in store for him, and that drove him almost to the brink of insanity; he began to imagine the unimaginable. And then one morning …"

"One morning?"

"One morning the mudir called your father to his office. He asked him politely, 'Do you know how your wife is doing?'

– I don't, said your father. I have had no news from her.

– We know that she is pregnant, said the mudir … five months along, am I right?

– Six, said your father.

– Will she have a son?

– We hope so, said your father.

– You wish to have an heir, yes?

– Yes, said your father.

– What will you call your son?

– We wish to call him Thovma, said your father.

– Thovma Khatisian, said the mudir, a true Armenian name.

– Yes, said your father.

– We have arrested your wife, said the mudir. She is now in the women's prison in Bakir.

– But that cannot be, said your father. That simply cannot be.

– And why can't that be?

– Because she has done nothing wrong.

– Many claim to have done nothing wrong, said the mudir … and yet still they are arrested.

– Yes, said your father.

– We will hold your wife hostage, said the mudir … and we will keep her until you have made your confession.

– Hostage?

– Yes, said the mudir.

– Don't be afraid, said the mudir. Your wife is under my personal protection. Nothing will happen to her. Only her unborn child will be killed if you refuse to sign.

– My son Thovma?

– Yes, your son Thovma!

– The mudir smiled and opened a drawer in his desk and took out a few things belonging to your mother. Her internal passport, which was known as a teskere, was there, as were a few pieces of jewelry that you father once bought for her. Her wedding veil was also there. They were all objects your father recognized. You see, said the mudir, it's true. We have arrested your wife. Do you believe me now?

– Yes, said your father.

– And by arresting your wife we have also arrested your son, even though he hasn't been born.

– My son Thovma.

– Your son Thovma.

– My son, said your father. My son.

– He goes wherever your wife goes.

– Thovma, said your father. My little Thovma.

– No harm will come to your son if you sign. Will you sign?

– Yes, said your father. I will sign.

Your father signed. He wrote his name right next to those of the others which were already on the page, confirming that they had witnessed the signatory sign with his own hand. The mudir was very friendly. He said, 'As I'm sure you are aware, that will not do. You will also go to Constantinople … where you will testify before the whole world.'

– Yes, said your father.

– And in Constantinople you will not retract your confession because we shall hold your wife hostage until you have confessed to everything in Constantinople.'

– Yes, said your father.

– And you know what will happen to your son if you retract your confession in Constantinople?

– I won't retract anything, said your father.

– Oh, there is one more thing, said the mudir. The day after tomorrow a few gentlemen will be attending my office. These gentlemen would like to hear with their own ears everything that is written in this confession. So, you will learn this written confession, that you have signed with your own hand, by heart and you will repeat it to the gentlemen word-for-word. Think of it as a general rehearsal so that we know what you will say in Constantinople; so that you don't make any mistakes, do you understand?

– I understand, said your father.

– Take a duplicate of the written confession to your cell, efendi, and learn it by heart. Confess everything to those men exactly as it is written here.

– Yes, Mudir Bey.

– There are still a few gaps in the written confession. Think of something to say and be sure to answer any questions either the gentlemen or I may ask. Answer them in no uncertain terms. Everything needs to sound credible and natural; it should in no way sound as though it has been memorized. Do you understand?

– Yes, Mudir Bey.

– And think of your little Thovma.

– Yes, Mudir Bey.

What would go on to take place two days later in the mudir's office was not quite a grand trial," said the storyteller, "because that, of course, had to take place in Constantinople. And because the gentleman in the mudir's office were no judges: they were simply witnesses. The mudir claimed it was purely a general rehearsal of a verbal confession, but in reality it wasn't even that. It was just a confession before several witnesses: the first in a long line of confessions that your father would have to make before he would give his final performance before the eyes of an investigative judge in Constantinople and then repeat it in the courtroom before the eyes of the whole world. Do you understand?"

"No," said the Last Thought.

"Well, listen," said the storyteller, "and I will explain. Your father is supposed to make a confession of which we – both you and I – know very little about. We only know that the mudir is the one who came up with it and that it has something to do with a mystical Armenian global conspiracy in which your father is allegedly involved. This confession, as I already mentioned, has been completely made up by the mudir with the complicity of the vali, the mutasarrif, the kaimakam and the chief scribe. Although it is complete fiction, it is based on certain suspicions they hold which are plausible. The mudir put his invented story into writing and had your father sign it. The other gentlemen, by that I mean, the vali, the mutasarrif, the kaimakam, and of course the mudir and the chief scribe themselves, have testified to the authenticity of the signature by giving their own, although they were actually made before your father even signed."

"I see," said the Last Thought.

"I've said it all already, but I'll say it again. And let me also repeat that your father is now supposed to verbally recount everything that is written in his confession so that he can give a similar story in Constantinople. It's a confession he will have to retell many times until it sounds so convincing that even those gentlemen in Constantinople will feel confident enough to put him on trial to testify before the entire world. This testimony in the mudir's office is therefore not a general rehearsal, even though the mudir calls it as such. It is merely the first of many rehearsals which will eventually lead to a general rehearsal and then to your father's actual testimony before the world."

"I'm just starting to understand," said the Last Thought. "But what will my father actually confess to?"

"You'll find out soon enough," said the storyteller.

6

"You have to picture the scene," said the storyteller. "There they are, all gathered in the mudir's office, everyone that the mudir has invited to be preliminary witnesses: the vali of Bakir, the kaimakam, the chief scribe, the mutasarrif, a handful of Turkish officers, and three Germans, including the small, queer lieutenant, the major – who is also a friend of the vali's – along with an Austrian journalist who has taken up quarters here close to the front. The kadi, a Muslim judge, is also there but only to watch and to observe; the purpose of this meeting is not to judge, but to listen. You also have to picture a room that is as smoky as a Turkish coffeehouse; the small, queer lieutenant – a non-smoker – coughs intermittently, as does the chief scribe, who is also known to be a non-smoker. You have to picture the coffee that is being served in dainty little cups … and the confectionary and the raki. Three Turkish officers and the kadi sit on the divan, whilst all the others sit on the floor, perched atop comfortable cushions. The three Germans are also on the floor, as is the Austrian journalist. They do not wish to attract any attention and so are happy that they have been allowed to sit on the floor and have not been encouraged to sit, say, on the divan or even on the two Frankish chairs at the desk. The three Germans and the Austrian are well aware that nobody ever dares sit on a Frankish chair. It simply isn't the done thing. There they stood: two needless, empty chairs. The only sounds to be heard in the room are muttering, the slurping of coffee and raki, as well as the odd smacking of lips. Some of the gentlemen help themselves generously to the baklava; others simply chew on the end of the chibouk pipe. The Germans and the Austrian cast an occasional glance at the prisoner, who is seated unchained next to the desk, seemingly ill at ease and anxious.

– What is the point of this whole spectacle? whispers the small, queer lieutenant to the major. He speaks in German, knowing that none of the Turks understand.

– The mudir wishes to make a name for himself in Constantinople, says the major. For months Constantinople has been trying to find someone to pin the blame on, but to no avail.

– What crime has the prisoner committed?

– We will soon find out.

– Efendiler, says the mudir. Sadly, I do not possess a map, although I have been requesting one for years. As you can clearly see, my calls have not been answered. Why, you may be asking yourselves? Well, the official in Constantinople who is responsible for Turkish maps is an Armenian, and he has obviously refused to honor my request.

The mudir pointed to the desk. Take a look at this desk. It is completely covered in dust. The saptieh responsible for cleaning it only dusts one side – the side where I always sit – and for years I never even noticed. – Just look at the amount of dirt of this desk! You can see for yourselves. There are even dead flies that have been here since 1912 and 1913 – since the Balkan Wars. They are covered in dust, almost embalmed, if you will. So, what do I do when I need a map? Well, what do you think? Let me tell you: quite simply, I draw the map in the dust on the tabletop with my finger. Here, take a look. You see this map of Turkey just here?

The men stood up to observe the map. The Germans in particular were astonished by what they saw: a hand-drawn map that had been traced in the dust, its lines running through a graveyard of dead flies that had been there since the Balkan Wars.

– As a Turkish patriot, said the mudir, I always have a map of Turkey drawn out in my head. Always. As such, you will find that this map is entirely accurate.

The mudir then began to pace backwards and forwards in front of the desk as the other men took their seats again. – And who is to blame for this state of affairs? said the mudir. Who is making us Turks feel so at ease and lulling us into complacency? Well, guess.

– The Armenians, said the vali.

– That's right, said the mudir. The Armenians are to blame for everything. They have us hypnotized.

– Precisely, said the vali.

The mudir called the men over to look at the map again. With his finger he drew a circle at the heart of Turkey.

– This land that lies at the heart of Turkey is what we call 'Anatolia'. But the Armenians call it Armenia, or Hayastan.

– The name 'Armenia' can be found on several maps, said the German major.

– It's written as Greater Armenia and Lesser Armenia, said the Austrian journalist. Greater Armenia is alleged to stretch beyond the Persian and Russian border, but I couldn't say exactly where; I don't know the regional maps quite as well as the mudir.

– Quite right, said the mudir, but at this very moment we are only interested in the Turkish part of this supposed Greater Armenian Kingdom.

– There once was a Greater Armenian Kingdom, said the Austrian journalist. It was in this region.

– But that was a very long time ago, said the mudir. It was such a long time ago that there's surely no longer any truth in it.

– So it's just a story?

– Yes. A story, said the mudir.

– But the Armenians wish to bring this tale of an Armenian kingdom back to life, said the mudir. They are hoping that, with help from the Russians, they will be able to establish their own Armenian state here, in the heart of Turkey.

– Is there any evidence of this?

– There are indications, said the mudir. Indications of Armenian treason which point towards specific evidence.

– Is there evidence or not?

– That is of no importance, said the mudir. All that matters is that we believe in the evidence we have: evidence, which is based on credible indications. Do you understand?

– Not quite, said the Austrian journalist.

Your father's tongue was laden with fear," said the storyteller, "and the knowledge that something could happen to his small, unborn son if he didn't say everything that the mudir wanted to hear, together with the few swigs of raki that the mudir had given him to drink, loosened the fear from his tongue and thrust it out into the room in the guise of a lie.

– I shot the Austrian heir to the throne and his wife in Sarajevo, said your father. I acted out of conviction and in the name of the Armenian people.

Your father was silent and gulped down a few small glasses of raki. The men were also silent until one of them broke the silence by laughing. It was the Austrian. But gentlemen, he said. That is ridiculous; it's complete and utter nonsense. I might only be a foreign correspondent for a Viennese newspaper, but I know about the facts that led to the outbreak of war. The Austrian royal couple were shot and killed by a Bosnian nationalist called Gavrilo Princip, a high-school student, a young hot-headed boy and deluded fanatic. And a group of Serbian officers, as well as a secret organization called *Crna Ruka,* the *Black Hand,* whose leading member is a colonel in the Serbian army, a man called Dragutin Dimitrijevic, were behind the attack.

– The press has got its facts wrong, said the mudir. The Bosnian fanatic, Gavrilo Princip, may well have shot at the royal couple, but the bullets fired by this Armenian were those that struck Archduke Franz Ferdinand and his wife.

– And how do you intend to prove it?

– This man will prove it.

– In 1898 I emigrated to America, said you father. I emigrated because I hoped to find work over there and to save money so that one day I could return to my homeland a rich man. I emigrated for no other reason. I did not emigrate because Armenians were being persecuted in this country because Armenians have never been persecuted here in Turkey. That is a lie perpetuated by the Armenian global conspiracy. They invented this lie to damage the reputation of Turks all over the world.

– But that's not true, said the Austrian journalist. Even the Young Turks and the incumbent government admit that the Armenians were persecuted under the previous, ousted administration.

– Under Abdul Hamid's government, said the German major.

– Are you referring to the alleged massacre of 1895 during which it is claimed that 300 Armenians were killed? the mudir asked in a very cautious tone.

– The figure given to me was 300,000, said the German major.

– They are just numbers, said the mudir. Numbers don't mean a thing.

– Perhaps we should leave the previous government out of it, said the vali. The former government, the one led by Abdul Hamid, is no more. Our new administration is modern, progressive and just.

– Yes, Vali Bey, said the mudir. I don't think anyone here could have put it better.

– Armenians have always had it good, said the vali.

– Who own all the major businesses in Turkey? Who are responsible for the trade and craft industries? Who gorge themselves on the fruits of the Turkish people's labor?

– The Armenians, said the mutasarrif. The kaimakam also nodded and said, the Armenians.

– And what right do the Armenians have to complain when they have it so good and always have done? And even if the previous government is said to have beaten a few of them to death or shot them or who knows what, the Armenians will have long made up for their losses. You see, these Armenians are highly fertile and thus have many children. And where do all these millions of them come from? And why are they still living here if things are or ever had been that bad?

— Too right, said the mudir.

— Life was good for us all, said your father. The Armenian persecution under Abdul Hamid was greatly exaggerated. Most of it is nothing but a pack of lies. And only the sinister minds of those behind the Armenian global conspiracy could come up with the idea to parade out these old lies again.

— What do you know about the Armenian global conspiracy? asked the mudir.

— Not much, said your father. In America I noticed that the Armenian charities were constantly collecting money. They also came to my apartment and asked me to make a donation.

— What for? asked the mudir.

— They said it was for orphans.

— But you, of course, know that it isn't true?

— Yes, said your father. There can't possibly be that many orphans. I knew from the very beginning that all those funds were to be used to purchase weaponry and that the money would find its way into the hands of Armenian nationalists.

— What sort of nationalists?

— The Dashnaks ... members of the national Armenian Dashnak party. They are also known as Dashnaktsutyun.

— How do you know that?

— I was told by my brother-in-law Pesak Muradian, a man I corresponded with and then later met in person.

— When did you meet?

— After my return. In 1914.

– This Pesak Muradian is one of the Dashnaks' leaders, said the mudir. He is a dangerous nationalist and a conspirator. He is one of those who wish to establish an independent Armenian state here in the heart of Turkey. We have been trying to find him for several months, but he has vanished without a trace.

– The Dashnaks! The Austrian journalist gave a laugh. The Armenian national party! This is just ridiculous, Mudir Bey.

– And what makes you say that?

– The Dashnaks are real, said the journalist. But as far as I have been told, the party in question is legal, or at least it was before war broke out. It was officially recognized in 1908 after the Young Turks came to power.

– True, said the mudir.

– The Dashnaks have long given up their quest for independence, said the Austrian journalist. They abandoned it when the Young Turks took over the government in order to cooperate with oppressed minorities.

– True, said the mudir.

– Because the Young Turks promised them equal rights. They promised equal rights for all Ottoman citizens, including the Armenians.

– True, said the mudir.

– So why would the Dashnaks need weapons?

– Because they are secretly in cahoots with the Russians, said the mudir. And because they are only pretending to go along with the Young Turks when really they are planning an uprising.

– Do you have any proof?

– We have indications, said the mudir.

– Whilst I was over in America, I didn't pay much attention to politics, said your father. But I found all those money collectors rather suspicious. I just couldn't imagine that they could really need that much money for orphans, particularly orphans that didn't actually exist.

– They raised billions, said the mudir. Armenian bankers and businessmen, not just in America but all over the world, offered up hefty sums.

– Yes, said your father. It's true.

– And how can he be so sure? asked the Austrian journalist.

– I already told you, said your father. I was told by my brother-in-law Pesak Muradian, although it is common knowledge amongst Armenians, even those who claim not to know anything.

– At that time I also didn't know anything specific about an Armenian global conspiracy, said your father, although I was sure that such a thing existed. But as I said, I didn't pay much attention to politics over in America.

– He is a poet, said the mudir. Poets believe that they are somehow superior, and that they don't need to bother with anything real or tangible in this world. But it is those exact same poets who become dangerous when they get mixed up in things that should be left to the pragmatists.

– Exactly, said your father.

– When did you become involved in the actual execution of the Armenians' objectives?

– Later, said your father. In June 1914 when I decided to shoot dead the Austrian heir to the throne.

– And his wife?

– And his wife.

– As a poet, you must have found this mission compelling?

– Yes, said your father. As a poet, I had a very ambiguous perception of the world and of those events which captivate the whole of humanity. The thought of being able to have some sort of influence gave me a thrill.

– And how did your involvement even come about?

– It was a coincidence, said your father.

– But efendi, said the mudir. There is no such thing as coincidence. Everything is predetermined by fate.

– In spring 1914 I decided to turn my back on America for a while, said your father. I wanted to see my family in Turkey again. I also wanted to marry, and I wanted to take a woman from my village as my wife.

– You had been married before, correct?

– Yes. But my first wife died during childbirth.

– And you didn't have an heir?

– No. I had no heir.

– You wished to have a son, correct?

– Yes, Mudir Bey. Most of all, I wanted to father a son with a woman from my village. A respectable woman that didn't show her legs off to everyone.

– Or her face?

– Or her face.

– The journey across took several weeks, said your father. I came on a German passenger ship called the *Graf Schwerin*. It was a very large ship – like a floating city – and it moved so quietly through the water, it felt as though we were on a lake: a still lake.

– Indeed, the Germans know how to build decent ships,

said the mudir, be it a passenger ship or a warship. Just look at the *Goeben* and the *Breslau*, two German warships that now sail under the Turkish flag. Not even the English, those sons of bitches, could build something quite as fine. Isn't that right, efendiler?

– Yes, said the vali. We used the *Goeben* and the *Breslau* to shell Odessa.

– Everything the Germans make is of the finest quality, said the mudir. It cannot be denied. And I can easily imagine that this enormous German ship, the *Graf Schwerin,* sailed as though she were on a lake.

– You can always rely on German efficiency, said the vali. I bet you that nobody suffers seasickness on one of those German ships, efendiler, and that even the roast pork served on board stays put in those infidels' stomachs as proof that Allah Himself, who is the greatest – praise be His name – is willing to turn a blind eye to the Germans so that nobody thinks to doubt their efficiency.

– It's true. Nobody on board suffered seasickness. You are completely right, Vali Bey.

– You see, what did I tell you, efendiler? said the vali.

– I met quite a few Armenians on the ship, said your father, but they were all harmless individuals who had nothing to do with the Armenian global conspiracy, at least so I presume. They were businessmen. I talked to them because they spoke Armenian. We met on the deck, in the dining hall during meals or to socialize during the evenings. The trip across on that large German ship truly was a pleasant journey.

– Like most tourists, I had taken a camera along with me, said your father, so that I could impress my friends and acquaintances – but mostly my family – back home with pictures of my travels … just a childish whim, nothing more. There was no political motive behind it, and I certainly had no intention to cause harm to Turkey or to take pictures of forbidden places, and I definitely did not intend to hand over any sensitive photographic material to the English or the French or the Russians. I honestly didn't, efendiler. I was nothing more than a harmless tourist; and besides, who could have known at the beginning of 1914 that a great war would break out? A war that could heap disaster upon so many people? No, efendiler, I knew absolutely nothing of these things when I took my camera with me on my journey. Believe me.

– At this very moment we are not interested in your camera, said the mudir. Tell us about Sarajevo.

– I took the train to Paris, said your father, and thought about taking the Orient Express to travel via Vienna and then on to Constantinople, but then I realized that I needed to travel via Sarajevo.

– Because you had an uncle there to whom you needed to hand over some money, correct?

– Yes, Mudir Bey. It was from his brother in America, my other uncle. I had promised him.

– A form of foreign exchange fraud?

– I hadn't even thought of that.

– A trivial offense?

– Yes, Mudir Bey.

– Go on.

– At first, I had no real desire to make a detour to Sarajevo, but then I thought to myself that perhaps it could be good fun, seeing as my uncle owned a coffeehouse.

– I didn't realize that one could have so much fun in a coffeehouse.

– Well, it wasn't really a coffeehouse; it was a kind of brothel.

– What do you mean by that, efendi?

– It was a coffeehouse with secret rooms called *séparées*. There were also girls who sat around in the coffeehouse that you could pay to go into one of these secret rooms with you.

– And you knew this?

– The entire family knew. My uncle was the black sheep of the family. He was only on good terms with his American brother. He occasionally lent him money and paid for him to travel to America when he first went over.

– I see, said the mudir.

Some of the men were now laughing. The Turkish officers were whispering amongst themselves.

– So you wanted to go to Sarajevo to not only deliver the money to your uncle, but to have fun? The mudir smiled warmly. I presume that a bit of fun … before remarrying … is good for the soul. A last taste of freedom, so to speak?

– That's right, Mudir Bey. I thought I would first travel to Sarajevo, drop off the money, then have a bit of fun … in my uncle's coffeehouse … after all, I had certainly earned it after all those difficult years in America: the hard work, the loneliness … I thought, 'Why not have a few days of carefree fun before going home, getting married and being tied down.'

– We understand, efendi, said the mudir.

– We understand, said the fat vali, who began to quietly and excitedly giggle away to himself, his plump face beaming. There are pretty girls in Bosnia, he said, although you can't find them as young as you can here in the brothels of Bakir, which are all in the hands of Armenians.

– Not all of them, said one of the Turkish officers.

– Tell us about Sarajevo, said the mudir to your father.

– I arrived in Sarajevo, said your father, just as headlines started appearing in the press about the imminent Austrian royal couple's state visit. A date for the visit had also been set: June 28, 1914. There was very little in Sarajevo to suggest that an event was about to take place that would change the course of history. Of course, it's true that the streets had been cleaned, and the dirt and rubbish had all been cleared away, particularly in the Muslim quarters of the city and in the narrow alleyways of the bazaars. It's also true that there were more police than usual on the streets, as well as units of the regional Austrian garrison, but any changes were barely noticeable in the days leading up to the state visit.

– What did stand out to you in particular? asked the mudir.

– I noticed that many Armenians had suddenly turned up in Sarajevo. Armenians that were not from the area.

– How did you know that these Armenians were not from the area?

– The waiters in the coffeehouse told me, as did my uncle, and of course the other guests, too. Particularly the girls. They talked about the foreigners.

– You see, efendiler, said the mudir, glancing around the circle of men triumphantly. On the day of the assassination, Sarajevo was crawling with Armenians. Armenians, who were not from the area. Where did they all come from? And why?

– But, Mudir Bey, said the Austrian journalist. It was a grand occasion: a state visit. Visitors came from all over the world, particularly members of the press. Even I wanted to travel to Sarajevo.

– Were you there?

– No, said the Austrian journalist. My newspaper sent another one of my colleagues. I still regret it to this day.

– It truly was a major event, said the vali.

– Yes, indeed it was, said the mudir.

– The Austrian heir to the throne had been warned, said the mudir. Even we Turks issued him with a warning. You see, these Bosnians are dangerous people. They are just as unpredictable as the Serbs. At that time we knew that there was a strong possibility that an assassination attempt would be made during a state visit in Bosnia. I would even go as far as to say that everyone knew that an assassination would, in fact, take place.

– Exactly, said the vali. Everyone knew. Even the Archduke himself knew. But the Archduke was too proud to turn back.

– He was a proud man, said the German major. The epitome of a German officer.

– Of an Austrian officer, said the Austrian journalist.

– He also knew that he wasn't popular, said the vali. And still he travelled to Sarajevo!

– It was a clear act of provocation from the Austrians, said the mudir, for nowhere else were the Austrians as unpopular as in Bosnia and Herzegovina.

– A provocation, said the vali, but also a necessary move. A mighty country showing a lesser one just who was in charge.

– Exactly, Vali Bey, said the mudir. Where would mankind

be if the mighty let the weak know they were afraid?

– *Nowhere,* said the vali.

– Look here, efendiler, said the mudir. Let me spell it out for you. Who did Serbia previously belong to? And who did Bosnia belong to, and Herzegovina? Well, can you guess, efendiler? I'll tell you: these provinces once belonged to us, the Turks.

– Exactly, said the vali.

– And who instigated an uprising in the 1870s? Was it the Turks? No, efendiler. It was the Serbs who instigated an uprising. And against whom? Against us Turks. And why, if I may dare to ask? Well, I'll tell you, efendiler. Out of pure wantonness. Without any due reason. You see, we always treated these subjects well, even though they bred pigs and let them run around in the open in a country that was being governed by believers of the true faith.

– Exactly, said the vali.

– Then the Serbs became independent, said the mudir, despite the fact that those pig breeders weren't even able to govern themselves, and those sons of bitches from Russia helped them along the way. That was at the end of the 1870s.

– Yes, said the vali.

– But the Austrians put a stop to it all when they invaded Bosnia and Herzegovina in 1878.

– They put a stop to it, said the vali.

– Because the Serbs wanted to annex Bosnia and Herzegovina as part of their new state, even though they couldn't.

– Because the Austrians suddenly came and occupied the two provinces?

– Obviously, said the mudir.

'Obviously.' The word was even repeated by the Austrian

journalist. 'We swept in and occupied those two provinces that the Serbs had proclaimed as theirs.'

– Those two provinces are rightly ours, said the mudir.

– Even the capital of Bosnia, the old city of Sarajevo, is a Turkish city. And still I sometimes laugh up my own sleeve when I think about how things were back then in 1878, when the two provinces were under Austrian occupation. I laugh with joy that the Serbs didn't get their hands on them.

– It was a kick in the rear for the Serbs, said the vali.

– A kick in the balls, said the mudir.

– Nothing filled the Serbs with as much bitterness as the loss of Bosnia and Herzegovina, said the vali. By occupying this territory, it was as though the Austrians had cut off the Serbs' balls.

– And that is why no other people on earth hate the Austrians as much as the Serbs.

– True, said the vali.

– Thirty-six years. That's how long tensions had been brewing in Herzegovina and Bosnia, said the mudir. Thirty-six years, efendiler. It was a powder keg that would eventually explode.

– Eventually, said the vali. Except no one knew when.

– Then, when the Archduke came to Sarajevo, the time had come.

– Exactly, Mudir Bey.

– Let's move on to Sarajevo!

– Yes, let's move on to Sarajevo.

– We have established that an attack on the Archduke was foreseeable, said the mudir. After all, how could the Bosnian nationalists tolerate such a provocative act? An official Austrian state visit in their capital!

– An outrageous provocation, said the vali.

– If I weren't Austrian, said the Austrian journalist, and loyal to the Kaiser, I could almost sympathize with those Bosnian nationalists. But what does all this have to do with the Armenians, efendiler?

– Explain to these gentlemen, the mudir said to your father, how the Armenians are involved and why the Armenian global conspiracy had a particular interest in the attack on the royal couple … even though it was, in fact, an internal affair of the Bosnian nationalists.

– I will explain, efendiler, said your father.

– Tell us!

– Yes, Mudir Bey.

– It is very important, efendi.

– Very important, said the vali.

Your father glanced around nervously. He was sweating and he wiped the sweat from his brow with the sleeve of his shirt. For a few seconds his eyes met those of the chief scribe, and in those eyes your father read the following words: 'This man is telling nothing but lies. And those lies are oozing out of all of his pores and gathering as beads of sweat on his forehead – these man's lies are so obvious that all of us here can see them. Lies! Even though he is now trying to wipe them away with his sleeve.' – But the chief scribe's glance didn't stop there: 'This man is afraid. If he doesn't say what the mudir wants to hear, his unborn son will be disposed of before he has even seen the light of Allah. This man is pitiful, but what choice does he have?'

– Efendiler, said your father. The Armenians who had travelled from many foreign countries and cities and arrived in Sarajevo shortly before the state visit were none other than henchmen of the Armenian global conspiracy!

– We know that, efendi, said the mudir. Why don't you tell us instead why the Armenian global conspiracy wanted to see the Austrian royal couple dead? And why did they choose you, of all people, to shoot the Archduke and his wife?

– Yes, said your father, I will explain to the gentlemen.

– The Armenian global conspiracy sent their agents to Sarajevo just before the visit to ensure that the assassination went ahead as planned.

– So the Armenian global conspiracy knew of an imminent assassination?

– The whole world knew, said your father.

– And what about in Sarajevo?

– Obviously people were aware of it there, too. Everyone knew. We all realized as soon as the press announced the state visit. I heard whispers on the streets, and saw people discussing it in coffeehouses. It was an audacious provocation of the entire Bosnian nation, the likes of which hadn't been seen in a long time.

– And what about the Armenians? asked the mudir.

– Sarajevo was suddenly crawling with Armenians, said your father. They met in restaurants and in coffeehouses, particularly in those run by Armenians. Some of these visiting Armenians met in my uncle's coffeehouse every single day.

– Were they official meetings?

– Yes, said your father. They met every afternoon, drank

coffee, played cards, and teased the girls, but sometimes they retired to one of the *séparées*.

– With some of the girls?

– No, without.

– And what did they do there?

– They planned a conspiracy.

– Before the assassination, I was staying in a hotel, said your father, but I spent the days sitting around in my uncle's coffee-house. A few days before the state visit, my uncle took me to one side and spoke to me.

– What did he say to you?

– I had once told him that I was a marksman, said your father. Although the Armenian farmers in my village were not allowed to carry weapons because, at that time – before the revolution – Abdul Hamid was still in power, and it was strictly forbidden for Armenians to bear arms. But we concealed a couple of rifles and revolvers in our villages which we needed to protect ourselves against Kurdish bandits. I once shot dead a Kurd as a young boy.

– Had you ever shot anyone else?

– No. Only that one Kurd. But I have also shot wild ducks and geese, and one time, just for fun, I shot a swallow out of the sky. The farmers in the village used to say, 'That Khatisian boy could shoot a fly from a swallow's beak.'

– So you were a marksman?

– Yes.

– And what did your uncle want you to do?

– He said the foreign Armenians, who were meeting in a *séparée,* were looking for a marksman.

– Did that surprise you?

– Very much so, said your father.

– Later the Armenians spoke with me. They said that Bosnian fanatics were planning to assassinate the Archduke with the backing of a group of Bosnian officers. They told me that they had connections to this group of officers.

– And what did they want from you?

– These Armenians said that neither the group of Serbian officers nor the Bosnian nationalists, who were all in cahoots with one another – that neither one nor the other was capable of carrying out a proper assassination because they were all too crazed or hot-headed. That's why, the Armenians said, an outsider had to do it, someone like me, someone nobody would suspect: a marksman, someone who would be able to carry it out. The Armenians also told me that I shouldn't be afraid as everyone would instantly point the finger at the Bosnians and the Serbs. They told me all I had to worry about was doing it properly: cold-blooded, with precision … an ambush attack … and then disappear into the crowd.

The Armenian conspirators made one thing clear to me: The murder of the Austrian crown prince and his wife on the orders of a group of Serbian officers – as would be the official version of events – would have to result in an invasion led by Austrian troops as the Austrian government had long been looking for an excuse to settle the score with the Serbs. However, given the fact that the Russians had a military alliance with Serbia, they said that such a move would immediately bring Russia into the fray. But a Russian mobilization would then be cause for alarm for the Germans, who would, in turn, mobilize their troops. England

and France would also be called to action. So the Armenians knew that murdering the royal couple on Bosnian territory – in Sarajevo – would trigger a world war. – Your father paused for a brief moment. Then he said, Of course, Turkey wouldn't be spared from a world war on this scale. And as the German military has been training the Turkish army since the last century, it was easy to predict that, sooner or later, Turkey would enter the war on the side of the Germans.

– These Armenian conspirators had exceptional foresight, said the vali.

– Yes, said your father.

– And what interest did the Armenians have in this world war?

– For the Armenians, said your father, the aim was to embroil the Turks in a war with Russia. They knew that if Turkey entered the war to fight alongside the Germans and the Austrians, this would lead to war between Turkey and Russia, too.

– That seems obvious, said the vali.

– However, a war between Russia and Turkey would free the Armenians from the Turkish yoke.

– What do you mean by Turkish yoke, efendi?

– I don't mean anything by it, Vali Bey, said your father. I am simply trying to explain how the Armenian conspirators saw it.

– And how did they see it?

– Well, in their eyes, what mattered most was the Caucasus front. No one, so they thought, could stand up to the Russian juggernaut. They thus reasoned that the Russians would pass through the Caucasus, invade Turkey and liberate the millions of Armenians living on Turkish soil.

– Anatolia would be occupied by Russian troops?

– Precisely. Anatolia would be occupied by Russian troops, and millions of Armenians in the border regions would be liberated.

– And what did the Armenians expect from the Russians and this so-called liberation?

– That an Armenian state would be established on Turkish soil. After all, this region once belonged to the Armenians.

– True, said the German major. Armenia really did once belong to them.

– Anatolia or Armenia or Hayastan. It's all one and the same.

– And this Armenian state, would it have been independent?

– Not entirely, said your father, it would have been an Armenian state but a Russian protectorate. But that was to be expected.

– And the Armenian conspirators would have agreed to this?

– Only as a temporary solution, said your father. They still wanted to pursue their goal of an independent Armenian state, but they also believed that such a young state would need Russia's protection, particularly in the current climate.

– Were Russian citizens also among the Armenian conspirators in Sarajevo? asked the vali.

– Some of the Armenians had Russian passports.

– And how did you find that out?

– They spoke an Armenian dialect that is only spoken on the Russian side of the border. My uncle told me that they were actually Russian-Armenians and that they also held Russian passports.

– Could it be that these Armenians with Russian passports were in fact members of the Russian secret service?

– Possibly, said your father.

– From the Okhrana, said the mudir.

– I don't know, said your father.

– It appears as though the Okhrana were somehow implicated in the affair, said the German major. After all, the occupation of Anatolia is of interest to the Tsar.

– That's right, said the mudir.

– And the Dashnaks, asked the vali, the Armenian nationalists?

– They were going to aid the Russians as they invaded, said your father.

– An Armenian uprising behind Turkish lines?

– Yes, said your father. They predicted that the millions of Armenians living in the border regions and in the rear area behind the front would turn on the Turks as soon as the Caucasus army of the Tsar made their move.

– And how do you know all this?

– I found some of it out from the Armenian conspirators, and my brother-in-law Pesak Muradian told me a great deal … but later, once I had connected all the dots.

– So the Armenian conspirators travelled to Sarajevo as soon as the Austrian royal couple's state visit had been officially announced? asked the mudir. And as soon as a date had been set?

– Yes, said your father.

– And, if I understand correctly, they had connections to a group of Serbian officers?

– Yes, said your father.

– But they didn't think that the group of officers and their henchmen were really capable of carrying out such an act. And that is why they wanted you to do it, is that right, efendi? You were supposed to shoot the Archduke and his wife dead?

– Correct.

– Because no one would suspect you? Because you were an outsider? And because the blame would be laid at the feet of the Bosnians and the Serbs?

– Yes, Mudir Bey.

– And you insist that you were the one who shot and killed the Austrian heir to the throne?

– Yes, Mudir Bey.

– And his wife?

– It's true, Mudir Bey.

– As I said, a few days before the state visit – it must have been four days earlier – the conspirators welcomed me into their inner circle. I assume it was because my uncle told them that I was a decent man, and that I was a patriot and also a poet.

The conspirators spent a long time trying to convince me. They told me that the salvation of the Armenian-Turks through a Russian invasion was in the balance, and that it was imperative to trigger a war. They said I could be the savior of the nation if I did it. I eventually gave in. I am a poet, efendiler. The whole thing gave me a thrill. In truth, I really did see myself as the savior of the Armenian people. And I pictured seeing my name later on in history books.

– Yes, said the mudir.

– The Armenian conspirators gave me a revolver, said your father. It was one they had bought from the Serbian officers, those they had connections with, and this revolver, a Browning, came from the Serbian armories.

– When did they give you the revolver?

– On the day that the royal couple arrived in Sarajevo.

– So shortly before the assassination?

– Yes.

– They say that all of Sarajevo was out on the streets that day?

– The city's streets were thronging with people, said your father, especially around the quay by the bridges. There were police everywhere. There were roadblocks everywhere. When the open car carrying the royal couple arrived from the direction of the city hall and turned into Franz-Joseph Street, I was standing nearby. I had my camera with me, as well as the revolver, which I had concealed beneath my jacket and behind my camera. The crowd was restless. You could see the hatred on their faces. As the colonnade approached, the crowd where I was standing broke through the police line and charged towards the open car where the royal couple sat. Of course, the crowds were pushed back by the police, but the car remained motionless.

– And it was at that moment that you shot?

– No, efendiler. I hesitated. The open car in which Franz Ferdinand was sitting, together with his wife on the rear seat, started up again, but it drove very slowly. I tried to run alongside the car, but I was repeatedly pushed back. I ran and I ran. I ran alongside the car and once again it came to a halt, this time on the corner of Franz-Joseph and Rudolf Street.

And suddenly I saw a young man holding a revolver in his hand. He looked like a student. He was standing very close to me. I saw him run towards the car, break through the police line and I saw him shoot at the royal couple.

– Those were the historic shots of Sarajevo, said the German major, the deadly shots fired by Gavrilo Princip, the man who shot the Archduke and his wife dead.

– On the orders of a group of Serbian officers, said the queer lieutenant.

– It must have been him, said your father, except he hit neither the Archduke nor his wife. Just a few seconds after this Bosnian fired his shots, I fired my revolver. But I was a marksman, and I hit the Archduke. I hit his wife, too, who was sat next to him.

– But that cannot be true, said the German major. We know who shot the royal couple. The bullets were identified. They came from the revolver of Bosnian nationalist Gavrilo Princip. There can be no doubt about it.

– You are forgetting that our prisoner had the exact same revolver as that Bosnian, said the mudir, provided by a group of Serbian officers and procured from the Serbian armories. The two weapons are identical.

– Are you suggesting that the bullets that were later removed from the body of both victims may actually have also come from this man's revolver?

– That is precisely what we are claiming, said the mudir.

– And where is your evidence for this? Said the German major.

– This man's testimony is the evidence.

– But that won't suffice, Mudir Bey. Where is his revolver?

– He threw it away.

– It's true, said your father.

– And the witnesses? said the German major.

– There are no witnesses, said the mudir. The Armenian conspirators are long gone, and we don't know any of their real names. And as for the prisoner's uncle, he has since died.

– He sadly passed away, said your father. And I don't know the real names of any of the conspirators. They were smart enough not to give them to me.

– And what about your uncle's family?

– They had nothing to do with it. Not a single one knew anything about it.

– And the waiters?

– The same.

– And the girls?

– The girls also knew nothing about it.

– Still, we should interrogate them.

– That would be a waste of time, said your father. Neither the girls nor the waiters could have known what was discussed behind the doors of the *séparées* – it could have just been any old business matter that we were discussing. And I acted alone when I carried out the assassination. Completely alone. No one noticed me in the mass of people. No one saw me.

– This is indeed a monstrous act, said the major. But this accusation is one without witnesses or evidence.

– This man is the witness, said the mudir.

– It is monstrous, said the major. But no one will believe his testimony.

– We will make sure that people believe it, said the mudir.

– After the assassination, I stayed in Sarajevo, said your father. No one had seen my revolver that I had hidden beneath the protective cover of my camera. Although the shots were audible, with all the jostling and noise, everybody believed they were the Bosnian attacker's shots. I then vanished into the crowd.

– It's true. I stayed in Sarajevo for a few more weeks, said your father.
    – Because he had a venereal disease, said the mudir.
    – I thought I had a venereal disease, said your father.
    – Did you have any other reason to delay your journey back to Turkey?
    – No, said your father.

– Of course I was waiting for the Austrian ultimatum, said your father. But there was no reason why I couldn't also wait in Turkey for the outcome. There was no political reason to delay my onward journey.
    – And what about the ultimatum?
    – They were supposed to announce the decision, said your father, but it was delayed. Weeks passed and nothing happened. At the last minute it looked as though the Austrians were too afraid of the consequences, and that the war that we all wanted to see happen wouldn't break out.
    – But the war had to happen?
    – Correct.

– At the end of July I finally decided to continue my journey, and so I arrived in Constantinople on July 25.
    – On July 25? Three days before the outbreak of war?

– Yes.

– Was that a coincidence?

– It was. Pure coincidence.

– You hadn't thought that this coincidence could arouse the suspicions of the Turkish authorities?

– No. I hadn't.

– You then took some photographs around Constantinople … on a steam boat trip. If I am not mistaken, you photographed the Bosporus Strait and all the way along the shoreline of the Sea of Marmara, up to the mouth of the Dardanelles?

– Yes, Mudir Bey. But I wasn't following anyone's orders; I did it purely on my own initiative.

– To what end, efendi?

– At that time I hadn't really thought it through, Mudir Bey. But I thought to myself, 'If war does break out, you could give these photos to your brother-in-law, Pesak. He has Russian contacts.'

– So that the Russians could land in the Dardanelles?

– I think so, yes.

– Or the English or the French, who have a better fleet?

– At that time I wasn't entirely sure.

– The Austrians and the Serbs mobilized, said your father, and a few days later their countries were at war. But on July 25 and 26, just a few days before the conflict broke out, there was little sign in Constantinople of what was about to take place. Tourists were still able to visit the Bosporus Strait, go on steam boat cruises and take photographs. It was as though the Turks were still deep in some kief-induced slumber. I stayed for a few days and took photographs. I also put my clothes in to be cleaned: a pretext to explain why I had needed to stay on in the capital for a few days if ever I was caught and interrogated.

    – You would claim that you had had to wait for your clothes?

    – Correct.

    – Because no man wants to return home in dirty clothes?

    – Yes, Mudir Bey.

– I then travelled home to my family.

    – To Anatolia? To Bakir and then on to Yedi Su?

    – Yes, Mudir Bey.

    – That's where you were married?

    – I was married.

    – And you went on a honeymoon along the Syrian coast?

    – Yes, I did.

    – And you took photographs there as well?

    – Yes.

– Particularly along the coastline, am I right? Although the coast is mostly lined with cliffs, there are a few bays where the enemy could land?

    – I photographed those landing sites.

    – That is high treason, efendi, said the mudir.

    – High treason, said the vali.

The mudir looked around the men in the room. 'We found a whole load of photographs in his apartment, efendiler, but they were harmless photographs. We did not find the most crucial ones.' The mudir gave a slight smirk, and it appeared to the men gathered in his office as though his glass eye was smirking, too.

    – Tell these gentlemen why we didn't find the most crucial

photographs, he said to your father.

– Because I gave them to my brother-in-law, said your father.

– Precisely, said the mudir contentedly. He gave them to his brother-in-law, Pesak Muradian, one of the Dashnaks' most-wanted leaders. As you are aware, he is one of those planning an uprising here behind the front. He is working together with the Russians. These people are simply waiting for the Russians to give them the signal: the signal to attack.

– That's right, everything the mudir says is correct, said your father.

One of the Turkish officers said, 'The Russians always attack over-land. Their fleet isn't strong enough to risk a successful landing.'

– But the English tend to approach from the sea, said the second Turkish officer. So it would be safe to assume that the Russians passed the photographs on to the English.

– Precisely, said the vali.

– An English landing on the Syrian coast, but also along the Dardanelles and on the Gallipoli Peninsula, would boost a Russian advance. So, it would be in the interest of the Russians for the English to get their hands on these photographs.

– Exactly, said the vali."

Suddenly the storyteller's voice filled the room, drowning out every other voice. The storyteller said, "Let them talk, my little lamb. Soon they will get hungry and call it a day. In the mean-time they will drink raki and coffee, and savor the sweet baklava, and smoke their chibouk and cigarettes and hookah. The mudir will clap his hands once more, the saptiehs will run to and fro, bringing fresh raki."

And the storyteller said, "Just as evening approached, they decided to call it a day. The saptiehs led the prisoner back to his cell and each man went his own way. The two Germans and the Austrian decided to take another stroll to the Gate of Happiness where a fresh group of Armenians was now hanging. This time, however, there were not three, but five bodies.

– What do you make of the accused's confession? asked the major.

– Nothing whatsoever, said the Austrian. That man was under pressure. His entire confession was nothing but one big lie. It was as though it had been dictated to him beforehand.

– By the mudir?

– I assume so.

– Constantinople is looking for someone to pin the blame on.

– Everyone's after someone to blame.

– Do you think that Enver Pasha will be able to use the accused's confession?

– No, I don't think so. It won't hold up.

– And the mudir?

– He's just a petty blowhard; another one of those intellectuals who have studied in the West and who wish to make a name for themselves in Constantinople.

– But he appears to have the backing of the vali, and the kaimakam, and the mutasarrif.

– Of course. Should the mudir be successful and manage to convince Enver, they will take the credit for it themselves.

– And if not?

– Then the mudir will take the fall.

– This mudir is an ambitious man.

— He certainly is.

As they spoke, the three men had come to a halt directly beneath the hanging bodies. The short, queer lieutenant pulled the major and the Austrian, who were taller than he was and towered over him by a head, to one side out of fear that the gray military caps of the two men could touch the dead men's feet.

— You see, said the Austrian. Many people are adamant that this whole business with the Armenian global conspiracy is true. But the whole thing is more mystical than tangible. The Minister of War, Enver Pasha, may well be a fanatic and an idealist of sorts, but he is not foolish; at least not so foolish that he, too, would blame the Armenians for the whole assassination business in Sarajevo, particularly as the whole world already knows who was really responsible. No, gentlemen, not even Enver Pasha could allow such a farce to take place, especially not in a public trial.

— You make a good point, said the major. Neither Enver nor anyone else in his government could.

— Talaat Bey, the Interior Minister, in particular would never let himself be drawn into such nonsense. Talaat is a staunch realist, a man with a cool head. He has no interest in terms such as *global conspiracy.* For him, the Armenians are nothing more than the enemy within.

— The enemy within. That may well be. But an enemy that has the support of exiled Armenians. And that, on the other hand, is certainly a global conspiracy of sorts, albeit one that hasn't been mystified.

— Either way, said the Austrian, the government will not agree to a trial that is both a farce and which would embarrass them.

– And what will the government do?

– They will find a convincing reason – one based on actual evidence – that will justify certain government actions before the international community, particularly before their allies.

– But there is no convincing reason that could justify actions taken against an entire people.

– Those men in Constantinople will come up with something.

– Don't you think that they're running out of time?

– What do you mean? asked the Austrian.

– Well, I mean … that the government has already set the ball in motion, and nobody really knows what crime the Armenians have actually committed.

– Yesterday I spoke with the German Consul, said the major.

– About the Armenians?

– About the executions and the high number of arrests.

– What did the Consul say?

– He has already informed Berlin, and lodged a complaint at the highest level. But Berlin has known about it for quite some time.

– Couldn't the Kaiser do something to put a stop to all these arrests and executions?

– The Kaiser will not interfere with matters here. And besides, we are at war; arrests happen every day.

– And executions?

– Those, too.

– But surely not on this scale.

– True. Not on this scale.

– Did the Consul say anything else?

– Yes. He said that the Turks are getting ready to stage a massacre.

– Against the Armenians?

– Yes.

– Massacres have always taken place here. That wouldn't come as a surprise.

– True.

– Did the Consul say anything else?

– Yes. He said the Turks were preparing to stage a massacre unlike any the world had ever seen. A massacre that will eclipse every other massacre in history.

– And how does he know that?

– His sources told him.

– So it will be a great massacre?

   – Yes.

   – When?

   – Nobody knows.

   – What are the Turks waiting for?

   – A credible charge.

   – So they can indict the entire Armenian people?

   – Yes.

– But surely the Kaiser must intervene?

   – He should.

   – After all, the Turks' bullets are fired from German guns.

   – True.

– The Consul should inform the Kaiser. He should send him a telegraph stating, 'A massacre unlike any the world has ever seen is about to take place. The victims are Christians.'

– It will be of little use.

– Why?

– Because the Kaiser is not interested in what might happen.

– You mean it has to happen first?

– Precisely.

– He needs facts? Actual reports?

– Exactly.

– Before anyone could convince him to step in?

– Yes.

– But then won't it surely be too late?

The two Germans and the Austrian discussed the imminent massacre for some time, then the young lieutenant left the other two to go to the Kurdish district to find himself a hamal – one of those strong, Kurdish laborers, whose spearheads, which they kept hidden beneath their dirty shalvar trousers, did more than just tickle. The German major and the Austrian journalist also went in search of some relaxation, and so strolled towards the city's brothels.

– Do you believe that a German sheath will offer protection against the French disease? asked the German major.

– You'll have to give it a try, said the Austrian.

– The Turks call syphilis the French disease.

– Yes, I know, said the major.

– Someone should also send a telegram to Kaiser Franz Joseph, said the Austrian.

– About syphilis and the threat to German troops?

– No. That's really Kaiser Wilhelm the Second's responsibility.

– So why do we need to send Franz Joseph a telegram?

– Because of the Armenians. Perhaps he could step in before it's too late?

… before it's too late!" The storyteller laughed out loud. "I'll tell you something, my little lamb. When the powers that be in this world are sitting too comfortably to set their asses in motion … or if the movement of this specific body part would be contrary to certain interests, the ass remains safely in its idle state: its movement is delayed and the conscience, located somewhere north of this static ass, dismisses the mind's concerns with a cry of: 'later!'. – And I assure you, my little lamb, it is always too late – and this time things will be no different."

And the storyteller said, "The two German officers and the Austrian have cottoned on."

"Cottoned on to what?"

"That the extermination of the Armenians in Turkey – the execution of an entire people – ultimately does not depend solely on the exterminators themselves, but on the silence of their allies.

The great massacre!" said the storyteller. "Everyone in this country knew that it would come, but very few could actually imagine what it would look like. What did the Turks have in mind for the Armenians? Would they slaughter them all just like sheep? And before the eyes of the entire civilized world? Who would come to the aid of the Armenians? Perhaps Kaiser Wilhelm the Second, who refrained from taking even the tiniest of actions for fear that it might upset his Turkish allies? Or Kaiser Franz Joseph, who was old and couldn't pee straight? Could the Russians help, or the

English, or the French? Were they not too far away from where it was taking place ... on the other side of the front? Or would their outrage go no further than headlines in the press, only to be thrown out in the trash together with the rest of yesterday's news? – But believe me, my little lamb. Regardless of what is about to be unleashed upon us, historians will laugh up their sleeves, particularly those in charge of recording contemporary history. You see, they need new material to punctuate their boredom, material that they can work with. Their lack of imagination will take them in search of figures: figures that will help them keep the volume of the slain in check – to record them, if you will – and they will try to find the words to describe the great massacre and to make sure it is inserted nicely and neatly into its proper place on the history shelf. They don't realize that every human soul is unique, and that everyone has a right to a name, even the local idiot in your father's village. They will call this great massacre 'mass murder', and the more erudite amongst them will refer to it as 'genocide'. Some know-it-all will call for it to be known as 'armenocide', and the goofiest egghead of them all will look through the dictionaries and finally proclaim it 'holocaust'."

Book Two

1

"Your father is now lying on the straw mat back in his cell. He knows that the mudir intends to take him to Constantinople so that he can testify to the Armenians' guilt in front of the whole world. Eventually he would be taken to Constantinople. This much was certain. But until then many days would pass, and during that time perhaps they would realize that they no longer needed his testimony at all. Perhaps those men in Constantinople would find others to testify in support of a completely different and much more credible accusation.

Your father cannot sleep. He is thinking of his unborn son Thovma, who will someday come into the world beneath a grapevine. And he realizes that he, too, was born beneath a grapevine, but the story didn't unfold as it did in the nightmarish version told to him by that voice of fear, where his mother's breasts were so full of milk that they burst. No ... no! That was just a lie! His mother's breasts never burst!"

The storyteller said, "His mother's breasts didn't burst. That was a lie."

"Do you mean my grandmother's breasts?"

"Yes, Thovma," said the storyteller. "Those are the fine breasts

I'm talking about.

Once upon a time there was a young boy," said the storyteller.
" ... he lay unborn beneath a grapevine. He was to be called
Vardan and this boy was your father.

Once upon a time there was a woman. She was nine months
pregnant. As the Lord God's impatience manifested itself in
pain – a phenomenon more widely known as *contractions* – and
when it felt as though her stomach was about to burst, she turned
to her husband and said, 'We must quickly fetch the donkey
and cart so we can go and collect our Vardan. He's lying under a
grapevine and cannot wait any longer.'
  – Where is his grapevine?
  – In the land of grapevines.

Once upon a time there was a donkey. He ran as quickly as
an Arabian horse. He whisked the pregnant woman and her
husband at lightning speed to the land of grapevines. As they
journeyed, the pregnant woman's breasts began to swell, but they
didn't burst. You see, the Lord God wanted the milk to wait.

Once upon a time there was a pregnant woman. She and her
husband arrived in the land of grapevines just in time. And she
saw a grapevine which had grown in the shape of a cradle for
the baby born beneath it. The woman saw the grapevine first as
a mother's eyes are sharper than those of the father. She rushed
towards the grapevine, and her husband ran behind her. As the
husband saw his wife take her son in her arms, he gave a little sob
and said, 'That'll be our Vardan.'

It was little Vardan. There could be no mistake as the woman was suddenly no longer pregnant.

– Your swollen belly has gone, said the man.

– The pain has gone, too, said the woman.

They washed little Vardan in the stream next to the grapevine. The wife laughed with joy. The husband did, too. Later on, when the wife held little Vardan to her milk-filled breasts, her nipples opened up.

And little Vardan drank his mother's sweet milk. And his parents thanked the Lord God for making the milk wait.

As they made their way back to their own village, their donkey took its time. They were travelling uphill. The landscape became increasingly barren; the hillsides were increasingly sparse and rugged; the bare cliff faces glistened in many different colors. Soon the land of grapevines lay far behind them. The narrow path on which they travelled disappeared into the high mountains, whose peaks lay above the clouds. They didn't whip the donkey; they didn't need to. Now they had time. They also didn't need to steer the donkey, for the donkey knew which way to go. A few hours passed by before they stopped to rest. The husband fetched the water pouch from beneath the sheep's-wool pillow, together with a wicker bread basket. They drank from the pouch which they had filled with fresh spring water in the land of grapevines, and they ate lavash bread which the wife had baked at home in her tonir. After they had eaten and drunk, the husband took the baby from his wife, laughed and held the child up high.

– Do you think our Vardan knows where he is?

– No, said the wife. Give him back to me.

– He needs to know that he is in the land of our forefathers, said the husband.

– I'm sure he couldn't care less, said the wife, taking the child back from her husband and pressing him against her breast.

– All this child needs to know is that he is with his mother, said the wife. That's all that matters.

– And what about his father?

– Of course, said the wife. He should know that he is with his father, too.

– If our Vardan already has thoughts in his head, said the husband, and eyes that know what they see, I would like to show him the landscape.

– But his eyes are still half stuck together, said the wife, because the Lord God doesn't want him to see too much at once. Otherwise he might get a fright.

– But you've already washed his eyes.

– I didn't wash them properly.

– When will he open them up fully to see the world for the first time?

– Perhaps in a few days' time, said the wife.

– If our Vardan could understand my words, and if he had the eyes of an eagle, I would now say to him, 'Look, Vardan. This is the land or our forefathers.' And I would point towards the east and say, 'Do you see that big, snow-covered mountain over there? That is Mount Ararat!'

– But he doesn't have the eyes of an eagle. And he has no idea what you're saying to him. What would be the point of showing him the land of our forefathers?

    – Not everything has to have a point.

    – So, you would show him Mount Ararat?

    – Yes.

    – And what else?

    – The city of Bakir, said the husband, pointing towards the southeast. And also the city of Erzurum, which is only a few days away from Bakir by cart. – And I would also show him the royal Armenian city of Ani: the city of a thousand and one churches. And I would say to him, 'Ani is a ruined city. Ani is as dead as the Armenian Kingdom, the kingdom of Goddess Anahit and the kingdom of the first Christian churches.'

    – The Kingdom isn't dead, said the wife. Our priest, Kapriel Hamadian, once said that the Armenian Kingdom wasn't dead.

    – And where is it then if it isn't dead?

    – It only looks dead, said the wife.

    – And who told you that?

    – Priest Kapriel Hamadian.

– And I would show our son Vardan all the Armenian villages and cities, all the ones in this region. 'Look, the Turks took all of this away from us. You see that city there? That's Urfa. And Diyarbakir is over there, and farther that way is the city of Konya. The city of Sivas isn't far from here: that belongs to the Armenians, too.' And if Vardan were to ask me what those mountains were called, I would say, 'I do not know, my son. Some call them the Kurdish mountains, others the mountains of Hayastan. But a researcher from Frankistan, who once came to our village and who showed our mayor, Mukhtar Ephrem Abovian, a very peculiar map, said that they were the Armenian Highlands. They lie within Turkey but stretch beyond the Russian and Kurdish borders, all the way to Kurdistan.'

And I would say to him, 'Do you see that river down there? That's the Karasu, and there's the Murat. And a bit farther on you will find the place where the Euphrates and the Tigris flow. And if we were to go down the other side of this mountain with our cart, we would reach Malatia. And at some point the mountains stop and the land becomes flat. The land is as flat as the palm of my hand and so hot that you need seven pouches of water just to travel across it. I believe it's called Mesopotamia.'

And I would say to him, 'There are Armenians everywhere, but many of them live here in our region. But there are also Turks living here, and gypsies and Kurds and Persians and Arabs and Jews and Greeks and devil worshippers called the Yazidis, and many others. You needn't be afraid of most of them. Just be wary of the Turks and the Kurds.'

– You're right, said the wife. As soon as he can see the world properly and perhaps understand what we say, and as soon as he has his first teeth and can walk – and isn't just kicking about – then we will say to him, 'Watch out for the Turks and the Kurds.'

– What about the devil worshippers? said the wife. Is it true that they can put a curse on our Vardan?

– No, said the husband. That isn't true. They're just as incapable of putting a curse on our Vardan as the gypsies.

– So who can put a curse on him? Perhaps the Turks, or the Kurds?

– No, said the husband. At best they can slit his throat. Or simply beat him to death.

– So who could put a curse on him?

– Only those with the evil eye, said the husband.

And they exist among every group.

– Even the Armenians?

– Even the Armenians.

– Well, I've always known it was true, said the wife.

– Then why did you ask? said the husband.

After they had eaten, the husband suddenly had an appetite for fish, so he turned to his wife and said, 'That lavash didn't satisfy my hunger. I could gobble up a whole fish, and I bet you our little Vardan could as well.'

– Well, I bet you he can't, said the wife.

– Each time I think about eating a fat, juicy fish, said the husband, it reminds me of that great Armenian lake, the one not far from the Russian border.

– You mean Lake Van? The lake just two smokes away from my brother's house?

– No, I don't mean that one, said the husband. I'm talking about a lake that I saw only recently. And how could it have been Lake Van? Had I been there, do you not think I would have been to visit your brother who lives practically on its shores? I haven't seen your brother in years.

– So it must have been a different lake?

– It was a different lake, said the husband. And I've gone and forgotten the name. But it doesn't matter, seeing as all the lakes in the region are Armenian. Let's just say it was just another

Armenian lake.

    – And what happened there? asked the wife.

    – Nothing special, said the husband.

And the husband said, 'It wasn't that long ago. You were two months' pregnant with our son Vardan. I took the donkey and rode for three days through the mountains. I passed through many fertile valleys. I passed rivers and streams, as well as a few lakes of various sizes.'

    – But that can't possibly be true, said the wife. You haven't left the village a single time in the last two years.

    – But that's what happened, said the husband.

    – Perhaps you only dreamed it.

    – Perhaps I did, said the husband.

And the husband said, 'So, I came across this huge lake, and there I met a fisherman who was just casting out his net. His name was Petrus, but he called himself Bedros because he was Armenian.'

    – Bedros?

    – Yes, Bedros.

    – And what happened with this fisherman?

    – Nothing special. He just said, 'Can you hear the fish talking to each other?'

    – No, I said. I can't.

    – They're all speaking Armenian, said the fisherman.

    – Then they must all be Armenian fish, I said.

    – Right, said the fisherman.

– The Turks claim that they're Turkish fish, said the fisherman, but I know that they're Armenian; I can understand what they're saying.

Yes, I said.

And the fisherman said, 'The flowers in this region also speak Armenian, as does the grass – and even the wind that rocks the tops of the trees sings Armenian lullabies to the leaves as they sway.'

– Do the Turks know? I asked.

And the fisherman said, 'They know, but they won't admit it.'

– And what about the fat, juicy fish? asked the wife.

    – Well, it was a fat, juicy fish, said the husband.

    – What kind of fat, juicy fish?

    – One the fisherman caught for me later that day.

    – Tell me about this fish? Was it really fat and juicy?

    – Yes, said the husband.

And the husband said, 'The fisherman told me a story. It was the Story of the Fat Fish.'

    – Tell me the story.

    – I will, said the husband. I will tell you the story that the fisherman told me.

– Once upon a time there was an Armenian goddess. Her name was Anahit. She was sitting on a rock in the Euphrates, combing her silky locks. And each time that one of her hairs fell out, the wind carried it away.

    – Where did the wind take it?

    – It carried it far away, but not too far as her hair never left the land of Armenia.

    – Did the hair get stuck somewhere? In the air perhaps?

– No, said the husband. Eventually the hair came down, and it always fell into water, either in a river or in a pond, or in a stream or in a lake. Sometimes it would even fall into the sea.

– And what did the hair want?

– It wanted to feed the fish in the water.

The husband said, 'Do you know what that fisherman said to me?'

– No, said the wife.

– He said, 'That is why the fish in this region are so fat and plentiful. You see, Anahit is the Goddess of Fertility.'

– How many children do you have? Bedros the fisherman asked me.

– Eleven, I said. And soon it will be twelve for my wife is pregnant again.

– Will it be a boy? asked the fisherman.

– I hope it will be a boy, I said.

– And what will you call him?

– I will name him Vardan.

– Vardan was an Armenian hero, said the fisherman. He fought against the Persian Kingdom in 401 with his army of 60,000 Armenians. Do you know what his battle cry was?

– No, I said. How should I know that?

– 'For Hayastan and for Christ.' That was his battle cry, said the fisherman.

– So he was an Armenian hero?

– One chosen by Christ.

– Do you wish your son to become a hero? asked the fisherman.

   – No, I said. Heroes die young. I want my son to grow old.

   – So you don't want him to be a hero?

   – Exactly, I said. I don't want him to be a hero.

– He should become a fisherman, said the fisherman. Like me. If he becomes a fisherman, he will never go hungry.

   – Well, I would like him to become a farmer, I said.

   – He should become a fisherman, said the fisherman.

– Life is not easy for an Armenian farmer, said the fisherman. He is at the mercy of the sun and the rain. And the Turkish tax collectors and the Kurdish Beys, who also charge their own taxes, and whose riders take away his livestock or kidnap his women or even set fire to the roof over his head.

   – True, I said. They might set fire to his house.

   – They might even force him off his field.

   – They could do that, too.

   – Believe me, it will be better if he becomes a fisherman.

   – So he shall.

   – Yes, said the fisherman.

And then the fisherman caught a fish for me, and it was the fattest fish that I have ever seen. He cut the head off and said to me, 'We will cook it on the spit and eat it now. Fish has to be eaten fresh.'

   – Yes, I said. Then I added, 'It's a shame that my son Vardan isn't here to enjoy this fish with us.'

   – There'll be other fish for him to catch and eat, said the fisherman.

   – I would like to keep this fat, juicy fish for Vardan, I said, but I know that I can't.

– It's true, you can't, said the fisherman. After three days any dead fish will begin to stink as much as the lap of a Kurdish girl in winter. You see, Kurds only wash in summer when they can bathe in the rivers.

– True, I said.

– And then the fisherman said, 'There will be other fish for your son Vardan to catch and eat.'

The wife said, 'A fisherman he shall be.'

– Yes, said the husband.

– After the christening, said the wife, we'll place a rod in his cradle.

– That's a good idea, said the husband. We should get him used to it as early as possible."

2

"And so it was," said the storyteller to the Last Thought, "that immediately after your father had been christened by Priest Kapriel Hamadian, his mother placed a child's fishing rod inside his cradle. Would you like me to describe the cradle to you? The cradle in which your father slept whenever he wasn't dozing between his mother's large, milk-filled breasts?"

"Yes, Meddah."

"At first glance, it looks like a completely normal cradle, my little dove. A type of crate with a drainage hole because, as you know, little children still soil themselves, even those called Vardan who have been named after a hero, although they aren't destined to become one. Your grandfather originally built the cradle for his first son. As time passed, all of his children ended up sleeping in it as it was passed down from child to child."

"So, there isn't anything special about it?"

"There is, my little lamb. You see, your grandfather carved a dove into the wood: a dove carrying an olive branch."

"What does it mean?"

"It was supposed to be the dove from Noah's Ark, the one that rose up from Mount Ararat to go forth and fetch an olive branch from the land that would someday be known as Hayastan – the land that lay at the foot of the mountain – as proof that the floods were over.

In the Khatisian household it was tradition for a newborn baby to be rocked during the day by its grandmother, perhaps because the mother had kept watch over the child during the night, or simply because she was exhausted from hours of her baby's joyous suckling. Grandmother Khatisian was used to rocking babies. And as she didn't always want to sit next to the cradle, she would tie a long piece of string around one of her legs and attach the other end to the cradle so that she could walk around all over the house or out in the yard, or sit in front of the house chatting to passers-by, and needed only to give the long string a little tug with either her hand or her foot to comfort the crying baby."

"Did my father have a grandmother?"

"What a question, my little lamb. All small children have grandparents.

This cradle really wasn't anything special," said the storyteller, "it was filled with soft sand that Vardan's grandmother would change once it had gotten too damp. Of course, the cradle also had a drainage hole, which I mentioned earlier, so that they would need to use as little sand as possible. It was a proper Armenian farmer's cradle – one built with love and care. So you see, there was nothing special about the cradle, or your father for that matter. Like all small children, he spent his time either crying or screaming or kicking around – or being quiet and peaceful. Mostly your father was a pleasant child. He slept through the first few days of his life, smiled as he slumbered and dreamed of his mother's large, milk-filled breasts; sometimes he also dreamed of the long piece of string his grandmother held and would occasionally tug. Perhaps he also dreamed of the dove carrying the olive branch, Mount Ararat and the land of Hayastan, although I doubt it.

And when your father's great-grandfather fathered his daughter – by that I mean, your father's grandmother – he said to his wife, 'If it's a boy, and I certainly hope that it is, we shall call him Tigran as that was the name of an Armenian king. However, if it's a girl, we shall call her Satenig. She was an Armenian princess.'

But then Vardan's great-grandmother said, 'It will be a girl: I can feel it. But she'll be no princess. We'd best call her *Hamest*.'

– Why *Hamest* of all names?

– Because my heart is telling me that *Hamest* is the only name we can give her, said the great-grandmother.

Hamest means modesty," said the storyteller. "And as she did in fact give birth to a girl, they called her *Hamest*."

"Was she a modest woman?" asked the Last Thought.

"No," said the storyteller. "That's exactly the point. She was anything but modest. As a matter of fact, she was a real dragon, one that marched around bossing everyone about. They should have called her *Zovinar*: a name that can mean both *nymph* and *lightning without thunder*."

"Was she like lightning without thunder?"

"She was," said the storyteller. "Her flashes of rage were not met with a roar of disapproval. No one cared when she cursed as there was no malice behind it."

"Was she good to my father?"

"She was good to your father.

And because she had been given the wrong name," said the story-teller, "one day, the day on which she was to conceive herself – her wedding night – she said to her husband, 'You know, they really ought to have called me *Zovinar,* but they didn't.'

And her husband said, 'If God punishes us and gives us not a son but a daughter, we shall call her *Zovinar.*'

But it was not to be," said the storyteller. "In the end none of their children were called Zovinar as the more they thought about the name, the less they liked it. Only when the Lord God bestowed a wife called Zovinar upon one of their sons – Hagob – did Hamest turn to her husband and say, 'Now, despite this and that and God knows what, we have a Zovinar in the family. Remember? That was the name I should have been given.'

And so it was," said the storyteller. "Hamest gained a daugh-ter-in-law whose name was Zovinar. And Hamest said to her husband, 'I'm sure she's been given the right name. I'm sure our Hagob's wife is like a lightning strike without thunder.' – But Hamest was wrong; Zovinar had also been given the wrong name. She was a modest woman who should actually have been called Hamest.

Despite her temperament – or perhaps because of it – your father's grandmother had an inconspicuous body. She was dwarf-like in stature, as skinny as a black Kurdish mountain goat, impetuous in her movements and as tough as a piece of *pastirma,* a dried meat, often found in farmers' pantries, that was notoriously difficult to digest. As she always wore a couple of cloves of garlic around her neck to protect her against the evil spirits and the evil eye, she always smelt of garlic, an odor which repelled some but which others found appetizing, given that garlic was and still is a popular condiment. Your father always started screaming whenever his grandmother came over to his cradle, bent over him with her cloves of garlic and said, 'Hi there, my fearless, little pasha. If you're not a good boy, the Kurds will come and get you.' Before softly adding, 'Or the big bear.'

This was just after his christening, so your father was still too small to be able to tell the difference between Good and Evil or even to know why his grandmother wore cloves of garlic around her neck. All he knew was that one of the women who took care of him smelt of garlic and the other one smelt of sweet milk, and so it was understandable that he had a tendency to only reach out for his mother.

His mother not only smelt of milk. She looked like a dairy cow, and thus the complete opposite of his grandmother. He could see her fat, portly frame, with her dugs sloshing from side to side, as she walked back and forth beside the cradle. When she leaned over the cradle, her gestures were like flowing milk, and the gentle words, which she whispered into Vardan's ear, babbled like the sound of a jet of milk being shot into a wooden pail. Her words were sweet, as was her smell. So it's no surprise that little Vardan was overcome with joy whenever his mother came close to the cradle, or whenever she tenderly took him in her arms to breastfeed him."

The storyteller's voice took on a serious tone. He said, "Every Armenian child is in grave danger during the first forty days of its life. During those first forty days the mother should never leave the child alone. Although the grandmother would rock the baby, and sometimes leave the room whilst doing so – employing the help of a long piece of string, as I previously explained – the mother was always sat somewhere close-by. It was also forbidden for a mother and child to leave the house during those first forty days; it was only allowed on the day of the christening when both had to attend church."

"Why is an Armenian child in such grave danger? During the first forty days, I mean."

"Because of the evil spirits, my little lamb. The Armenians recognize many spirits. There are the *Wishaps* and the *Dews* and the *Alks* and many more. Of course, there are also the *Djinns,* which the Turks also believe in. Many of these spirits go after the livers of small children, which they devour in an instant once they are left alone by their mothers. There was once an incident in the village that people talked about for many years."

"What kind of incident, Meddah?"

"Are you sure you want to know?"

"Yes, Meddah. Tell me."

"In the past," said the storyteller, "when the Armenians became the first people in the whole world to adopt Christianity as a state religion, Saint Gregory ordered the temple of the Persian fire worshippers in the city of Etchmiadzin to be torn down, and on that exact same site he built the world's first state church. It was a building of such magnificence that even the architects of the royal palace were green with envy. The city and the church still stand today. And that is where the holy oil of *meron* comes from, which is used to anoint each tiny Armenian child when they are christened. – Well, my little lamb," said the storyteller, "it came to pass that the Khatisians' neighbors had a child: a little girl who was christened *Takouhi,* which is the equivalent of *queen.* People had warned the little girl's mother. People told her, 'Do not let that child out of your sight during the first forty days. Remember that the spirits live in the darkness and they are surely vexed that you have such a beautiful baby, and one called Takouhi at that.' – But the child's mother laughed and said, 'Nothing can happen to my little girl: Priest Kapriel Hamadian has anointed her with meron, the holy oil.'

And when people asked, 'Have you washed the child since?' She would laugh and say, 'Of course I have.'

– And was there oil in the water?

– Of course there was. What was left of the meron washed off into the water.

– Was it holy water?

– Of course it was holy water.

– And what did you do with the holy water? Did you throw it away?

– I sprinkled it around the house.

– To keep the Djinns away?

– Of course to keep the Djinns away.

– And you believe that the Djinns are afraid of holy Christian water?

– Of course they are.

And so it was," said the storyteller, "that the mother often left her child alone. She had placed a Bible inside the girl's cradle and hung garlic cloves before the door, as well as a few horseshoes in the door frame – and she made sure they were hung upside-down so that the ends pointed towards the floor as was done by everyone else in the village in order to protect the rooms of their houses from evil spirits. She even placed a broomstick in front of the cradle because the Djinns were afraid of brooms and sticks, but it was no use."

"Why was it no use?"

"Let me tell you, my little lamb," said the storyteller. "One day – just as the woman was returning from the well where she had stayed for quite some time, chatting with the old women – she came home and saw …"

"Saw what?"

"That the child has vanished."

"Vanished?"

"Into thin air. No one ever saw her again.

I can picture myself," said the storyteller, "sitting next to your father many, many years ago. He is barely three weeks old, and he is looking at me with his large, dark, Armenian eyes. 'Hey there, you little tyke,' I say to him. 'Are you scared?'

And your father, who can't even speak, tells me, 'What is there to be afraid of, Meddah? My grandmother is here rocking me at the end of her long string. And my mother has just gone to the stable to pee, but she'll be back in a moment to feed me.'

– True, I say to him. You're quite right about that. But didn't anyone tell you that mothers should never leave their children alone during the first forty days? A single second is all it takes for a child to vanish for all eternity.

And your father asks, 'Because of the Djinns?'

And I say, 'Yes. The Djinns are after your liver. You better be careful. Your mother is in the stable peeing, and when she returns, you'll have vanished because the Djinns will have come and taken you away.'

But your father just laughs and says, 'No, the Djinns don't have any power here because Priest Hamadian anointed me with holy meron oil at the christening, and because my grandmother bathed me afterwards and took the bathwater, which contained traces of the holy oil, and sprinkled it around the house. The Djinns can't break through this protective circle. And do you know why?'

– No, I say. I don't know why.

– Because Jesus Christ is protecting me.

– Well, I'm not so sure about that, I say. Christ is not always there when you need him. Many Armenian mothers tried that trick with the oil and still the Djinns have come and stolen their children.

I tell your father about the time when his mother conceived for the twelfth time.

– There is a narrow path that leads out of the village, I say. And if you walk towards the sun for fifteen smokes in the early morning, you will reach the hut where old Bulbul lives.

– Bulbul? asks your father.

And I say, 'Yes. She's named after the nightingale. Bulbul. And do you know why?'

– No, says your father.

– Because she's a midwife and she sings whilst the mother screams. She sings so hauntingly that the soon-to-be mother believes it is her own voice she can hear … and she sings until the child is born.

– Does she sing like a nightingale?

– No, my little lamb, I say. Her voice is as ugly as that of a donkey, an animal which the Prophet once said had the ugliest voice of all Allah's creatures.

– Many feel a chill run down their spine – as the saying goes – I tell your father, and in their minds many make the sign of the cross when that nameless donkey shows up, carrying bow-legged Bulbul. But you needn't be afraid of her, even if people claim that she has been bewitched by the Djinns and turned into a figure of mystery, parading around on two gnarled legs with a rough, manly voice and a little gray goatee on her chin.

In any case, no one really knows who she is and where she comes from. People say she comes from the wild Hakkari mountain lands and that she is the daughter of a Kurdish sheikh and one of his many wives. Her father, the sheikh – so they say – could neither read nor write, but he had a great thirst for knowledge, which is why he occasionally had a *hafiz* – a Muslim who has memorized the entire Qur'an – kidnapped. Sometimes his people would also kidnap storytellers from the bazaars of the larger cities, tie them up and bring them into his tent. The sheikh had the hafiz recite to him the wisest of verses from the Qur'an until he had had enough, and then the storytellers would have to tell him all the stories that they knew. They say that Bulbul always listened in when she was a small girl, and eventually she herself knew the most important parts of the Qur'an's suras off by heart, and she also knew all of the stories and fairytales that the meddahs had told. One time, so they say, the Kurdish sheikh had captured an old storyteller, one who already had one hundred years to his name. And because he was so old, he would sometimes fall asleep while telling a story. But Bulbul, the little girl who was sitting right next to him, picked up where he left off, and she was just as good as the old man – sometimes even better. She recounted the tale all the way to the end.

– And why is Bulbul no longer with her clan?

– Because one day the clan cast her mother out, and Bulbul left with her. Bulbul cursed her father. And she cursed the clan. They travelled far away. Sometime later, Bulbul's mother died of cholera. They say that Bulbul, who was ten years old at the time, was captured by gypsies, and travelled through the land with them for a while until they cast her out, too. She then moved around numerous villages and cities – no one knows where – and when she showed up one day in Yedi Su, she was already bow-legged and hunchbacked, and the first gray hairs were starting to sprout from her chin, although she wasn't even that old. She came on a nameless, gray donkey, had a sack and a cane in her hand, and – so they say – all manner of jewelry and gold. And she built herself a hut up in the mountains and has lived there ever since with her pets: animals that she has acquired over the years. Bulbul is afraid of no one and no one would cause her any harm as even the wild Kurds up in the mountains are afraid of her magical powers."

And the Meddah said, "I tell your father, 'When your mother became pregnant with you, Bulbul rode into the village on her nameless donkey. And she said to your mother: You must not look into the mirror for nine months.'

– I've never looked in the mirror when I was pregnant, said your mother. Not once in all my pregnancies.

– Good, said Bulbul.

– My mother always warned me against it, said your mother.

241

Each time I was pregnant she would say: Do not look in the mirror for nine months.

– She was right to warn you, said Bulbul

– But my mother never explained to me why.

– Well, that is a good question, said Bulbul. I assume that it's because unborn children are curious … but also wary … and because the child sees everything its mother does from within her womb.

– Everything that I do?

– Everything that you do.

And Bulbul said, 'When you look into the mirror, your unborn son will mistake your reflection for his actual mother. And because your reflection is reversed, he will turn inside your womb and lie the wrong way around. And when that happens, both will die: mother and child … they die during birth. The child dies without making a sound, but the mother will die in a cacophony of screams. I've seen it with my own eyes. One mother, whose child lay the wrong way around inside of her, howled as loud as the swine of the infidels when they drive in the knife.'

And so it was," said the storyteller, "that your father's mother did not look in a mirror for nine whole months. And so when the time came for little Vardan to make his way out of the womb so that he could see his mother from the outside, she had no idea how she looked.

So, there I am, sitting next to your father's cradle," said the storyteller. "And I say to him, 'Do not be afraid. The evil spirits aren't coming to get you. Those are just stories. The Turks and the

Kurds, now that's where the real danger lies. When you're bigger, make sure to dip your little winkle, which will someday be a proper, adult cock, in holy meron oil. You see, the Turks and the Kurds have the terrible habit of cutting the cocks off Armenian men, particularly when the *great tebk* comes.'

And your father asks, 'What is the *great tebk?*'

And I say to him, 'A tebk is a tebk. It translates as *a rare event,* but really it means a massacre.'

– Do not be afraid, I say to your father, caressing little Vardan, who is but three weeks old, with my storyteller's voice. I say to him, 'At this very moment in time, there is no tebk, at least not in this region. Right now the only threat to you are the villagers and their superstitions.' And I say to him with a smile, 'Listen, my little lamb. Someone just died in the house next door. And soon your mother will come back from the stable. And she will take you in her arms.'

– And then?

– Then she will flee up to the roof with you; you see, all Armenian houses have flat roofs.

– But why do I have to go up to the roof with her?

– Because the dead take small children with them when they are carried to the cemetery. But they can only take them when the children's little legs are close to the ground. But up on the roof it's different. The dead have no power there.

And I say to little Vardan, 'There is only one coffin in this village and it is over one hundred years old. Soon they will carry the dead body past. And soon your mother will return from the stable and take you up to the roof.'

You must be wondering why there is only one coffin in the village, I say. And one that is over a hundred years old at that.

– Yes, says little Vardan. Tell me about the coffin.

– Every inhabitant of the village is given the same coffin, I say. You see, the coffin is only used to carry the dead to the cemetery. Afterwards they bring the empty coffin back.

– So how do they bury the dead?

– They are buried without a coffin, my little lamb. They are simply wrapped in a linen cloth. That's how all of your ancestors were buried.

– And what happens with the empty coffin that the villagers carry back?

– It is left for the next one, my little lamb. Perhaps it will be used by your grandfather, for he is already very old, or by one of your neighbors.

– And what will happen with me?

– You still have time, my little lamb. You are only three weeks old. If you don't die sooner, at the hands of the Turks or the Kurds, say, or because of some sort of horrible disease, you will live to a grand old age. Perhaps you will live to see a hundred, or even a bit more. And when they close your eyes, people will say, 'This coffin is over two hundred years old; it was already a hundred years old when this dead man was born.' – But you can be sure of one thing: that coffin will still be as sturdy as it is now. You see, Armenian craftsmen are the best in the world. Everything they make is built to last.

Someday your mother will lay you down on the floor so that you can kick your legs out without the confines of the cradle, but she will make sure that nobody treads on you. And she will heed those words of caution given to her by everyone, including Bulbul: Beware the first forty days. Be careful, Zovinar, not to step over him as that is bound to stunt his growth. And if you do step over him, be sure to take the same step backwards – back over him, in the opposite direction – in order to break the spell. Then he will grow normally again.

– Listen, my little lamb, I say to your father. You will suffer many illnesses, as all small children do, but have no fear. Your grandmother will press goat's horns into your skin; they are sawn in half and heated in the tonir, then the sawn through, cup-shaped part is placed onto the skin until it turns blood-red. Then your grandmother will scratch all the red spots with a sewing needle and attach leeches that will suck out all the bad blood, and with it all the germs. Once the leeches are so full that they look as though they might burst, your grandmother will pull them off and throw them into a jug filled with salt water so that they spit all of your blood back out again. And just to make sure, your grandmother will massage them and squeeze them until the leeches have spat all of the blood back out into the jug of salt water. Then she will place them back onto your skin at exactly the same spot as before. And they will suck out your blood until you are well again.

– And what if it doesn't work? asks Vardan.
    – Then your grandmother will take off all the clothes that ever came into contact with your sick body, and she will hang the clothes from the holy tree, the one that stands alone by the village square. If the holy tree does not cast off the clothes from

its branches, any diseases that were carried out of the house with them will vanish.

– Is there really a holy tree … here in Yedi Su?

– Of course there is, my little lamb. Each village in this region has a holy tree.

– Why is the tree holy, Meddah?

– No one knows, my little lamb … or no one can really remember how and when a tree was deemed to be holy because in most cases it happened too long ago. All it takes is for a dervish to have once slept beneath it, or Saint Sarkis.

– Did he come to this region?

– Of course he came here.

When you have your milk teeth and if you happen to have toothache one day, your grandmother will treat you with raki, or she will use Armenian oghi liquor which comes from the land of grapevines. She will massage the liquor into your gums and she will say, 'This boy's teeth will last until he's one hundred and twenty years old. Well, my boy, what do you say to that?'

I say to your father, 'Hi there, little tinkler. Have you ever been to the Armenian cemetery in Yedi Su? Of course you haven't, not yet.' I tell him that the best time to go is on the first Monday after Easter as that's when the whole village is there. 'The Kurds and Turks and gypsies are there, too; they come down from the mountains into the valley and set up their stalls in front of the cemetery entrance. Yes indeed, my little lamb. The whole place looks like a bazaar, and in fact that's what they call it: The Easter Monday Bazaar. People diligently go and pray in the cemetery and then everyone partakes in a big feast. As it is customary on this day for the priest to be allowed to take all the left-over baklava home with him, it is also known as *Priest's Baklava Day.*

Would you like me to tell you another story, my little lamb? How about the story of how your great-grandfather was buried?'

And your father, who was three weeks old said, 'Yes, tell me!'

– Your great-grandfather had just been placed inside his freshly dug grave, say I, the storyteller. But they hadn't covered him with soil. Just as they were about to begin shoveling, your great-grandfather's son, your grandfather to be precise, quickly placed a bottle of liquor into his father's grave – it was either raki or oghi, a decent and well-respected brand in any case – because he believed that an Armenian's soul needed three days to be released from the grave. White souls go directly to heaven, but black souls could not cross the threshold of pure thought that lay before the gates of paradise. And so your grandfather thought that the liquor might help the soul of his father, who was a drinker in life, as well as a glutton and a fornicator, to make that final leap over the barrier of purity.

Yes, I say. And then your grandfather took a second bottle of liquor out of his pocket, along with a silver cup, filled it to the brim and downed it in one. Everyone stood watching said, 'Bravo!' And they said, 'May all the days that he never lived be added to your life.' – But your grandfather said, 'No … not to my life: they should be added to the life of my grandson Vardan, a boy Hagob and Zovinar have yet to conceive, but who will come into this world one day.'

– And have Hagob and Zovinar decided to have him at least … this little Vardan of yours?

– Of course, said your grandfather … but only after my many hours of persuasion.

– And so everyone had a taste of your grandfather's liquor and toasted, 'our little Vardan, who is yet to be born.'

– Had I really not been born then? asks Vardan.

– Not at that time, say I, the storyteller.

– You don't even know where you are, I say to Vardan, who had just that second pissed in his diaper again and softly began to cry. Hey, little one, guess where you are?

– I'm lying in my cradle, Vardan tells me, in my cradle with the dove and the olive branch. I just peed in my diaper and I'm waiting for my mother.

– You are lying in your cradle, I say. True. But you don't know where your cradle is.

– No, I don't, says Vardan.

– Your cradle rocks on its short legs and it is three long steps away from the tonir, which is in the middle of the living room.

– I didn't know that, says Vardan.

– The farmers of Yedi Su call their living room their *oda;* only the mukhtar calls his a *selamlik.*

– Do all living rooms smell as peculiar as mine?

– Yes, they all smell similar, I say. They smell like a stable because the stable is just next door, and to get there the animals need to cross the living room.

– Why is that?

– I don't know exactly, my little lamb. But I presume that the Armenians once kept their animals in their oda because the tonir's fire wasn't warm enough, especially in winter. And I say,

'A stable isn't the only thing you can smell in here. It also smells of smoke. That's because the house doesn't have a chimney. And it also smells of spices and *pastirma* … you remember pastirma? That dried meat that gives small children hiccoughs? … And it smells of butter and cheese, and the remnants of the honey cake that your mother recently baked.

When Hayk, the first Armenian, walked to Mount Ararat with his trusted followers – an event which happened long ago, my little lamb, long before our time – he came to this village, which at that time wasn't a village, but a deserted valley. At the exact same spot where that tonir stands today, Hayk came to a halt and said, 'One of my descendants will settle here, and he will dig a fire hole and call this hole *tonir*.'

And that is exactly what happened. One day a man riding a donkey came through this valley, a man who also went by the name of Hayk. As he was too tired to continue his journey, and as he was also hungry and thirsty and freezing cold, he decided to stop. The donkey's good nose led them to one of the seven sources and its refreshing water. Once they had both quenched their thirst, the man returned to the same spot that he had just ridden by, the place where your oda now stands. He dug a fire hole, lit a fire inside and said, 'I shall call this fire *tonir*.' He then heard a voice that came down from the clouds and said, 'This tonir is holy. Build a house over it. And take a wife and marry her before this tonir.'

And I point to the tonir with my storyteller's voice and say, 'You see, my little lamb. Hayk was married before this very tonir. And he built his house over it.'

When Hayk's family consisted solely of father, mother and children, he called his family *entanik*. Later, after it had grown in size to include grandchildren, aunts, uncles and cousins, they would refer to themselves as a *kertastan*. At that time Hayk lived with his wife, children and animals all in a single room. But eventually Hayk built a wooden wall that ran lengthways through the large, windowless room: a solid wall supported by crossbeams, to keep man and animal separate. And as the space became increasingly crowded and less and less comfortable, despite the separate rooms, Hayk's descendants built individual rooms with individual walls and individual roofs that were attached to the main patriarchal house. That all happened a long time ago, but every villager knows the story. That is why some people who pass by the village point to the houses of Hayk's descendants and say, 'Look, that's where the Khatisians live ... the whole clan ... or at least those who stayed and haven't yet moved away.'

My little lamb, I say. You don't even know what your village looks like. And I say, 'It looks like most Armenian villages, which are cleaner than Kurdish and Turkish villages. The houses are made of clay, crushed stone and rock, and they are covered in white tiles. They have flat roofs made of poplar branches. The largest house of them all belongs to Mukhtar Ephrem Abovian, a man who has been mayor of Yedi Su for a number of years. Of course, the streets are only mud roads and who would expect anything different? But the village has a holy source in which Saint Sarkis bathed many centuries ago. And it has seven wells, one of which is called *Gatnachpjur:* the well of milk.'

And I say, 'My little lamb, there is no milk in the Gatnachpjur well, but mothers whose milk has run dry need only pray once at the Gatnachpjur well, cross themselves and then dip their breasts into the water and their breasts will instantly begin to swell.'

I bet you would like to know, my little lamb, what your mother did when her long, doughy, but dry breasts began flopping sorrowfully from side to side every time she moved? Well, my little lamb, she prayed and prayed fervently ... and she crossed herself ... of course, all before the Gatnachpjur well, and then she dipped her breasts in the special water, and shortly afterwards they began to swell and became fat and juicy.

Any foreigner to these parts riding along the caravan road between Bakir and Erzurum who reaches the crossing with signposts pointing towards Van, Bakir, Moush, Kayseri, Konya and Diyarbakir would have no idea that this village existed: a village lying just half a day's ride away in one of the plateau's valleys, concealed between the bleak mountains and situated fifty-five smokes away from the Kurdish camp of Suleyman Agah, a man also known as Suleyman Bey. And should any foreigner dare stray from the caravan road and ride straight across the impassable mountain landscape for half a day, he still wouldn't see the village, even if he accidently passed close by. You see, the first houses of the village hang hidden in the rock face like birds' nests on high, invisible to any foreigner who unwittingly rides along the rough, winding path that leads to Yedi Su.

    – You mean, you can't even see the roofs of the houses?

    – No, my little lamb. Or you only see them once you are above them.

    – Why would anyone be above the roofs?

    – Because the very end of the rough trail winds into the

valley above the village roofs. And a foreigner would have to look down to see the roofs along the rock face, and most riders look straight ahead.

    – Does that mean you shouldn't look straight ahead?

    – Of course you should, my little lamb, but not always.

When your mother was three months pregnant with you, a Kurd rode into the village. He was riding into the morning sun. At the entrance to the village his horse stumbled, slipped off the winding road and fell – but it wasn't a great drop or a deadly fall – and so it was that the Kurdish rider and his horse landed on the roof of your house.

    – Just like that?

    – Yes, my little lamb.

    – Didn't it scare my mother?

    – She was scared out of her wits! You see, the roof, which was made of poplar branches, collapsed and the Kurd and his horse fell straight into your living room – into the selamlik or the oda. That's right, my little lamb. Your mother was just taking a nap when it happened. She suddenly heard an almighty crash, woke up and saw the Kurd and his horse fall through the living room ceiling, landing just next to the tonir.

    – And what did my mother do?

    – She didn't do a thing, my little lamb. She just starred at the Kurd and his horse in complete shock.

    – And what did I do, Meddah?

    – Your mother's shock was so great that you almost came tumbling out of your mother's belly.

    – You mean it was almost a miscarriage?

    – Almost, my little lamb. Your mother very nearly lost you

in that moment, and then there would be no Vardan. And this Vardan, who was never born, would never go on to take a wife and father a son with her, whom he would name Thovma.

– Will I have a son one day, Meddah?
– Of course you will.
– And will I name him Thovma?
– You shall!

– And what happened with the Kurd and his horse?
– Everything I just told you.
– So, the Kurd was riding into the morning sun?
– Yes.
– And his horse tripped? Fell off the path? Fell down the edge of the cliff? And landed on the roof of our house?
– That's right.
– And he and his horse fell into our living room, a room also known as a selamlik, or an oda? And both horse and rider landed next to the tonir where cow shit was burning and flickering and smoldering?
– Yes, my little lamb.
– And my mother had a fright so terrible that she almost lost me?
– Exactly.
– And that would have meant that I would never be able to become a father … as I would never have been born?
– Yes, my little lamb.
– And there would be no son called Thovma, who will one day be born.
– Precisely, my little lamb. There would be no Thovma either.
I softly chuckle to myself and say, 'As you can see, nothing

serious happened. The only person who came was your grand-mother, who entered from the next room, looked at the Kurd, looked at the horse and took hold of a poker lying next to the tonir which was, in fact, not a real poker but a long iron rod designed to poke cow shit. She took the instrument in her hand and began waving it violently at the Kurd and his horse. Believe it or not, the Kurd was terrified and so he galloped out of the living room and suddenly he was gone.

– What a woman! said little Vardan, who was only three weeks old and who couldn't even speak. My grandmother is actually quite brave. Who would have thought it?

– Yes, my little lamb. Your grandmother's heart is in the right place.

– Is she the first Armenian woman to dare thrash a wild Kurd with a poker?

– You mean … in all the thousands of years that the Arme-nian people have existed?

– Yes, Meddah.

– I don't know, my little lamb. That's a question for a histo-rian. All I can tell you is that, I, the Meddah, know of no similar case.

And I, the Meddah, say to little Vardan, 'Your grandmother didn't always play the nagging wife, my little lamb. But when you lay eyes on her for the first time, it's hard to imagine that she was ever any different.'

– Different? In what way, Meddah?

– You know, just different, my little lamb. Many, many years ago, when she married your grandfather and moved into this house, your grandmother was a small, anxious bride. She was twelve, had barely any breasts and very little hair between her legs, but she did have large ears and no mouth at all.

– But, Meddah, that cannot be?

– Oh yes it can, my little lamb. That's exactly how it was. You see, after the wedding night, her mother-in-law said to her, '*Gelin*' – that's the Turkish word for *young bride,* even though the Armenians have their own word for that. She could just as easily have said *hars* … which simply means *bride* … but the Turkish word is harsher on the tongue, sounds a little shrill, instills a sense of respect, perhaps also fear, and is considered more sophisticated and effective when used for communication between two women of different social standing. You see, my little lamb? And so the mother-in-law said *Gelin!* – 'Gelin,' she said. 'From now on, you shall have ears but no mouth. You may only speak with small children, and you may only speak with your new husband when the two of you are alone and only when he addresses you, do you understand? You may speak to no one else, especially not with your father-in-law or your husband's brothers, otherwise people will say that you tore the veil.'

– And when will I be able to speak to them? asked your grandmother.

– Only after your first child is born, said her mother-in-law. And when that time comes, I will say to you, 'Gelin, you now have your mouth back.'

The Armenians call this trial period for a young daughter-in-law *nor harsnutiun,* and the vow of silence is called *moonch.* In truth, I, the Meddah, ask myself, why the Lord God bestows tongues on young brides only for their mother-in-laws to forbid them to speak. Even the mother-in-law's mother said to your young, twelve-year-old grandmother, 'Gelin, swallow your tongue!'

In truth, my little lamb, it is easy to side-step the law when it is written down on paper … but there is no way to fight the unwritten laws of the family. Your young grandmother knew that and so she obeyed the old traditions. Only once her first child was born did she begin to speak again.

As the youngest woman in the household, your grandmother had to perform all the lowly tasks. One of her daily duties was to make everyone's bed first thing in the morning, including those of her sisters-in-law. You see, in the kertastan none of the women made their own beds. The youngest gelin had to do it. And the neighbors would stand in front of the door peeking in to see if she actually did.

– And if she hadn't done it? asks little Vardan.

– Well, then people would have said, 'Look there, in that kertastan everyone makes their own bed. *That family is pregnant,*' which means: 'That family is falling apart.'

The more children your grandmother had, the more her position in the kertastan improved. She gave birth to fourteen children overall. You father, my little lamb, was the youngest of them. She was almost forty when she gave birth to him. And you, my little Vardan, are also your mother's youngest child, even though you are only her twelfth. And so it should come as no surprise, my little lamb, that your grandmother is now rather old, and she has also become the matriarch.

– Does everyone in the family obey her?

– They do indeed.

– Then surely she must be the eldest woman in the household?

– No, my little lamb. Your great-grandmother is the eldest. But no one takes her seriously anymore as the woman has become senile in her old age. All day long she does nothing but sit next to the tonir and doze – if you lift your little head, you can see her.

My little lamb, your grandmother's breasts are as wrinkly as her hands and her face. The fire in her eyes, however, blazes with as much intensity as the jets of flame in the tonir. Her tongue is equally vibrant, always saying whatever the heart tells it to. It's as though her fiery mouth is making up for all those years of silence; no one can curse like your grandmother.

My little lamb, can you guess what your grandmother said to that Kurd as she chased him out of her living room with that iron rod?

– How should I know, Meddah?

– You son of a bitch, she said. You grandson of a rabid sheep. You stinking, Kurdish ballsack. Tell your Bey that he and his band of lowlifes can go to hell! I hope each of his men's cocks rot. The Padishah in Constantinople should have you all hanged. May your children die of cholera and your men succumb to that disease from Frankistan that people get in brothels and whose name I've forgotten in my old age. May the Djinns and the Alks gobble up your children's livers, and may the great floods descend upon you.

– Tell me, Meddah. Why do the Kurds fill my grandmother with so much rage?

– Well, she has her reasons, my little lamb.

Armenian mothers are more afraid of the Kurds than the Turks, even though the Kurds are relatively harmless in comparison to the Turks. So, as I said, they are afraid. And even unborn children can sense when their mothers are frightened. Mothers know that, which is why they say to their children, 'Watch out! If you don't behave, the big bear will come and get you. Or the Kurds!'

– Which Kurds do they mean?

– Not those Kurds who live in the cities, my little lamb, and not those who live in the semi-nomadic villages. It's the wild Kurdish mountain tribes that the women fear. They sometimes kidnap women, massacre the men, loot the villages and burn people's houses to the ground.

– Why do they do that, Meddah?

– I honestly don't know, my little lamb.

Listen, my little lamb. It's all very complicated indeed, but I will try to explain it to you. First there's the whole business with taxes.

– What are taxes, Meddah?

– Well, my little lamb. Taxes are taxes.

You see, my little lamb, it's like this. The Kurds don't pay any taxes to the Turks because they don't believe in them. Only recently the Padishah in Constantinople sent five thousand riders out to the Kurdish mountains to collect taxes, but would you believe it, those five thousand riders were never seen again. You see, it was very simple: The Kurds waited until the soldiers had climbed up to the narrow mountain roads, and then they shot them down one by one, stole their horses – as well as their boots and uniforms – and threw their naked bodies down into the ravine. – And because the Padishah in Constantinople has no desire to lose that many horses and soldiers again, he leaves the Kurds in peace, and instead demands two or three times more tax from the Armenians.

– But I don't understand, Meddah.

Look here, my little lamb. The Turkish tax collectors practically bleed the Armenians dry. Not only must they pay the infidel tax, known as *rayah tax,* they also have to pay poll tax, along with plenty of other taxes and duties. I'd rather not list each one. But the most important tax of all is the exemption from military service tax, known as *bedel.* No Armenian can get away without paying it, not even you, my little lamb.

– Why, Meddah?

– Because the Armenians are not allowed to bear arms and thus are not allowed to serve in the military.

– But they still have to pay bedel?

– Exactly.

– And what does that have to do with the Kurds? – I think it's perfectly in order that the Kurds don't want to pay taxes and that they completely refuse to acknowledge them as a civic duty. I honestly do. I can't say I think much of taxes myself, even though I'm only three weeks old and don't really know what taxes are.

– Well, let me explain, my little lamb. The Kurds may not pay the Turks any taxes, but they demand their own taxes from the Armenians.

– I thought the Armenians only paid taxes to the Turks?

– But they have to pay taxes to the Kurds, too.

– So they pay double the amount of tax?

– More than double, my little lamb. And when they can't pay, people come and burn their houses down, chase them off their fields and, to top it all, lock them up in prison.

– And what about the Kurds?

– Let me explain, my little lamb. In this region there is a bey who is also a sheikh. His name is Suleyman. This sheikh believes that the whole land, all the way up to the Euphrates, belongs to him. He doesn't recognize the Padishah in Constantinople, or any other ruler. He believes that everything belongs to him, even the villages in this mountain valley and everything that its inhabitants own. This sheikh, however, is not stupid. He allows the Armenians to cultivate their fields, and has no objection to them rearing livestock and so on. But every now and then he comes to the Armenian *millets* – the word used to describe Armenian regions – and takes whatever he needs. He leads the livestock away, takes grain from the granaries or even objects he likes the look of – sometimes he even takes pretty girls. He has a few thousand riders at his disposal, and whoever protests ends up a head shorter.

Your father recently said to your mother, 'The Kurds are the stupidest people in the world; they can only count up to ten.'

– But I know a Kurd who can count up to twenty, your mother said.

– You mean, he's learnt to count on both his fingers and his toes?

– Exactly, said your mother.

You see, my little lamb, say I, the Meddah. Regardless of whether the Kurds are clever or stupid, one thing is certain: They are not to be trifled with. Either you give them what they want, or you will wake up the next morning with no roof over your head, or, if you're unlucky, with no head at all.

– Meddah, now you're just being silly. How can anyone wake up in the morning without a head?

– The Kurds also collect a bride tax from the Armenians.

    – What's that?

– Well, it's exactly that. A bride tax. When an Armenian marries, he must give half of the dowry to Suleyman, the leader of the Kurds.

    – If I get married one day, will I have to pay it, too?

    – Of course you will, my little lamb.

    – And what if I don't?

– They'll hack your head off, my little lamb. Or something even worse.

    – What, Meddah?

– The Kurds will kidnap your wife before you have taken her virginity.

    – Is that worse than death?

    – It is worse than death, my little lamb.

And now you need to sleep, my little lamb. Tomorrow is another day. Your grandmother, the one who rocks you with her long string, will be here shortly. And your mother will soon be back from the stable where it would seem she unexpectedly had to go for more than just a pee. And I'm sure she's taking her time giving everything back to the Lord that her body doesn't need. Why else would she be taking so long? – And soon, my little lamb, your father will be back from the field. Shall I sing you a lullaby?

– Yes, Meddah.

But I say to Vardan, 'Before I sing you a lullaby, I will tell you about the day you were born.'

– But I know all of that already, Meddah, says Vardan.

– So, how did it happen, my little lamb?

– You know, Meddah. I was born under a grapevine.

But then I, the Meddah, say, 'Oh no you weren't, my little lamb.'

Those are only stories that people tell little Vardan. Do you want to know what really happened? – And I say, 'Yesterday Bulbul rode into the village on her nameless donkey. And she rode into this living room, left her donkey next to the tonir and crouched down next to your cradle. She said to you: Well, well, my little lamb. I bet you're wondering how you came into this world?

You said: Bulbul, I know how I came into this world. I was born under a grapevine.

But then Bulbul laughed and said: No, my little lamb. I know the real story, for I am Bulbul, the midwife.

And Bulbul tells you the story. She says: It happened three weeks ago, my little Vardan. I was riding into the village on my nameless donkey when I heard your mother wailing. It's coming from the stable, I thought to myself, the Khatisians' stable. And so I rode to your house. And I rode through the open entrance into your oda. I left my donkey next to the tonir and went into the stable. And guess what I saw there?

– I don't know, Bulbul, says Vardan.

– I saw your wailing mother sat crouched next to the cow. – What's the matter, my little dumpling? I said. Did the cow put a curse on you while you were milking it? Is the Devil in her udder? Did you drink some of her milk? And is the Devil now inside your belly?

– Little Vardan is inside my belly, said your mother. I think he wants to come out.

I said that things could be worse.

And your mother said: True, things could be worse.

And suddenly your mother started writhing in agony again. But I held onto her tightly, ran my fingers along her neck, and along her back and over her hair.

– Should I lie down on my back, Bulbul?

– No, Zovinar. Only the women in Frankistan lie on their backs when they drop their young.

– Should I carry on squatting here next to the cow?

– Yes, Zovinar. Hold on tightly to her teats.

– And what else should I do, Bulbul?

– You should push, Zovinar. Just push.

– Push, Bulbul?

– Yes, Zovinar. Imagine you have just had a pee and now you have to lay an egg … And you push a little bit, you know?

– Yes, Bulbul.

– And I'll run my fingers over your back and along your neck. And I'll hold on tightly to you and stroke your hair. And you'll just push a tiny bit, my little dumpling.

– Yes, Bulbul.

– And I caressed your mother and comforted her. And I hummed a song with the voice of a nightingale that sounded like the voice of a donkey. And your mother moaned and pushed, and kept on pushing until you slipped out.

And all of a sudden, there you were, lying in the straw next to the cow. Your mother breathed a sigh and I said: It's over now.

When you let out your first cry, your grandmother came into the stable. She watched as I bit through the umbilical cord and she asked me: How do you do that, Bulbul? You don't have any teeth left.

– I do it with my lips, I said.
– And why don't you have any teeth left, Bulbul?
– Because my husband knocked them all out … why else do you think?
– And why did he do that, Bulbul?
– Because I showed my face to other men.
– Did you show them your teeth, too?
– Yes, those too.

And your grandmother bathed you in salt water. And as she bathed you, she sang an old Armenian song. The song told of good salt that strengthens the limbs and of the Lord God, who had blessed the Armenians' children with large, dark, velvety eyes.

A short while later your father entered and he saw the severed umbilical cord. It was lying in the hay, next to the cow's legs. He also saw the placenta which was also lying in the hay next to the cow's legs.

– What about the placenta? asked your father.

– Nothing, Hagob Efendi. What about it?

– And the umbilical cord?

– Nothing, Hagob Efendi. What about it?

– Tell me, Bulbul … did you at least wipe some of the blood from the umbilical cord on my son's cheeks just as my mother did with me and my grandmother did with my father?

– Yes, Hagob Efendi, I said. I did. I did it so that he will have rosy cheeks when he's older. Look at this child. Do his cheeks look white to you?

– No, Bulbul. They are nice and red from all the good blood.

– And what shall we do with the umbilical cord? asked your father.

– We should bury it in the cemetery, said your mother. But we will bury it so deep that the dogs can't find it and eat it.

– In the cemetery? asked your father.

– Yes, said your mother. In the cemetery.

I asked your mother: Why in the cemetery? – And she said: So that one day he will become a good Christian.

Afterwards I realized that the cow in the stable probably was possessed by the devil, or even had the evil eye, and as I wasn't sure whether or not it was true, I went into the village, entered seven different houses, taking a different needle from each one, came back, entered the stable, stuck each of the seven needles into the placenta to kill the evil inside it, pulled the needles back out, spat on them and buried the placenta and the needles behind the house.

Bulbul said: Don't be afraid, little Vardan. The Djinns won't come and get you. The only thing you need to fear are your milk teeth. You see, when they start to grow, they will hurt.

– What will happen, Bulbul?

– Well, let me tell you, little Vardan. One day every human being gets their first tooth.

– Why, Bulbul?

– Mainly because Allah wants to show us that we can be penetrated, both from outside and from within.

– But I don't understand, Bulbul.

– Well, look here, little Vardan. This is how it works. Man is made of flesh and blood, and anything made of flesh and blood can be penetrated. The growing tooth penetrates you from the inside, whether or not you want it to and regardless of how much it hurts. The tooth grows and grows and penetrates your flesh.

– And what about if I pray to Christ?

– It's no use. Not even Christ can stop a growing tooth from penetrating your flesh.

– Does that mean I'll be penetrated from the inside?

– Precisely.

– And how can a person be penetrated from the outside?

– There are many different ways.

– Like what?

– You could be penetrated by a Kurd's knife. Or a Turk's knife. Or perhaps by a bullet.

– Are there any other ways?

– There are many, little Vardan. So many.

And Bulbul said: Even I have been penetrated. But it was a long time ago.

— What happened, Bulbul?

— Well, let me tell you, said Bulbul.

And Bulbul said: The story goes like this, little Vardan. It happened when I was eleven. I had thorns between my legs and where those thorn bushes grew less dense lay the Gate of Expectation.

Bulbul smiled. She said: The Gate of Expectation lay between two spying, interrogating and questioning earlobes whose task was to spy on possible intruders, to check their intentions and to ask whether the intruders knew that all dreams and desires lay hidden behind the locked Gate of Expectation. These spying, interrogating and questioning lobes were dainty, nowhere near fully mature and, to tell you the truth, no bigger than the earlobes of an unborn sheep. And concealed between these earlobes lay my apparent guardian ... a thin bit of skin that was as delicate as the petal of a young rose, but as defiant and impenetrable as the taut goat's skin on the drum of the munadi of Bakir: a man who is a loud-mouthed drummer and one of the city's criers.

— A drummer and a crier?

— Yes, little Vardan. A drummer and a crier.

— And one day, said Bulbul, a prince on a white horse arrived to kidnap a poor, little orphaned child. That orphaned child was me. Eventually we were married before an imam. And I remember the imam saying: Marry your virgins. Peace be with our Prophet Muhammad, who loves the poor and the orphaned.

And Bulbul said: The prince took me to his tent where he showed me what he had between his legs, and it was a terrible sight; it looked like something dead that had suddenly sprung back to life.

As he rammed this living death between my legs, I cried out to my father in heaven, but my father laughed and said: See, it is not death but pain from which all life is created. You should have rubbed some beeswax between your legs, my little dove, or mutton fat, so that those thorns lose their barbs and those fearful, tightly-nestled earlobes open up … and so that bit of skin, that is as tender as the petal of a young rose and supposedly as tough as the skin on the drum of the munadi of Bakir … well … to make that soft, too, so your body can let the pain in.

– And so, said Bulbul to little Vardan, I was penetrated, and in that moment I realized that human beings are merely flesh and blood: they can be penetrated.

– What can't be penetrated? asked Vardan.
    – Souls, said Bulbul. And thoughts.
    – How does that work? asked Vardan.
    – Well, sometimes it's like this and sometimes it's like that, said Bulbul.

– And what will happen when I get my tooth? asked Vardan. Will it be the same living death that will penetrate me from inside?
    – Yes, my little lamb, said Bulbul. Later on your little teeth will mash everything that comes between them. They will kill for you so that you can live.
    – I'm afraid, Bulbul.

– Do not be afraid, said Bulbul.' "

Then the storyteller's voice became soft. The images faded away somewhere into the past.

"We are alone," said the storyteller. "You and I: the Meddah and the Last Thought."

"Is this where the story ends?"

"Which story?" asked the storyteller.

"The story of my father?"

"Of course it's not the end. It's only just begun."

3

"When your father's first tooth penetrated him from the inside, appearing suddenly in his gum, and his mother realized that this boy was no longer a toothless being but a human who could bite and crush ... and also kill ... she said to him, 'Soon you will no longer need my milk. I will sprinkle pepper over my nipples to wean you off; to take away your desire to suck for many years to come. And I will chew proper food for you and place it inside your mouth, and I will say to you: You are not a sucker anymore – you are a biter.' And your father's mother smiled, put her finger in his mouth, felt the tooth and said, 'Now it's time to celebrate.'

The Armenians enjoy celebrations," said the storyteller. "More fun is had at their celebrations than at those of the Turks. But for your father, the celebration that marked the appearance of his first tooth was the first to be held in his honor. Just after Vardan was born, Hagob had handed out raisins, nuts and liquor to people in the village, whilst Zovinar and old Hamest welcomed anyone who poked their head through the open door and into the oda with an additional serving of sweet rice pudding and fresh water from the well mixed with mulberry syrup. But today, *hadig* would be cooked all day long, and the neighbors would come by to help in the task. Hadig is made from chickpeas and bulgur, as well as cinnamon, sugar and nuts and other delicious ingredients which Zovinar and Hamest preferred not to reveal. Even Hayk, the first Armenian, treasured hadig; he knew that the dish resembled blancmange and that – when cold and solidified – it took the shape of a wobbly cake: the best cake in the world. That is why Hayk turned to his wife that day on Mount Ararat and said, 'If harissa, that gristly, fatty, overcooked meat and barley stew, is to become Armenia's first national dish, then that sweet hadig – my favorite dish – must be the second.' And Hayk said, 'When my descendants' first teeth start to come through, their mothers shall celebrate with a feast of hadig. And they shall invite anyone who is or who could be a mother to join the celebrations.'

And that is exactly what came to pass," said the storyteller. "When news spread that the rumor about your father's first tooth was indeed true, the women of the village left their huts and houses and flocked to the house of the Khatisians to celebrate the feast of hadig.

Just picture the scene: There's little Vardan sitting in his cradle, biting his teeth together – the ones he doesn't yet have, which must mean that he has one! – he bites his lips together because he doesn't want to show his one, little tooth. But he has to. You see, whoever lays eyes on that first tooth is guaranteed to never lose any of their own teeth.

– Why won't he open his mouth? asks the grandmother. He's supposed to show us his little tooth.

– I don't know, says Vardan's mother.

– We have to make him laugh!

– But he's a serious child; he doesn't laugh.

– That would be laughable … a child that doesn't laugh. You'll have to do what my mother did with me.

– What's that?

– Hold a hadig cake underneath his nose and place a second on his little head.

– Will that make him open his mouth?

– Of course. He will laugh and show everyone his first tooth.

And that's exactly what happened," said the storyteller. "Vardan's mother waved one round hadig cake to and fro under the baby's nose and placed a second on his little head. And Vardan, who was a serious child, suddenly began to laugh and so showed everyone his first tooth.

– May his teeth last until he is one hundred and twenty, said his grandmother. And all the gathered guests mumbled, 'Until one hundred and twenty!' And one by one they approached the cradle and said to Vardan, '*Atschket louis*' which means *light in your eyes*. They said the same thing to Vardan's parents. Some cried as they embraced Zovinar and uttered the exact same words: Atschket louis."

"What does *light in your eyes* mean?" asked the Last Thought. And the storyteller said, "In fact, what it actually means is: may your eyes shine."

"Is that the best wish you can offer someone?"

"Yes," said the storyteller. "If someone has dark eyes, you know he's in a bad way. But if a man's eyes shine, you know he has made it through the night. It is as though the bright light of day burns on in his heart.

When a child starts taking its first steps, the Armenians mark the occasion with their *Shekerli celebration:* the celebration of the first steps. You see, Armenians believe that the direction a child walks when it takes its first steps is a sign of what it will become later in life.

At the celebration of Vardan's first steps, it felt as though the entire village was gathered in the Khatisians' oda, although there wasn't enough space for them all. But anyone who couldn't be there in person was there in thought, or they had said to their relatives or neighbors, who were able to attend, 'Tell me what happens so that afterwards I can say that I was there.'

And so it was," said the storyteller. "Vardan's mother had baked a heap of baklava in the tonir and laid them out on copper *sofras:* useful little trays, which were handed around by your father's grandmother and his older brothers and sisters. His mother took the final piece of baklava out of the pan – one that had turned out rather small – and tied it to Vardan's tiny right leg with red thread. Vardan sat crying in the middle of the room, his tiny hands grasping on tightly to his mother's legs as if to say, 'What sort of strange celebration is this? What do you all want from me?'

– Today you will decide the path you will take later on in life, his mother said, lifting him up and standing him on his two little legs. Off you go, my fearless, little pasha, she said, before winking at him, turning her head, winking to the guests and saying, 'Now, let's see what he'll be!' – But she didn't let him go.

– Why aren't you letting him go, Zovinar? asked one of the guests.

– I don't know, said Zovinar.

– I recently had a dream, said Hagob, who was standing next to Zovinar. I dreamed that our Vardan would become a fisherman.

– Nonsense, said the grandmother. Dreams can't decide his destiny.

– And who should?

– His own little legs will decide.

– And why his little legs?

– Because his head decides where his legs go.

– Well, we'll see about that, said Hagob. And he said to his wife, 'Let the little pasha go!'

But Zovinar didn't let him go.

– What's the matter? asked the grandmother.

– Nothing is the matter, said Zovinar.

– Hagob, the father, started to laugh. He turned to the guests. Everyone, look over here, he said. The Shekerli game is about to start.

Hagob gulped nervously and had stopped laughing. He softly whispered to his guests, 'We set a pail of water next to the tonir. If our Vardan walks to the pail and touches it, or even puts his hands in the water, then he will become a fisherman!'

– And if not? asked one of the guests.

– Well, then he won't, said Hagob. Hagob said, 'If he walks past the pail, however, and stumbles towards the fire – the fire in the tonir where my wife baked all the baklava – if he stops there, well … that means he will be a craftsman.'

– Yes, a craftsman, said Zovinar. That would also be good.

– And if he touches the Bible, the one lying next to the

cradle, said the grandmother, then he will be a pious man, or perhaps even a priest.

– Yes, a priest, said Vardan's father. A few people clapped their hands and cried out, 'A priest! A priest!'

It seemed Hagob had run out of suggestions. He glanced around with a look of uncertainty, and scratched his broad farmer's head.

– If he goes to the stable, he will become a farmer, said Zovinar.

– That's right, said Hagob.

– He will tend to his fields, and wait for the rain and the sun to arrive.

– That's right, said Hagob.

– But if he goes to the door and stumbles outside, he will be an adventurer.

– An adventurer?

– Yes.

– What's an adventurer?

– I'm not entirely sure.

One of the guests said, 'An adventurer is someone who takes risks in life, such as a businessman.'

– So he'll be a businessman?

– Absolutely.

– You mean a real businessman?

– Of course.

And then your father's great-grandmother, who was sat watching next to the tonir – a woman already in the grips of senility – laughed. She had suddenly woken up. 'A businessman,' she giggled. 'He will be a millionaire.'

Hagob nodded awkwardly. A millionaire?

– Why not, said Zovinar. That's not a bad suggestion. Perhaps he really will become a businessman … and earn millions … and make all of us happy.

Zovinar was still holding on to her son, even though little Vardan had started to cry again and was waving his arms and thrashing his legs about for he was desperate to be released.

– Well, what do you think? asked Hagob. He was now asking everyone in the room. What do you think? Should he be a farmer or a craftsman, or a fisherman, or a priest, or a businessman?

The people gazed excitedly at little Vardan who had just been released by his mother. Vardan wasn't crying anymore. Suddenly he was standing alone on his own two, wobbly legs. He looked around and stumbled towards the pail, which stood next to the tonir. Someone must have given the pail a push beforehand as strange circular ripples appeared on the water inside, and as the morning sun shone warmly into the room, adorning the rippled water with a smile, it looked to Vardan as though the water was actually smiling, and so it came as no surprise that Vardan made a beeline for the pail to get a closer look at this smiling, brightly shimmering pail of water. But the pail stood close to the tonir, and as the grandmother had thrown a great deal of tezek into the fire, it was now crackling and burning brightly, distracting little Vardan.

– He's going to be a fisherman, cried his mother. Look, he's going towards the pail, and I bet you he's going to put his hands inside.

– He shall be a fisherman, said Hagob, the boy's father.

But then someone in the crowd shouted, 'No. He's not going

to stop in front of the pail. He's going towards the tonir. The fire has caught his eye.'

And then someone else cried, 'He's going to be a craftsman.' Then everyone shouted, 'A craftsman! A craftsman!' Everybody clapped their hands, some whistled, others laughed or giggled. 'That's a reliable job,' someone shouted.

But Vardan stopped before neither the pail nor the tonir. He also didn't stop next to the Bible that lay next to his cradle. He started to move towards the stable as he could hear the voices of the animals inside.

– He's going to be a farmer, shouted the grandmother. I knew it. To be a real Khatisian, you have to be a farmer.

– That's true, said Hagob. That boy has my blood in his veins.

– He has mine, too, said Zovinar.

But Vardan didn't run into the stable, even though he was tempted by the voices of the animals. He turned around and ran towards the open doorway where he could see the sun's early morning rays advancing over the threshold. And the early morning brought with it the scent of the meadows, flowers and trees, as well as the chirping of the birds, which sounded far more dulcet and enticing than the dull voices of the animals in the stable.

– He's about to fall, somebody cried. And then someone else cried out, 'No, this boy is not one to fall flat on his face before he knows what he wants in life.'

– Look, he's running towards the doorway!

– He's going to be an adventurer!

– A businessman!

– A businessman!

Even Vardan's great-grandmother cried out, 'Yes, a businessman. He will make millions.' And she stretched out her ancient hands towards little Vardan and shouted, 'Atschket louis! Light in your eyes, my little lamb.'

And in fact," said the storyteller, "your father stumbled towards the doorway and for a brief moment it looked as though he was actually going to go outside. But it wasn't to be."

"What happened, Meddah?"

"Your father stopped on the threshold," said the Meddah. "He stood stock-still and looked outside with his large, baffled eyes and took not one step more.

Everyone was disappointed," said the Meddah. "They cheered your father on, but he didn't want to go any farther. He just stood in the doorway as though he were afraid of the big world outside. The priest was also amongst the guests that day and Hagob asked him what it meant. And the priest thought about it for a time and then said, 'He won't be a business man, and he won't be a proper adventurer either; he's too afraid to even go out into the real world.'

– But he's looking out to it, said Hagob.

– True, said the priest. He's someone who looks but doesn't act.

– He also didn't go into the stable. And he also wasn't interested in the tonir, or the Bible or the water pail.

The senile great-grandmother then cried out, 'My Vardan is peeking!'

And everyone laughed and said, 'He's standing on the threshold and peeking out. Do you reckon that's all he'll do?'

One of the guests spat into his hands, rubbed the spit into his eyes, laughed and said, 'He'll be a peeper.'

And another said, 'A dreamer.'

And then the priest said, 'Perhaps he will become a poet?'

When the priest uttered those words, Vardan's mother began to tear at her hair and stagger towards the tonir with a look of despair. It looked as though she was about to throw hot ashes over her head. Hagob rushed to hold her back. There could be no mistake: the jovial bubble had now been burst. The guests stood there shocked. Hagob didn't even hear what they said as they quietly whispered to one another, nor did he hear the comforting words that some guests called out to Zovinar.

– It's not all that bad, he said, trying to console Zovinar. Better a poet than nothing at all.

– But he won't be able to feed his family.

– Then we will feed them for him, said Hagob.

– His children will starve.

– No, they won't starve, said Hagob.

The mayor of Yedi Su was also among the guests that day," said the storyteller, "Mukhtar Ephrem Abovian: a man easily recognizable on account of his enormous moustache, which he styled like the Kurds, and his red, spotless fez which concealed his completely bald head."

"Why does he hide his bald head under a fez?"

"Because any self-respecting man always has a fez on his head. But he also wears it to keep all the flies and their tickly legs at bay; you see, Mukhtar Ephrem Abovian is a very sensitive man."

"And what about his spotless fez?"

"It's the only clean fez in the village."

"So, he's quite persnickety?"

"It has to be said."

"Is there anything else that's special about his fez?"

"Yes, my little lamb. His is a very famous fez."

"Why is it famous?"

"Well, let me tell you," said the storyteller. "When a new mayor is chosen in the village, all of the candidates place their fez upside down on a copper sofra. The oldest men in the village and the heads of each household place a nut in the fez of their chosen candidate. The man with the highest number of nuts in his fez becomes mayor."

"Does that mean Ephrem Abovian had the highest number of nuts in his fez at the last election?"

"He certainly did," said the storyteller. "The richest man is always the most powerful.

If you really want to see everything that I see," said the storyteller to the Last Thought, "and if you try really hard to imagine it, you will now see Vardan's mother retrieving fresh baklava from the tonir, piling them onto the copper sofras and handing them out to the guests. As you can see, my little lamb, she serves the mayor and his wife first before going from guest to guest. The last person to be served is Hovhannes, the water carrier. He is the poorest person in the village and has neither a wife nor children. He is dressed in rags, smells like a donkey's fart in a windowless stable, stutters, is slightly cross-eyed, has a twitch and is generally a pitiful being. I have never understood why the children in the village ridicule and set their dogs upon him."

"Is he also the village idiot?"

"Yes, he is the village idiot.

The mayor's wife is pregnant. If you look, you will see her nudge her husband, whisper something in his ear and point towards the water carrier.

– But that cannot be, says the mayor.

– It's true, says his wife. The water carrier has the evil eye.

– So what if he does? says the mayor.

– He's been staring at my belly this whole time, says the mayor's wife. I bet you that will bring bad luck.

– What do you mean by 'bad luck'?

– Perhaps our child won't be a boy but a girl.

– So? says the mayor. Don't we already have seven boys? The eighth shall be a girl.

Vardan's mother passes by once more with her sofra.

– Would you like another piece of baklava? she asks the mayor's wife.

I've suddenly lost my appetite, says the mayor's wife. Can't you chase that water carrier out of the house?

– Today he's our guest, said Vardan's mother. I couldn't do that.

– Zovinar, don't you think that devil has the evil eye?

– No, says Vardan's mother.

– But he won't stop staring at my belly.

– He also looked at my belly a few times, says Vardan's mother, and as you can see my little Vardan turned out to be perfectly normal. He's a beautiful boy and already walks like a boy of two, even though he is only 18 months.

– Yes, he is a beautiful and strong child. But do you think it's normal that he wishes to become a poet?

— No, I don't, says Vardan's mother.

— Perhaps it has something to do with the evil eye?

— You mean the water carrier …

— Anything's possible.

— I'll have to ask my husband what he thinks first.

And Vardan's mother asks Hagob, 'Do you think that the water carrier has the evil eye?'

— I'll have to ask the priest, says Hagob.

And Hagob asks the priest. And the priest is not quite sure and says, 'Anything is possible, Hagob Efendi. After all, the water carrier has no wife. And as priest of this village, I am not aware of him ever having one. I also caught him at it not that long ago.'

— Where did you catch him?

— In the stable behind the church. He was mounting my donkey.

— Mounting? In what way?

— You know what way I mean, Hagob Efendi. He was fornicating with my donkey – although actually it's not a donkey, it's a jenny.

— That's unbelievable, Vartabed.

— Perhaps he does have the evil eye; after all, everyone knows that a man should never be intimate with an animal."

4

"In the night that followed the celebration of Vardan's first steps, Hagob and his wife tossed and turned, and had many a strange dream. When they woke up the next morning, Hagob said to his wife:

– I dreamed that the water carrier's evil eye had turned that little boy in the mayor's wife's belly into a little girl.

– I dreamed the exact same thing, says Zovinar.

– It is tradition, says Hagob, for little girls to be betrothed while they are still in their swaddling clothes, at least that's what happened to you; you were betrothed to me before you even knew your own name.

– On the day after my christening.

– On the day after your christening.

– You were older than me, my dear Hagob, you were already three and you could even count.

– I could count to three, says Hagob.

– Yes, says Zovinar.

Zovinar says, 'Your father came to my father and asked for my hand on your behalf. And the two men exchanged coins, threw them into the tonir and finally sealed the engagement with a handshake.'

– Precisely, says Hagob.

And Hagob says, 'I didn't know that the water carrier had the evil eye, but if we dreamed it, then it must be true.'

– Yes, says Zovinar.

And Hagob says, 'Indeed.'

And Zovinar says, 'Perhaps it wouldn't be such a bad thing if the water carrier's evil eye turns that little boy in the mayor's wife's belly into a little girl. After all, the mayor is a rich man and he could betroth his little girl to our Vardan, who was also cursed whilst still in his mother's belly. Why else would he have decided to become a poet?'

– You're right, says Hagob, before adding, 'I will speak with the mayor tomorrow.'

But as it so happened, the mayor's wife gave birth not to a girl but a little boy. Only when Vardan was three years old did the grapevines bestow a little girl upon the mayor and his wife.

On the day immediately after her christening – which was nine days after her birth – Hagob set off for the mukhtars' house to ask for his daughter's hand in marriage on behalf of Vardan. Although the mayor initially remarked that he had no desire to give his daughter away to a ne'er-do-well boy who would go on to become a poet, Hagob reassured him, explaining that the Khatisians' land crossed into that of the mayor and mukhtar and with the situation being as it was, their children's marriage would ensure that in future there would be no disputes about whose pastures belonged to whom and so on and so forth. Besides, Hagob argued, he owned a rooster named Abdul Hamid, and it was the best rooster in the whole village of Yedi Su, and if the mayor and mukhtar so wished, Hagob would, as Vardan's father, be more than willing to lend this rooster – the one and only Abdul Hamid – to them without any further ado, providing that was the mukhtar's wish and, of course, that of his wife, too.

And so it was," said the storyteller. "The two men exchanged two coins, threw them into the tonir and shook hands. They then drank some liquor and raised their glasses to Vardan's health and to the health of his bride, who had been christened the day before by the name of *Arpine,* the Armenian name for 'the rising sun'.

Everybody in the house congratulated your three-year-old father on his engagement. Even the neighbors came into the oda, took your father in their arms and said, '*Atschket louis*'. Some of the neighbors said, 'May Jesus Christ protect your bride from the Kurds.'"

"Were they afraid that the Kurds would take her virginity before my father had known her?"

"That's right, my little lamb.

Of course, your three-year-old father was too young to understand what was going on and why everyone was congratulating him – and too young to grasp what a hymen was and why his bride was saving it for him. And he also didn't know that as his father had exchanged coins with the mayor, he had said to him, 'Take good care of my daughter-in-law, Mukhtar Bey. Make sure nobody takes her virginity.'

And the mayor said, 'Hagob Efendi. Your son will wed a virgin. That I promise you. No Kurd will kidnap her or have it off with her. I'm on good terms with Suleyman, the Kurds' sheikh. I pay him my taxes on time and give him cattle and grain, and I will also pay the bride tax, which is half the dowry you will give me for my daughter when the time comes.'"

"I don't understand, Meddah? Are the Kurds really so keen on little girls who aren't even old enough to walk?"

"No, my little lamb. They're only interested once the girls are sexually mature, which only happens after they turn ten or eleven … sometimes even twelve.

As I have already explained to you, my little lamb, it's not those city-dwelling Kurds that the Armenians fear, and not even the semi-nomads who live in their dirty Kurdish villages. It's the wild, marauding mountain clans they fear. They have spies everywhere. They know precisely what is happening down in the Armenian villages: who has money and who doesn't; who has sons and who has daughters. They know how old the girls are and when they will be sexually mature.

Then they simply come and take them away. Believe me. That's just how it is. That is why the girls are married off as soon as possible for they are only prized as long as they are virgins.

For those Christian virgins living in the isolated, unprotected villages of the elevated plains, the wild Kurd is a kicking, punching, thrashing, door-breaking masculine brute from head to toe. Everything about him is brutal. Even his dark, piercing gaze. When the Kurds gallop through the village just after harvest to collect the taxes owed to the sheikh, the virgins are so terrified and alarmed that they piss their tightly-knotted shalvar trousers. However, for some, the piss only trickles down the inside of their bare thighs as the virgin is so afraid that those earlobes between her legs clamp shut. No more do they spy, interrogate or question; they just become spasmodically sealed. Some of them close so tightly that no one can pull them apart again. It is as though the Virgin Mary herself had sewn them together as a measure of precaution.

I can see the questioning look in your eyes, my little lamb. But believe me, that's really how it is. The Armenians cannot protect their women as they are not allowed to bear arms."

"Because they are Christians?"

"That's right."

"And the Kurds?"

"The Kurds are Muslims. Every Muslim has the right to bear arms."

"And what about the Turkish authorities? Why don't they protect the Armenians from the Kurds?"

"Because it is not in their interest to do so, my little lamb. They fear the insubordination of the infidels and therefore have no objection to the Kurds intimidating them. The Kurds are almost like the long arm of the Sultan, keeping the Armenians in check."

"And what about the courts?"

"What courts?"

"I mean, what happens when a Kurd is brought before the court?"

"That might occasionally happen in the cities, but not in the isolated villages. Look here, my little lamb. Even the few saptiehs that there are in the villages are afraid of the Kurds. If they can't arrest the Kurds and bring them before the court, who can? And even if there were any courageous saptiehs, do you think they would be able to take on an entire Kurdish clan by themselves? Or chase after the Kurds? Through the narrow paths and ravines of the mountains that lie somewhere between the two seas?"

"So it's not possible?"

"It's not, my little lamb. And even if someone did manage to bring a Kurd before the court, it would be pointless. You see, before a kadi, all Christians and infidels are considered to be liars, unless they have two Muslim witnesses."

"Which I imagine they don't?"

"Most of the time they don't, unless they buy two false witnesses."

"Is that allowed?"

"It is. But in the case of a young girl being kidnapped and losing her virginity, it would bring little solace to either the girl or her father."

"Why, Meddah?"

"Well, why do you think, my little lamb? Do you think that winning a court case would restore the girl's lost innocence or even her hymen that will have vanished into thin air? And why would any self-respecting Armenian man want to marry such a girl? So that they could commit the sacred act together and he could father Christian children with her who would then carry his name?

You see, even a successful court case would be practically meaningless.

So, the mayor had promised to deliver a virgin to your father. He promised to look after her and to protect her from the Kurds.

Even the sole saptieh in the village, the flat-footed, pockmarked Shekir Efendi, who was sat drinking raki in the coffeehouse with the mayor shortly after the engagement, promised to do his very best to protect the child.

– You never know, Mukhtar Bey, he said to the mayor. They say those Kurds don't lay a finger on babies or put their fingers or anything else inside of them – the thin bones of a young lamb, say, or the twigs of an oak tree, or even the stalks of flowers or anything of that kind. But I did hear just recently that they do kidnap babies.

– Why do they do that? said the mayor.

– To fatten them up, and keep them until they are big and bleed all by themselves.

– Bleed? In what way, Saptieh Agah?

– Every month, as women do.

– And then?

– Then they take their virginity, but they don't use rods or the thin bones of a lamb, or even the stalks of flowers or anything of that kind.

– How do they do it then, efendi?

– Well, how do you think, Mukhtar Bey? The Kurds use the thing they have between their legs, which is usually quite considerable in size.

They drank their raki followed by a sweet coffee served in a small bowl. The mayor thought to himself, 'He's only saying that to scare me so that I'll give him a regular tip, even though I already pay him baksheesh, as well as give him meat and wheat flour and fruit from my garden.'

– And you really will watch out for her, Shekir Efendi?

– As if she were the apple of my eye, said the saptieh. With

Allah as my witness. And the next time the Kurds come to lead away our cattle, I will stand guard in front of your door so that they don't take your child with them, too. And the saptieh tapped his old gun with his knuckle and said, 'I will guard her as though she were my own daughter.'

– But you don't have any children, Shekir Efendi. And you don't have a daughter.

– It's sad but true, said the saptieh. My wife ran away. Who knows where she is now.

– Why did she run away, Saptieh Agah?

– Because she couldn't have any children, said the saptieh. And because I threatened to kill her if she didn't have any.

– The mayor nodded. He said, 'Yes, Shekir Efendi.' And in his head he secretly hoped that the saptieh wouldn't lay a hand on the child while he was standing guard over her. After all, this man had no wife and would sometimes have it off with donkeys. He would mount them from behind just like the water carrier, who was possessed by the Devil and had the evil eye.

There was another man in the village who people said also had the evil eye: the red-haired blacksmith Kevork Hacobian. You see, many women in the village would dye their hair with henna and so if you looked beneath their veils, you would find red hair. But the blacksmith used neither henna nor any other artificial dye from Frankistan on his hair. His hair color was a gift from God. But that was precisely what made him unusual, and therefore suspicious. What person of Armenian descent has genuine red hair? Had the Lord God punished the unborn child while it was still in its mother's womb so that it would be born with red hair? Or was it the work of the Devil? Had the blacksmith's mother got mixed up with the devil worshippers perhaps? Or the gypsies, who everyone knew had the evil eye? Or was Priest Kapriel Hamadian right when he once proclaimed at the cemetery, 'Yes, it is true. I know what caused his red hair. The blacksmith's mother confessed everything to me.'

– But she never goes to confession, Vartabed.

– True. But I dreamed she confessed to me.

– And what did you dream, Vartabed?

– I dreamed, said the priest, that the mother of this red-haired devil had come to confession.

– And what did she confess?

– She said to me, 'Vartabed, do you remember the red-haired Irish missionary who once came to this village before my son, the red-haired blacksmith, was born?'

– Of course, I said. I remember.

– Well, back then that false saint wanted to convert all your little sheep to Catholicism, even though everyone knows that our Savior Jesus Christ cannot have a dual nature, as the Catholics believe; logic dictates that he can only have one: he is God. And everyone knows that our Gregorian faith is the one true faith.

– Right you are, I said. And what do you wish to confess, my daughter?

– I dreamed, said the mother of the red-haired blacksmith, that that red-haired Irish missionary climbed on top of me while I was sleeping, although I can't be sure because back then I was very young and slept very deeply: so deeply that I wouldn't have noticed a thing.

– Then it's possible that this false saint climbed on top of you, or could have done?

– Yes, Vartabed.

— And that might explain your son's red hair?

— Yes, Vartabed.

Either way," said the storyteller, "this red-haired blacksmith ended up becoming the most important man in Vardan's life beside his own father."

"Why?"

"Because he was Vardan's godfather."

"His godfather?"

"That's right, my little lamb. That red-haired blacksmith was godfather to your father. You see, back then, during the christening, Hagob couldn't find anyone else for the job."

"Wasn't Hagob afraid of his evil eye?"

"No," said the storyteller. "You see, everyone said that little Vardan's grandmother could see through others, and she told Hagob, 'Hagob, the blacksmith will be the perfect godfather: he has kind eyes. There is not a trace of the Devil in them.' And if she said it, it must be true.

Everyone in the village knew that the Armenian blacksmiths were in fact the true saviors of the world, although anyone who envied or loathed them didn't like to admit it."

"Why are Armenian blacksmiths the saviors of the world?"

"Because that is what the Armenian stories proclaim, especially those that speak of Mount Ararat."

"How do they go, Meddah?"

"Well, listen and I'll tell you, my little lamb …

There is a giant trapped inside Mount Ararat … a Persian giant by the name of Meher. He is chained to a rock face deep within the mountain. Horns grow out of his forehead. Wild dogs, black ravens and poisonous snakes keep watch over him. They say that one day, on the eve of Ascension, he will break loose from his chains and come forth from the mountain to destroy the world."

"How does he plan to do that, Meddah?"

"You see, my little lamb, the earth is a sofra made of clay, a semi-circle shaped tray on which the Lord God has laid out his delicious treats: everything that he holds dear. This sofra is carried by angels who regularly take turns bearing it. All the stars in the sky orbit this clay sofra that we people call earth. If the giant breaks free from his chains and comes forth from the mountain, roaring with all his fury, he will simply upend the sofra with his large, frightful hands, and all that God holds dear will fall into the abyss and die."

"Even the flowers?"

"Yes, even the flowers."

"And the trees?"

"Yes, even the trees."

"But aren't they rooted in the soil?"

"Yes, they are, my little lamb. But they'll fall just the same."

"I thought only those things not rooted down could fall. I mean everything that flounces around and moves."

"No, my little lamb. If that giant upends our sofra, everything on it will disappear."

"Everything that God loves?"

"Yes, my little lamb. All that God loves will perish. And the whole world itself will perish, for what would be the point of the world if everything that God loves was no longer here?"

"It would all just disappear?"

"That's right."

"And what does that have to do with Armenian blacksmiths?"

"It has a lot to do with them, my little lamb. From Easter Monday to Ascension the blacksmiths in this region strike their hammers on their anvils three times early in the morning. This allows the giant's chains, which have weakened over Easter, to be secured once more, ensuring that he does not escape and that the world does not perish."

"Does that mean that Armenian blacksmiths are the true saviors of the world?"

"That's right."

"Even the red-haired blacksmith Kevork Hacobian, the man who is my father's godfather?"

"He's one of the most important ones; you see, he doesn't just pound his hammer on the anvil three times early in the morning between Easter and Ascension: he does it all year long."

"Every morning?"

"Yes, my little lamb. Just to be sure. Every morning.

And seeing as we're talking about the time between Easter and Ascension, let me quickly tell you another short story.

On the Day of Ascension the Armenians in Yedi Su celebrate a peculiar festival of Pagan origin that has very little to do with the Ascension of our Savior. And yet it is in some way related; you see, I am certain that Christ would be happy if he knew that on the exact same day as his Ascension, the children in the village of Yedi Su counted all the stars in the sky."

"What happens, Meddah?"

"Well, let me tell you," said the Meddah. "On the Day of Ascension all the children come together early in the morning on the village square. They then separate into groups and go out onto the meadows and fields where they pick flowers to decorate their hair and clothes. This festival is called *Widjak* and it has something to do with the sun god *Mir*."

"Is it a flower festival?"

"No, my little lamb. Surprisingly, it isn't. It is a celebration of chance, destiny and counting stars."

"What happens, Meddah?"

"Well, let me tell you," said the Meddah. "After all the children have adorned themselves with flowers, the little girls go to fetch earthenware jugs. They then take them to the seven wells. As they walk there, they may look neither sideways nor backwards. But the girls from the village of Yedi Su take the water carrier with them as it isn't easy for little girls to pull up water from seven different wells."

"What does the water carrier do?"

"He lowers the heavy water pail down into the depths of the seven wells, brings the pails – full to the brim with water – back up to the light and places them in front of the little girls who may look neither sideways nor backwards. Once that's done, the little girls, who are covered in flowers from head to toe, bend forward, cross their arms behind their backs and fetch their own water … taking it from the pail before them, of course … but they take it with their mouths."

"With their mouths?"

"Yes, my little lamb. The little girls look as though they are drinking the fresh water, except they're not: they spit it out into the earthenware jugs made of brown clay which they carried to the seven wells. They fill the clay jugs, place a small stone or whatever object they can find inside, and make their way to church where Priest Kapriel Hamadian waits on the Day of Ascension to bless the little girls' water which they have collected in their jugs. After doing just that, he leads the little girls and their jugs around the church seven times."

"Then what happens, Meddah?"

"Then the little girls go home and hide the clay jugs containing the holy water. Once night falls, they take their jugs up to the roof, place the jug next to the chimney and leave it there so that the holy Widjak water inside the jug can count the stars."

"Does the holy water really count the stars?"

"It does, my little lamb. Just like the sun god Mir, who counts the stars in the sky every single night in order to make sure that all his children are still there."

5

"When Vardan was three years old, the older boys in the village took him with them out onto the meadows and fields on the Day of Ascension. They adorned him with flowers and carried him on their shoulders. They then followed the girls all the way to the seven wells, taunting them and pelting them with birds' eggs which they had collected beforehand. One of the boys said to Vardan, 'Listen up, kipper. The girls will hide the jugs containing the holy water. We'll try and find their hiding place before they take the jugs up to the roofs so that they can count the stars. Listen up, kipper. You're going to steal a jug and then you're going to order the girl to perform a forfeit. Otherwise you won't give her the jug back.'

And your three-year-old father, who had no idea what a forfeit was, asked, 'A forfeit?'

And the older boy laughed and said, 'Yes, kipper. A forfeit. The girl has to give you a kiss, otherwise she won't get her jug back, get it?'

And your father laughed, even though he had no idea what they meant.

During that Widjak festival, when the boys in the village challenged your three-year-old father to demand a forfeit, and with it a kiss, something else took place which would stay with your father for years to come."

"What happened, Meddah?"

"The incident with that stupid water carrier."

"What happened to him?"

"The boys spent the whole day looking for the place where the girls had hidden their clay jugs. During their hunt, they came across the water carrier just as he was mounting the Khatisians' jenny. It was early in the evening."

"A jenny?"

"Yes."

"Was she nameless, like Bulbul's donkey?"

"No. Her name was Ceyda."

"How did the water carrier manage to get into the stable to mount Ceyda? I thought you had to go through the living room to reach the stable?"

"Ceyda the jenny was not stood in the stable because Vardan's grandmother had left her outside, tied up, of course."

"And what happened with the water carrier?"

"The boys caught him, pulled him down from the jenny, tied him up and dragged him up to the flat roof of the Khatisians' house. Your three-year-old father saw it all."

"He even saw the water carrier having it off with Ceyda?"

"That, too."

"And did he see them tie up the water carrier and take him to the roof?"

"Yes, my little lamb. He saw it all. And he also saw the dripping member of the wailing water carrier, which the boys, being sadistic as young boys often are, grabbed hold of and used to pull him down. He saw them push it back inside his filthy shalvar trousers before dragging him up to the roof. As you can see, he's just a poor, clumsy village idiot. One of the boys said to your father, 'Let's leave Hovhannes the water carrier on the roof overnight as punishment so he can count the stars.'"

"Did the water carrier really spend the night on the roof? And did he really count the stars?"

"No, my little lamb," said the Meddah. "It's not good for a man with the evil eye to count the stars together with the holy water. That is why Vardan's grandfather came to bring the poor fellow back down.

I haven't told you anything about your father's grandfather yet because the man was completely overshadowed by the grandmother of the family. Very much unlike his wife, Hamest, he was a quiet soul. They say he used to be good fun, always cracking jokes, but then he changed."

"Did something happen to my father's grandfather – my great-grandfather – that turned him into a quiet person?"

"Yes, my little lamb," said the Meddah.

And the Meddah said, "In winter the wild Kurds, who live high up in the mountains, send their old and their sick down to the Armenian villages to stay there during the colder months. These old and sick Kurds are unbidden guests, but no one dares refuse them. Once inside, they spend most of their time in the stable, taking whatever they want to eat – from the Armenians' pantries, of course – before retreating back to the stable. Once spring arrives, they vanish."

"Why doesn't anyone dare chase them away?"

"Because then they would be lumbered with the entire Kurd clan: but they wouldn't come to spend winter in their stables; they would come to take vengeance for their old and their sick. The sheikh of the Kurds would send his riders down into the village to cut off the men's cocks, rape the women and burn their houses to the ground.

One day, in 1846, your father's grandfather refused to allow some of the Kurds' elderly and sick relatives into his stable. But it was a very unwise decision indeed. You see, the very next day as many as one hundred armed Kurdish riders stormed into the village. They dragged Vardan's grandfather onto the market square, undressed him and were just about to cut off his cock when his wife, Hamest, came running to them, wailing and begging the Kurds for mercy. The Kurds decided to take pity and so spared him his cock, but they did cut off his earlobes and gave him several lashes. Your father's grandfather never forgot the lesson he learned that day."

"Didn't the villagers fight back?"

"They never fight back, my little lamb. The village's only saptieh trembled with fear, gnawed his filthy fingernails and grinned stupidly as one of the Kurds took his gun away. The Kurd then said to him, 'Don't fret now. This gun is older than you. The government will give you a new one.'"

"And what about the Armenian men in the village?"

"They stood silently around the village square.

My little lamb, it should come as no surprise that, in the eyes of the Turks and the Kurds, Armenians are the most cowardly people on earth. It's almost as though they were born to present their backs to the whip and their cocks to the blade – just as the slits of their women seemed to exist purely for the enjoyment of believers of the true faith and their circumcised cocks.

After the incident with the Kurds, his public shaming and the terror he suffered, Vardan's grandfather developed a high-pitched voice … and it was as though the Kurds' threat of castration had actually come true and their curved knives had indeed severed your great-grandfather, who was still a young man at the time, from all his masculine glory. Let me explain something to you, my little lamb: A man's dignity, as well as his pride, dangle between his legs. But a man's dignity and pride also reside in his head. You see, there's a secret bond that exists between a man's head and that glorious bundle hanging between his legs, and so it should come as no surprise that some men, who suffer the humiliation of defenselessly losing their masculine dignity, eventually end up believing that their propagator genuinely has been taken away.

As I said, Vardan's grandfather was a quiet soul; he stood in the background, lost his deep voice, spoke without power or intonation, squeaked like a sick bird whenever he tried to protest against his wife's dictatorial character or her stormy temperament, took up drinking and finally wound up a drunk. – But I won't bore you with such things, my little lamb, by that I mean your great-grandfather's propagator that he thought he'd lost, or his high-pitched voice. I'd rather tell you about all the goodness that lay in his heart … and the unusual blanket that he gave to your father one day.

As I've already mentioned, Vardan was the youngest grandchild, and perhaps that was the reason why his grandfather was particularly fond of him. One day he gave Vardan a colorful, hand-knotted blanket, and he said to him, 'This jorgan dates back to the days of Sultan Ibrahim; it was made in 1642. You should have it, my little lamb. And you will give it to your first-born son.' – And your father, who wasn't even four years old, asked, 'My first-born son?' – And his grandfather said, 'Yes. Your son, my little lamb. You shall call him Thovma … just like me: Thovma.'

And his grandfather said, 'This jorgan really does date back to the days of Sultan Ibrahim. Do you know who he was, my little lamb?' – And as your father didn't know who he was, he told him: 'Sultan Ibrahim was a man with a tired, old driver between his legs. You see, this Sultan had too many women in his harem. Like every man, the Sultan carried all his *Sturm und Drang* underneath his clothes inside two small, hanging sacks. They were quite sweet little pouches that were once taut and firm, but over time had become soft and limp. His propagator had become limp, too, along with everything that was brutal and gristly and which once jutted out yearningly from beneath the two pouches. He started to grow tired of his wives, for not only were they many, they were also all very keen. Still, the Sultan was jealous as he considered each wife to be his own personal property. One day the Sultan heard that one of his wives had been having it off with a eunuch, although it seemed highly unlikely as everyone knew that eunuchs didn't have any balls. Do you know what balls are, my little dove?'

And your father, who was just under four years old, said, 'Yes, Abdul Hamid the rooster lays a ball every day.'

And his grandfather, who seldom laughed, suddenly guffawed

and said, 'Abdul Hamid the rooster doesn't lay the balls, my little dove, the hens do. And besides, they're called eggs.'

And then he said, 'So, let me tell you what happened to Sultan Ibrahim's wives. One of them had had it off with a ball-less eunuch. Well, the Sultan tried to find out which one had committed the adultery, but he simply couldn't get a word out of anyone; you see, all the wives in his harem stuck together and kept their lips tightly sealed. So guess what the Sultan did?' – And as your father couldn't figure it out, his grandfather said, 'Well, let me tell you. One day the Sultan had all the women in his harem tied up, all two-hundred and eighty of them – for that's how many there were – had them stuffed into large sacks that were weighed down with stones, ordered the sacks to be taken to Constantinople and for them all to be thrown into the river so that the women would drown. And that's exactly what happened.'

– Is that really true, grandfather?

– It is, my little lamb. You see, Turkish history is full of tales of such cruelty, and that is why it's no surprise that the Franks from Frankistan, who are also cruel in their own way – worse even – consider the Turks to be the cruelest people on earth.

–This jorgan harbors several generations of dead fleas, said his grandfather. But dead fleas don't bite, my little dove."

"And what about living fleas, Meddah?"

"You get used to them," said the Meddah. "The Khatisians' house was teeming with fleas. They jumped across the carpets and rugs, over clay jugs, oil lamps and various other objects.

And they were also living in your father's new jorgan, which was already very old. As a child, your father would try and catch some of them with his mouth, and he was always delighted whenever he finally got one. Of course, by this time your father was no longer sleeping in the cradle with the dove and the olive branch; he now had his own bed lined with lambskins.

When his grandfather gave him his jorgan, he said, 'The cradle with the dove and the olive branch will stand empty for now, but one day your son will sleep in it.'

– My son? Asked your father.

And his grandfather replied, 'Yes. Your son, Thovma.'

Your father sometimes played with himself, as all little boys do, without having any idea how dangerous it was.

One time your grandfather caught him at it and said, 'Don't you ever do that again, otherwise your son Thovma won't be born.' He then added, 'You will become as loony as that water carrier Hovhannes. He, too, played with himself when he was a little boy.'

Your father said, 'But I'm no water carrier.'

– I didn't say you were, said his grandfather. And he said, 'Your little winkle is a dangerous toy. Playing with it won't just send you loopy, it can also turn the most level-headed of men into *parvanas*.' And as your father, who wasn't even four, didn't know what parvanas were, his grandfather explained, 'Well, my little lamb. A parvana is a moth from the East of which there are many here in this region because we have plenty of sun and flies and mosquitoes. Now, when a man plays too much with his little soldier, the one between his legs, his head will grow heavy with love, and he will believe that every girl is his beloved. And often he can't tell them apart from the flames of the tonir.'

– What happens then? asked your father.

– The man, who has become obsessed with love, believes himself to be a moth, and he blindly plunges into the flames which he mistakes for his beloved.

– And what happens then? asked your father.

– Then that's the end of him, said his grandfather.

And his grandfather laughed and said, 'But fear not, my little lamb, my little pasha, my little dove, my little sperm bearer, carrying the seed of my great-grandson Thovma. You won't need to play with your winkle later on when things get serious and you can feel a great longing in your little balls to be with a woman. And you won't need to mount a donkey, like Hovhannes, the water carrier. And you won't need to become a parvana, so tortured by love that you plunge into the flames of the tonir. You won't need to do any of that because we have picked a wife for you. She may still be peeing in her diapers, but she's waiting for you, my little lamb. Her father, who is our mayor, will make sure she has plenty of meat on her bones. And she will have a plump rear, but one that's a sensible size. And you too will be sensible and enter into the holy bond of marriage with her. And you will father a son with her and you will call him Thovma.'

But there was still a way to go before your father's marriage," said the storyteller. "The conception of his son Thovma still lay in the stars. Even as your father celebrated his fourth birthday, he still had no idea how serious a business fathering children was, or about the duties of an Armenian man, his responsibility to his family, and his fears. At the age of four, your father didn't even know who Abdul Hamid was, the man who had assumed the sultanate just two years before your father was born in 1876. All he knew was that his father's rooster carried the name Abdul Hamid and that from now on all their roosters would be called by that same name. You see, every rooster is destined to have its head chopped off, and every Armenian wanted to see Abdul Hamid's head roll, for rumors had started to spread … rumors that Abdul Hamid had plans to wipe out the entire Armenian race.

Your father was still living in a fairy-tale world and indeed his grandfather told him the most wonderful fairytales and stories. For instance, there was the story about Noah's Ark, the angel and our Savior's cloth. Would you like me to tell it to you, my little lamb?"

"Yes, Meddah."

"Well, it goes like this and it goes like that," said the Meddah.

"One day," said the Meddah, "the Armenian King Abgar fell sick with leprosy. A voice came to him in a dream and it said, 'Only the sun god Mir can save you from leprosy, O Abgar. Climb up to Mount Ararat, right up to the highest peak where you will be close to the sun and Mir.'

And so it was," said the storyteller. "The King climbed up the Armenian mountain, but as he reached the very top, the sky darkened, and the sun was nowhere to be seen. The King stumbled around, and suddenly he came across the wreckage of a ship that resembled an ark. And as he had never heard of Noah's Ark for he had read neither the Bible, which had already been written, nor the Qur'an, which had yet to be written … when he saw the wreckage, he was bewildered and thought to himself, 'How on earth did a ship get up here on this mountain?' And behold: no sooner had he asked the question did an angel appear before him and say, 'One day, long ago, a dove flew from this place down to the land that would one day be known as Hayastan, and there it found an olive branch.'

– An olive branch? asked the King.

– As a symbol from the Lord, said the angel, who had returned to save the world again.

And the angel said, 'There is no sun god known as Mir. And there is no use standing here on the highest peak of this Armenian mountain in order to be closer to the sun. The sun cannot cure leprosy.'

– Who can? asked the King.

And the angel said, 'Jesus of Nazareth.'

– Jesus of Nazareth?

– Yes.

– Where can I find this man?

– In Judea, said the angel. There he wanders the land, looking for souls to fish.

– So, he's a fisherman of souls?

– Yes.

– And a miracle healer?

– That, too.

– If I find him, will he restore me to health?

– Only if you truly find him, said the angel.

– And how do I truly find him?

– You have to believe in him.

– If I believe in him, will my health be restored?

– Yes, said the angel.

But the King was suspicious and so first sent his spies out to Judea in order to find out if what the angel said was true: if there was indeed a man called Jesus of Nazareth who really could cure leprosy.

And so it was," said the storyteller, "that the spies of the Armenian King arrived in the Holy Land just as Jesus was preparing to hold his Sermon on the Mount. And as the King's spies followed the people who flocked to the mountain, they came to witness the Sermon on the Mount.

Once Jesus had finished giving his sermon, one spy turned to the other and said, 'He certainly is a peculiar saint; one who blesses the meek and the poor and the witless, even promising them the kingdom of heaven. How should such a man cure our King of leprosy when his Majesty is neither meek nor poor or even witless? And we already know that he has a place in heaven next to the gods.'

And they wanted to turn around and leave, but one of the spies said, 'That lying saint is walking back down the mountain. Do we not have a letter for him from his Majesty, King Abgar? We must give it to him.'

And they handed the Armenian King's letter over to Jesus. And Jesus read the letter and said, 'Your King wants to believe in me and requests that I travel to Hayastan to cure him of leprosy. But I do not have the time to undertake such a long journey by donkey; I still have a lot of work here in Judea. And I must also travel to the City of David, a place people there call Jerusalem, to drive the traders and money changers from the temple.' And Jesus said, 'I must also journey to the cross that will soon be fashioned for me.'

His speech was quite remarkable, and the spies did not know what to make of it. When Jesus of Nazareth saw the confusion on the faces of the King's spies, he untied the cloth which he had wrapped around his head before giving the Sermon on the Mount. Jesus said, 'I perspired a great deal during my sermon. You see, it is not easy to persuade stubborn minds that those who are meek and poor and witless will reach the kingdom of heaven. Take this cloth drenched in sweat and give it to your King. If you do this, his health will be restored.'

The spies took the cloth and rode off with it. Once they had left Judea and as they were making their way towards Hayastan, riding through the cedar forests and gorges of Lebanon, they were ambushed by robbers: men who were the forefathers of today's wild mountain Kurds. They slayed the spies of the Armenian King, threw their bodies into the ravine and stole their clothes, shoes and horses. In fact, they took everything, except the Savior's dirty, sweaty cloth, which they threw down into one of Lebanon's deepest ravines, where it still lies today."

The Lord's cloth … the Last Thought thought to itself. So even to this very day the cloth lies in a ravine in Lebanon? Why didn't the Lord God stop the King's spies from being killed? Why did they have to die and lose the cloth?

"Tell me, Meddah. What happened to the Armenian King?"

"He died a miserable death, my little lamb."

"And what would have happened to him if he had received the cloth?"

"He would have been cured of leprosy, my little lamb. He would have converted to Christianity in the days when the Savior was still alive, and all his people probably would have done, too. But, as I just told you, the story didn't end that way. He never received the cloth and so Armenia remained a Pagan country. Only in the year 301 did Armenia, or Hayastan, become a Christian state.

And at that time," said the storyteller, "King Tiridates the Third was ruler of Armenia, a ruler also known as Tiridates the Great. One day, he was told of a certain Gregory the Apostle, a man whom the people called Gregory the Illuminator. He journeyed around Hayastan, preaching Christianity. It was said that he was the son of the man who murdered the former king – the then father of the current king – before fleeing, and who was on a mission to atone for the sins of his murderous father. But as King Tiridates was afraid that the son of the man who had murdered the late king could also murder him, he had Saint Gregory arrested, put in chains and thrown to the lions.

And really that should have been the end of Saint Gregory. But it wasn't. You see, when the King's soldiers threw Saint Gregory into the lions' den, the Lord God transformed the lions' hearts to those of lambs, and Gregory was able to survive many years in the den. Clandestine Christians came and brought him food and water. King Tiridates, however, went mad. Not long after, he began to crawl around on all fours, just like those wild beasts with hearts of lambs inside Gregory's den.

On one of the rare days when King Tiridates had regained his senses – which happened every now and then – his sister Chosroviducht told him, 'Gregory is still alive. He has turned the hearts of those wild beasts into those of lambs. He can work magic, and I'm sure he could make your madness disappear.'

And so the King's soldiers came and fetched Saint Gregory from the lions' den and took him to the King and his sister, who said to Gregory, 'Can you cure my brother, the King of the Armenians, of his madness?'

– Yes, said Gregory. You see, the King is merely possessed by the devil.

– How will you cure him, Gregory?

– With the Bible, said Gregory.

And so Gregory swung the Holy Scriptures around the mad King's head three times, and he spoke words similar to those the Savior had used when healing the sick and the invalid. And before his mind descended into chaos once more, he asked the suffering King, 'Do you believe in the Son of God, who healed the invalid and the sick?'

And the King replied, 'Yes, I believe.' – And from that moment on, he was cured.

When the Armenian King Tiridates adopted Christianity, the entire royal family converted, too. The people soon followed suit. And so it came to be that, in the year 301 of the Common Era, Armenians became the first people in the world to adopt Christianity as a state religion.

Armenians were destined to suffer for Christ like no other people on earth," said the storyteller, "and among the many stories that your great-grandfather told your not even four-year-old father about how the first Armenian Christians suffered were the stories of *Yazdegerd* and *Shapur*."

"Who was Shapur?"

"He was a Persian king, my little lamb. A fire worshipper: a true devil incarnate. A Christian Armenian slave once tried to convert him to Christianity while in his bed, but it did little good. You see, her Pagan rival, the woman who shared King Shapur's bed the following night, whispered a different story in his ear."

"What, Meddah?"

" 'If you adopt Christianity,' she said to Shapur, 'then your war elephants will go the way of the lions in the den of Gregory the Convertor: He turned all the lions' hearts into those of lambs.'

– But that would be bad, said Shapur. How should I wage war against my enemies if my elephants have the hearts of lambs? – And as the King was afraid that the Christians might persuade him to turn to their faith, he decided to have them all killed.

Just one week after first hearing those persuasive words whispered across the pillow by his Christian slave and then, the following night, the spiteful arguments of her rival, King Shapur's troops invaded neighboring Armenia. The King unleashed a massacre upon the occupied territory. He ordered thousands of men to be slain, the Armenian cities were razed and the severed heads of priests and Armenian notables were mounted on the city wall. In the Armenian capital he ordered the women to be rounded up on the main squares, raped in broad daylight and then trampled to death by his war elephants."

"That's a terrible story."
    "It is, my little lamb."
    "Shapur?"
    "Yes, King Shapur."
    "And who was Yazdegerd?"
    "He was another Persian king. He was a fire worshipper like Shapur, and also a pretty horrid fellow.

This Yazdegerd was just as cruel as Shapur," said the storyteller, "but he was smarter. Yazdegerd knew that the only way he could force the Armenians living in the Persian-occupied provinces to obey him permanently would be to destroy their religion. That is why he told his elephant handlers, 'The force of our elephants will not be enough to destroy the religion of these people.'
    – And how do you plan to destroy them, Great Yazdegerd? asked the elephant handlers.
    – By converting their priests, said Yazdegerd. And turning them into fire worshippers.

And so it was," said the storyteller, "that Yazdegerd decided to address a letter to the Armenian priesthood which read as follows: If you choose to adopt my religion, We shall bestow great rewards and honor upon you. However, if you choose not to convert, We shall erect fire altars throughout the whole of Armenia, and our magi and mobeds will rule the land. And should any man try to stop us, that man will be killed together with his family. – And do you know, my little lamb, what the Armenian priests replied?"

"No, Meddah."

"They wrote a letter to King Yazdegerd, which said: No one can take our faith from us. Take from us all that you wish, Great Yazdegerd. Our earthly goods we give to you, and we are willing to worship you as the sole King on earth. But Jesus Christ is our Lord in heaven.

The older children in the village often played games where they pretended to be King Yazdegerd or King Shapur. And they also played at being Armenian kings: King Abgar and King Tiridates. A particularly thrilling game was the one that involved King Abgar and the cloth of the Savior, which one of the King's spies tried to protect from the marauding Kurdish forefathers until he wound up dead at the bottom of one of Lebanon's ravines, right alongside the Lord's sweat-covered cloth.

In times of drought the children played the rain game with a puppet called *Nuri,* which was, in fact, nothing more than a Christian cross made to look like a puppet. They took the puppet from house to house and everyone was obliged to give them something – sometimes eggs and oil, mostly hadig, and occasionally pokhint, a sweet dish similar to hadig but made out of nuts, honey and flour. As they went, the children sang an old Armenian rain song that all their ancestors who had gone before them had sung: Dear Lord … Dear Lord … You satisfied our thirsty souls with Your glorious power, now send down water to quench our thirsty flowers … Let the rain fall, Dear Lord … let it rain … let it rain. – And the children implored their cross-shaped puppet to work its magic, collected hadig and pokhint, oil and eggs, pushed and pulled their puppet along and sang,

'Dear Lord … Dear Lord: let the rain fall.'

Of course, the boisterous boys' favorite game was Turks, Kurds and Armenians. The Armenians were always valiant and brave; the Turks and the Kurds were always underhanded and cowardly. However, the Turks and the Kurds were always armed, whilst the Armenians could use only their hands and legs, and, of course, their heads, to defend themselves. But in the end it was always the cowards who won over the valiant; you see, even the strongest arms and the finest of minds made little difference when faced with an armed enemy. At the end of the game the brave Armenians lay dead on the floor, whilst the Turks and the Kurds whet their wooden swords and danced with joy.

Although your father was only four, he was already taking part in the game. Once the boys grabbed hold of the blacksmith's youngest, red-haired son, who was even smaller than your father, and sent him out onto the field to steal a lamb. 'You're a Kurd now,' they said to him. 'Now you're going to go into that field, steal a lamb, and bring it back to us here.'

The blacksmith's son, who bore the name Avetik, did as he was told. As all of the sheepdogs on the neighboring fields recognized little red-haired Avetik, they only barked a little when Avetik took one of the lambs. They growled and snarled, and even began to howl, but did him no harm.

Avetik brought the lamb back to the boys. One of the boys was pretending to be the old saptieh Shekir Efendi, another was a Turkish captain and a third was the kadi. The saptieh arrested the Kurdish thief although all the boys knew that Shekir Efendi the saptieh was far too cowardly to ever dare arrest a Kurd. But that's how the scene was played out: The saptieh grabbed the small, red-haired boy by the collar, gave him a bit of a throttling and then dragged him before the Turkish captain.

– Where is the owner of this little lamb? asked the captain.

All the boys pointed to your four-year-old father, who knew the game and laughed. As the older boys had taught him how to play the role, he also knew exactly what he had to say and do. First, your father gave a small tip, a baksheesh, to the saptieh. He then gave another, larger tip to the captain, and he showed the biggest tip of them all to the boys but kept hold of it as it was reserved for the kadi, a Muslim judge.

They dragged your four-year-old father before the kadi, and your father had to say what the boys had told him to say. 'Kadi,' he said, pointing to little red-haired Avetik, 'this Muslim Kurd stole my lamb, and every Armenian in the village saw it and will testify.'

– Armenians are Christians, said the kadi. And witness statements made by Christians count for nothing. You must bring me two Muslim witnesses.

– But there weren't any Muslims who witnessed it.

– Then that's just bad luck for you, you son of an infidel whore who sired a bastard with an infidel blasphemer.

Your father then slipped the kadi the large tip he had kept for him and whispered something in his ear. And the kadi nodded and said softly, but loud enough so that everyone could hear, 'There are Muslim witnesses for hire stood in front of the hukumet. Go and pay two of them to be your witnesses. And I swear by Allah the Almighty that I have seen and know nothing … and that will be another two silver piasters.'

Your father slipped the kadi two silver piasters before going to the hukumet, which the children had built using two boxes stacked one on top of the other.

There he found the two false witnesses standing around: two pathetic-looking figures played by barefooted children. Your father looked the two false witnesses up and down before choosing one and saying, 'Efendi, will you come with me to the kadi to testify what you have seen?'

– What am I supposed to have seen, *chelebi?*

– Well, listen and I'll tell you, said your father, without showing how flattered he was. You see, the word *chelebi* means 'distinguished gentleman'. Listen and I'll tell you, efendi. You just saw a dirty Kurd steal my lamb. You saw it with your own two eyes.

– With my own two eyes, chelebi?

– Of course, you idiot. You didn't see it with my eyes, did you?

– And what kind of lamb was it, chelebi? Was it one with a black marking around its neck? Or one with several markings? And how old was the lamb? When was it dropped by its mother?

– I'll have to find out first, efendi.

– But surely the lamb is still in the police station.

– Well, then I'll make my way to the police station.

And then your father came back and said to his false witness, 'It's true, the lamb does indeed have black markings: one around its neck and one on its snout. And its mother dropped it exactly two weeks ago.'

– Am I supposed to have seen its mother giving birth to it, chelebi?

– No, you idiot.

– So what is it that I am supposed to have seen, chelebi?

– Well, what do you think, you idiot! You saw this filthy Kurd steal my lamb, the one with the two black markings that was dropped by its mother two weeks ago.

– And what did this filthy Kurd look like, chelebi?

– It doesn't matter what he looked like. The kadi will show him to you and you will say, 'That's the man!'

– But that must mean that I saw his face when he stole the lamb. The one with the two black markings that was dropped by its mother two weeks ago.

– Of course you saw the Kurd's face!

– As he was stealing the lamb?

– Of course, you idiot.

– And how much will you pay, chelebi?

– Half a piaster.

– But, chelebi. I won't swear a false oath and sell my soul for just half a piaster.

– Then I'll give you a few paras as well.

– But, chelebi, do you expect me to sell my soul for half a piaster and a few paras?

– Then I'll give you a silver piaster. What do you say to that?

– Now that's more like it, chelebi. You see, I'll do anything for a silverling. But you're forgetting that Allah will demand alms from me.

– What alms?

– You see, chelebi, if I commit a sin by swearing a false oath,

I will have to either fast for seven days or pay alms to the poor. Only then will Allah forgive my sins.

– Then fast for seven days.

– But, chelebi, how am I supposed to fast for seven days? Can't you see how emaciated I am already? Do you think it's right that I should be forced make myself even thinner and suffer the mockery of my wife and my thirteen children?

– Then I suppose you will have to pay alms to obtain Allah's forgiveness.

– But, chelebi, how should I pay alms with just one single silver piaster? You will have to pay me another silver piaster: one for me, one for Allah.

– Alright, let's make it two.

– But, chelebi, two piasters means I only saw the Kurd's back. I didn't see his face. How do you expect me to have seen both his back and his face for just two silver piasters?

– How much will it take for you to be able to tell the kadi that you saw his face, too?

– Three silver piasters, chelebi. Mere pocket money for an educated and wealthy chelebi such as yourself. Do you wish to poke fun at my misery? Is it not disgraceful enough that I, a practicing Muslim, have to give a false oath for an uncircumcised giaour and rayah like you? And all for just three lousy silver piasters?

Your father now started bawling and clamoring and tearing at his hair. The other children laughed and whispered something in his ear. Your father screamed at the false witness. 'Efendi, you are ruining me! I'm ruined. You see, I have to pay the same to the second witness. And I also bribed the kadi, and the captain and the saptieh. And this whole thing is costing me more than that lamb was even worth. I'm ruined. Can't an uncircumcised man find any sympathy in this world?'

There was one boy playing the game who was older than the others. Although he had been christened Garabed, as time went by everyone simply began calling him Garo. He was ten and the youngest son of Kupelian, the saddle maker, a man who once had his entire herd stolen from his stable by the Kurds.

Now, this son of Kupelian the saddle maker, this Garo, he was a strange customer, a trouble-maker and a spoilsport. Whenever they played war games, he would always take on the role of the valiant yet unarmed Armenian, and he staunchly refused to ever change role and play one of the cowardly yet armed Kurds or Turks. He also never wanted any of the cowardly Kurds or Turks to pretend to kill him – which, of course, was part of the game. Instead, he simply pretended to join in and waited for the Kurds and Turks to attack him with their wooden swords, at which point he would furiously set about defending himself by punching and kicking. He would take the wooden swords away from his enemies and beat them with it until they ran away crying. People said that this Garo boy was not only a spoilsport: he was a future Armenian freedom fighter, most likely one whose life would end on the Turkish gallows. He would be a nationalist.

The nationalists!

In the 1880s everyone was talking about them. One of them even came to the village once to speak with the priest, the mayor, the blacksmith and a few other men. He even spoke with Vardan's father, Hagob. But he didn't stay for long, and he and his mule were soon on their way.

Vardan didn't know who the nationalists were and what the man on the mule wanted. But his grandfather soon explained. 'He wanted us to allow his people to bring guns into the village, which the mayor would then have hidden, most likely in the cemetery.'

– But that's where the dead are buried?

– Yes, my little lamb.

– Are the guns hidden on top of the graves?

– No, my little lamb. They are hidden inside the graves. Right alongside the dead.

– Can the dead still sleep with guns in their graves?

– Of course, my little lamb. They'll sleep even more soundly because they know that we need the weapons to defend ourselves against the Kurds.

– Are the dead afraid of the Kurds?

– They used to fear them, my little lamb. And they are glad to see that we, the living, no longer wish to be afraid either.

– Did the man on that mule actually bring some guns here?

– No, my little lamb.

– And why not?

– Well, why do you think, my little lamb? It is forbidden, that's why. Do you think we all want to get sent to the gallows?

There were rumors in the village that the nationalists had hidden guns in many villages. The red-haired blacksmith said, 'It's time for the Armenians to fight back.'

And Garo said, 'The next time the saptiehs come by with the

tax collectors, followed by Sheikh Suleyman's Kurdish riders, we should blow their heads off.'

But Priest Kapriel Hamadian, who always attended these meetings, said, 'No, no, that would bring about misfortune.'

And the mayor said, 'The Turks would send troops here and it would be the start of a new tebk.'

– True, said the mayor's wife. A new tebk. Heaven forbid.

– The nationalists are our misfortune, said the mayor. The Turks and the Kurds are just waiting to find weapons here in our village. It will give them an excuse to kill us all.

The priest said, 'The great tebk! I can see many gallows. And I can see fire and smoke.'

Once as many as one hundred saptiehs rode into the village with a yuzbashi to search for guns. They rifled through the Armenians' houses, dug up the fields and the courtyards; they even went into the graveyard to lift up the stone slabs resting on top of the graves. But they didn't find a single gun anywhere."

6

"The older you become," said the storyteller, "the faster time passes you by. Just look at Vardan's great-grandmother; she stopped counting the years moons ago. Recently she said, 'Oh, our Vardan is already hopping about like a young foal. He's jumping around the courtyard like a flea on a kilim rug, and he rides like a big boy … on Ceyda, I mean, that shameless jenny that allows herself be mounted by the water carrier. And yet it wasn't but one year ago that he was still peeing in his diaper. And do you remember, Zovinar, my sweet little granddaughter, that time when my daughter Hamest bathed him in saltwater? It wasn't that long ago' – But grandmother, Vardan's mother said. That was years ago.

Vardan, who was growing up so fast, was also starting to realize that time stood still for no one, and noticed that his third pair of shalvar trousers, which his father gave him for his seventh birthday, were growing shorter by the day.

– Those trousers aren't getting shorter, his father once said. It's your legs: they're getting longer.

The same thing was happening to the other children, too, especially Avetik, the red-haired son of the red-haired blacksmith. He appeared to be growing much faster than most, and already towered over all the other children his age in the village. At age nine, Avetik was already wearing his father's clothes and trying to ignore the rumor going around the village that when he was small, he had drunk the milk of a gypsy who, in turn, had drunk from the teat of a long-legged dog. – Be that as it may, one thing had become clear: The Lord God does not share out time equally, and although it seemed to be passing his great-grandmother by in leaps and bounds, for Vardan, time was moving much more slowly; it plodded along just like Ceyda the jenny whenever Vardan led her through the nearby gorges.

Not much happened in the village. Visitors from neighboring villages and small cities came by every once in a while. Sometimes they came from one of the larger cities, such as Moush, Erzurum, Diyarbakir, Van or Bakir. Once a man even came from Constantinople. He was stylishly dressed and wore a western suit. Vardan's grandfather said, 'One day your uncle from America will come here, too: my son Nahapeth, who works over there as a rag seller. He's a wealthy man.'

– How many uncles do I have in America?

– A bunch, my little lamb. But I can only remember the names of two.

– And who is the second?

– My son, Krikor. The arabadji.

– But I have another uncle who's an arabadji in Bakir.

– True, my little lamb. One is an arabadji in Bakir, the other an arabadji in New York.

– Does my uncle in New York have a mule to pull his araba?

– No, my little lamb. He has a proper horse. An American mustang, no less.

– What kind of a horse is that?

– A Native American horse, my little lamb.

– And what kind of araba does he have?

– He has one with wheels that turn around an axle.

– But, Grandfather. The wheels of an araba don't turn around an axle. I've seen it on our araba. They're nailed on to the axle. I even did it myself once.

– We live here in Hayastan, my little lamb. We still use the same arabas as those of our ancestors.

– And in America?

– Everything is completely different over there, my little lamb. All the wheels in America turn around an axle. And believe it or not, the arabadjis over there don't put dry flour onto their arabas when they start to squeak as we do here. They rub them with oil: a devilish oil that they dig out of the earth.

– Does Uncle Krikor do that, too?

– Yes. That's exactly what he does.

– What does Uncle Krikor look like?

– I can't remember, my little lamb. I only have a photo of your other uncle: Nahapeth, the rag seller.

– And what does he look like?

– The image isn't very clear. All you can see is a big hat … a hat with a wide brim. Vardan laughed. I've heard people talk about those strange hats, but I've never actually seen one.

– Well, you won't have to wait long, said his grandfather. When your uncle from America visits, you'll lay your eyes on a hat just like it.

Of course, people from the village of Yedi Su sometimes travelled themselves, mostly to the neighboring villages, but sometimes to the larger cities. They came back with bizarre stories of enormous bazaars, beggars, brothels, city walls, sprung horse-drawn carriages and beautiful women that smelt of rose and lily water. Everyone admired and envied those who dared travel outside the village, but there wasn't always cause for jealousy; those who passed along lonely, narrow mountain paths and were subsequently robbed, or even killed, by the Kurds were envied by no one."

The storyteller said to the Last Thought, "Do you see that bare, white, chalkstone hillside just where the village ends? The people call it *Ak Bayir:* the white hill. And just three donkey's farts away from that hill – which isn't even half a smoke – three donkey's farts, and no farther, lies *Gobekli Tepe,* the potbelly hill, the one where the children play their war games … It's the perfect site. And there, between Ak Bayir and Gobekli Tepe, stands an old hut. You can even see it."

"Yes, I can see it," said the Last Thought, "because I see everything that you see. And I, too, can see the white hillside that the people call Ak Bayir, and the potbelly hill called Gobekli Tepe. And I can hear the war cries of the children as they play. And I can even see the old hut and the tonir's smoke that wafts out through the open door and into the air."

"There is no tonir in that hut," said the storyteller. "It's a Turkish oven that looks just like an Armenian tonir but which the Turks call by a different name."

"What name?"

"They call it *tandir.*"

"Who lives in that hut?"

"The only Turkish family in the village."

"You haven't mentioned them until now."

"I forgot, my little lamb. I quite simply forgot."

"And why, Meddah?"

"I don't know, my little lamb. The word *Turk* is like a terrible illness, and people only ever mention terrible illnesses when they feel threatened by them. But you see, these Turks living in Yedi Su are a threat to no one; they have been living peacefully side-by-side with the Armenians for many years. People in the village have grown so accustomed to them that they no longer even notice that they're there."

"Do the Turkish children play with the Armenian children on the vast playground on the side of the potbelly hill that they call Gobekli Tepe?"

"But of course, my little lamb."

"And do they join in the dancing at Armenian weddings?"

"Yes, my little lamb."

"And no one thinks anything of it?"

"No one thinks a thing.

The only thing that the Armenians didn't like about these peaceful Turks," said the storyteller, "were the names of their men and boys as they were the same as those of the Turkish tax collectors, saptiehs, officials and Kurdish robbers: all of them men who made the villagers feel uneasy and whom people wished not to be reminded of. Thus the villagers simply gave anyone with one of these unpopular names a nickname, a Turkish one of course, and these new names were more fitting than the original ones, avoided any embarrassing mix-ups and reflected the unique character of the people they were bestowed upon. And so it was that the head of this Turkish family, whose name was Suleyman – the same as the dreaded leader of the Kurds – came to simply be known as *Tashak*."

"Tashak?"

"That's right."

"What does that mean?"

"It's the term used to describe what a man carries around in his scrotum."

"And what does Suleyman have in his scrotum?"

"The same as any other man, my little lamb, only his are a little more conspicuous. You see, this Suleyman once carried a heavy sack of flour on his back and suffered a groin hernia. And believe it or not, people now say his scrotum hangs down to his knee, although no one has ever actually seen it because Suleyman never lowers his shalvar trousers in front of others, not even when he's working in the fields and has to urgently answer the call of nature as one occasionally does. And as there isn't a public hamam in Yedi Su where the villagers could go to take a steam bath together, nobody has been able to confirm whether or not it is actually true."

"So how do people know that Suleyman's scrotum hangs right down to his knee?"

"You can tell by the way he walks. You see, Suleyman walks as if he has several sacks of whey hidden between his legs."

"You don't say."

"That's right."

"But that must be quite embarrassing."

"Indeed, my little lamb. Particularly when the tax collectors come to the village. When they're there, poor Suleyman daren't even cross the street for fear that the tax collectors might think he has something hidden inside his trousers."

"Inside his trousers?"

"Yes."

"A mysterious, dangling ballsack?"

"That's right."

"Tashak?"

"Tashak.

Tashak's eldest son was named *Bodur,* which means 'short-legged man'. Like his father, he too waddled around but for a very different reason and in a completely different way. His strange gait was caused by his slightly bowed, outwardly-curving and excessively short legs. Bodur was already fifteen and hoped to soon marry. People teased him and said he should be careful that his future wife didn't step over his future son without making sure she took the same step backwards, otherwise their child would end up just like his short-legged father whose little Turkish legs stopped growing because his mother had stepped over him as he played on the prayer rug when he was less than forty days old and had forgotten to take a precautionary step backwards.

Bodur's younger brother was called *Tiryaki* – the addict – a name usually used to refer to chain smokers. The small children would run behind him on the street shouting *fosur-fosur,* which means something like, *puff, puff.* Fosur-Fosur Tiryaki couldn't afford to buy any tobacco himself, and so he would smoke anything he could lay his hands on, mostly the hairy, sun-dried silks found on ears of corn, but he would also smoke hay, limp grass and the occasional dried cabbage leaf, the exact same cabbage leaves which the women in the village used – either dried or fresh – to make delicious stuffed cabbage filled with meat and rice and covered in a thick sauce. The Armenians called it *patat.* The Turks called it *sarma.*

Yes," said the storyteller. "It makes your mouth water just thinking about it. Would you like to hear more about the Turks? Well, there were also a few little girls in this Turkish family and they all wiggled their backsides when they walked, which was a dangerous thing indeed. You see, none of the Armenian boys dared lay a hand on those rears as they wiggled by, for they knew that a Turkish man's dagger isn't just for decoration, and this was particularly true for the brothers of these young girls. The ten-year-old was called *Hulja,* the dreamer, the nine-year-old *Shirin,* the sweetie, and the seven-year-old was called *Meral,* the doe. Tashak's wife was simply called *Neshee,* which meant joy, most probably because she was always in a good mood and was never without a smile, or because people said that she came into this world with a cry of joy. Tashak's youngest son, who was in charge of the hens, was given the nickname *Gog-Gog* and was three years older than your father.

Gog-Gog was the name used to describe the call given when feeding hens. When the sun came up, Tashak would kneel before his front door on his prayer rug with his Turkish head facing toward Mecca. Whilst Tashak twisted and turned into all the positions of a pious Muslim carrying out his morning prayers, Gog-Gog ran around the house and called the hens over with cries of 'gog-gog-gog'. Anyone passing by the Turks' house early in the morning would know the exact routine: the rooster would crow, Tashak would pray to Allah and Gog-Gog would beckon the hens.

Just imagine the scene: The boys are standing on Gobekli Tepe playing a game to see who can pee the fastest. Your father is four and standing next to Gog-Gog. For the first time in his young life he lays eyes on a circumcised cock. He is so shocked and appalled that he pees on his own knee and runs home crying.

– Why is he crying? asks Hamest.

– He just saw a circumcised meat hook, says Vardan's grandfather.

– What do you mean, a meat hook?

– You know, a meat hook!

– Many years ago I witnessed a circumcision in a Turkish village, says Vardan's grandfather. It was like a wedding.

– Like a wedding?

– Like a wedding.

– Well, I can't remember it so well now, says Vardan's grandfather. But what I do recall is seeing the men in the village and the little fella, whose little sausage they were going to slash, gathered in the house of the mukhtar. Everyone was talking and smoking. Then I saw the father of the boy appear from the mukhtar's stable with a white horse. He took the little boy by the hand and placed him on top of the horse. The boy rode from house to house and everyone wished him good luck. A little prince atop a white horse; a prince dressed in white clothes with red stripes and golden embroidery. On his head he wore an embroidered, blue kepi.

– Yes, *and?* said Hamest.

– And the boy's father led the horse by the reins. He led it all the way to the house, where the *sunnetshi* was already waiting.

    – Who's that?

    – The man who performs the circumcision.

    – And then what happened?

    – At first, nothing, said Vardan's grandfather. Then suddenly a group of other men appeared. They grabbed the small prince, yanked his shalvar trousers down, and the circumciser grabbed the bird dangling between the prince's skinny little legs – grabbed it, just like that – pulled it all the way out of its hiding place and suddenly he held a sharp knife in his hand.

    – And then?

    – Then he cut off the little bit of skin.

    – Is that all?

    – That's all.

– Of course, the sunnetshi applied a bit of flour to the wound, and the father took the crying boy in his arms and sat him on top of a large cushion by the front door so that everyone in the village could see him. And outside the drummers and flute-players played their tunes. Some people began to dance, and then, before they knew it, the whole village was dancing.

– It seems our Vardan had quite a shock when he saw Gog-Gog's stump.

    – Yes, said Vardan's grandfather.

    – He must have thought it was a bird's beak without any skin?

    – But Hamest, birds' beaks don't have any skin.

    – Then he must have thought it was a frog's head.

    – A skinless frog's head? Perhaps one that had been scalped?

– Precisely."

7

"There are things a man won't do for fear of losing his dignity. Collecting cow pats is one of them. This task was often left to the women, but mostly it was done by small children. In summer the tezek was left out to dry in the sun on the flat roofs of the houses; in winter they were simply slapped against the walls of the living room where they were left to dry by the heat of the tonir. Once they were dry, they would simply fall off the wall; all that was left to do was pick them up. At the age of four, Vardan was already running after the other children as they went out onto the fields to collect tezek. He copied them and sobbed loudly when they pushed him away. Later on, when he was older, he would push back and get into fights with the other boys and girls who tried to get ahead of him on the field. He was often assisted in the task by the red-haired Avetik. They collected and shared out the spoils evenly. Avetik said that perhaps they needn't take all of their tezek home; perhaps they could sell some of it instead, but that would be a job for a shrewd tradesman who knew a thing or two about business. He once said to Vardan, 'Well, what do you say? You want to become a poet, don't you? Got an idea where we could sell our tezek?'

– In the city, said Vardan. The people in the villages already have plenty.

– And how will we get to the city?

– By donkey, said Vardan.

– Then we would need another sack.

– I can steal one from my father, said Vardan. He won't even notice it's gone.

– And what if the Kurds steal the sack from us?

– You mean when we're riding through the mountains?

– Yes, exactly.

– The Kurds don't steal tezek.

– How do you know?

– I just do.

But the boys still weren't brave enough to venture out of the village on their own.

– When we're older, said Avetik, then we'll be strong enough to take on the Kurds if they ever do decide to steal our tezek.

– Then we could take Garo with us, said Vardan. He's sure to have muscles as big as those of the blacksmith in a few years' time.

– You mean as big as my father's?

– Yes.

– That's not a bad idea.

– Or we wait until I'm officially engaged. Then I'll be grown up and old enough to go on business trips whenever I wish. Before then I doubt my father would let me go down to the city by myself.

– You've got a point there, said Avetik. I'm sure mine wouldn't let me go either.

– Well, there you have it, said Vardan.

– And what's happening with your engagement? I thought

you got engaged years ago?

– Well, obviously I got engaged years ago, said Vardan, but the official engagement party will only take place once my bride starts bleeding from between her legs all by herself.

– Who told you that?

– My father.

– How old is your bride?

– She's three years younger than me. She's now five.

– And when will she start bleeding from between her legs all by herself?

– Only when she's old.

– How old?

– Well, I think around eleven or twelve.

– But our tezek business can't wait that long.

– You're right there.

Once Vardan's father took him in the donkey-drawn cart to the mill. It was the first journey he ever took. The mill was located in a neighboring Armenian village called *Piredjik,* which translates directly into Turkish as *nest of fleas.* And Piredjik lay in *Sinek-Dere,* the Valley of the Fly. Piredjik wasn't far away. If the road there were a straight caravan road, you could perhaps reach it in twenty smokes. But as it was, travelers had to navigate mountain roads and steep ravines, and so the trip actually ended up taking several hours. The mill, operated by an Armenian, stood at the entrance of the Valley of the Fly and only ran when water levels were high: either in spring, when the snow up in the mountains would melt, or on days of torrential rain. And as there was neither rain nor high water on the day that Vardan and his father journeyed to the mill, the miller said to Hagob, 'Hagob Efendi, how should I get the mill to run when there is not a flake of snow in the mountains or even a wisp of cloud in the sky? Perhaps you would like me to fill up the stream with my pee?'

– Now you mention it, where is the stream? asked Hagob.

– The earth swallowed it up, said the miller.

– And when will the earth spit it back out again?

– When it rains, said the miller. Or next spring when the snow up in the mountains melts.

– How about, asked Hagob, how about if all three of us pee into the stream, my son Vardan, you and I? Perhaps then the stream will spring back to life, and the earth will spit back out all that it has swallowed up?

On their way back from the mill, they crossed paths with Bulbul, who was riding home on her nameless donkey – all the way back to her hut, high up in the mountains. She was sitting slumped on its back. Bulbul had tied a headless rooster to the donkey's tail and with every step the creature took, drops of blood would drip down from the spot where the animal's head had been chopped off, leaving red dots on the narrow mountain path below.

– Why did you cut the rooster's head off before you got it home? asked Hagob.

– Because the donkey was afraid of it, said Bulbul, and because he was becoming agitated and was just about ready to throw the rooster off, and me with it. You see, that rooster was a raucous creature, and it was screeching and flapping around on the donkey's tail where I had tied it.

– Who gave you the rooster?

– Old Hamest, your mother, said Bulbul.

– Is that our Abdul Hamid?

– No, said Bulbul. You can see that it's not him. This is a stray rooster that flew into your chicken yard not that long ago to stir up a whole lot of trouble. You know, Abdul Hamid can't stand to have another rooster near him.

– But perhaps this rooster was stronger than Abdul Hamid; perhaps we should have kept him?

– He wasn't stronger, said Bulbul. Abdul Hamid would have pecked him to death if old Hamest would have let him. Trust me, Hagob Efendi, two roosters in the same chicken yard is even worse than two women stood at the same tonir.

Once Bulbul had left, Vardan asked, 'Is it true that Bulbul is a midwife, and is it true that she helped bring me into this world?'

– Yes, it's true.

– Did she breastfeed me, too?

– No, she's no wet nurse.

– She's a Kurd. How does it work with the Kurds? Do they breastfeed their children?

– Of course.

– And what's their milk like?

– It's as sweet as any mother's milk.

– Is it as sweet as my mother's milk?

– Yes, said Hagob.

They spoke about Bulbul for quite some time. They spoke of her lonely hut high up in the mountains where she lived alone with her nameless donkey and her hens, and they wondered whom she must talk to as darkness falls on one of those long, lonely nights by the tonir. Finally, Hagob said, 'She talks to her animals, and I bet you, my son, that she never bores of their company. You see, animals are better listeners than humans.'

– And why doesn't she have a husband?

– They say she used to have one, said Hagob ... before she came to this region ... but her husband chased her out of the house.

– Chased her out? Just like that?

– Yes.

– Is that something only Muslims do?

– No, said Hagob. Sometimes Christians do it, too.

– And what about the Armenians?

– You know, I'm not entirely sure, said Hagob. But I've never heard of it happening to any of our friends or family. Come to think of it, I don't remember a single time when it happened in Yedi Su, even if the husband and wife had argued: What God has joined together, let no man put asunder.

One day something took place in Yedi Su that Vardan would remember for the rest of his life. There was an Armenian trader who lived close to the Khatisians. He had an aquiline-nosed wife who people claimed needed a good seeing to every night. The trader and his wife already had thirteen children, and one night the trader turned to his wife and said, 'That's enough.'

The trader was rarely home as his business took him to the vast bazaars of Bakir. Most of the time he would return with a mule-drawn cart filled with gifts.

No one knew exactly what type of business the man dealt in. They said he stood around the bazaars of Bakir with a Jew and a Greek. The Jew had a gray horse, the Greek a gray donkey. As the light faded and it became difficult to tell the difference between the two animals and their similar gray coats, the Armenian would hastily find a trusting Turk to buy the gray riding horse from the

Jew, and in the hazy light of dusk he would deftly swap it with the Greek's donkey by distracting the Turk or deceiving him with some other trick. The Jew and the Greek would help him pull off the move. Once the deal had been done and they had helped the Turk up onto the donkey, the three would scarper, spend the night in the Greek's house and the next day they would buy a similar donkey that cost less than the amount the Turk had paid for the horse and share out the profit – the surplus value, no less – fairly between them. But, of course, the pitcher will go to the well once too often. One day the three were caught and arrested.

Of course, there was a trial. The only teacher at the village school, who suffered from consumption but was an educated man, even arranged for a lawyer from Van, who was a relative of his, to defend them. This lawyer, at least so the teacher told the farmers of Yedi Su, had tried to prove to the court that the surplus value that the three crooks had made had nothing to do with the Theory of Surplus Value put forward by a certain Karl Marx and that the three men were indeed loyal Ottoman citizens and that they had nothing to do with the radical ideas of an infidel Frank of German-Jewish descent that had been brought into Turkey by the vagabonds, the conspirators, the deadbeats, the loons and the leftist students from that deplorable land of Frankistan. But the Armenian lawyer's plea was of little use as the crooks couldn't scrape together the bribe they needed to pay the High Court. And so the inevitable happened: the three were taken to prison, but only for one year and the few days between Ramadan and the Bairam festival.

So, the Armenian handler's aquiline-nosed wife, who needed a good seeing to more or less every night, waited patiently for her husband to return. But one day her patience ran out, partly because of her aquiline nose, for people said that those with aquiline noses simply could not hold on, particularly when the tickling between their legs was all too much to bear.

In 1889 the woman suddenly fell pregnant, even though her husband had been in prison for months. Priest Kapriel Hamadian said that Armenians did not commit adultery and suggested that perhaps the Holy Spirit had taken pity on the aquiline-nosed woman because He knew she couldn't wait and so had planted His seed within her, for only the God of the Jews was a chastising God, but the God of the Christians was compassionate, not unlike Allah, the God of the Mohammedans, whose compassion Tashak often spoke of.

When the child was born and word got out that it was a little red-haired girl, the priest said that she couldn't have been fathered by the Holy Spirit as the Holy Spirit would never father a red-haired child as such infants were possessed by the Devil. Some people in the village suspected that the red-haired blacksmith had put a curse on the woman, whilst others said that perhaps the blacksmith's eldest son, who, although dark-haired, still carried his father's genes, had fathered a little red-haired girl with the trader's wife. The reason for their suspicions was the fact that the blacksmith's eldest son pestered all the girls in the village, but not only that: He also stared at the rear of the handler's aquiline-nosed wife every time she went to fetch water from the well, even though she already had thirteen children and was no longer a girl. To cut a long story short, the blacksmith's eldest son was accused of having fathered the little red-haired bastard with the trader's wife.

For whatever reason, Mukhtar Ephrem Abovian denounced the woman, ordered her head to be shaved and had her and the bastard child sit backward on a donkey. The donkey was slowly led through the village, passing from house to house. The woman sat crying with the small bastard in her arms. People spat on her, rubbed mud on her face and showed no mercy to the small bastard, who was also spat upon and smeared with mud. What Vardan remembered most vividly about that day was that it was mainly the old, nagging women who seemed to be filled with the most rage. Their venomous spit seemed to have no end. When the whole spectacle was over, Vardan's father said, 'The old women are the worst. They are jealous because they too would have liked to have had a taste of that blacksmith's son's cock.'

It's true: It wasn't the men in the village who seemed particularly vexed by the episode, it was the old women. It was they who were the true guardians of morality. And it is also true that the trader didn't chase his wife out of the house upon his return. People said she slept alone in a corner of the oda. They said she cried out and cursed loudly in her sleep. And they said that the little red-haired bastard didn't sleep in its cradle but with its mother, and at night it would crawl around beneath the jorgan where its small hands would play with the ear of corn between the legs of its crying, cursing mother.

Your father's childhood … the village of Yedi Su … the menacing eyes of the Kurds high up in the mountains … the death lurking in the files of the Turkish officials that would someday rise up from its pages to cleanse the forgotten provinces ... the Sultan in Constantinople, who didn't like Christians, particularly the Armenians ... stories ... somewhere out at the ends of the earth. Nobody had even noticed the first signs of a brewing storm that would descend up them like the biblical floods.

So," said the storyteller. "All sorts of things are whirling around in my head, and I've just been saying the first thing that pops into my mind. I don't know why but I haven't told you anything about your father's brothers and sisters. Blame it on my constant jabbering."

"My father's brothers and sisters?"

"All older than him as he was the youngest, but you know that already."

"I certainly do, Meddah."

"One was three years older than your father. His name was Dikran, just like the man the Turks would have hanged from the Gate of Happiness years later."

"Dikran, the cobbler? The one with the yellow boots? The most beautiful boots in the whole of Bakir?"

"Yes, that's the one."

"Is he the same Dikran?"

"He is the same man. When he was just seven years old, he said to your four-year-old father, 'When I grow up, I will become a cobbler.' Then he added, 'I will move to Bakir, to the big city, and I will make a pair of yellow boots that will be the most beautiful in all of Bakir.'

– Bakir? your father asked.

– Bakir, said Dikran. Many of our uncles live there and one of them is a cobbler. He will teach me the trade.

– Do you mean Uncle Levon?

– No, he's the arabadji. Uncle Dro is the cobbler."

"Is that true?"

"It is indeed, my little lamb. Uncle Dro was a cobbler in Bakir and the man who would later train Dikran as his apprentice. Dikran became a good cobbler. He married, set up his own business, fathered many children and one day he made a pair of yellow boots out of goatskin leather – wonderful, genuine goatskin leather – that looked so elegant that people said they were the most beautiful pair in the whole of Bakir.

The gypsies in particular were amazed by Dikran's yellow boots. One of them once tried to trade a young foal for the pair, but Dikran refused to let them go.

I remember how it happened," said the storyteller, "The gypsies came from the horse market and trotted through the Armenian artisan district. They stopped in front of Dikran's house. Dikran was sitting behind his workbench cleaning the pair of yellow boots.

– I'll give you a foal for those boots, said one of the gypsies.

– But these boots are not for sale, said Dikran

– Everything a man owns can be bought, said the gypsy. It's just a matter of finding the right price. How about I throw in a goat?

– But I don't want to sell them, said Dikran. The gypsy said, 'What's so special about those yellow boots? Do they give you magical powers, like Aladdin and his lamp?'

– Something like that, said Dikran. Looking at them cements

my faith. And when I am sure of my faith, I get more enjoyment out of my work and I do a better job.

    – Of which faith do you speak, efendi?

    – Of my faith in my art and my faith in myself.

– Let me explain, said Dikran. These boots have brought me good luck. You see, the thought that one day I would be able to make such a magnificent pair of boots spurred me on to work harder, and so it's thanks to these boots that I became a good cobbler.

    – They brought you good luck, you say?

    – Yes.

    – Then let us read your palm so that we can see if those boots really are lucky.

    – You want to read my palm?

    – Yes, said the gypsy.

But the gypsy had no idea how to read palms and so he called over his old mother, who then came and read Dikran's future.

I see a hanging man, said the old gypsy. He's wearing the same boots as this fella.

– What else do you see? asked Dikran.

    – I see a blind beggar, said the gypsy. And he's placing your boots inside his old sack.

    But Dikran just laughed and quickly retracted his hand. He said to the woman, 'You just want to scare me because I won't trade you my boots for the foal and the goat.' "

The storyteller said, "This story, the one that told of a hanging man wearing Dikran's boots, and of a blind beggar and his old sack – this story quickly became the talk of the town. Even Priest Kapriel Hamadian got wind of it, but he responded simply by saying, 'That's just nothing but gypsy drivel. A good Christian should cross himself three times before he asks a gypsy to tell his fortune.'

– And what should my son Dikran do now? Hagob asked the priest.

– He should cross himself if ever the gypsies show up at his door again.

– And if they don't show up again?

– Then he should rub garlic into his boots, said the priest. And afterwards he should leave them for seven days, no more, no less, then he should touch the Holy Bible with his right hand while putting the boots back on with his left.

Many years later," said the storyteller, "your father was on his way back from visiting a relative in Bakir. As he was passing under the Gate of Happiness with his donkey and cart, he saw a sick, blind beggar lying by the side of the road. The passing traffic didn't seem too concerned about running him over where he lay, and the man would have almost certainly been crushed and trampled to death by the animals and carts had your father not taken pity on him. Without hesitation, he invited the man to join him in his cart and took him back to Yedi Su where the Khatisian family nursed him back to health. Your father brought him back to the Gate of Happiness some weeks later. That blind beggar was called Mechmed Efendi.

Back then Mechmed Efendi said to your father, 'You have saved my life. One day I will do the same for you.' And then he said, 'I know your brother, Dikran. He often passes by the Gate of Happiness to give me half a piaster and to chat with me a while. Your brother Dikran is a good man, that's why I always offer him some good advice.'

– Then surely you've heard the story about the old gypsy's prophecy?

– You mean that business with the hanging man ... that's supposed to happen sometime in the distant future ... a hanging man wearing Dikran's yellow boots?

– Yes, Mechmed Efendi.

– And the business with the blind beggar and his old sack into which the hanging man's boot are said to disappear?

– Yes, Mechmed Efendi.

– What about the old sack?

– It could be your sack, Mechmed Efendi, said your father. As he said those words, he placed the blind man's hand on the old sack that he always dragged around with him. But Mechmed Efendi just shook his head in bewilderment and said, 'But, Vardan Efendi, there are many blind beggars, and there are also many old sacks. Besides, I heard that your brother Dikran used garlic and the Bible to break the curse on his boots long ago.'

– Do you believe in our Bible, Mechmed Efendi?

– I believe in the word of the Prophet, Mechmed Efendi said, and they say he gave an interpretation of the Bible, albeit a slightly different one.

I hope you're not expecting me to tell you the stories of all your father's brothers and sisters," said the storyteller, "or even the stories of his aunts and uncles or any of his other relatives, some of whom were part of the kertastan in Yedi Su but most of whom lived in Bakir and other cities in Turkey and the country's former provinces, such as Greece and Bulgaria, Romania and Hungary, or even in Serbia and Bosnia, or in cities such as Sarajevo, which was once a Turkish city itself, or even the stories of those who have journeyed over the ocean, like so many Armenians; Armenians who the Turks say subvert minds just like the Jews, turning up everywhere in their invisibility cloaks and masks to strike terror into people's hearts. Where would the tale end if I stopped here to regale you with every single story? And how will I ever get around to finishing my own story in what little time there is left? You see, Thovma Khatisian is nearing the end; he doesn't have much time. And I'm sure he still wants to hear as much of the story as I can possibly share with his Last Thought. That is why you should heed my words when I, the storyteller, say that time is running out. But if you like, I suppose I could tell you a few more stories, about two of your father's sisters and three of his brothers who were particularly close to his heart and so deserve a mention."

And the storyteller said, "One sister was fourteen years older than your father and was already married when he was born. Her name was *Makrouhi,* the clean one, although she was anything but clean. People said she, like the Kurds, only washed in summer, but that she had a heart of gold. Makrouhi came by every day to visit as she lived on this side of the village square, by that I mean on the Khatisians' side, barely half a smoke away. She helped her mother and grandmother around the house and played with your father. She really did have a heart of gold for she would feed your father treats when he was still lying in his cradle, bathe him in salt when his grandmother was away and clean his cuts when, later as a young boy, he fell over or hurt himself playing *Kurds, Turks and Armenians.* This Makrouhi was married to Armenag the master saddle maker. Yes, that's right: Armenag, although people tended to call him quite simply Armen. And this Armen had large, rugged, powerful hands ... and they were righteous hands, too, for they beat Makrouhi every single day. They beat her until she started to wash regularly and she did justice to the name Makrouhi once more.

Another one of your father's sisters was called *Aghavni,* which means 'dove', and she certainly lived up to her name for she really was as gentle as a dove. One day she flew away to marry Pesak, the son of a rich carpet seller from Bakir. This Pesak was an unremarkable man, despite the fact that he wore glasses and had studied in Stambul for a time. Who would have thought that at the turn of the century this Pesak would become a Dashnak and then, later, one of their most-wanted leaders?

I'm sure you'd like to hear how her marriage to Pesak came about? – Well, my little lamb, it happened thanks to Manoushag, the marriage broker, a woman known in the village as *Mietsnort Manoushag,* which means something along the lines of violet, the matchmaker.

No, my little lamb. Manoushag, the violet, was neither young nor pretty. She was what the Armenians call *duhne menatzaz,* and very aptly so. You see, *duhne menatzaz* means 'stayed at home' or, in other words, an old maid.

Now, I know what you're going to ask, my little lamb. You'd like to know whether your father's engagement with his future bride, the daughter of the mayor, was arranged by Manoushag. Well, my little lamb, you know perfectly well that it wasn't; Hagob arranged the engagement himself, which was unusual but that's just how it happened. And that was also the reason why Manoushag, the marriage broker, was quite angry at Hagob when she found out that he and the mayor had gone behind her back and exchanged engagement coins before the sacred tonir.

One of your father's brothers was called Sarkis. He became a goldsmith in Bakir. This Sarkis married an aquiline-nosed woman who was just as randy as the aquiline-nosed wife of the Armenian trader in Yedi Su. It was also the reason why Sarkis was pale and hollow-cheeked; you see, his wife just couldn't get enough of the bone that Sarkis had between his legs and which – so they said – the Lord God had bestowed upon him mainly for the purpose of peeing rather than procreating. But Sarkis the goldsmith had to have it off with his wife every single night if he wanted to have peace and quiet in his tonir. Of course, he didn't want his wife to end up beneath another man, which would most certainly have led to another head-shaving, or, as Hagob would say, 'That woman will end up sat facing backwards on a donkey with her head shaved, just like the aquiline-nosed wife of that Armenian trader from Yedi Su,' even though the goldsmith's wife had yet to give birth to a red-haired bastard like the Armenian trader's wife: a bastard child who enjoyed playing with ears of corn, particularly between its mother's legs, although they had no business being there as they were God's fruit from the field and not the bone of a man.

However, the goldsmith's wife was not only hungry for sex; she was also hungry for money. And so she often said to Sarkis, 'Why do you slave away at your workbench from morning till night? Why don't you do the same as the money changers in the alleyways between the bazaars? All they have to do is count money: They don't sow, they don't reap, and yet the heavenly father still makes sure they don't go hungry.'

Another one of your father's brothers was called Boghos. Boghos was a good-for-nothing who claimed to work in the carpet shop with his sister Aghavni and his brother-in-law Pesak, when in reality he would spend his days walking the streets of Bakir in the company of the worst possible people: failed students from Constantinople, Ezurum and Van who had, at some time or another, returned home to sponge off their relatives in Bakir. These disreputable men spread leftist ideas of equality and fraternity which had gone to their heads, and Boghos', too. One time, when Boghos was back in Yedi Su, he turned to his father and said, 'Do you know what Huntchakians are?'

– Yes, Hagob replied. They are crazed fools.

– They are Armenian nationalists schooled in Marxist thinking, Boghos replied. And then he asked his father, 'And do you know what Dashnakzagan are?'

– They are also crazy, Hagob said. Just in a different kind of way.

– They are radical right-wing Armenian nationalists, Boghos said.

But Hagob simply shook his head and said, 'I don't know anything about all that.'

– And do you know what Marxists are?

– No, Hagob said.

– They are egalitarians, Boghos said. Just imagine a world in which everyone is equal!

– But people aren't equal, Hagob said.

He was a very strange fellow, this Boghos. Whenever he had a craving for his mother's or his grandmother's delicious cake, he would come to Yedi Su for an extended visit. Often during the evening he would sit by the tonir with Hagob where they would smoke a chibouk together. Once Boghos said to him, 'You know what? All of you are reactionaries.'

– What's that? asked Hagob.

– You just want everything to stay as it is.

– What we want doesn't matter, Hagob said. All that matters is what the Lord God wants.

– And what does the Lord God want?

– He wants everything to stay the same.

And Hagob said, 'Should the rooster crow at midnight instead of first thing in the morning? And should the poor have plenty to eat whilst the rich starve? And should the Armenians beat the Turks and the Kurds instead of the other way around? Everything has its place. You just have to accept it.'

Your father had another brother whom he loved almost as much as Dikran, the cobbler. He was twenty years older than your father, his name was Hajgaz and he was the eldest of Hagob's children. This Hajgaz was short and bald-headed, red-cheeked and obese – he was even a little asthmatic, as well as short-legged and ungainly. He had fat fingers: chubby fingers, fingers adorned with gold rings, rings that held emeralds and diamonds. Even back in 1858 when Hajgaz shot out of his mother and plopped down onto the jorgan – his grandfather's jorgan, which Vardan would later inherit and which Zovinar had squatted over: that same jorgan filled with straw and sheep's wool, swarming with lively fleas and many generations of dead fleas, and surrounded by clouds of bluebottles and mosquitoes – what I mean to say is that even in that moment when Hajgaz plopped onto this jorgan, he was the only asthmatic infant in the entire Khatisian clan. When his first cry came out of his small, toothless mouth, it was wheezy and punctuated by coughs. But he wasn't sick; just a few minutes later, as his grandmother was bathing him in saltwater and giving him a good scrub, while Hajgaz coughed and cried, she turned to Zovinar and said, 'Your first-born isn't sick. He's just coughing because he's impatient.'

– What do you mean? asked Zovinar.

– Well, let me tell you, his grandmother said. This little squirt, whom we shall name Hajgaz after my father, who is still alive and whose days will be added to young Hajgaz's life. Well, my little dove, this little squirt is just coughing because he's impatient.

– Impatient for what? asked Zovinar.

– Well, let me explain, said his grandmother. Your Hajgaz just can't wait to do business.

– What business?

– You know! Business! It's written all over his face: One day he will be a rich man.

– And how can you tell?

– I can tell by the way he's puffing out his cheeks and knitting his brow.

– So you think he will become a rich man?

– Absolutely.

And, of course, Grandmother was right; even at the Shekerli celebration, the celebration of a child's first steps, it became apparent
that Hajgaz was an impatient and energetic child for when he
took his first steps, he rushed neither to the tonir nor the water
pail nor the stable and not even to the cradle with a copy of the
Bible that his mother had placed inside it … no, no: the first
thing he did was run on his little legs all the way outside, through
the oda's entryway and right onto the sunny village street.

Hajgaz also began trading with tezek – in other words, run-of-
the-mill cow shit – when he was a little boy, just like Vardan
and many other children. But once he reached the age of seven,
things took a different turn when Hajgaz started travelling to
neighboring villages to buy things that weren't available in Yedi
Su so he could then sell them at a profit. When he was ten, he
ran away from home, moved in with his uncle, the one who was
an arabadji in Bakir, spent his days walking around the large
city's bazaars, striking up deals, and trading with other sellers
and buyers before finally starting his own business selling watermelons from Diyarbakir.

At the age of thirteen Hajgaz owned one of the largest melon
stalls at Bakir's melon bazar. Travelers returning from Bakir told
the villagers that although Hajgaz still coughed and wheezed like
a thirsty camel, he was also as rosy-cheeked as ever and had cheeks
like the fattened up heinie of a child who had been left out in the
sun by its heartless mother. They said that Hajgaz also had quite
the belly and chubby fingers, although they lacked jewelry as he
said he would only buy such adornments when his brother Sarkis
could make them for him at a cheap rate – although people said

Sarkis was still learning and yet to become a fully-fledged gold-smith. In short, Hajgaz was on his way to becoming a successful man, and his melons, according to what people said, really did come from the region of Diyarbakir and were so big and heavy that one could only wish they might fall on the heads of the Armenians' enemies.

People often spoke of Hajgaz, and his melon stand provided plenty of material for the rumor mill. In the village café next door to the tobacco shop, men dealt joke after joke about Hagob's short, fat, asthmatic son who had gone to Bakir to make his fortune. There was talk that Hajgaz, who was only thirteen years old at that time, wanted to marry an older woman, a veiled lady of thirty-five who would pursue Hajgaz doggedly every evening as he was taking down his stand and was making his way home with his donkey and cart.

And so it was that one day Hajgaz announced his engagement, and a year later he married a widow named Vartouhi, a name which implied its bearer was as tender as a rose.

– How can a woman over thirty-five be as tender as a rose? Hagob said to his wife. And what could a woman, who is older than many a grandmother in Yedi Su, possibly want from my son? My son, who is short and has a drooping belly, and who coughs and wheezes when he talks … and even when he doesn't … because that's just the way he is … even though we bathed him in salt … and scrubbed him with it, too … with saltwater I mean … what could such a woman possibly want with my Hajgaz, whose seed is still so young and has barely been sown?

– What could she possibly want? asked Zovinar. Yes, that's what I'd like to know, too.

– And Priest Kapriel Hamadian, who was sitting next to the pair said, 'The question, Hagob Efendi, is not what she wants from him, but what he wants from her.'

– Yes, that is the question, said Hagob.

– That is the question, said Zovinar.

– This woman is said to be very rich, said the priest.

– I've heard that, too, said Hagob.

– Her late husband was the richest money changer in all of Bakir.

– I've heard that, too.

– And your asthmatic son, Hajgaz, is a businessman!

– Well, he's certainly no fool, said Zovinar.

– Well, he is my son after all, said Hagob.

– That's right, said the priest.

As anticipated, after his marriage to Vartouhi, the widow, Hajgaz became a serious businessman. But he didn't become a money changer like Vartouhi's first husband. As he was obese, red-cheeked and drawn to all sorts of culinary delights – a connoisseur and a glutton by nature – and thus probably, for this reason or that, Hajgaz began trading in a diverse range of delicacies. He became a restaurateur. And as he had chosen this path, or, as the Muslims say, as *kismet* – where everyone's destiny is foretold – dictates, it came as no surprise that this new restaurant, an establishment dedicated to all things delectable and which Hajgaz named *Hayastan,* soon became the most famous eatery in the whole of Bakir. It was said that in the *Hayastan* it was impossible for guests, even the Turkish ones, not to fall in love with Armenia if but for a brief moment of time, for Vartouhi conjured up Armenian delicacies for every visitor that proved that even one of the wisest sayings – *the way to a man's heart is through his stomach* – could still ring true in Turkish-occupied Hayastan.

Now, let's return to your father," said the storyteller. "As a young boy, he had already begun trading in tezek. When he and Avetik were slightly older and more mature, they travelled to Bakir more frequently to sell the dried cow dung they had collected. Sometimes they took Garo with them, but most of the time they just took Gog-Gog, the Turkish boy, because he was a skilled donkey driver. Even if the creature protested, Gog-Gog could still get it to pick up the pace. However, as Ceyda, the jenny, was a female donkey, Gog-Gog didn't just entice her with fragrant hay which he would teasingly wave to and fro beneath her muzzle; he would also talk to the creature, whispering sweet words into her ear and stroking her private parts. Sometimes Gog-Gog would pinch Ceyda on a particularly sensitive part of her backside and bellow with laughter when she suddenly sprang forward.

– Do you at least know the right people in Bakir who will buy some tezek off you? Gog-Gog asked one time when Ceyda was having one of her moods.

– Of course, said Vardan.

– He even knows someone who will pay a decent price, said Avetik.

– An Armenian?

– An Armenian!

– And he doesn't tell lies? He doesn't say that the tezek is actually goat dung?

– No, this one doesn't.

Who is this Armenian in Bakir that buys your tezek?

- My eldest brother, Hajgaz.
- Him! The one they say is filthy rich?
- Yes.
- Doesn't he have any wood to burn?
- He does. But dried cow shit is cheaper."

8

"At the end of the 1880s," said the storyteller, "strange schools that were run by nuns and priests were set up by the Franks across the whole of Hayastan. They were called missionary schools, and their purpose was to teach true Christianity to the Armenians, who were followers of the Gregorian Church. Then the Americans arrived, who were essentially Franks, too, except that they lived on the other side of the pond. They taught their pupils all manner of things and those who studied under their tuition could even gain entry into one of the main universities of Stambul or Frankistan. Many Armenians sent their sons and daughters to one of these schools, but not the families living in Yedi Su.

In Yedi Su nothing changed. The boys still attended the village school while the girls stayed at home. The previous mukhtar of Yedi Su, who was even more revered than the current man in office, Ephrem Abovian – this former mukhtar, a man who people said had personally taken the virginity of all his female domestics and who was very wealthy and well-respected, this mukhtar once said, 'An educated woman will be the undoing of her family.' Yes, those were his very words. – And how right he was, this mukhtar, for there were plenty of cautionary tales to support his argument. Even the priest himself recently said to the virgins of the village, 'Just take a look at the educated women of Bakir. Learning has taken hold of their minds and arrogance has set up camp between their legs. The fires go out in their tonirs and domestic tranquility deserts their odas. Their men are lackluster and tame – and they are afraid. They are afraid for truly the darkness lurking within their women is enough to make the bone of even the finest man recoil.'

The priest then added, 'I once met a man in Bakir who had an educated wife, and he confided something to me. Do you know what he said?'

– What, Vartabed?

– Vartabed, he said. My wife is no more. Her well has dried up. The Djinns have taken refuge in the brambles between her thighs. Her empty chalice resembles a malkin and her warm, slippery chasm of joy is now as tight as a pair of nose spectacles that scold silently.

Your father attended the village school," said the storyteller. "He could read and write but little more. However, he did know how to play the wooden flute that Gog-Gog the Turk had whittled for him. Whenever your father drove the sheep too high up the mountain as he was watching over them, he needed only to play a few notes on his flute to call them back.

It's true, very little happened in the village of Yedi Su," said the storyteller. "The only event of any real importance was the incident with the trunk of books."

"What trunk of books?"

"You know, the incident with the trunk of books.

Listen, and I'll tell you," said the storyteller. "There was a teacher suffering from consumption in the village school who died when your father was nine years old. Shortly afterwards another teacher came to Yedi Su who also suffered from consumption and wore rimless glasses, just like his late predecessor. People used to say to the teacher, 'Whenever you ride up into the mountains on your donkey, Hodja Efendi, you'd do well to leave your glasses at home. You see, the Kurds think anyone who wears glasses is a spy. Many bespectacled men have been slain by their hand.'

But the new teacher didn't listen to the warnings of the people and often rode up into the mountains, until one day he didn't return. People said, 'He suffered from consumption: perhaps he became so weak that he slid off the donkey and is now lying somewhere.' But there were others who said, 'No, no, he was wearing his glasses. Didn't the Kurds slay a man wearing glasses in seventy-four because they thought he had been sent by the Sultan to spy on the Kurdish territory for the saptiehs and the tax collectors? They've almost certainly killed him. His body is lying at the bottom of a gorge and that teacher's soul is somewhere with Christ.'

– And where is his donkey? people asked.

– The Kurds have taken it.

– But a proud mountain Kurd doesn't ride on a donkey.

– True.

– Perhaps they slaughtered the donkey and ate it long ago?

– Or perhaps they just killed it and its body is lying next to the teacher in a gorge.

– Then the donkey's soul would also be with Christ.

– Quite possibly.

Indeed, it really was a mystery. The teacher was never found. He left nothing behind, well, nothing of any value. All he left was his trunk of books.

It's true. When the teacher moved to the village, he dragged with him a trunk of books so heavy that only the strong arms of the red-haired blacksmith and Garo, the saddle maker's son, could carry it. As the teacher was lodging with the blacksmith at the time, and solely because space was very limited in his lodging, the trunk was kept behind the foot-operated bellows in the blacksmith's generously-sized workshop, which is where it stayed. Now ... after the death of the teacher, the blacksmith had wanted to burn all of his many books as that would ultimately save him having to burn a load of good, carefully-dried and combustible cow shit. In other words, it would save him valuable capital. But it wasn't to be.

It wasn't to be because the following happened," said the story-teller. "Just as the blacksmith was about to burn the books ... just at that very moment ... his godson, Vardan, walked through the door of the workshop.

Vardan said, 'I'll give you three sacks of tezek for the books.'
– What do you want the books for?
– I want to read them, said Vardan.
– People say you want to become a poet.
– Yes, said Vardan.
– Is that why you need to read all these books?
– Actually, it isn't.
– Then why do you want to read them?
– No reason, said Vardan.

And so they fetched Garo, the saddle maker's son, and together they carried the trunk – this time with six hands instead of four – into the Khatisians' oda. Hagob didn't protest, and neither did Zovinar as their oda was now spacious since the little ones had grown up and many of their older children had moved away. And so it was that Vardan, who could play the flute and command his sheep on the mountainside, also began to read books. There were plenty of good books in the trunk – books of which the teacher once said, 'Many were written in Armenian, many are translated … and all of them try to explain the world.'

– All those books will twist that boy's mind, Hagob said to Zovinar. Think about it: Who else has a twisted mind? The water carrier!

– But not from reading books, said Zovinar.

The consumptive teacher once said to Vardan, 'If I die one day, you can have all the books in my trunk.'

– Do I have to read them all if I want to become a poet?

– No, the consumptive teacher replied.

And the consumptive teacher said, 'I've seen the way you command your sheep with your flute. Each time you play a few notes, they stand stock-still, walk away from the edge of gorges and return to the safety of the valley.'

– Do you think it's a sign that I will become a poet?

– No, the consumptive teacher said.

And the consumptive teacher said, 'If you want to become a poet, you will have to learn to play a different flute.'

– But, Hodja Efendi … what kind of flute do you mean?

– An invisible flute, my little Vardan. One that is not of this world.

– And how will I be able to hold it in my hands, Hodja Efendi, or blow into it with my mouth if it doesn't actually exist?

– Nobody said that it didn't exist. Listen, my little lamb: Just because something is not of this world, doesn't mean that it doesn't exist.

– And how will I know it when I see it, Hodja Efendi?

– You don't need eyes to see it, my little lamb.

– What do you mean?

– Well, what do you think, my little lamb? You can sense it of course. One day you will see this flute that can be neither seen nor felt, but you won't see it with your eyes. And you will take hold of it, but not with your hands, and you will never let go of it again.

One day an old shepherd had told him that he once knew a cripple who couldn't find a wife. And as he was so very lonely, he began to sing about love and so became a poet.

– Can you only become a poet if you're a cripple?

– Yes, the old shepherd replied.

The consumptive teacher, however, told Vardan that it wasn't true. Poets were no cripples. Poets, so the consumptive teacher said, were, in fact, gypsies, except these gypsies didn't read mystical signs on people's foreheads and hands; they deciphered the language of people's souls and transformed it into melodies of words.

– When will I be able to decipher the language of the soul?

– When it is time for you to take hold of the invisible flute, the consumptive teacher said.

– And when will that be?

– Someday, said the consumptive teacher. And he stroked Vardan's mop of curly hair, smiled and then said, 'Someday the time will come when the invisible flute will send forth its messengers.'

Once Vardan became sexually mature, he believed he could see the invisible flute's messengers in his dreams. A tremendous feeling of sorrow grew in his heart, as did a tremendous feeling of fear, but he was also filled with a tingling sense of joy and fiery expectation. The messengers of the invisible flute would play for him, and in his dreams he heard a thousand and one melodies. What he had previously only been able to sense, he now knew with certainty. It was as though torrents of water were breaking free from sources he never knew existed, swelling to the size of rivers, lakes and seas. The angels blew into their trumpets with their red lips. In his dream Vardan saw Bulbul the Kurd's wrinkled breasts. They hung like sacks over the back of her nameless donkey. The farther Bulbul rode, the more her breasts metamorphosed, and when the donkey reached the edge of the village, her breasts were like the warm, soft and delicate, milk-filled breasts of his mother, until they transformed once more: Now Vardan saw the breasts of his bride, which he had yet to lay eyes on. They were small, but as hard as pomegranates, with enticing, succulent nipples. 'Go on, touch me, my groom,' the breasts said. And the breasts laughed as his hands were shaking, then they said, 'It's alright, you're allowed.'

And Vardan touched them.

– Don't push too hard, said the breasts. You must be gentle.

Do it softly – nicely and softly.

 – Should I just use my hands?

 – No, my groom.

 – How should I do it, gelin, my little bride?

 – Use your lips, my groom. Your lips.

And Vardan began to suck, just as he had sucked when he was a baby. Sobbing, he lustfully clung on to the breasts of his bride. The more he sucked, the smaller they became, until they finally disappeared completely.

 – They're gone, he said to his bride.

 – You devoured them, his bride said.

 – What should I do now?

 – Keep sucking, my little groom.

 – But what should I suck?

 – Anything your lips touch, my little groom.

 – Even your hands?

 – Even my hands.

 – Even your feet?

 – Even my feet.

 – And what else?

 – Everything, my little groom. Everything.

 – Do you have lips between your legs, too?

 – Yes, my little groom.

 – Are they really as slender as the earlobes of an unborn sheep?

 – Yes, my groom.

 – Or are they big and ridiculous, like a pair of donkey's ears?

 – Why don't you find out for yourself?

 – Should I really?

– Yes, you should.

– Are we already married?

– I don't know.

– Perhaps this is our wedding night?

– Yes, perhaps.

As this tingling sense of joy swept aside his fear, together with his misery and his shame, and Vardan was carried away by a freedom he had never felt before, he awoke with a cry.

– It's nothing, said Hagob, as Zovinar showed him his son's wet *doshek* – a mattress filled with straw and sheep's wool which was not quite as old as the jorgan Vardan had been given by his grandfather.

– What do you mean 'nothing'? said Zovinar.

– He's a man now, said Hagob.

– And what about the doshek?

– It's wet, said Hagob.

– Your son is squirting out valuable seed, Zovinar said. Instead of giving it to his wife, he's squirting it senselessly into his bed.

– But he doesn't have a wife.

– That'll have to change.

– It's time for him to be wed.

– Yes.

– When will you speak to the mayor?

– Soon.

But it wasn't quite time for wedding bells yet," said the story-teller. "Only the following year did the mayor's daughter leave a few spots of blood on her straw and sheep's wool doshek: spots of blood that did not come from a wound.

– It's time, said the mayor's wife when she discovered the blood on the doshek early the following morning. Now we have to officially announce the engagement with the Khatisians' youngest son.

– But she's only eleven, said the mayor.

– Eleven isn't ten, his wife replied. What are you waiting for? Do you want her to become an old maid?

– It is tradition, said the mayor, for the marriage to take place one year after the girl bleeds for the first time. But that isn't possible.

– Why not?

– Because we need to fatten her up. Do you think the Khatisians' youngest son will want to marry a girl that's all skin and bone just because his father and I exchanged coins all those years ago?

– How long will it take to fatten her up?

– Usually two years.

– We should have made a start sooner.

– Yes.

– Two years, you say?

– You heard correctly.

– Well, I suppose we'll just have to make it happen in a year.

And so it was," said the storyteller, "that an engagement first sealed many years ago, back when the two fathers exchanged coins and the bride was still in diapers and had no idea of what had taken place; an engagement that was more discreet than usual, a simple promise and a matter of honor between two men – Hagob and the mayor – was now publically announced by both fathers the day after the bride's sexual maturity was confirmed. Now it was set in stone: Hagob's son and the mayor's daughter would become a married couple. Now it was irrevocable. The mayor told everyone that his daughter now bled and that the blood did not come from any wound: She was now a woman. The whole business with his daughter's fattening up was also no secret. People said that this slender, little girl, who bled from no wound, this being made of fragile bones was to be fattened up to a respectable woman within a year. People said that the mayor's wife had sworn a promise to all the saints. They also said that Vardan's mother had told the mayor's wife, 'I will send your daughter forty sofras filled with baklava on the day the engagement ring, which my other son Sarkis, the goldsmith, has made and sent, arrives.' And she added, 'Forty sofras, no more no less, for I want people to say that the bride received forty sofras as is tradition when the children of respected members of the village are engaged to be married.'

The mayor's wife allegedly replied, 'Forty: no more, no less. Forty sofras filled with baklava. And each time my daughter empties the sofras of their baklava, I will refill them.'

– In the name of the Lord, Zovinar said. She shall be fat and respectable. Fatten up my daughter-in-law so that my son doesn't become a laughing stock.

Vardan had rarely laid eyes on his bride. Although they often played together as children, it was not acceptable for a future husband and wife to be seen alone together, to look at each other too brazenly or to even touch each other whilst playing. 'Be sure never to stand too close to her,' his mother used to say. 'Otherwise tongues will start wagging.'

– And what will happen then?

– Then people will say, 'His bride doesn't respect the veil.'

– But she doesn't wear a veil?

– But she will wear one someday, you stupid boy.' And his mother said, 'Be careful! Don't you ever go near her until she has a ring on her finger. What people think of her is also what they think of you, and of your children and grandchildren.'

The process of fattening the bride provided plenty of material for the gossiping old wives and the cruel tittle tattlers in the village. Some said that the mayor's daughter would never gain weight *because she had never seen salt as a child.* As the people in the village washed not with soap but with sodium from Lake Van, which roving Armenian traders would sell to the farmers every now and again, and as the mayor possessed a large stockpile of this sodium, the rumor was that his daughter had never been bathed in table salt, as was common and proper: She had been bathed in a soap substitute, which was basically water containing sodium from Lake Van. However, people said that such water would weaken the body of an infant during its first forty days which, as everyone knew, wasn't the case with table salt. But the mayor just laughed off any accusations and said, 'Listen, it makes no difference if it's sodium from Lake Van or table salt. I'll make a bet with anyone willing. I bet thirty sheep that on the day of her wedding to the Khatisians' youngest son, my daughter Arpine will be so fat that she couldn't fall down the Gatnachpjur well even if she tried.'

– And what do you mean by that, Mukhtar Bey? Anyone who tries to fall down the Gatnachpjur well falls down it. There's no two ways about it. Where else would she fall if she jumped straight in? Alongside it?

– What are you talking about, you idiots! Why on earth should my daughter fall alongside the well if she jumps straight into it? Why can't you understand what I'm saying? I mean that her rear end will be so fat that the walls of our beloved milk well will be too narrow for her backside to fall into the depths. That's what I mean.

– But nobody's backside can be that fat, Mukhtar Bey. Do you understand what we're saying? No one could ever have a backside that fat.

– I will prove it to you, said the mayor.

– And how do you plan to do that, given that your daughter has never seen salt and has been bathed in soap from Lake Van?

– I'll prove it to you somehow.

– And how much baklava will she have to eat until her rear – her rear that is destined to remain thin because the girl has never seen salt – how much will she have to eat for it to become as fat as you claim?

– Well, if you wish to know, efendiler, she will eat forty pieces of baklava every day. *Forty, no more, no less.* And do you know how many pieces of baklava my poor wife, may God keep her by my side for years to come, will have to bake to turn my daughter into a respectable woman?

– No, Mukhtar Bey. Only someone sick with consumption could work that out, someone like our former village teacher. But he's now dead and lost in the mountains together with his donkey, may God rest his soul.

Yes, that's what happened," said the storyteller. "Everyone followed the fattening of the bride with excitement and intrigue, especially the two families at the heart of the action as the mayor and Hagob's honor was at stake. Over the course of a year, so much baklava was baked in the mayor's house that the scent of those sweet little cakes could be smelt throughout the entire village. Eventually the aroma even wafted all the way up to the Kurds high in the mountains. And so it was that Suleyman, the sheikh of the Kurds, turned to his sons and said, 'A wedding will soon take place in that village. If what my spies tell me is true, it will be a marriage between the daughter of the bald-headed Mukhtar Ephrem Abovian, and the youngest son of Hagob, the farmer. Woe betide them both if they refuse to pay the bride tax to me and my tribe.' "

9

"Vardan could hardly wait for the day of the wedding to arrive. The fatter his bride became, the greater his desire grew for a backside that would block the entrance to the Gatnachpjur milk well and be larger and more impressive than a pair of Diyarbakir watermelons. In his dreams he could hear the voices of the sellers at a melon bazar in some far off city: 'Melons made of flesh and blood. Larger and fatter and juicier than the largest and fattest and juiciest Diyarbakir melons. Can't fall in the Gatnachpjur well. Oh, Allah, You who have created the water in the well and the flesh of the melon. Tell me, why can't this melon fall down a well?'

In his dreams Vardan could see the people standing in front of the melon stall. One curious bystander was a rich Turk with a golden pocket watch which he wore for all to see beneath his open waistcoat.

– Hey, you … melon seller! Why can't that melon fall down a well?

– I don't know, efendi. But I presume it's because Allah built wells that were too narrow for a melon as fat as this.

– But Allah doesn't build wells, you blithering fool. Allah simply sends us the water that goes inside. It is man who builds the wells.

– Yes, efendi. With Allah as my witness, it is true. You speak the truth.

– Who built the well that is too narrow for the fattest of watermelons?

– The Armenians, efendi.

– Those infidel dogs.

– That's right, efendi. They deliberately built the well to be narrow so that fat melons such as this would get stuck.

– And why?

– I don't know, efendi. But I presume they did it so that people would see just how large the melon is, and how juicy and fat … so fat that it can't fall down the well – that damn well the Armenians call Gatnachpjur and whose walls are too narrow for their Armenian watermelons.

– So, it's an Armenian watermelon, is it?

– It is.

– And why is such a melon growing in Turkey?

– Because the Armenians claim there is no land known as Turkey, at least not here in this region. This land is called Hayastan. All of it is Hayastan. And everything that grows here belongs to the Armenians, including the melons.

– And what if you sold me that single melon in exchange for my golden pocket watch?

– I'm afraid I can't, efendi.

– You see, I want to tear it right open. And then I want to stick my tongue inside it. And I bet you, you jackass, that I could lick out all of the honey inside using only my tongue.

– But, efendi, there is no honey inside.

– Of course there is, you idiot. There's honey inside that melon. I bet you there is.

– But, efendi, I can't sell it.

– And why not, you son of a miscreant? I'm offering you a golden pocket watch!

– Because this melon has already been sold.

– I bet you've sold it to an Armenian.

– I have, efendi.

– Those dogs take everything right from under our noses.

– Yes, efendi.

– And what's the name of this Armenian dog?

– His name is Vardan Khatisian, efendi, and he is the fourteen-year-old son of Hagob Khatisian.

– I hope this Hagob and his son drop down dead. May Allah bring these infidels to their senses with the power of the fire and the sword. Can't you see? They're taking everything from us, even our finest melons.

In his dream Vardan could hear the voice of the market crier and the voice of the rich Turk with the golden watch, and he could hear the murmur of voices on the grand bazar, and he could smell the various aromas of the stalls' thousand and one delicacies. Then, suddenly, he saw the large melon, which was the backside of none other than his bride, rise up into the air and set off for Yedi Su on the back of a flying carpet, landing right underneath his jorgan. And the fat melon said to him, 'I belong to you. Soon we will be married. But you must remember to pay the bride tax, which is half of the dowry.'

– What if I forget?

– Then the Kurds will take my virginity.

– But that can't be allowed to happen.

– Oh yes, it can.

In his dream Vardan took hold of the melon and, even though they were not yet married and it was actually forbidden, he stroked the chubby flesh and his fingers discovered a forest of thorns hidden beneath the melon that opened and parted, just like the waters of the Red Sea before the staff of the patriarch.

– I feel a mouth behind the forest of thorns. It's opening its lips.

– The lips are only the sea, my groom. Do you have your staff?

– Yes, gelin, my bride.

– The sea has disappeared, my groom. Can you feel it?

– Yes, gelin, my bride.

– All that is left are the lips, opening up for you.

– Yes, gelin, my bride.

– They are as delicate as the earlobes of an unborn sheep.

– No, gelin. You're lying. They're as big as the ears of a fully-grown donkey.

– Well, it doesn't matter, does it, my groom? How can I help it if they've grown so big and fat from all the baklava I've eaten?

– I don't know, little gelin, my bride.

– Or would you rather have a skinny, little rag doll?

– No, little gelin.

No man will ever admit the number of times he has unloaded into his jorgan in his sleep," said the storyteller. "But I would wager that the amount of precious seed that your father wasted while his bride was being fattened up would have been enough to fill all the empty clay pots stood around the walls of the oda; that is, if the pots were empty of course, and not filled with whey, cheese, preserved green tomatoes, peppers and other provisions.

Needless to say it was enough to attract the attention of both his grandmother and his mother.

– Didn't I tell you not to touch your thing? Do you want to turn out like the water carrier?

– But I didn't touch it, Mother. It all happens when I'm asleep. What am I supposed to do when a giant melon made out of flesh and blood and honey comes chasing after me in my dreams?

– You see it in your dreams?

– Yes, Mother.

– And what about your man's bone that's actually still the bone of a boy? Who rubs that in your dream?

– No one, Mother.

– The Lord God perhaps?

– I don't know, Mother.

In Yedi Su marriages always took place after the harvest. It had been that way for as long as anyone could remember. When the wind blew down from the mountains of Hayastan, just as the farmers were threshing their crop, and carried the chaff far out over the Armenian land, the old women used to say, 'Soon there will be another *harsanik-pilav*,' by which they meant the Armenian wedding rice which the Turks also knew, except they called it *zerde-pilav*. It was clear that the old women knew what was to come. It was the same procedure every year. As soon as fall arrives, the goddess Anahit walks soft-footed through all the towns and villages of Hayastan to entice the brides out of their parental homes and into the homes of their husbands-to-be. And that was exactly what came to pass in 1893 when Anahit appeared to Hagob in a dream and said to him, 'Hagob, the time has come to lead your youngest son to the altar. Behold, Hagob, his bride has been fattened up. She will be a fertile hassock for your son, one which he can sow and reap.'

The impending marriage was the talk of the village. Old men stood around the seven wells cracking jokes whilst the old women giggled bashfully.

– Hagob wanted him to be a fisherman, the old women said. But he has become but a simple farmer and a shepherd, who also takes himself for a poet.

– He's a fisherman, the old men said. You see, he's hooked himself a fat, juicy wife. And the old men laughed and said, 'To catch such a fat fish, you need a strong rod. You think the Khatisians' youngest son has a fine, strong rod – one that could keep such a fat fish on the end of its hook?'

Then the old women would blush beneath their headscarves and say, 'We don't know about that. But his rod is young. May God bless him with many children.'

Seven days before the wedding, Bulbul rode into the neighboring district capital, Gokli, on her nameless donkey to deliver a message to Nazim Efendi, the town crier. This crier, Nazim Efendi, a Turk with a lame leg and one deaf ear, was responsible for seven Armenian and two Turkish villages in the region.

– I come on behalf of Hagob Khatisian, Bulbul said to the town crier. His son Vardan will marry the daughter of Mayor Ephrem Abovian next week in Yedi Su. Can you deliver this message to the seven Armenian villages and tell them that every villager that is free from cholera and the French disease is invited?

– Why didn't Hagob Efendi come to tell me this himself? said the crier.

– Because he sent me, said Bulbul.

– And what price will the Armenian pay for such a service?

– A pair of new boots that his son, Dikran, will make for you.

– And how can I be sure that what you say is true?

– How long have you known me? asked Bulbul.

– More than twenty years, said the crier.

– And how many times have I come by over the years to bring you messages?

– Several, said the crier.

– And have I ever lied to you?

– No, said the crier.

The crier knew everyone who lived in the seven villages," said the storyteller. "And, of course, everyone knew him, too. Whenever he limped through the streets in his tatty clothing and shoes, with his fur cap askew, his goat-skin drum swaying above his waistband and two sticks in hand, ready to announce the Sultan's latest proclamation to the people on the village square, the children would cry, 'The munadi is coming! The munadi is coming!' Some of them taunted him loudly or yelled obscenities into his deaf ear. As the crier could neither read nor write, he always took a literate Armenian along with him who could read the Arabic script in which the Turkish words were written. The literate Armenian would then whisper the words he had read into the still functioning ear of the lame and partially deaf crier, who, in turn, would hold the parchment beneath his nose and pretend to read it effortlessly, yelling the Sultan's words to the gathered crowd. The munadi's voice was so powerful that people were terrified even if the news was good. They said that the munadi screamed his words with such force so that the echo would reverberate all the way up to the Kurds in the mountains, even though the munadi knew perfectly well that they couldn't care less about the Sultan's decrees.

One day, back when Hagob's wife was pregnant for the final time, the munadi came into the village with his Armenian and Hagob took him to one side and asked, 'So, Nazim Efendi. What's news?'

– You'll soon find out, the munadi said.

– Sure you can't just tell me now, Nazim Efendi?

– No, Hagob Efendi.

– Not even for a small tip ... you know, a little bit of baksheesh?

– I'd have to think about it first, Hagob Efendi. Before carefully adding: Hagob Agah.

– And what about if I gave you a generous baksheesh?

– A generous baksheesh, you say, Hagob Agah? Did I hear correctly, Hagob Bey?

– You did indeed.

– Well, Hagob Pasha. If it's a generous baksheesh we're talking about, I'm all ears. I'll even tell you more than I know.

– Hagob Pasha, the munadi said. The Russian-Turkish war is over. The Russians are withdrawing. There, now what do you say to that?

– What war, Nazim Efendi?

– You know, the war, Hagob Pasha! I think it's the one from seventy-seven and the one from seventy-eight ... the one we lost,

I believe, even though the Russians have suddenly started to retreat again.

- Did such a war really take place?
- Of course, Hagob Pasha.
- But we didn't see any soldiers here.
- No Russians either?
- No, we didn't see them.

Do you have any other news, Nazim Efendi?

- I do, Hagob Pasha. But it's not good.
- Can't you keep the bad news to yourself?
- No, Hagob Pasha, I'm afraid I can't. It seems you Armenians will have to pay the military tax again, by that I mean bedel … because you cowardly dogs are too feeble to carry arms for the Sultan.
- But we're not all that feeble, Nazim Efendi.
- You aren't hiding any weapons here, are you?
- God forbid, Nazim Efendi.

- Tell me, Nazim Efendi. Can you announce something to the people that isn't written on your parchment? What I mean is, could you announce that the Sultan wishes to congratulate me on my son, Vardan?
- And where is this son of yours, this Vardan, Hagob Pasha?
- He's not here yet, but he will be soon. My wife's pregnant, you see.
- And when will he be born, Hagob Pasha?
- When the first leaves fall from the trees, Nazim Efendi.

— Alright, listen here, Hagob Pasha. I'll tell you what I'll do. Perhaps the Sultan did say something that he didn't actually say. With Allah, anything is possible. Perhaps the Sultan really did congratulate you and just isn't aware of it.

— Precisely, Nazim Efendi.

— And after all, Hagob Pasha, if you think about it, why should the news about the withdrawal of the Russian troops be any more important than the imminent arrival of your son, Vardan?

— That's right, Nazim Efendi.

— And how much baksheesh are we talking?

— Well, Nazim Efendi. That depends on how you say it.

— What do you mean, Hagob Pasha? Do you mean the news about the Russians withdrawing and the news about the war and the news about the bedel?

— None of them, Nazim Efendi. I mean the news about my son.

— Oh, that news?

— Yes, that news.

That was a very long time ago," said the storyteller. "And now that selfsame crier made his way around the seven villages to spread the news that Vardan, the son of Hagob, whose imminent birth he announced in the name of the Sultan years ago, had not only long been born but was now to be married to none other than the daughter of Mayor Ephrem Abovian from Yedi Su."

10

"Exactly two days before the wedding, Uncle Nahapeth from America arrived. He brought along his eldest son Howard, whose real name was Hovhannes, just like the witless water carrier, and who was – believe it or not – still a bachelor, even though he was five years Vardan's senior. The two Americans' arrival in Yedi Su was such an unusual event that even the sparrows on the rooftops fell silent in awe – but only for a moment, for once the two men had stepped down from their arabas in front of the Khatisians' house, the sparrows perched atop the flat roofs began twittering even more animatedly than before, filling the air with a cacophony of noise.

– That's Hagob's brother, people said. He's a rag seller from America and a millionaire.
   – And his son?
   – That's his heir.
   – Why is that rag seller wearing a hat with a brim?
   – That we don't know.
   – His son's wearing a similar hat, too.
   – Yes, we've noticed.
   – The Turks will beat them to death when they see them walking about the streets in hats with such large brims.

– But that won't happen in our village.

– Do you think they walked around Bakir looking like that?

– I suppose we'll have to ask.

– Did they even go to Bakir?

– They did. They spent a couple of days with Hagob's eldest son, Hajgaz.

– The one who owns the *Hayastan?*

– Yes.

– I heard that Hagob's eldest son had sent the rag seller a telegram. To tell him about the wedding.

– Yes, I heard that, too.

– That rag seller must have given the American telegram carrier a hefty baksheesh, otherwise it would never have gotten to him.

– Yes, true.

– Those telegram carriers in America must earn a fortune in tips. Just imagine how much baksheesh you would pocket delivering telegrams to all those millionaires every day!

– Perhaps we should all go over to America and become telegram carriers.

– I bet you anything that even the telegram carriers are millionaires over there.

Whilst the women had gathered at the seven wells to share the latest gossip and, above all, to talk about the two Americans, with their checkered jackets and ironed trousers and large brimmed hats, as well as the bride, who was to be taken to the Gokli hamam the next day, on the eve of her marriage, to be bathed and cleaned in the famous steam bath that lay in the neighboring district capital, the two Americans sat in the local café where they enjoyed the curious admiration of the village's men.

– Do all men in America really walk around in public with such large hats? the mukhtar asked.

– Yes, the rag seller said.

– And nobody beats them to death?

– No.

– Tell us again about the whole business with your hats, said Hagob. I mean, what it was like in Bakir when you two were walking the streets with your big, brimmed, American hats.

– But I've already told you.

– But not everyone here has heard.

– Very well, then I'll tell you all again.

But Uncle Nahapeth didn't seem to be in a hurry to tell them all the story of the hat. Instead, he told them about America, the land of freedom, where Kurds, Turks and Armenians lived peacefully side-by-side; where there was no military tax; no internal passports; no bride tax; where common words such as 'bedel' and 'teskere' were unheard of; where Muslims didn't get upset when Christian men refused to have their cocks circumcised. He said that over there everybody was the same, and everybody had equal rights. The only exception were the Negroes, he said, because they were not real people; they were simply tamed apes as that's what a southerner once told him. Would you believe it? 'Now, listen to this,' he said. 'This southerner also told me that one of those tamed, black apes once laughed at a white woman in his town. And then, of course, white men wearing black hoods came to his house, dragged the ape out of his bed in the middle of the night and strung him right up. It's true.' But he explained that otherwise life over there was good. That there was money on the streets but it could only be seen and pocketed by those who worked hard and, of course, by those people with brains. Everyone else stayed poor, for which they had only themselves to blame. Anyone could get rich quickly if he was made of the right stuff and had the Lord God on his side.

– And what about those big, American hats? Hagob asked.
– What big, American hats?
– The ones you and your son went out walking with in Bakir.
– Oh, you mean those hats?
– Yes, those hats.
– Well, listen and I'll tell you, the uncle said. Now, just let me think.

Vardan's uncle from American sat chubby-cheeked between the other men. His red drinker's nose looked like it was laughing, as did his narrow, black, mischievous eyes. 'I was born in Hayastan,' the uncle said, 'but this one here, my son Hovhannes, whom we call Howard, he was born in America.' With those words, the uncle pointed mockingly at his son, a slim, pale and slightly intimidated figure sat between Hagob and Vardan, sucking sheepishly every now and then on the hookah pipe that Hagob had placed next to his cushion. 'This American sap,' the uncle said, still pointing almost accusingly at his son, 'can speak neither Kurdish nor Turkish, and can only say a few words of Armenian that are so pitiful, you have to laugh when you hear them or else you'll cry.'

– And what can he say?
– He can just say *Ingilizce.*
– And why can't he speak any Turkish or Kurdish, or even

proper Armenian?

– Because he is a real American, the uncle said. And because he believes that everyone in the world only speaks *Ingilizce,* a language that makes people sound like they have pebbles and shit in their mouths.

– Anyway, there we were, walking through Bakir with our large hats on our heads, the uncle said. And I was really quite scared that the Turks would beat us to death, but as you can see, we are still alive.

– Indeed, said Hagob.

– So, we went walking with our hats, the uncle said, and I was afraid that they would beat us to death but we are still alive.

– You've already said that, Hagob said.

– True, said the uncle.

– So, we took our hats for a walk in Bakir, said the uncle, and people gave us stupid looks, especially the Turks, but other Muslims, too.

– I can just picture it now, said Hagob.

– Some people said *sinek kagidi;* they said it loudly so that we could hear.

– What does that mean? my son, this American sap, asked. It means *flycatcher,* I told him. What do they mean by that? And why are people saying flycatcher to us?

– Let me show you, I said.

– We walked along the alleyway where all the shopkeepers were, the uncle said. There was a Turk among all the Armenian shopkeepers. He was sat sleeping in front of his shop, catching flies.

– How could he have been catching flies if he was sleeping?

Hagob asked.

– So, there we were, stood in front of the shop and the sleeping Turk. Do you see all the bluebottles? I said to my son in Ingilizce. Do you know where they all come from?

– No, father, he said.

– Neither do I, I said.

– Listen, let me tell you something, I said. There is a city here called Turkhal. It is the dirtiest city in the whole of Turkey. In summer there are so many bluebottles there that the Turks even have to fish them out of their wedding soup.

– Wedding soup? he asked me, this American sap.

– You know, wedding soup, I said. The Turks call it *dugun chorbasi.*

– And why are there so many bluebottles there? he asked.

– Because the city's original streets lie three meters deep.

– And what's on top of the original streets?

– Nothing but dirt, my boy, I said to him. You see, for centuries people have been throwing their rubbish out onto the street, along with their shit and God knows what. Dead cats and dogs lie there, too; even the odd beggar has rotted out on the street. And for centuries all the layers have been flattened down and compacted by traffic and people's dirty feet.

– And what about here in Bakir?

– Here it's even worse, I said.

– So Bakir is the dirtiest city in Turkey?

– The dirtiest – and the most beautiful, I said.

– And then I pointed to the sleeping Turk. Look, my son, I said to him. Every time he feels the legs of a bluebottle tickle his face, he wakes up.

– Yes, Father, he said. I see.

– And he watches it with his half-closed eyes.

– Yes, Father.

– And he waits for the fly to creep a little higher – over his nose, over his forehead – he waits until it climbs above the edge of his fez.

– Yes, Father.

– Only then does he strike it dead. Did you see it, boy?

– Yes, Father.

– That way he doesn't get any blood or fly stains on his skin. He delights in crushing it slowly against his red fez and then flicks the dead fly onto the street with his fingers.

– Yes, Father. I saw.

– That's why the Turks don't wear hats with brims, I told my son. For how should a Turk be able to flick a dead fly from the edge of his fez using just one finger if that fez has a brim? It would be impossible; the fly would stay stuck inside the brim.

– Is that why brimmed hats are called flycatchers?

– Precisely, my boy.

– But the Muslims only became really nasty when we walked past one of their mosques with our hats, Vardan's uncle said. Here, the faithful no longer cried *sinek kagidi,* but *shapkali.* My son asked, 'What does that mean?' And I told him, 'It's a Turkish word which means *hat man.* It's a dangerous word, my boy.'

– Why is it dangerous, Father?

– Yes, that is the question, my boy. I don't know either. It just is. And I told him, 'As a boy, I would often walk around Bakir, whiling the day away at the bazaars and staring at women,

women who wore black charshafs and double-layered veils. And once I saw this English man wearing a hat similar to ours and the people insulted him and said *shapkali.* The next day they found the English man outside the walls of the city. His head had been cut off. And next to his head lay his large hat, but the brim had been removed. And I assume that whoever cut that man's head off also cut off the brim of the hat because he was so bothered by it.

– Why? My son asked.

And I said, 'You sap. It doesn't matter *why* it bothered him. Isn't the fact that the brim annoyed him reason enough?'

The priest, who until that point had been sat listening silently next to the rag seller, now joined in the conversation. 'There is a reason,' the priest said.

And the priest said, 'When people say *flycatcher* to a man in a large brimmed hat, they mean no harm. They are simply using the hat as an excuse to dish out a few words of mockery. They would neither beat the hat wearer to death nor would they cut off his head, or even the brim of his hat for that matter. But when people say *hat man,* now that's a different matter entirely. *Shapkali!* That is not a word of ridicule. You see, by saying this word, they are implying that the wearer of the brimmed hat has come here not only to challenge the faithful but, more than anything, to taunt the *Mahdi.*'

And the priest said, 'The Mahdi lives in Paradise for the faithful and was a saint even when he was alive. Sometimes, so the Muslims believe, Allah allows the Mahdi to return to earth for just a few seconds to reveal one of the many secrets of Paradise to the true believers. The Mahdi always appears to the faithful after they have fasted and cleansed themselves, but only during prayer and at the precise moment when the believer presses his forehead to the dust on the ground and speaks the name of Allah. When the Mahdi appears, the believer, who is kneeling before Allah, need not stand; he must simply look upwards: then he will see the Mahdi.'

– And what does all that have to do with the brim of a hat? Hagob asked.

– Plenty, said the priest. For how should a believer look upwards when he is kneeling on his prayer mat with his head in the dust ... how should he see the Mahdi when the brim of his hat blinkers his view? Hats are not made of glass, you see.

– True, they're not made of glass, Hagob said.

– Right, said the priest.

– Is that why the Muslims don't wear hats with brims?

– It is the one and only reason, said the priest.

– Those large hats really are dangerous, said Hagob. Tomorrow my eldest son Hajgaz will arrive in the village. I will ask him to arrange some respectable headwear for both my brother and his son.

– Good idea, said the priest. Bakir has a good selection of sensible, brimless hats. Your eldest son should procure them straight after the wedding, I mean once he's returned to Bakir, then he should send them back here with an arabadji as quickly as possible. A turban would work well and be the least conspicuous, but I think that a red fez would be more befitting such fine gentlemen as your American brother as his son. Don't you think, Hagob Efendi, that you should tell your eldest son that a red fez would be best for the gentlemen?

– Yes, said Hagob.

In the coffeehouse the men drank endless glasses of raki, as well as Armenian oghi liquor, ate sweet delicacies and drank spiced tea and sweet coffee. Vardan's uncle laid his arm around him and whispered something into his ear. Vardan blushed, and so the uncle repeated his words. He did it very quietly so that no one other than Vardan could hear.

– Tell me, my nephew, have you ever had a woman before?
– No, Uncle Nahapeth.
– And do you know what you'll have to do on your wedding night?
– No, Uncle Nahapeth.
– And your bride? Does she know?
– I don't think so.
– Then we'll have to have words later.

No one had seen the bride's bare backside; not even the water carrier who sometimes watched the women of the village when they went to the stable to relieve themselves. Even Vardan found it hard to imagine what it might actually look like in real life. The accounts of the women who accompanied his future bride to the steam bath on the eve of the festivities were the only possibility he had to find out something about her backside, or anything else of hers for that matter. It must be said that the bride's visit to the hamam was not only a matter of great intrigue for Vardan; anyone unable to take part was also filled with curiosity. The men spread fierce rumors in the village, and some of the women, who hadn't gone with the girl to the steam baths, frantically exchanged tale after tale. When the accompanying women finally did return from the hamam in the evening, together with the bride, they were bombarded with questions.

– Did you see her backside?

– No, she had it wrapped up in towels.

– But the attendant, the *hamamdji,* surely she saw the bride's backside as she was helping wrap her up in the towel?

– Yes, she saw it.

– And what did she say?

– She said it was a decent backside. Even the hips were strong and chubby. The hamamdji said, 'She'll have many children, this one.'

– And what does her backside look like?

– The hamamdji said it looks just like her face: a fat lump of flesh.

– But that can't be. A backside doesn't have eyes or ears, or even a nose.

– True. What she meant is that it looked just like a face if you imagine it without the ears and the eyes and the nose.

– And what about the mouth?

– Her backside has a mouth, except that it's shaped like a long slit and it runs from top to bottom. You know, the other way around.

– The other way around?

– Yes, like I just said. The other way around.

– And what about her breasts? Do they really look like pomegranates? Or are they like big cheesecloth sacks that people use to squeeze whey?

– Her breasts resemble neither pomegranates nor bulging cheesecloths, said the women who had seen the girl's bare breasts in the hamam. Her breasts are like featherless doves but with a red beak, and – believe it or not – even though they have no feathers, those little doves looked as though they might fly away at any moment.

– Then it's high time we got the marriage celebrations underway, the men said. And high time for Hagob's youngest son to grab hold of those breasts so that they don't fly away.

– Exactly, said the women.

– But Hagob's youngest son wishes to become a poet, the men said. His hands are soft and don't really know how to grab hold of anything.

– Then he will have to be taught, said the women.

And the men said, 'Yes, absolutely.' "

The storyteller said, "God created the world in six days, and on the seventh day His creation was crowned with the Sabbath. And so it won't surprise you to hear that Vardan's wedding lasted a whole seven days and that the church service took place on the seventh day: on the day of Creation's crowning glory. It would be on a Sunday as that was the day on which Christians celebrate the Holy Sabbath.

Even on the day before the marriage, the day on which the bride was taken to the hamam, relatives of the Khatisians began to arrive in their arabas. Some had travelled far, from cities such as Belgrade and Sarajevo: cities that once belonged to the Ottoman Empire. Among them was a man called Ghazar Khatisian, the coffeehouse owner from Sarajevo, who arrived with his wife and their six children, as well as his brother-in-law Khachatur Babaian, who owned a textile factory in Belgrade. I won't sit here and list all of the Khatisians' relatives that came from neighboring villages and cities both large and small, some in donkey-drawn carts, some in arabas that were pulled by oxen, mules or horses, for time – as we both know – is of the essence. All I can promise you is that all those whom your father loved dearly were there."

The storyteller said, "Some of the guests were robbed by the Kurds along the way, and they arrived without gifts; some of them even arrived naked and barefoot. The relatives from Bakir, however, arrived under escort as Hajgaz was on good terms with the authorities who, in exchange for a substantial baksheesh, provided the owner of the *Hayastan* and his caravan of relatives in their arabas with twenty armed saptiehs who accompanied the caravan through the Kurdish territory.

Yes, the scene was set," said the storyteller. "On the first day of festivities the village was so overcrowded that Priest Kapriel Hamadian had no other option but to shelter the guests, for whom there was no longer any space left in the village's dwellings, stables and barns, in his church. The Armenians from the seven villages had also come, as had some Turks from the neighboring Turkish village of Keferi Koi, who were relatives of Yedi Su's Turkish family. Persian, Russian and Arabian salesmen suddenly showed up in the village, as did some semi-nomadic Kurds and a few Chaldean Nestorians, who were the last surviving members of an ancient Christian sect living in caves close to the seven Armenian villages. The village was also suddenly overrun with unwelcome guests, mainly devil worshippers, gypsies, beggars and paupers who always made an appearance when generous helpings of food and liquor were available for the taking. People said that word of Vardan's wedding, which had been announced by the blistering drum of the munadi, had spread far beyond the borders of the seven villages, carried by an echo and the wind. Among the beggars was also the blind man who sat next to the Gate of Happiness, Mechmed Efendi, who simply hitched a ride with Dikran, the cobbler.

In Yedi Su people always used to say that a daughter is lost on the day of her wedding, but not a son. You see, when she marries, the bride leaves her family home to move in with her groom's family. The groom's parents are the only ones who don't lose a child; they gain a daughter.

Thus the mood in the Khatisians household was understandably lighthearted, whereas loud clamoring and wailing could be heard from the mukhtar's house.

– The bride will have already started packing her things together, people said. She's breaking her mother's heart.

Now, I'm not so sure," said the storyteller, "whether the bride really was breaking her mother's heart. If they were so devastated to lose her, why were the Abovians in such a hurry to veil their fattened up daughter in the first place? The truth of the matter is that all the clamoring and wailing that could be heard while the bride was packing up her dowry and preparing to leave were all part of the custom of decency; the bride's parents had to show the village just how upset they were to lose their beloved daughter. It was for this very reason that two ballad singers from Bakir, whom Haigaz had brought with him on the mukhtar's orders, stood before the mukhtar's house – sometimes in front of the holes serving as windows, sometimes before the open front door – singing their satirical songs: *Go with God, my daughter,* sang one, imitating the voice of the bride's mother … *Go with*

God, my daughter and never forget us.

– *How could I forget you, Mother,* sang the other in the high-pitched voice of the fattened bride … *How could I forget you, Mother, you who have fed me with your sweet milk.*

– *Go with God, my daughter,* sang the first … *Go with God, my daughter, you who have drunk my milk.*

Yes, that's what took place," said the storyteller. "Hagob paid a thousand piasters for the right to his daughter-in-law's milk, a sum not unusual for a respectable family. He also paid the dowry which was known as *ozhit.* On the day before the festivities began, Zovinar had brought her daughter-in-law a dish containing henna. It lay inside a clay dish which rested on a wooden plate garnished with plenty of fruit. Henna and fruit were symbols of the goddess Anahit, and the bride who ate from the fruit of her mother-in-law on the eve of her wedding, before painting her finger and toe nails with henna – well, her fertility would be ensured and she would bestow many grandchildren upon her mother-in-law. As Zovinar handed the dish over to her daughter-in-law, she said, 'A fat backside guarantees nothing. You have to eat my fruits, gelin, my daughter-in-law … and you must paint every nail that the Lord God has given you on your little fingers and toes with this devilish red color. And after my son, who is healthy and who has good blood in his veins … after he has impregnated you … with God's help and the help of our Savior … remember to place a bible next to your bed and to hang garlic in front of your door.'

Hagob had slaughtered more sheep and lambs than the herd could bear, and the mukhtar, too, had contributed a substantial number of his own livestock.

– We don't have any more animals left to pay the bride tax to the sheikh of the Kurds, Hagob said to the mukhtar.

And the mukhtar said, 'That Kurdish sheikh and his bride tax can go to hell.'

– Let's hope that the sheikh has forgotten all about the business with the bride tax.

– We can but hope, the mukhtar said. Sweet and spicy scents wafted through the village. Every now and then the wind would blow the smoke rising from the spits up over the flat roofs and high into the mountains.

– The scent might reach the sheikh's nose, said Hagob.

– Let us hope that the wind changes direction before then, said the mukhtar.

On the day before the church ceremony it was custom for the groom to be shaved and have his hair styled by a respected hairdresser. This was considered a sign that the groom took the marriage seriously and was prepared to lead a proper, domestic life. The more respected the hairdresser, the greater the groom's commitment to his pledge. It was usually the godfather's responsibility to procure a barber of adequate standing – if possible, one who could also sing ballads while he was shaving and cutting the groom's hair: old Armenian songs that told of wedding celebrations, an abundance of children, modesty, bliss, money and joy. As Vardan's godfather, the red-haired blacksmith, didn't know of a barber who would meet the Khatisians' expectations, Hagob had no other option but to ask his eldest son, Hajgaz, to bring a suitable master barber from Bakir along with him, for everyone knew that even well-respected, singing barbers could be found in a city as large as Bakir. And the owner of the *Hayastan* didn't disappoint, but the man he brought along in his araba wasn't just any barber: He was famed Armenian barber Vagharshak Bahadurian, a pedigree wedding barber who regularly groomed the heads of the rich and who knew the hair and beards of their sons better than their mothers and wives. This famous barber had once worked for Hajgaz – back when he wed dear old Vartouhi – but his most sensational assignment came a few years ago when his scissors and blade prepared the former Armenian mukhtar of Bakir (a widower, who was marrying for the second time) for his marital bed. It was no easy task considering that the former mukhtar was as bald as Ephrem Abovian, the mukhtar of Yedi Su, had wayward facial hair, suffered from bloating and hiccoughs, especially when being attended to by a barber, and emitted anxious gases whenever anyone touched his skin or his hair with a sharp instrument. But the famed barber Vagharshak Bahadurian not only expertly sculpted and arranged the graying ringlets that hung over the mukhtar's ears and temples, he also softened them with rose oil and ironed them flat. It was a masterpiece, a true work of art. Even when it came to the mukhtar's stubble, so the story goes, the man was able to deliver a completely clean shave. People said this barber could sing like a chorus of birds in the early morning, and that his voice brought everyone health, happiness and virility, a statement that could only be true for each man whom he had prepared for his marital bed was still full of vigor and had brought many a child into the world – yes, even the former mukhtar of Bakir, even though everyone knew he had been no spring chicken when he married for the second time, suffering as he did from suspicious bloating, enduring hiccoughs, and anxious gases, which he shared with the world.

For seven days and seven nights I wandered the streets of Yedi Su unseen and unheard," said the storyteller. "Nobody knew I was there and yet I felt as though I had eaten and drunk together with all the wedding guests, and sang and danced with them in the narrow alleyways and on the village square. We were very lucky with the weather for the Lord God had blown the approaching clouds back up into the mountains. And so naturally the yellow sun, which the wild Kurds high up in the mountains captured every night and hid inside a black tent made of goat's hair, hung unfettered in the sky during the day, smiling down on the land of Hayastan, and at its most welcoming, or so it seemed to me at least, here in this region, where the village of Yedi Su stood with its small Gregorian-apostolic church, its market square and coffeehouse, the blacksmith's workshop, its few narrow and dusty alleyways, its white-tiled clay huts and scattered houses built with rubble and rock – the village of Yedi Su with its flat roofs facing up to the sky: roofs where villagers would go to sleep on hot days, where washing and cow pats, or tezek, were hung out to dry and where women would spread the juice of mulberries and grapes out over thin syrup trays and expose them to the sun's rays, as well as the swarms of mosquitoes and flies. The women's traditional clothes were colorful, their saffian leather slippers dainty and the jewelry that adorned their arms, ears, necks and double-layered veils glistening. They made the men's bulky boots seem all the more coarse and their sleeveless jackets, their white, gray and brown shalvar trousers, and their black fur caps all the more ungainly. What would it have been like, I thought to myself, if it had actually rained during the festivities? What would have happened to all the joy that thrived out in the open air? How would people have been able to dance beneath the protective roofs of the houses when the space inside was already so confined? How would they have been able to dance in the gloomy rooms? Would they have stayed out on the streets where they would have gotten wet and sank into the mud? And where would the musicians have played? In the rain?"

As the festivities entered their sixth day, I lay exhausted on the eastern pointed arch of the village church. My imaginary shadow was beside me, or someone who looked like him.

"How do you like the weather?" I asked.

"I like it very much," my shadow replied.

"The Kurds could have kept hold of the sun to annoy the Armenians."

"But they didn't."

"True."

"True," repeated my shadow.

"Or the Lord God could have run out of puff, and it would have been a sad day as he wouldn't have been able to blow away the clouds, and the clouds would have covered up the sun and their rays wouldn't have been much use if it had rained."

"True, it was a possibility."

"But it can't rain at an Armenian wedding!"

"Why?"

"Because Christ is among the guests."

"How do you know that?"

"Everyone knows that," I said. "Christ is present at every Armenian christening and every Armenian wedding."

"Are the Armenians his favorite Christians?"

"Yes, my little lamb," said I, the storyteller. "The Armenians are his favorite Christians for they are in great danger living here as they do in the land of the Muslims."

"In great danger?"

"In great danger."

"Because of him?"

"Because of him."

Hagob's entire face is beaming," I said to my own shadow, "as at this, the marriage of his youngest son, everything – absolutely everything – seems to be going without a hitch. And I don't just mean the weather, I mean the music, too."

"I have never seen so many musicians at a farmer's wedding."

"The baglamas and drums come from Yedi Su," I said, "as do the young fellows who know how to play them ... the others, those holding Anatolian wind and string instruments, come from neighboring villages, as well as the munadi's city, and some of them have even come from Bakir. Hajgaz brought them all on his araba, together with the wedding barber."

"I also spotted some gypsies: men and women dressed in rags."

"Did you see their fiddles?"

"Yes."

"They're from Russia," I said. "They're smugglers who bring Armenian liquor across the border from Yerevan into Van. Sometimes they also come as far as this region. They never travel without their fiddles, and even though they can't read music, they know just how to transform desires and dreams into melodies without recognizing a single note. Fiddles have a language all of their own, and when they tell the tales of people's desires and dreams, women's eyes begin to well up, while those of the men become even fiercer."

And I said, "The hubbub created by the musicians below is being carried by the wind all the way up to the ears of the Kurds in their camps. And because my ears can hear exactly what the Kurds hear, let me tell you: the Kurds are on the lookout. Their spies are already on their way."

"Will the Kurds attack the village?"

"I don't know."

And I could hear the mother of the Kurds' sheikh as she tried to persuade her son: 'My son, those Armenians are making such a racket; your godly father must be spinning in his grave.'

– But my father should be resting in peace, said the sheikh.

– But those infidels won't allow it.

– You're right.

– They're celebrating another wedding. Hagob's youngest son will wed the daughter of that bald-headed mukhtar, Ephrem Abovian.

– I know.

– Have Hagob and the mukhtar already paid the bride tax they owe you?

– No, not yet.

– Then you should go and get it.

– That's exactly what I'll do.

– When?

– On the seventh day of celebration.

– Will you kidnap the bride?

– Of course.

– And who will take her virginity?

– One of my sons will do it.

– Which one?

– I don't know.

The old woman nodded. She then laughed and said, 'We'll teach those infidels a lesson they won't forget. Then everyone in the seven villages will know the punishment that awaits an Armenian who doesn't pay his bride tax.'

"Hagob isn't holding back on the liquor or the wine," I said to my shadow. "Can you see? Even the Turkish guests are getting stewed."

"And why not?" my shadow said. "There is nothing in the Qur'an about Armenian liquor and Armenian wine. Why shouldn't the Muslims pickle themselves silly?"

We then talked for a while, my shadow and I, before my story-teller voice took a brief nap. It soon woke up again and rubbed its invisible, imaginary eyes. Around midday on the sixth day, I, the storyteller, took off from the church's pointed arch together with the figure I imagine to be my shadow to hover over the village before settling on the market square, directly in front of the coffeehouse, where the blacksmith was toasting the health of his godson.

– We'd better get going, said the blacksmith. It's almost time for everyone to watch Vardan being shaved and having his hair cut.

– Will they do it on the market square?

– No, in front of the Khatisians' oda. Outside, just before the door.

– Then we'd better hurry if we want to get a good spot.

And so I followed the line of men making their way to the oda. The women were right behind us. Everybody wanted to be there to watch the whole procedure and, of course, admire the famous barber Vagharshak Bahadurian … a man whom everyone had already heard much about … as he worked his magic.

Hagob had placed two sacks of grain in front of the house's open door, each holding up a side of a thick carpet on which Vardan sat like a young king atop his throne. He was surrounded by a throng of people who all chattered away to one another. Every now and again cries of 'Where is the barber?', 'Where is Vagharshak Bahadurian … Vagharshak Efendi?' could be heard.

My shadow and I, we forced our way through the crowd and sat ourselves next to Vardan. We noticed that he was restless. He was also slightly embarrassed and confused for he wasn't used to receiving so much reverence and attention. In all his modesty, it had probably never even crossed his mind that he, Vardan, might one day take center stage and have all eyes on him. Vardan's eyes searched for his bride but they couldn't find her. Blinded by the burning light of the midday sun, all he could see were the brightly colored clothes of the many wedding guests who surrounded him; he could smell their sweat as well as their liquor- and wine-tainted breath, and probably thought to himself, 'Soon the barber will be here to make sure you're perfectly groomed for your wedding night, and tomorrow you'll be wed in the church, and then after that … well, after that you will have to take your bride's virginity and hang the blood-spotted sheet in front of the door so that everyone can see that you married a virgin. And she has to be a virgin; it's a matter of honor.'

 – We Armenians call honor *pativ,* Vardan once told Gog-Gog, the Turk. Honor is everything. And the bride's honor is also the honor of the groom.

And Gog-Gog, the Turk, replied, 'It's more or less the same for us Turks.'

So, as I was saying, my shadow and I were sat unseen next to Vardan. When the barber finally arrived and started to snip away, the two of us quickly scurried away and went to stand amongst Vardan's relatives.

"Where is the bride?" my shadow asked.

I said, "The bride will be hidden by her relatives. But I'm sure she will be here soon so that the priest can bless the bride and groom's wedding clothes. The church ceremony isn't due to take place until tomorrow, on the seventh day, but the wedding clothes are to be blessed today, on the sixth day."

"Will the priest bless their clothes today?"

"Of course," I said. "Today … next to the holy tonir."

"After Vardan has been shaved and had his hair groomed?"

"Straight after that," I said.

"Did you see those gypsy women?" my shadow asked. "One of them just put a curse on the barber's scissors and his razor blade, too."

"She spat on the blade and the scissors," I said. "But that only means good luck."

"Good luck?"

"And kind, well-meaning thoughts."

"The gypsies know everything," I said. "We should ask them when the great tebk is coming."

"The great massacre?"

"Yes."

"Or at least ask whether the Kurds will come and kidnap the bride, which the Kurds generally do on the seventh day of festivities, just after the church ceremony … but only if the bride tax hasn't been paid."

"Why don't they take her before the ceremony?"

"Because the act of taking the bride's virginity is more powerful and delivers a bigger blow to the groom if the bride already has his ring on her finger and thus bears his name."

"So the Kurds will come and kidnap the bride?"

"Well, actually they have to," I said. "It's a matter of honor. But perhaps the sheikh of the Kurds has other things on his mind and has completely forgotten about the whole marriage business. Anything's possible."

"We can only hope," said my shadow.

And I said, "Indeed."

Then I made one last comment on the gypsies: "For five whole nights they have slept out in the open under the holy tree because they believe it holds magical powers."

"Five whole nights?"

"Yes. And tonight will be the sixth."

We then turned our attention to the barber, who skillfully worked his way around the groom's head. Soon he would begin shaving his face. The barber deliberately went about his work slowly. Every now and again he would lower his scissors to collect the tips that were, in accordance with tradition, thrown to him by guests. It rained copper, silver and gold coins. As he collected the coins, the barber's face didn't move an inch. He also didn't say thank you.

Only once the barber had begun shaving the groom, applying shaving soap – genuine, scented, foaming Frankish soap – to his face, did he start to sing and it was true: his voice really did sound just like early morning birdsong. Even the musicians reached for their instruments again and accompanied the barber as he sang.

"Where have the gypsies gone?"

"They're here, my little lamb," I said.

"Why aren't they playing on their fiddles?"

"They are waiting, my little lamb," I said.

As the Russian gypsies began to play, all the other instruments fell silent, and the barber's voice became softer. The fiddles' sorrowful tune carried the pair of us away, me and my shadow. And with us and the magical notes emanating from the fiddles' souls and the souls of the gypsies, the entire village seemed to rise up into the air: the market square and the dusty alleyways, the crooked houses and the tezek on their roofs. And Christ was among us, for he had been there the entire time. We journeyed up to heaven and then we journeyed back down again, and suddenly, as the fiddles ceased playing, we all found ourselves back where we started.

"Among the crowd of onlookers, I see people," my shadow said, "whom Priest Kapriel Hamadian said belonged to a sect of devil worshippers. Their men look fierce and are wearing turbans, and their women are wearing colorful traditional Kurdish dress."

"I see them, too."

"At night they sleep on the blacksmith's roof."

"Where else should they sleep?" I said. "Everywhere else is full."

"Would the priest have let them into the church?"

"I don't know."

"I dread those devil worshippers," my shadow said.

"They're all harmless," I said.

"Do they really believe in the Devil?"

"They believe in God," I said, "but they also believe that the battle between Good and Evil is yet to be won."

"Do they pray to God?"

"No," I said, "they don't pray to God because they believe that God is so kind that we would never punish anyone. And as He isn't a punitive God, there is no need to appease Him."

"And whom do they appease?"

"The Devil for He is evil. And they are more terrified of Him.

However, they also worship *Melek Taus*," I said. "It's a bronze bird of which there are only seven in the land. The *qewels* carry this bird from village to village for the creature embodies the Spirit of God on earth."

"Who are the qewels?"

"They are the priests of the devil worshippers."

I said to my shadow, "Those qewels don't have it easy; the poor creatures are plagued, they truly are. For you see, not only do they have to drag a heavy bronze bird from village to village, they also have to mount the wives of their followers as every devil worshipper sees it as an honor to have his wife receive the Spirit of God through copulation with a qewel."

I said to my shadow, "And the devil worshippers have their children christened just like the Christians, but they also have their boys circumcised, like the Jews and the Muslims. They are a strange people."

"They seem more like a fearful people to me."

"What do you mean?"

"Well," I said to my shadow, "it seems as though they don't want to get on the wrong side of any of the three religions, and are afraid to upset either the God of the Christians, the God of the Jews or of the Muslims."

"Perhaps, my little lamb."

"How are these Turkish subjects treated by the Sultan?"

"Well," I said. "A short time ago the Sultan was hunting them down and would have their men publically impaled. But for now he's decided to leave them in peace."

We talked at length about this, that and the other, my shadow and I … and hadn't even noticed that the famed barber had already completed his task and that the two of us were now sitting alone next to the single carpet covering the two sacks of grain.

"Where have all the people gone?" my shadow asked. "And where is that famous barber? And, most of all, where is Vardan? He was sitting right there on those sacks of grain but a moment ago, looking like a king."

"His family have taken Vardan into the oda," I said. "You see, the bride has now arrived accompanied by a whole procession of her relatives and, of course, her godmother, her *ginka mair*. The priest has now arrived, too."

"Will the priest now bless the clothes?"

"Yes," I said.

"I noticed," my shadow said, "that before, when Vardan's hair was being snipped, styled, straightened out, serenaded, soaped up, shaved and perfumed – you know, as he was sitting there on those two full grain sacks, a carpet beneath his rear – I noticed that he was wearing his oldest clothes."

"There's a reason for that," I said. "Even the bride, who has just been led into the groom's oda by her procession of relatives, was wearing her oldest dress."

"Why?"

"That's just how it is," I said. "Vardan is sitting next to the tonir and his bride is standing behind him. She is silent and may not utter a word for soon Boghos will arrive and bring two small packages with him. They are wrapped in a sackcloth and contain a secret."

"What secret?"

"Well, beneath the sackcloth lie the couple's new clothes … The one package contains those of the groom and the other holds the wedding dress and the new veil. The priest will bless the new clothes as well as the new veil. And he will pray for quite some time and then he will place the right hand of the bride into the right hand of the groom. Then the bride and the groom will leave to take a bath in the stable – but not in the same stable – Vardan will enter the Khatisians' stable while the bride enters the mukhtar's stable. There they will put on their new clothes and then, and only then, will they be formally introduced to the wedding guests." And I said to my shadow, "I can tell you right now that the bride will be wearing red. Her wedding dress is red. And her outer veil is red, the outer veil that will cover the inner veil whose sole purpose is to conceal her mouth and her chin. Her shoes will also be red, by that I mean her saffian leather slippers that are so dainty, you won't believe your eyes."

"Why? What's so unbelievable about them?"

"That they are able to carry all that fat that the bride amassed while she was being fattened up."

"And Vardan?"

"Vardan won't be wearing shalvar trousers," I said, "nor will he be wearing boots or a sleeveless jacket. He won't even have his usual fur cap."

"What will he be wearing?"

"Modern things that his eldest brother, Hajgaz, bought in Bakir: a Stambul suit, a red tie from Van, the Armenian garden and citadel city, low-cut shoes from Erzurum and a genuine fez from Bakir – stiff and solid and red."

"He's going to look like a dandy!"

"But he's no dandy."

As Zovinar and Hamest, and Zovinar's daughters, walked among the guests with their sofras filled with sweets, acting offended whenever anyone said, 'No, thank you. I'm full.' … as the women walked around with their sofras in this way … we two, by that I mean my shadow and I, felt as though we too were partaking in the sweets, especially the baklava that Zovinar had baked, and we also felt as though we were holding out our glasses to be filled with liquor and wine by Hagob and by Vardan's grandfather, and later on we truly felt as though we were drunk out of our wits. In our imagined drunken state, we soon fell into a deep sleep and when we awoke, the sixth day was already over.

And so it was that the sun rose on the seventh day, the day of the marriage ceremony. During the ceremony the two of us, my shadow and I, stood guard over the small Gregorian village church.

"We should do something if the Kurds come to kidnap the bride," my shadow said.

"Yes," said I, the storyteller.

"But what?" said my shadow. "We don't even exist, you and I. I mean, you're a storyteller and I'm your shadow."

"You're absolutely right about that," I said. "Or maybe you're not. Perhaps we do exist; it's just a different kind of existence."

"And what would we be able to do?"

"Keep standing guard," I said. "And continue to bear witness for those in the world of imagination."

"For Thovma Khatisian?"

"Precisely."

"OK," my shadow said. And as he uttered those words, the two of us intently fixed our eyes on the winding village road that ran above the roof of the Khatisians' home right up into the mountains ... right up to the black tents of Suleyman, the sheikh of the Kurds.

"A horse carrying a Kurdish rider once slipped and fell whilst walking along that winding road at a spot just above Hagob's house," I told my shadow. "And both horse and rider fell through the roof and landed next to the tonir."

"I know the story," my shadow said. "When they come to take the bride's virginity," I said, "we should ask the Lord God to make them all fall through the roof. Perhaps they will break their necks."

"Or perhaps they will fall straight into the tonir," said my shadow.

And so, while we kept watch and talked, we heard the liturgical songs of the priest and the congregation through the door of the church that was slightly ajar. And from amongst the many voices, we heard Zovinar sob with joy. And we also heard the mournful sobs of the mukhtar's wife, who was losing her daughter.

"Bride and groom will now be stood facing one another," I said to my shadow. "Soon the priest will touch their heads and press their foreheads together, and, as is tradition, he will wind a pearl amulet – the *narod* – around the foreheads of the married couple for them to wear for a week. It's supposed to ward off evil spirits, and it's even more effective than garlic or upside-down horseshoes."

"And what about the crosses?" my shadow asked.

"Everyone present wears a small wooden cross," I said. "Only the blacksmith, Vardan's godfather, is wearing a large cross. And he holds that large cross protectively over the heads of the young couple."

"And what about the wedding rings?"

"What about them?" I said. "The priest will present the rings to them on a plate, and Zovinar will sob even more loudly, as will the mukhtar's wife, and the hands of the bridal couple will shake as once those rings have been placed, there is no going back. Then the couple may only be parted by death."

"Will their ring fingers shake, too?"

"They will shake most of all, my little lamb."

Whilst we two, my shadow and I, were on the lookout for the Kurds, the wedding ceremony was completed inside the small church. Soon after the doors sprang open and the laughing, newly-wed couple walked out onto the street. We saw Vardan's eldest brother Hajgaz, who had stopped just before the church door, place a fragile plate before the feet of the couple and we saw Vardan stamp on it with his foot. And we heard some people sob and some laugh. Hagob was laughing particularly loudly. Vardan's grandfather was laughing, too, and with his high-pitched, squeaky voice, he pronounced the old Armenian phrase: *The shards have been broken … long live the bride and groom!*

Then the two of us, my shadow and I, flew off. We just left.

But we returned not long after to follow the merry marriage procession as it made its way through the village.

"I, the storyteller, almost managed to grab a squeeze of the bride's backside; you don't see rears as plump and as young as that every day. Like a fully-filled wine pouch on short legs, the fattened bride waddled through the streets of the village between her relatives and godparents. Everybody gazed in amazement at her expensive wedding dress with its golden embroidery, her small, red women's fez with its white and red veil, her golden jewelry and pearl necklace made of silver coins. Here once more the procession of women walked behind the procession of men. As the married couple exited the church, the musicians struck up another tune. The wives of the devil worshippers, the Muslims and the gypsies began a loud *talil*, a trilling sound made using the tongue that goes straight through any devout Christian. The wives of the devil worshippers standing on the blacksmith's roof, who preferred to follow the procession of men and women from where they stood, were particularly loud, and trilled even more powerfully and piercingly than the wives of the gypsies and those of the Muslims, as if trying to reach the ears of the

Devil as well. The wedding procession often stopped before a house to joke with the old women, who were sitting just by their doors, or to receive gifts. Some of the old women had smeared flour paste onto gold, silver and copper coins so that they could stick them to the bride's forehead, which she allowed them to do before thanking the women and removing the coins just so that she could throw them to her godmother who hid the money beneath her apron. Yes, it truly was a moment of unadulterated joy. It took almost half the afternoon for the wedding procession to finally reach Hagob's house.

The previous year Hagob had had a separate room built behind the stable where Vardan would live with his young wife. The room even had its own tonir and a window, which was not common, but Hagob had said, 'A window, just like the rich in the cities have in their odas and in the rest of their rooms.' In Frankistan, so Hagob said, apparently even the poor had windows in their odas. 'Now when my son wakes up early in the morning … with the will of God … he shall step to the window so he can breathe in the fresh air and inspect the weather.'

As the wedding procession finally reached Hagob's house, they found a bound lamb lying before the front door. Vardan's eldest brother stood next to the animal with a knife in his hand.

It all took place as it had at Hagob's wedding, and back then his father had also said to him, 'Yes, that's exactly how it was for me and your mother.' And that's how it was for their parents, and their parents before them. In fact, this is how things had always been and why should they ever be any different?

The wedding guests threw grains of wheat over the heads of the married couple, and some applauded when Vardan took the knife from Hajgaz and stroked the lamb's throat with his left hand at exactly the spot where he would make the swift cut. Vardan then spat on the knife and slit the lamb's throat, jumping to the side as the stream of blood gushed out and rushed against the front door, dragged the twitching lamb away from the door, stuck his index finger in the animal's open, bleeding wound, dabbed a few spots of blood onto his wife's forehead and his own, brandished an old sword that he had hidden beneath his jacket, and raised it – as a sign of his protection – above his young wife's head, who then slipped into their new home under the protection of his sword.

The musicians, who had briefly paused, now started playing again even more loudly and more merrily than before. The wedding guests talked among themselves; some clapped along in time to the music. The talil also grew in volume as some of the female devil worshippers had climbed down from the blacksmith's roof and were running towards Hagob's house, their tongues in full trill, followed by two gypsy women who copied them. The mayor then came running. He had brought the holy fire from his own tonir and handed it over to his daughter, who had stepped back outside again. And so it was that the bride took hold of the cauldron containing the holy fire from her parents' tonir. She cried as her father gave her the cauldron containing the fire, and she kissed his hand, returning to her marital home with tears running down her face. There, in her new tonir, she lit her own fire.

Vardan and his bride had just walked three times around the tonir when Hagob and Zovinar entered their new room. Zovinar had a white bed sheet draped over her arm.

– Your mother has brought you the white bed sheet, Hagob said to Vardan. We will now leave you two alone so that you can fulfil your manly duty. Don't think about it too long, just do it, and do it quickly. People are waiting impatiently in front of the house.

– What are they waiting for?

– To see the blood-spotted bed sheet, said Hagob, that you will hang in front of the door later to show everyone that your wife was still a virgin.

– Does it have to be now?

– It has to be now, said Hagob. Once night falls, people won't be able to see the blood.

– Can it not wait until tomorrow morning?

– No, Hagob said.

– For God's sake, said Zovinar. Do not dilly dally, my son. And do not bring shame upon this family.

– She's right, said Hagob. Do it now for by the time the rooster crows tomorrow morning, it may already be too late.

But Vardan was far too confused to take his wife's virginity now. And so he took her by the hand and led her to the front of the Khatisians' house once more. And he led her even farther, to the market square, in order to buy them both a little time.

'Later,' he thought to himself. 'You can do it later.'

Hagob and Zovinar were right; there are some things in life that shouldn't be put off until the next morning when the rooster crows. Just as Vardan and his wife were coming back from the market square, no less than one hundred armed Kurdish fighters galloped into the village. Their shrieks were even louder and more piercing than the women's talil. The Kurds shot wildly in the air, drove the crowds apart, rode to Hagob's house and then to the market square and back again. Suddenly they spotted Vardan and his bride. They surrounded the pair, hit Vardan over the head, grabbed hold of his screaming bride, pulled her onto one of their horses and galloped away."

11

"The village elders had gathered in the mukhtar's house, including a handful of men from the bride and groom's families as well as those of the godfathers and godmothers. The priest was also present. The men sat in the selamlik smoking around the tonir.

– Why didn't you pay the bride tax? The red-haired black-smith asked.

– I don't know, said Hagob.

– I don't know either, said the mukhtar.

– I'll tell you why, the priest said. You thought that the sheikh of the Kurds would forget about the wedding.

– We did. It's true, said the mukhtar.

– The Kurds won't take the bride's virginity if we pay the ransom promptly, said Hagob. The only problem is that the ransom will now be much higher than half of the dowry.

– The bride tax, said the blacksmith.

– The bride tax would have cost less, said the priest.

– We need to saddle up our three best horses, said the mukhtar, and ride after the Kurds. If we catch up with them and offer them a reasonable ransom, we'll be able to redeem my daughter's honor.

– By the time we catch up with them, the Kurds will have taken her virginity, said Hagob.

– That might well be, said the mukhtar.

– And what will that mean for my son's honor?

– I don't know, said the mukhtar."

The storyteller said, "Once upon a time there were three riders who saddled up the three best horses in the village and rode after the Kurds. One of the riders was Vardan's brother-in-law Pesak, another was his brother Dikran and the third was Avetik, the blacksmith's son.

When the three riders returned to the village, dusk had almost descended.

– Did you catch up with the Kurds? the mukhtar asked.

– Yes, Pesak said. They were waiting for us in one of the gorges because they knew that we would offer to pay a ransom.

– And is my daughter still a virgin?

– She is still a virgin.

– How can you be sure?

– The Kurds gave us their word.

– Do the Kurds want us to pay the bride tax?

– No, they only want the ransom.

– And how much do they want?

– They want twenty sheep for the bride returned alive, but she will no longer be a virgin.

– But we want her back a virgin.

– Then you'll have to pay one hundred sheep.

– But one hundred is too much. Where do they expect us to

find a hundred sheep?

– Then just give them twenty, Mukhtar Bey. Twenty sheep for your daughter's life.

– I can afford twenty. And as I'm sure Hagob will contribute half, I will only have to give up ten.

– Exactly, said the priest. Twenty sheep between both families will not make either of you poor.

– Right you are, said the mukhtar. But what will my daughter's life be worth if she is no longer a virgin? Her children will be ostracized, and her children's children. And how should my son-in-law carry on living? Should we allow him to become the laughing stock of the village? And who here will speak to my daughter? The old women will spit in her face, and the younger ones will turn their heads away. And how will I be able to continue as mukhtar? This shame will tar both of our families.

– You are right, Mukhtar Bey, said the priest. Give them fifty sheep, and Hagob will give them fifty more.

– But what will become of our herds? said the mukhtar.

– And Hagob said, 'Yes, what will become of our herds?'

On that exact same evening the families of both men herded one hundred sheep into the mountain lands of the Kurds. The sole woman to ride with them was Bulbul, the Kurd. She sat on her nameless donkey and hurried both the men and animals along.

– Hey, Bulbul, Hagob said. Why do you always want to be involved in everything?

– Why shouldn't I be involved? said Bulbul.

– Yes, good point, said Hagob.

– And why shouldn't I be involved? said Bulbul. I suppose you would rather be the one to verify whether or not your daughter-in-law is still a virgin?

– Do you want to do it?

– If not me, who will? said Bulbul. Or would you rather give the Kurds one hundred sheep before you know for certain whether or not she is still a virgin?

– No, I wouldn't want to do that, said Hagob.

– For if she is no longer a virgin, said Bulbul, one hundred sheep will be too many.

– Yes, one hundred will be too many, said Hagob.

– Then you'll just give them twenty, said Bulbul.

Bulbul and the men returned with the bride later that night. Vardan and the rest of the family were standing at the door when the strange, eerie procession arrived. The oil lamps were still burning down in the village.

– Hey, Bulbul, said Vardan.

– Hello there, my little groom, said Bulbul.

– What's going on, Bulbul?

– Nothing, said Bulbul.

It was already rather late, but the villagers hadn't gone to bed; even the guests on the roofs of the houses were still awake. Fortunately, the Turkish crier and drummer – the lame, half-deaf munadi – was among the wedding guests.

– Fetch your drum, Hagob said to him, and let all the people know that she is still a virgin; the honor of both our families has been saved.

– Pativ? said the Turk.

– Pativ, said Hagob.

– Shall I tell the people anything else?

– Yes, said Hagob. Tell them that first thing tomorrow morning, shortly after the rooster crows, they shall see a bloody bed sheet hanging in front of my house.

– Do you think the rooster will crow tomorrow?

– The rooster always crows at daybreak, said Hagob. He even crowed on the very first day when God created the earth.

– That must mean the rooster was here before Creation?

– Precisely, said Hagob.

The bride was so exhausted and frightened that she fell asleep as soon as she lay down on the bridal bed – she even fell asleep before her wedded husband could carry out his most sacred of duties. Vardan wouldn't have done it anyway as he too was dazed and shocked, and he had a terrible headache from the blow he had received. He simply lay down next to his bride and fell straight to sleep.

Vardan only woke up once. It was the middle of the night. 'What will people say tomorrow when they see that there's no blood on the bed sheet,' he thought to himself. With his hands, he searched for his wife's fat rear. 'You have to wake her up,' he thought to himself, but he didn't dare.

Vardan tried to picture just how many pieces of baklava she must have eaten to make herself so plump. 'Forty pieces every day,' he thought. 'And over an entire year.' He tried to calculate how many pieces of baklava that would have been. But as he was a poet and not a mathematician, he couldn't work it out. He tried to count each individual piece of baklava as you would sheep, and that made him feel so drowsy that he didn't get very far in his tally. Later on, after all that counting had sent him to sleep, he dreamed of a mountain of cake.

Zovinar caused quite a scene when she came in early the next morning and saw that there was no blood on the bed sheet. Hagob also rushed into the room.

– People will think the Kurds took her virginity instead of my son, he said.

– Our honor is lost! cried Zovinar.

– Lost, said Hagob.

– What happened? Hagob said to his son. Tell me, is she still a virgin?

– She is, said Vardan.

– Can you prove it? said Hagob.

– No, I can't, said Vardan.

– Didn't I bring you into this world with a healthy man's bone? asked Hagob.

– Yes, Father, you did, said Vardan.

– So why isn't there any blood on the bed sheet?

– Because she was asleep, said Vardan.

– And what kind of man doesn't even have the nerve to wake up his own wife?

– I don't know, said Vardan.

Shortly after the rooster had crowed for the seventh time, Bulbul arrived and knocked on the door, as if she already knew where her precious advice could be of service – and nowhere was it more urgently needed than in this house.

– The bed sheets are as white as snow, said Hagob. What will people think of us?

– Doesn't your son have a man's bone between his legs?

– Yes, yes. He does, said Hagob.

– You helped bring my Vardan into this world, said Hagob. All those years ago in the stable. Do you remember?

– I remember, Hagob.

– And that is why, Bulbul, I'm thinking that perhaps you'll be able to come up with something to help restore his honor.

– Perhaps I'll come up with something, Hagob. I always seem to.

– Can anything be done?

– Now, Hagob, let me have a think.

And Bulbul had a think and said to Hagob, 'I want you to slaughter that rooster Abdul Hamid. And with that rooster's blood I want you to color the bed sheet red. Then you will hang the red and white sheet in front of the door.'

– That's what I should do?

– Yes, Hagob.

– And what will people say?

– They will be glad, said Bulbul. They will say, 'Looks like the Kurds didn't take her virginity after all. Vardan did. And now we have the proof. There are spots of blood on the bed sheet. And that Vardan is a real man. He has a good, strong bone between his legs. May God bless him. And his parents, who gave him such a fine bone. And his in-laws, who made sure that his bride's thin bit of skin remained intact.'

– Right you are, Bulbul, said Hagob.

– Fetch that rooster, Abdul Hamid, said Bulbul.

– You shall have him, Bulbul, said Hagob.

Bulbul slit the rooster's throat, but only after she had let it crow a few more times. Then she sprinkled a few drops of its fresh, red blood onto the white sheet and held the sheet over the fire in the tonir so that the blood would dry. Then she said, 'Right, Hagob Efendi. Now let's hang the bed sheet up in front of the door.'

On the afternoon of the eighth day Vardan took the blood-stained bed sheet to the house of his mother-in-law. His grandfather had told him that back when he married Vardan's grandmother, he had journeyed for two whole days with his donkey and cart to bring his blood-stained bed sheet to his mother-in-law, who lived far away. That was how it was done, and it was also a sign of respect and of gratitude. 'I bring you this bed sheet,' his grandfather had said upon reaching the house, 'and with it proof that you raised your daughter properly. She was pure and unspoiled on her wedding day.'

And his mother-in-law said, 'Who would expect any different, my son-in-law. My daughter comes from a decent family, does she not?'

– There is no girl in this land from a better or more decent family, he replied, who is deserving of marriage to a Khatisian.

And his mother-in-law shed a few tears, sniffed the bed sheet and said, '*Atschket louis.* May your eyes shine, my son-in-law, and may God bless you.'

'You will say the same thing to the mukhtar's wife as Grandfather said to his mother-in-law,' Vardan thought to himself. 'And when she sniffs the bed sheet and says that it smells of rooster, well, then you'll simply tell her it isn't true.'

As he was on his way to the house of his mother-in-law, he bumped into his uncle from America and his son, who could speak neither Turkish nor Kurdish and could only say a few words in broken Armenian.

– This sap, his uncle said, pointing to his son. This sap refuses to marry a girl from this village even though I told him that they are the finest and most dependable.

It took Vardan seven days and seven nights to get to know his wife.

– The well between her legs is all dried up, Vardan had said to his father.

And his father had replied, 'It's not that her well has dried up. It's up to you, my son, with skill, patience and a great deal of tenderness, to dig until you find water – and the source will soon come to life, you'll see.'

– But it's not working, Vardan said.

– Then you'll have to take some mutton fat, my son, for when the earth is brittle and the drill between your legs too hard, you need some of that fine fat to smooth the way in.

And Vardan heeded his father's advice. He got to know his wife and she fell pregnant.

– If she gives birth to a boy, Vardan's grandfather said, you shall call him Thovma.

Well, it just so happened that Thovma would have to be born to another woman, and not to Vardan's first wife. You see, her lifeline was short – so short that the gypsies recoiled in fear when they read her palm.

Vardan's grandmother had warned his wife never to look in the mirror during her pregnancy. But Arpine simply laughed at the old woman. You see, she wasn't fond of Vardan's grandmother and was jealous of her privileged position in the kertastan. As she was naturally vain, defiant and lazy, and as she increasingly began to neglect her household chores and everyday duties with each passing week of her pregnancy, Vardan's wife increasingly found time to gaze into the mirror, which she did more often than she should have done. And her unborn child saw the mirror image of Arpine and mistook it for its real mother, and so it turned itself the wrong way around.

– Be careful, Vardan's grandmother warned. You've no idea what you're doing.

– But nothing bad can happen to me, Arpine said. You see, not only have I hung two horseshoes before the door of our bedroom ... and a bible next to my bed ... and hung garlic up in all the corners and over the front door and even around my neck, just like you, Grandmother. I've even rubbed butter around the wall of the well outside the house. How could the Djinns possibly put a curse on my unborn baby now?

– At least hang your small, golden cross in front of the mirror.

– But I'd rather wear it so that it hangs between my breasts.

– Between your chubby sacks of milk that aren't even full yet?

– Yes, said Arpine.

And so the story ended as it was doomed to end: After nine months of pregnancy, Arpine died giving birth.

She died at a time when the trees across the land of Hayastan had long unfurled their leaves and the Lord God had adorned the entire vilayet with a colorful carpet of flowers in honor of Ascension Day for the enjoyment of everyone in the region, including the Muslims and the Jews, the gypsies and the devil worshippers. The sparrows on the flat roofs of Yedi Su were already heralding the start of summer.

– It's almost as though the Yazidis are right, Vardan said to Priest Kapriel Hamadian. Those foolish devil worshippers who believe that the battle between Good and Evil is not yet won. What else am I supposed to think when the will of the Djinns in the cursed mirror of my godly wife was stronger than the will of God?

– It is a sin to question the Lord, the priest said. Surely the death of your wife was God's will. Otherwise she would have lived through the birth.

– And why did my Thovma have to die with her?

– That child was not your son Thovma, said the priest.

It was a nameless, stillborn child. – And surely it is God's will that you take another wife and father another child with her. A child that you shall name Thovma.

– Thovma?

– Yes, said the priest. Thovma.

One week after the funeral, Vardan's great-grandmother died, too, but as the senile old woman used to spend hours sat motionless next to the tonir, no one noticed she was gone. She just nodded off. Only in the evening, when the animals came back from the fields and trampled past the tonir on their way to the stable and one of the creatures knocked the grandmother with its swinging tail so that the dead woman fell off her chair, did Hagob realize what had happened.

– Her death was long overdue, people said. After all, she was over a hundred.

– She must have been grieving for my stillborn grandson, Thovma, said Hagob. Someone must have told her about it.

– But the priest said … the priest said it wasn't Thovma who died, said Zovinar. It was a nameless child. Our Thovma is still waiting to be conceived."

12

And the storyteller's voice appeared and said, "It was the year 1894, the year in which drummers and criers took to the squares across the land of Hayastan to announce reforms in the name of the Sultan: tax breaks and other benefits for rayahs and giaours and basically any infidel that Allah – blessed be His name – has condemned for all eternity. The Sultan promised more self-determination for the *millets,* the Christian rural communities. The munadis took great pleasure in pounding their drums and shouting these new promises over the heads of the masses. Of course, the Armenians would still have to pay the military tax – the Sultan's *bedel* – as they always had done. And they were still also forbidden from carrying weapons with the exception of a few Armenian saptiehs who, along with the Muslims, would ensure law and order in the millets. The Sultan promised the Armenians representation in government and commanded all Armenian traitors from the 77/78 wars to exchange their secret Russian passports for Ottoman documents. The munadis were well practiced criers, and so their promises sometimes sounded so sweet, you would think they had mouths full of honey.

In the village of Yedi Su only a few people understood what the Sultan's words actually meant, and so it was that Hagob approached the munadi after his announcement and asked,

'What does the Sultan actually mean?'

– I don't know either, said the munadi.

And so Hagob asked the literate Armenian who was, as always, at the munadi's side.

– It means nothing, Hagob Efendi, the munadi's Armenian assistant replied. Nothing at all, Hagob Efendi.

– But it must mean something?

– Well, said the Armenian. It does have some meaning. Have you ever heard of the Congress of Berlin, Hagob Efendi? I mean the one from 1878?

– No, chelebi, said Hagob.

– At this congress the Sultan made certain concessions to the great Christian powers, particularly in terms of reforms, and he promised to allow greater freedoms to the Christians living in the Ottoman Empire, as well as protection from the Kurds and from arbitrary discrimination by Turkish officials.

– We haven't seen much of those changes around here, said Hagob.

– Yes, I know, said the munadi's educated Armenian assistant.

– And what do the great Christian powers have to gain when our lives here improve? asked Hagob.

– Nothing, said the educated Armenian.

– So why are they fighting for our rights?

– It's just a pretext, said the educated Armenian. A pretext to intervene in our affairs. It serves their political interests. Do you see what I mean?

– No, chelebi, said Hagob. I don't.

Later that day in the coffeehouse, the educated Armenian told Hagob, 'The great powers are using the Christians as a pretext to provide their crutches to *the sick man of the Bosporus.* You see, they want to hobble alongside him and have as much control over him as possible, do you understand?'

– No, chelebi, I don't, said Hagob. And who is the sick man of the Bosporus?

– Ask the munadi, said the educated Armenian. He knows.

But the munadi didn't know either.

During one of his sermons, the priest said, 'When the Sultan announces reforms, it means he is planning a small massacre.'

– Why, Father? asked somebody in the congregation.

– Because he is annoyed by his own generosity, said the priest. Or because he wants to annoy the great Christian powers that he only recently pacified with the announcement of his planned reforms.

– And who will be massacred?

– Well, who indeed? said the priest.

At the end of 1894 massacres took place in remote Anatolian villages, but there were none in the seven villages or close to Yedi Su. People heard about the massacres from travelling Armenian traders. One of them said, 'The Kurds are slitting the throats of Armenian farmers, and they even burned some of them alive.'

– What type of Kurds were they? asked the priest.

– They were some of the 150,000 Kurds that the Sultan recruited. People call them the Hamidiye. Haven't you heard of them?

– No, said the priest.

– The Sultan is paying the Kurdish Beys a whole load of money for their fighters.

– So, the Beys need money, eh?

– That's right, Vartabed.

– And what does the Sultan need the Kurdish Hamidiye regiments for?

– I don't know exactly, said the Armenian trader. I presume to keep the minorities in check, and perhaps to scare the hell out of the great powers.

Very little happened in Yedi Su and its neighboring villages," said the storyteller. "Even in 1895, as the number of massacres grew, there was still no sign of trouble here in Yedi Su. The village's old Turkish saptieh still sat chattering away in the coffeehouse or napping outside in the sun whilst the children kept an eye on his gun, which was even older than he was. Suleyman's armed riders only made an appearance when taxes were due, but they were generally peaceful as long as they got what they wanted. And even the Turkish officials only came by when they needed money. Once one of the traders brought an English newspaper into the village which nobody could read.

– And what does it say in the newspaper? asked the priest.

– That the Hamidiye have massacred 300,000 Armenians, said the trader. Even those in the cities. In Constantinople there are dead Armenians lying in the street. And in Urfa they burned 1,000 Armenian women and children to death inside a cathedral.

– But that can't be, said the priest. Do you believe everything the papers write?

– Yes, said the trader.

– And did you see any of this with your own eyes?

– Yes, said the trader. In one small town I witnessed a slaughter. Kurdish Hamidiyes were there. Turkish civilians as well.

    – Did they slaughter sheep?

    – No. They slaughtered Armenians.

But in the village no one really believed the terrifying stories told by the Armenian traders. The few Turks who lived there were their friends, and everyone had long been acquainted with their relatives who came to visit. They were no better or worse than the Armenians, even though they didn't believe in Christ, but not one of them was a murderer. Not one of them would tolerate a massacre, or even stand by and watch as the Christians' throats were slit, or their women and children burned to death in a church. And the same could also be said of the sole Turkish saptieh in the village. He played cards in the coffeehouse like the other men, and occasionally joined them in a traditional game of *tavla* or backgammon. He drank no more and no less, smoked the same tobacco and sometimes farted when he had eaten too quickly or too much. Everyday life in the village continued as normal, despite the terrible stories.

Shortly after Christmas, a festival which Armenians celebrate at the beginning of January, Hagob said to his youngest son, 'You really should think about getting married again. What do you say, my son? Would you like me to speak with Manoushag? She's a good marriage broker; she set your sister up with the son of a rich carpet seller in Bakir.'

    But Vardan didn't want to think about asking the marriage broker for advice.

January 21 is the day of Saint Sarkis, who is also the patron saint of lovers. On Saint Sarkis Day the bachelors of the village would walk to the Gatnachpjur well to scatter birdfeed. The men needed only to throw a few breadcrumbs at the foot of the well and wait for a hungry bird to swoop down and snap up the crumbs with its beak … and then watch as it flew away. If they walked in the same direction as the bird, they were sure to find a bride. All they had to do was follow the bird and then they could be certain that they would meet the right woman, the one they had been waiting for all their lives.

On this Saint Sarkis Day, Vardan was amongst those who paid a visit to the Gatnachpjur well to scatter food for the birds. But he approached the tradition more shrewdly than the others: He cleverly built a trap in front of the well, caught a small sparrow who had already taken Vardan's crumbs in its mouth, threw a sackcloth over its head, carefully took hold of the animal, tied a small ring around one of its feet and then let it fly away. Now he could make no mistake. He would see which direction the bird flew in, follow it and look for a bird with a ring around its foot, which would land somewhere close to his future wife.

On that day Vardan wandered around the snowy mountains for several hours, always walking in the same direction as he had seen the bird fly. In the afternoon he reached the foothills of Yazidje and its snow-covered fields. It was the smallest of the seven villages and, in fact, nothing more than a hamlet of a few houses.

The village had been burned to the ground. Two Kurdish women in colorful headscarves picked their way through the rubble.

Their horses whinnied as Vardan approached.

– The Hamidiye were here, said one of the two women. We saw the smoke from up in the mountains.

  – Are there any survivors? asked Vardan.

There weren't. Or it at least from the looks of things the Sultan's Kurds had done a very thorough job. It was difficult to tell whether the Kurds had shot the villagers, or beaten them to death or killed them in some other barbarous act, for the dead bodies of the men, women and children had been thrown onto a pyre and left to burn. Not all of the corpses were charred beyond recognition. Vardan could see that some of the men were lacking heads; others were missing genitals.

  – Did you see what they did? asked Vardan.

  – No, said one of the women. We just saw the smoke.

Vardan searched through the rubble of the burnt-down houses but found no sign of life anywhere. The two Kurdish women followed him. Their faces were red from the icy cold and the biting wind. As they walked, they held on tightly to their headscarves with their hands. They clearly came from one of the semi-nomadic Kurdish villages of the elevated plains, and neither they nor their menfolk had anything to do with the Hamidiye. Vardan repeatedly turned around to check on them, but was satisfied that they meant him no harm. As he reached the last of the village's seven houses, he spotted a dead, dark-feathered bird in the snow. It was his Saint Sarkis bird. It had frozen to death. The ring, which he had attached to its foot so he could recognize it, was still there.

And Vardan suddenly heard a noise. The Kurdish women heard it, too. A soft whimper. It was coming from the burnt-out house in front of which the dead, dark-feathered bird lay.

– One of the women gave birth yesterday, said one of the Kurds. I was down here selling a rooster to her husband.

'Life is a miracle,' Vardan thought to himself.

The Kurdish women rubbed the child with snow and then dried it off before massaging it repeatedly. One of them gave the child her breast and the other fetched a horse blanket and wrapped the infant up in it.

– It's a little girl, said the one who had breastfed the child. We will take her.

But Vardan said, 'No. I'll take her.'

And so it was," said the storyteller, "that the black-gray bird sent by Saint Sarkis had brought Vardan to the village just in time to save the life of Anahit, the name that would be given to the girl who would one day carry Vardan's son, Thovma.

Vardan's tale of what happened that day and the sight of the burned child, whose eyes seemed to be the only living part of her body, spread fear and disgust throughout the entire village. People locked themselves up in their houses.

Vardan handed the small girl over to Priest Kapriel Hamadian who, although it was an unusual move, called for Bulbul the Kurd as she, so the priest said, had medicinal herbs in her hut, could work magic and, despite the fact that she was a Kurd, had safe, reliable hands that could be trusted to take good care of the small Armenian girl.

The villagers locked their front doors and as there was nowhere for them to flee should a massacre occur, other than the impassable, high mountains where they would all die a miserable death, starving and freezing in the snow and ice, they could do nothing but wait. But as they all knew that a locked front door can do little to protect anyone from the Hamidiye or the Djinns, it didn't take long before people unlocked their doors again, tentatively stepped outside and carried on with their lives as before. Whatever was coming, would come; no one could do anything to stop it.

– Trust in God and Jesus Christ, said the priest.

– I will defend myself and my people with my axe, said Garo, the saddle maker's son who wanted to become a Dashnak like Pesak, Vardan's brother-in-law.

– I'll chase those devils away with my hammer, said Avetik, the blacksmith's son.

And Vardan said, 'I'll use my ceremonial sword.'

Even the Turks in the village promised to fight alongside them. We are Muslims, Tashak said, and are allowed to bear arms. And I still have an old gun that I keep in my stable. I'll blow the brains right out of the heads of those Hamidiye dogs, and when they're dead, I will personally crush the balls of each and every one of them.

There was a lot of talk in the coffeehouse about the Hamidiye. The village's old, dozy saptieh, who strutted around between the tables, smoking and occasionally erupting in a loud burp or fart, said, 'When they come, I will chase them all away. After all, I am the law around here. Those Hamidiye are nothing but vicious irregulars, no better than the bashi-bazouks, and I have no idea why Sultan Abdul Hamid has given his name to those cowardly dogs.'

But they didn't come. The only danger the villagers faced were the heavy winds that blew down from the mountains and threatened to blow their poplar-branch roofs clean off, and then, when spring arrived, the snow melted in the mountains, sending down torrents of water that almost washed the village's small, crooked houses away. Everything remained quiet. Journeying traders, who returned to the village along with the more favorable weather, carrying with them beautiful silks, exotic jewelry and fruits from faraway lands, said that the world's press had kicked up an almighty fuss ... because of the Armenians, of course.

Hagob asked one of the traders why the world's press wasn't coming to help the Armenians, but the man just said that newspapers were made of nothing but paper and ink, and the letters on their pages were pitiful soldiers who helped only the great and the powerful in whose names anything and everything was printed, and that those angry words the newspapers shouted out to the world were no better than the loud-mouthed, hypocritical sing-song that came from the mouths of the market criers of Bakir.

Many more journeying traders came to Yedi Su, and each one told a different story. When the mulberries began to ripen, the traders said that people had stopped talking about the Hamidiye because the Sultan had sent them to Arabia. The Russians, so the traders said, believed the Hamidiye to be Kurdish Cossacks and were just waiting for those irregulars to defect to their side once the next war came around. People said that the Tsar had made no end of promises to the beys and agas, including better weapons for their riders, better horses, bigger fur caps, golden rubles, women and other spoils, if they joined him. The traders laughed, reassured the villagers and told them that instead of worrying they should stock up on provisions for the massacres were finally over. The traders assured the farmers that it would be wiser to remove the nuggets of gold from their boots, their cotton jackets, their earthenware jugs and even from the holes in the stable floor and wherever they had been hidden in the fields so they could invest in silks, beautiful jewelry or strange fruits that were perfect for preserving. One of the traders asked Hagob, 'Is it true that your youngest son is going to America?'

– Who told you that? asked Hagob.

– The mail carrier told me. I carried the fella with me in my araba a bit of the way.

– And who told the mail carrier?

– Well, I guess he read the letter that was in his mail sack.

– Do you mean the letter from America? The one from my brother Nahapeth?

– That's the one.

– He was here not that long ago, said Hagob. At the wedding. He came with his eldest son. A sap who couldn't even speak proper Armenian.

– And this brother of yours wants to help Vardan get to America? That's what was written in the letter?

– That's what it said, said Hagob. And he added, 'Not that long ago I gave that mail carrier a generous baksheesh so that he wouldn't open my letters.'

– But the mail carrier told me that you only paid him baksheesh so that he would deliver your letters on time. You didn't say anything about opening them.

– That could well be, said Hagob. And he said, 'To hell with the mail carrier. What does it matter if he knows what my brother writes in his letters? It's nothing secret. And I'm sure the Sultan doesn't care whether or not my brother turns my youngest son's head, you know, with this trip to America.'

And so it was," said the storyteller. "The uncle meant what he said about Vardan coming to join him in America, and Vardan himself had no objections to going; after the massacre in the village of Yazidje, Vardan suddenly had no desire to stay in Hayastan.

In the fall of 1897 another man wearing a large, peculiar, brimmed hat came to the village. He said he came from America and had brought money from Hagob's brother, Nahapeth, money that was meant for Hagob's youngest son, Vardan. And true to his word, he did indeed have money with him that he had hidden under the brim of his large hat.

I remember," said the storyteller, "that Hagob counted the money and then said, 'But this won't be enough for such an expensive journey.'
    – It's exactly half, said the American.
    – What do you mean? said Hagob.
    – Well, what do you think I mean? said the American who, although he wore a brimmed hat, actually came from Hayastan and still spoke just like the people here in these parts do. Even his manner and gestures were the same. What do you think I mean, Hagob Efendi? It's enough for half a ticket for the ship.
    – Is it possible to travel to America with only half a ticket?

asked Hagob.

– No, said the American.

– Are you saying my son should travel halfway and then get off the ship even though I know full well that you can't leave a ship when it's out in the middle of the ocean?

– No, said the American. Vardan should take the money and you will see to it that he gets the rest. Your brother said that you should dig up the gold nuggets from the *bak*. And the American, who wasn't really a proper American, pointed to the courtyard where the hens, ducks and geese were running around.

– So that's where I should get it from?

– Yes, said the American.

And so Hagob dug up a couple of nuggets of gold, gave them to his son who, in the spring of 1898, set out for America. Hagob took him to Bakir on his donkey-drawn cart. From there he joined a caravan of Greek, Jewish and Armenian traders, whose arabas were escorted by saptiehs. When Vardan arrived in Constantinople, some of his uncles and aunts whom he had never met before were waiting for him. He was terrified to be in such a large city but luckily for him an Armenian always has aunts and uncles everywhere who are there to take care of him. He stayed with his relatives and they even took him to the port, a place which terrified him even more than the big city, on the day he was due to leave."

Vardan didn't know that the storyteller was standing next to him at the ship's railing. And he also didn't notice the storyteller jump back down as the ship's enormous funnels gave the signal to pull away with clouds of steam and a blast of the horn. The storyteller jumped down just as all the ship's joints began to shake impatiently, driven on by its fiery ovens and the sweaty, coal-shoveling stokers in the boiler room. As the ship finally set off, the storyteller simply watched it leave from the shore before vanishing along with the passing time. He eventually reappeared again though, at the end of the year 1899, showing up just in time to witness the turning of the next century.

Book Three

1

No one knows why storytellers are sometimes in a hurry, why they blow the pages off of calendars and only mention what they feel important. And I, the storyteller, am no exception. And so I won't explain to you why I chose to casually skip through the first few years of the new century. There was the overthrow of Abdul Hamid in 1908, the Hamidiye regiments were disbanded and the Young Turks came to power. And then there were the Russians, who had set their sights on the Bosporus, the English, who were dreaming of finding the shortest route to India – a route which would run straight through Turkey – and then there were greater and lesser powers, hungrily eyeing up the rotten cake that Abdul Hamid had left behind. Everybody wanted a piece of it, including the Germans, and they were the smartest of all. You see, they knew how to hide their hungry eyes behind cold monocles – monocles made of thick, gray glass: monocles that were opaque. The Germans delivered weapons and sent their military officers to train the Turks. Their mediators lived in Pera, Constantinople's upmarket district, which had modern shops and refined hotels. They also built the Turks the ideal railway, which they named the Bagdad Railway. With a devious grin, they built a railway made out of iron, steel and fire: a sign of their efficiency, but also of their progress and good will. And so it was that among the many crutches that were eagerly sent from powers both great and small to aid the sick man of the Bosporus, the crutches sent by the Germans were the most useful.

During the Balkan Wars, I briefly flew to Bulgaria, but soon turned around and came back again to follow the German officers as they made their way to Bakir following the historic shots of Sarajevo. Once in Bakir I circled over the city, my eyes searching, before I came to rest together with my shadow on the Gate of Happiness.

"I heard shots a few days ago," said my shadow.

I said, "They were the shots of Sarajevo."

"Oh, those shots," said my shadow.

"Yes," I said.

"Why weren't we there?"

"Because I didn't want to watch the Austrian heir to the throne and his wife bleed to death in front of the crowds."

"And what difference would it have made?"

"None whatsoever."

The hangings had yet to take place. The black hooks protruding from the Gate of Happiness were still empty and seemingly pointless. It would stay that way for a few more weeks to come.

"The hangings have yet to take place," I said to my shadow as the summer drew to a close.

"Who will be hanged?"

"The Armenians."

"When?"

"Someday." I said, "Someday. I don't know when. Today the Turks mobilized their troops. It's August third, 1914."

"How was Vardan's trip to America, the one he went on back in 1898?" my shadow asked.

"Well, sometimes it was like this and sometimes it was like that," I said.

"And what happened to Anahit?"

I said, "The priest and Bulbul took care of the burned girl. It was true what they said: She no longer had a face. Just eyes. But her eyes shone brightly, as though she had seen Christ. And as her eyes shone so brightly, it wasn't hard for the priest to find her adoptive parents who would raise the child to be a Christian. Not that the priest didn't trust Bulbul of course, but she wasn't Christian.

And so new parents were found for the little girl: a childless married couple who lived on the outskirts of the village.

The little girl's adoptive father was the silk farmer, Yeremian, and her adoptive mother was his wife, a woman who couldn't have children and whose breasts, it was claimed, had been dry all of her life. A wet nurse would also be found for the little girl as well as godparents, who would accompany her to her christening.

And back then Priest Kapriel Hamadian said to Hagob, 'Christ has saved this little girl. And it was His will that someone pure of heart find little Anahit.'

– Do you mean my son, Vardan?

– I do. I mean your son, Vardan.

– My son wishes to marry this girl when the time comes, said Hagob. For it would appear to be the will of our Savior that these two come together as one.

– Then he shall marry her when the time comes, said the priest.

– But this child should not be breastfed by the same woman who breastfed my son, for that is forbidden if the two shall one day be married.

– Then find another wet nurse.

– And the red-haired blacksmith can't be her godfather either, nor can his wife be her godmother, as both are godparents to my son.

– It is forbidden to have the same godparents, said the priest, if the two are destined to be wed.

– Then I will see to it that Anahit has a different set of godparents, said Hagob. And I will speak with the blacksmith as he has already told some people in the village that he would like to be the girl's godfather.

– Yes, do, said the priest. And explain to the blacksmith why he cannot be her godfather.

And so a new wet nurse and different godparents were found for the girl. She was christened Anahit as that was the name given to the goddess of fertility. If something survives, it should be fruitful in order to prove to the Devil that God does not sow His seed in vain.

Hagob symbolically exchanged coins with the silk farmer. And together they threw their coins into the holy fire of the tonir, fished them back out again, blew into their hands, spat on their hands and their coins, and returned the coins to their pockets.

When Vardan travelled to America, Anahit's adoptive father said to Hagob, 'Your son is engaged to my daughter. What does he want to go to America for?'

– I don't know, said Hagob. He said he wants to become a poet.

– And because of that he has to go to America?

– No, not really, said Hagob.

And Hagob said, 'Perhaps he's just afraid of the great tebk that will one day come; a great massacre that none of us will survive. – Or perhaps he felt compelled to move far away because he is young and still doesn't know that the roots are more important than the golden fruit that dangle from the branches of those American trees.'

– Perhaps he wants to become a millionaire? said the silk farmer.

– Of course he will become a millionaire, said Hagob. Everyone who travels to America becomes a millionaire. And then he will come back to fetch Anahit.

– He'll have to wait a few years though. Until the first drops of blood – blood that comes from no wound – appear between my daughter's legs, showing us all that she is a woman.

– He will wait, said Hagob.

– But there are many women over there, said the silk farmer. And they show off more than just their legs.

– True, said Hagob. But I know my son. He will return.

– And it won't bother him that his wife only has eyes and no face?

– He knows, said Hagob. He doesn't mind.

– Will he take Anahit back to America with him? asked the silk farmer. Or will he return to Hayastan with his millions to settle here with Anahit?

– If the great tebk doesn't come, said Hagob, then perhaps my youngest son won't return to America with his millions after all. He will marry Anahit and buy a mansion here.

– But there aren't any mansions here in this region, said the silk farmer.

– Then he'll have one built, said Hagob. Or he'll buy one in Van, perhaps in the Armenian garden quarter or right on the shores of Lake Van where a wealthy relative of mine lives.

– It's a beautiful lake, said the silk farmer. Isn't that where we get our soap from?

– It is, said Hagob. If you live by the lake, you need only fetch some water, leave it to evaporate and the salt that's left is the purest soap you'll find.

– Does that mean he won't need to buy any more soap, he'll just fish it out of the lake for free?

– Yes, said Hagob.

The night before he left, Priest Kapriel Hamadian appeared to Vardan in a dream, and he said, 'If what they say is true, my son, that the wheat over there in America is made of pure gold, then take hold of a scythe and go out onto the fields of that great country and harvest those thick, golden grains of wheat before the locusts eat them all up. And if it is also true, my son, that there are stacks of money simply lying on the streets of those big American cities, then take hold of a broom and quickly sweep it all up before the rats come. But if you realize, my son, that those golden grains of wheat and stacks of money on the street are filled with nothing but leeches with an ice cold bite that suck the warmth from your heart and all the magic from your soul, then yank the handle from your broom and your scythe and throw those useless tools away. And then go to your little room, where no one can see you, and take hold of the poet's goose-feather quill and transform it into a rod.'

– And what should I fish, Vartabed?

– Fish the songs from your heart, my son, and the magic that neither the locusts, the rats nor those icy leeches can devour.

The witless watercarrier had heard from the other villagers that Vardan had saved little Anahit's life. But he had also heard the priest when he said, 'Our Savior, Jesus Christ, saved the girl's life.' And as the water carrier was one of those considered to be *poor in spirit,* as well as slightly muddled in the head, he thought that Vardan and the Savior were one and the same person. And so every time Vardan appeared, the water carrier began to stutter loudly and crept along behind him, gesticulating with his hands. Once he followed Vardan all the way to the Gatnachpjur well and because he had heard that the Saint Sarkis bird had taken flight from that very well to lead Christ to Anahit, he fell to his knees before Vardan and stuttered as he kissed his feet. It just so happened that the priest was passing by the well that day. A few other people then appeared, too. They jeered at the water carrier, grabbed hold of him and pretended to throw him down the well. Hagob also came running but arrived just as the priest was shooing the people away and trying to console the water carrier, who was in tears.

Later on, Hagob asked the priest, 'Did you understand, Vartabed, what the water carrier was stuttering after you had managed to calm him down?'

– Yes, said the priest.

– What did he stutter?

– He said something about Christ. And then he pointed to your youngest son and asked me whether he would be walking over the Sea of Galilee again any time soon.

– And what did you tell him?

– I told him that that fellow would soon be walking over the big pond, all the way to America.

Hagob didn't cry like the others as he bade farewell to his son. He just said, 'Never forget that you are from Hayastan.'

– I won't, said Vardan.

– And that a good tree should never be transplanted.

– I'll remember that, too, Father.

– A true tree would never even allow itself to be transplanted, said Hagob, and not even the most fertile of foreign lands could change that.

Initially, people in the village often spoke of Vardan, but as time went on, they mentioned him less and less, until eventually his name only crossed their lips whenever he sent a letter. At the beginning Vardan wrote often. They were long, detailed letters. But the more time passed, the shorter his letters became and one day they stopped coming altogether. Whenever Hagob complained about his son, people would say, 'When a man becomes rich, he forgets those he loves. The more millions a man has, the more forgetful he becomes.'

And so, as Hagob and his wife waited for post from America to arrive, trying to think of a reason to explain their son's long silence, and as year after year went by, and they grew older and more tired … they barely noticed that Anahit, the girl without a face, had blossomed into a young woman. The silk farmer had sent his adoptive daughter to go and stay with a relative of his in Bakir so that she could attend school there as the city was home to some American and Frankish missionary schools that also accepted girls, even those of the Gregorian faith. Anahit returned to the village just as the Young Turks seized power. The year was 1908 and a few years had passed since the first spots of blood had begun to appear between Anahit's legs – blood that came from no wound.

– Vardan needs to come back now, said the silk farmer. Anahit is almost thirteen and she's been bleeding for such a long time now that I fear she will soon be too old to find herself a decent man.

– She doesn't even have an engagement ring yet, said his wife.

Before people were not afraid to look directly into Anahit's burnt face, but now they all averted their eyes and whispered cruel comments behind her back.

And so it was not entirely unexpected that Manoushag, the marriage broker, said to the silk farmer and his wife:

– Would you like me to ask around to see if I can find her a husband?

– No, said the silk famer. I have promised her to Hagob's son.

– But no one has heard from him.

– We will hear from him soon.

– The longer she waits, the worse her chances will be, said the marriage broker. Who will want to marry an old maid, especially one without a face?

In 1909 another American with a large hat arrived. He brought with him a golden ring for Anahit and a few words from Vardan.

– He didn't want to send the ring by post, said the American.
– How is my son? asked Hagob.
– He's not bad, said the American.
– I receive letters from my brother Nahapeth, said Hagob, and from my other brother and my other relatives in America: not one of them mentions my youngest son.
– It's because he hasn't made his millions, said the American.
– Will my son ever come back?
– Yes. He told me that he would.

Now, I don't know," the storyteller said to his shadow, "I mean, I don't know why it took Vardan such a long time to make his way back home, but I presume it was because he couldn't afford the journey and had to save up to buy the ticket first. Or perhaps he had the money for the ticket and wanted to save a little more so that he wouldn't return to his native village a beggar. In any case, Vardan didn't return until 1914 when, on an early summer's day, he decided to embark on the *Graf Schwerin*, a German ship that would bring him safely back to Europe.

And that's what happened," said I, the storyteller, to my shadow, who was sitting restlessly by my side on the Gate of Happiness.

"In the early summer of 1914, Vardan was standing at the railing of the German ship, looking back at New York's harbor. The ship travelled past the Statue of Liberty, who was neither smiling nor waving. The torch in the statue's hand looked like a drawn sword, still displaying a banner from the previous December: Happy New Year 1914!"

"Happy New Year 1914?" – My shadow began to giggle, but not in a malicious way. – "Is that supposed to be some sort of bad joke, Meddah?"

"No," I said. "That's just what people say at New Year."

"Do you think Vardan had any idea?"

"Any idea of what?"

"Of the firestorm that would engulf the world just a few weeks later, changing it forever?"

"How could he have known? The only thing on his mind was Anahit and their upcoming wedding. Perhaps he also thought about the son he would father with her, Thovma. And surely," said I, the storyteller, "surely in that moment, as he sailed past the Statue of Liberty, he thought of the nameless, numbered streets of that huge city, streets that – at least to him – after so many years had finally grown faces. But in his heart he felt a longing for Hayastan."

"Vardan spent sixteen years in America," said my shadow. "That's a hell of a long time."

"Yes," I said.

"And yet … why did he choose to come back right before the outbreak of the Great War? He couldn't have picked a worse time."

"True," I said. "But still it was lucky that he didn't wait any longer. You see, if Vardan had decided to come back a little later, he would never have come back at all. The country was at war just a few weeks after that, and the great massacre wasn't far behind."

"Which massacre do you mean?"

"The imminent massacre ... that one I call holocaust."

"Holocaust?"

"Holocaust.

Some things are a blessing in disguise," I said to my shadow. "Let's presume that it would have been unwise of Vardan ... or careless ... I mean just plain careless, to leave a harbor as safe as America in order to return to Turkey and end up careening straight into the path of war and with it a holocaust that he could have avoided entirely. You could definitely call that unfortunate. But is this misfortune not also a blessing? You see, had Vardan delayed his return by just a few months ... he never would have seen his family again: not his father, not his mother, not his brothers and sisters or any of his other relatives and friends. He would also never have seen Anahit again and their marriage would never have taken place because everyone he cherished, everyone who meant something to him, was to be taken away by the holocaust. And then he never would have fathered Thovma, who is listening to this story."

"Thovma?"

"Thovma."

"A blessing in disguise?"

"Absolutely."

"So he was destined to bear witness to it all?"

"He was indeed."

"And you would call that a blessing?"

"I certainly would.

Vardan was surprised to see how much things had changed since he left. Wherever he went in Hayastan people assured him that things had never been better for the Armenians. Even the Armenian merchant who took him in his araba from the final stop on the Baghdad Railway all the way to Bakir assured him that it really was the case. After the overthrow of Abdul Hamid, so the merchant said, the new Young Turk government had solemnly pledged, in the name of Enver Pasha, Talaat Bey and Djemal Pasha, that from now on all Ottoman citizens, be they Muslim or non-Muslim, would have exactly the same rights. Most of these rights, so the merchant said, currently existed only on paper … and they were particularly hard to enforce in the remote provinces … but at least now Armenians were allowed to bear arms and serve as soldiers and officers in the Turkish army, something that would have been unthinkable in the past. – 'The authorities,' the merchant said, 'have even sent weapons out to the remote Armenian villages so that the villagers can protect themselves against the Kurds. And with my own ears,' said the merchant, 'I even heard a Turkish tax collector say to an Armenian cattle trader: It's about time, efendi. You Armenian crooks have always paid the highest taxes.

You have to admit it, efendi. And if you fill our public coffers with your dishonest money, you should have the rights to go with it.'

– We deserve to have our rights, said the cattle trader.

And the tax collector said: It's true. With Allah as my witness, the words you speak are true.

– Did he say anything else? asked Vardan.

– Yes. He said: I have heard, efendi, that the Russians over there on the other side of the border are mistreating your people. They are persecuting your priests and closing your churches. And they have even forbidden your language in their schools.

– It was like that for some time, said the cattle trader. It's true. And may God punish me if it wasn't. But the Russians recently promised their Armenians that they would change many things for the better.

– Well, you know full well, efendi, said the tax collector, that all Russians are liars. Can you think of anyone who tells bigger and bolder lies than the Russians?

– No, the cattle trader said.

'The two whispered together secretly for a time,' the merchant said, 'and I couldn't hear any of what they said. But then they started speaking loudly again, and I heard the tax collector say to the cattle trader: Well, efendi. The new government is treating you well. You have to admit it. And when the Russians see that we treat our Armenians better than they do, they will start to become nervous and fear that their Armenians will defect to our side when war comes.

– Yes, it's true, said the cattle trader.

– You see, the triumvirate isn't stupid. Particularly Talaat Bey. He is a very cunning man, and Enver Pasha and Djemal Pasha are too in a way. They know exactly why it's wise to treat the Armenians well and to even give you dogs weapons.

– Yes, said the cattle trader.'

– So, things are much better for the Armenians now? asked Vardan. Even better than they are for the Armenians over on the Russian side of the border?

– Precisely, said the merchant. Those terrible times we suffered under Abdul Hamid are over and done. The new government looks favorably upon the Armenians, and their policies exceed all our expectations. Hope is in the air everywhere you go. And so is change. It's small wonder that even the Dashnaks have started working together with the Young Turks, encouraging their people to support the new government.

– And what about the Dashnaks' dreams of re-establishing an Armenian state?

– It looks as though the Dashnaks are willing to trade their dreams for civil liberties.

– Are you sure it's true, efendi?

– That's what everyone is saying.

– And what if it leads to war with the Russians? Will the Turks trust us? Are you sure they won't think that the Dashnaks don't really mean what they say about being willing to settle for civil liberties as part of a large Ottoman nation? Won't they assume that the Dashnaks are still clinging on to their secret dream, their dream of independence … and that the Russians might help them achieve it?

– Nonsense. The Turks know full well that the Tsar would never give away territory he has already conquered to the Armenians because he wishes to keep it all to himself. The Tsar would never allow the Armenians to establish an independent state in the liberated territories. And the Dashnaks are just as aware of this as the Turks. In fact, it's a secret to no one. And every Armenian knows it, even the most stupid. No Armenian has ever put his trust in the Russians. And the merchant laughed. Do you know, efendi, he said. I once knew an Armenian fish seller who wanted to travel to Russia to sell salted fish along the coast of those big Arctic seas of theirs. And do you know what I told him?

– No, said Vardan.

I told him, 'Never trust a Russian, efendi! Think of all those empty promises their Tsar has made! You want to go and sell fish over there? Haven't you heard about what goes on with the Russian fish that they promise to the Armenians?'

– No, the fish seller replied.

– Well, it's like this and it's like that, I told him.

– What do you mean by that, efendi? the fish seller asked.

And I told him, 'Well, let me put it this way, efendi: Whenever a Russian promises you a fish, he'll just give you a piece full of bones in the hope that you'll choke on them.'

– Is that true? the fish seller asked.

And I told him, 'Yes, it's true.'

And it really was true," said the storyteller. "At the time when Vardan returned to Turkey, people said that the Armenians over on the Russian side of the border were looking over at their relatives in Turkey with a certain sense of envy; you see, for a while it seemed as though their relatives in Turkey were having a much easier time than they were."

2

"Vardan's wedding took place after the harvest, and the whole event followed almost the exact same procedure as the first. For seven days and seven nights revelers celebrated in the narrow streets of Yedi Su. They played the same music of old, and the sounds of the horns and the strings, the rhythm and whirling beats of the drums, but most of all the magical song of the gypsies' fiddles, climbed up high into the clouds ... clouds that contained not a single drop of rain for lest we forget: rain was not welcome at an Armenian wedding. The lambs and sheep were slaughtered in accordance with tradition and hoisted over the smoking fires by Hagob and his helpers. Others were busy baking and cooking, and the smell of a thousand and one delicacies hung in the air over the small church and the flat roofs of the houses. And yet this second wedding was different from the first because the people in the village were less afraid of the Kurds. The men of the village were now armed, and the Kurds up in the mountains knew. Thus attacks were now rare. And yet Vardan still insisted on paying the bride tax to Sheikh Suleyman, who was now an old man, for it would have been foolish to directly challenge the sheikh and his sons and grandsons as their riders would still outnumber the farmers of Yedi Su, weapons or no weapons."

"So they paid the bride tax?"

"Yes, the bride tax was paid."

"And nobody kidnapped the bride?"

"Nobody kidnapped the bride. The Kurds also didn't go against the church and take her virginity without its blessing. The wedding went off without incident. As I said, the celebrations lasted seven whole days and nights. And the seventh day was the day of the wedding ceremony and also the day on which the blood-stained bed sheet, just as in ancient times, was to be hung before the front door."

"Did Vardan have the same problems getting to know his wife as he did the first time? And did Hagob have to enlist old Bulbul's help to slaughter a rooster in order to fool the villagers?"

"No," said I, the storyteller.

And I said, "Back when he married his first wife, the fattened up daughter of the mayor, the well which needed to be opened was dry – if you ask me, I would say it was completely dried up – and during those first few days of marriage neither the desire of the wielder of that mighty bone nor his finest efforts could breach the walls of the hidden source he so desperately needed to find. And the thorn bush that lay before the dried up well was so unruly that it pains me to speak of it. But this time it was a completely different story.

No, Anahit was not fat, although they had tried to fatten her up. For some reason all the baklava she was fed by her adoptive parents and all the gentle coaxing of the silk farmer and his wife had no significant or noticeable effect. Although Anahit was by no means skinny, the fact that she was tall meant that the odd bits of chubby flesh that had formed around certain areas and curves of her body weren't all that obvious. Anahit towered over all the women in the village and was a head taller than most of the men. She was not a beautiful woman; she had no face, and her body was covered in burn wounds and scars. But Anahit moved with grace and pride, and the eyes that sat in her burnt face still shone fiercely for they had seen Christ.

Vardan got to know her the very first night they were together. And there was no dried-up well, and no unruly thorns. There was a grateful, sensual source that wanted to give and receive all at once. And everything about a man that was brutal and hard and merciless, so they said, became gentle, and even that elusive passion that was trying to find itself, found the other and became tender. It was as though Christ had brought man and wife together, and so they would stay as long as they still had breath in their bodies.

When war descended upon the country, all the men in the village who were fit for service signed up of their own free will before the drummers and criers came and the individual enlisting orders made their way through the slow Turkish post. The rich were still able to pay their way out of enlisting through the bedel, which applied as much to Muslims as it did infidels, but in the village even the sons of the rich refused to pay it and moved to the barracks in Bakir. And even I, the storyteller, am astonished to say that it was no different in all the other villages and cities … or perhaps I should say, it was a similar story. There was the odd deserter and draft dodger here and there: Muslims and Christians alike. But the vast majority of the young Armenian men couldn't wait to take hold of their flags and their weapons."

"What did the Dashnaks do?" my shadow asked.

"They ordered their people to fight for the Young Turks."

"And Pesak, Vardan's brother-in-law?"

"He put on a Turkish uniform and became a soldier."

"Hadn't he become one of the Dashnaks' leaders by that point?"

"He had."

"And he too wanted to swap dreams for civil rights?"

"Yes," said I, the storyteller. "The mood in the country had changed, especially among the Armenians. The idea of one day becoming equal Ottoman citizens was more enticing than the risky business of re-establishing an Armenian state which, in any case, would have been too small and too weak to survive long between two colossal powers such as Russia and Turkey. All the ordinary Armenians wanted was to be safe. They wanted to be able to go about their business and to provide for their families. All they desired was something calm and stable, and the Dashnaks were aware of that."

"And the Young Turks had every intention of bringing this dream of a safe haven to life?"

"That's what the new government had promised." I said.

"And what did the Armenian priests do when war broke out?"

"They ordered their congregations to go and fight for the Turks. And they prayed for the Padishah."

"Which Padishah?"

"You know, I'm not entirely sure, but I think they prayed for the Turkish one."

"And Priest Kapriel Hamadian?"

"He said, 'It's the right thing to do. The new government has given us rights, and now we have to fight for them as several exist only on paper. Now we have the opportunity to show the Turks that we are loyal citizens. And never in the whole of history have we had a better opportunity for the Young Turks have given us weapons, and our men are now Turkish soldiers just like all the others.'

Munadis from other parts of the country began coming to the village to call out their messages to the beat of their drums. A few weeks after war broke out with Russia, the senile, half-deaf and half-lame munadi Nazim Efendi came to the village to proclaim the army's momentous victories and give the villagers news of the war on behalf of Enver Pasha, Talaat Bey and Djemal Pasha, in other words the ruling triumvirate of the Committee of Union and Progress, and on behalf of the Sultan. Before he walked out onto the market square with his drum, Hagob had invited him to a glass of oghi liquor, handed him a generous baksheesh and whispered a secret into his one good ear. Later on, as he stood on the market square, the munadi announced that Vardan's wife was pregnant and that the Committee of Union and Progress, the triumvirate of Enver Pasha, Talaat Bey and Djemal Pasha, as well as Sultan Muhammad the Third sent their best wishes to Vardan and his wife, as well as their future son, who would be called Thovma. Furthermore, the munadi announced that the Turkish army had occupied Tabriz and that the Russians had been defeated; he said that Enver Pasha, who was also on the front, leading his troops no less, would soon free the Caucasus region along with every Turkish man and woman; he said that their German allies had long been at the gates of Paris, a sinful city in Frankistan, and that Allah was on the side of the righteous.

In winter there wasn't much to do. The farmers played cards or tavla and in the evening they dozed in front of their tonirs. Of course, they still had to take care of their animals and keep their households in order, but there was no work to be done in the fields. And so all winter long the farmers dreamed of spring and fresh furrows. They wondered whether the storks would be back again next spring, and whether after the war, which would surely be over by then, everything in Hayastan would still be the same as it always was during the days when they would sow as the spring winds blew.

And one day, when the marmots began to wake from their deep winter slumber and the snow was close to melting, a troop of saptiehs came to the village and stopped in front of Hagob's house. The saptiehs' uniforms were spattered with snow and mud, and their boots didn't look much better. They searched Hagob's house and all the neighboring buildings that belonged to the Khatisian family. They didn't find much, just a couple of harmless photos that belonged to Vardan and his papers, which he didn't take with him when he went down into the village; papers with foreign stamps and visas that were inside a casket together with the photos.

Later when they rode away, they took Vardan with them. The corporal, a chubby and good-natured looking chiaus, said to Hagob, 'It's a mere formality. Your son is an American citizen. The mudir of Bakir simply wants him to sign something.'

– When will my son come back? asked Hagob. And as he

sensed that something was amiss, he added, 'Tell me, Chiaus Agah, will I ever see my son again?'

The chiaus didn't answer Hagob's last question," said I, the story-teller, to my shadow. "For how could a run-of-the-mill chiaus answer such a question honestly? But Hagob's question echoed inside the chiaus' mind all the way through the Taurus Mountains. And then later, when the chiaus handed Hagob's youngest son over to the mudir of Bakir and he asked the mudir the exact same question, the mudir said, 'This Armenian will never see his family again.'

– His wife is pregnant, said the chiaus. She told me she was expecting a boy.

– This man won't see his son either, said the mudir.

– But a father should at least be able to hear his son come into the world, said the chiaus. Just once, I mean that moment when his son lets out his first cry ... his very first cry, even though he doesn't even know that the world, which Allah has made for us all, exists.

– That Armenian with his American passport, said the mudir ... that one right there ... will only hear the sound of his own screams, and they will be so loud that his son will hear them in his mother's womb.

– May Allah have mercy on his soul, said the chiaus.

– Many of these traitors will scream, said the mudir. Some will scream loudly, others less so. But every time they scream, those righteous souls in paradise will cover their ears. And the mortal remains of the true believers, which smell of musk and lavender, will rest more soundly in peace. The Prophet has cursed these infidels. May their mothers shudder at the sound of each of their son's cries.

– Yes, said the chiaus. And as he walked out of the mudir's office, he whispered, 'May Allah have mercy on their souls.' "

3

Two weeks before Vardan was arrested, the first Armenians were hanged from the Gate of Happiness, and we, my shadow and I, bore witness to the act. And the number grew. Every single day the Turkish authorities had some Armenian fellow hanged; sometimes several. The number didn't matter.

"Ever since Vardan was arrested," said my shadow, "there have been more and more of them. Do you think it has something to do with his arrest?"

"It's more the opposite," I said. "His arrest has something to do with the government's new policy, which also explains their use of hanging as a scare tactic."

"Those hanging men look as though they are sneering."

"They are simply confirming the government's fears."

"Whatever happened to the promises the Party of Union and Progress made?"

"The country is at war," I said.

"I mean the whole business with equal rights."

"That was before the war," I said.

I said, "Franz Joseph of Austria wanted to meet the German Kaiser in Paris, but by the looks of things it didn't work out."

"Perhaps the Austrian Kaiser is too old to undertake such a

long journey," said my shadow, "particularly as he has had trouble peeing for quite some time now. That must make any trip quite difficult."

"Perhaps," I said.

"And what about Enver Pasha? Didn't he want to meet with the German Kaiser, too?"

"Indeed, he did."

"And where?"

"In Saint Petersburg."

"And what became of the meeting?"

"Nothing," I said. "Enver first wanted to conquer the Caucasus and to liberate all the Turks from the yoke before travelling to Saint Petersburg. But that all came to nothing."

"And the German Kaiser?"

"He, too, has postponed his trip to Saint Petersburg. For tactical reasons, they said."

"And what's the situation on the Turkish-Russian front?"

"It's not looking good for the Turks," I said. "Enver Pasha's army is practically defeated. And someone has to take the blame."

"Who?"

"The Armenians."

"But I thought they were courageous soldiers. And they were loyal. They said so in the Turkish newspapers. Even Enver himself admitted it."

"They retracted that claim long ago."

"Did they give a reason why?"

"There is always a reason why."

"And where can it be found?"

"In their own fears."

"But surely their innocence will eventually come to light?"

"That would just make them all the guiltier. It would mean challenging a historical representation that others have created for them. That is a sin. And it is wrong. It's true, it would cast doubt over absolutely everything … all the justifications of Turkish history and those who wrote them."

"So, they have to be guilty?"

"Exactly."

We spoke for a while, my shadow and I. Then we heard something flutter past us. Both of us heard it, my shadow and I, the storyteller.

"Something just fluttered past us," says my shadow.

"That's just the Last Thought of Thovma Khatisian," I say.

"Really? His very last thought?"

"No," I say. "His very last thought is still inside his head, waiting for the signal to take flight."

"So which last thought is this then?"

"Only the last thought from the Story of the Last Thought … the story I'm telling a man who is lying on his death bed so that he knows how it will feel when his last thought passes through his mind, or how it might be … when it finally takes flight … escaping to some other point in time."

And I, the storyteller, can hear the Last Thought sigh. And I hear him ask a question:

"Will my father be released from prison today?"

"He will, my little lamb," I say. "He will be released today.

And fifty-five saptiehs are already waiting out in the prison yard."

"To take him to Constantinople?"

"That's right."

"To face trial?"

"To face trial."

And I show the Last Thought the sack of the blind beggar who is sitting on the side of the street in front of the Gate of Happiness.

I say, "In his sack that blind beggar has the boots of your uncle, Dikran, a man who was a cobbler, the best in the whole of Bakir."

"I know," says the Last Thought.

"I bet you'd like to know why he isn't selling them."

"Yes," says the Last Thought.

"So would I," I say. "But let's listen in to see what the blind man has to say.

– The truth is I actually wanted to sell these boots, says the blind beggar, Mechmed Efendi, to his grandson, Ali. But I've thought about it. You see, these are by no means the best yellow goatskin leather boots in this whole city, even though I always thought they were. It was all nothing but a story.

– Why, Dede? Why can't they be the best boots if you were always so sure that they were?

– Things are not what they used to be, says the blind beggar. And things that once had value are now worthless. It's the same for the best boots in Bakir that are made of the finest, yellow goatskin leather. Once they were new. And today they are in tatters. Just look at them: the leather is shabby and covered in scratches, there are holes in the soles, the heels are askew and all the parts that once gave the boot its shape and held the wearer's foot inside are now pitifully loose and limp.

– And what about the nuggets of gold that every Armenian has concealed in the heels of his shoes?

– There wasn't any gold in the heels, my little lamb. This Dikran fella was either too poor to put a little gold aside, or he didn't have enough foresight to.

– What'll you do with the boots, Dede?

– Well, I can't give them back to the dead man, can I, my little lamb? But I could give them to his wife. Or his brother! Yes … perhaps I should give them to his brother? That would be the most sensible thing to do. Then he could wear them himself.

– Which brother?

– Vardan Khatisian.

– He's being released from prison today, you see, my little lamb. The saptiehs told me. They are planning to take him to Constantinople. For his trial.

– His trial?

– His trial.

– Will you give him the boots today?

– No, not today.

– When will you give them to him?

– When he needs them.

– And he won't be needing them today?

– No, not today."

And I, the storyteller, say, "Do you see those Kurdish riders? They're coming from the direction of the grand bazaar, and now they're riding towards the Gate of Happiness."

"Who are they?" asks the Last Thought.

"They are highwaymen and bandits. Sometimes they come into the city to raid the bazaars, but it wasn't worth their while today because of all of the saptiehs and military officers that are currently roving around the nearby streets."

"Do they really make a living off stealing?"

"The clan itself also owns a flock of sheep but they can't survive on rearing sheep alone. The elderly Kurds, as well as their women and children, tend to the animals while the young men are away. They're a small clan that lives high up in the mountains. They are relatives of the Hartoshi Kurds and take their orders from Sheikh Halil the Righteous. As I said, they are a small clan, on the verge of being wiped out."

"What do you mean?"

"Well, you know how these things come about." I say, "Three hundred years ago, the son of the then sheikh stabbed the son of another sheikh to death. His brother, however, had to avenge his death because the unwritten law of revenge dictated it so – and this law was sacred. From that moment on the two clans were at war. They killed one another and still do. Now there aren't many of Sheikh Halil's, who is known as Halil the Righteous, family left."

"How many are there?"

"I couldn't say for certain. All I know is that they only have roughly fifty fighters and a handful of horses."

"Why are you telling me this?"

"You'll find out soon enough."

And I say, "Look, do you see? The Kurds are stopping in front of the blind beggar. And one of them – the sheikh's son – now dismounts his horse, walks towards the beggar and throws a silver medshidje into his collection cloth."

"I can see him."

"The Kurds and the beggar are old friends."

"How did they become friends?"

And I say, "Those wild Kurds can neither read nor write. They also don't believe what the newspapers write. The blind beggar is their most reliable source of information. Whenever the Kurds come to the city, they go to the beggar to hear the latest news."

"Can the beggar read the newspapers?"

"No, but he has good ears which he always keeps open.

– How are things progressing with the war, Mechmed Efendi? the sheikh's son asks.

– Well, says the beggar. The question is, for whom?

– For Enver Pasha's army?

– No.

– For the Tsar's army?

– Precisely.

– When will the Tsar's riders be in Bakir?

– Not by this summer, says the beggar. But they will come.

– And what about those damned Armenians? Will they all be strung up?

– Not all of them, Son of the Righteous One.

– Why not?

– Because they want to drive them all out. They will force their old, their women and their children into the desert. And all the men who have any juice left in their balls will be shot.

– How do you know all that?

– It's what I heard.

– And what will happen to the Armenians' houses, their land, their livestock and their businesses?

– They will find people to take them over, Son of the Righteous One. And these newcomers will be in a rush to move in. They always are. And believe me when I say that these people are already waiting to make their move. And their patience is wearing thin. It seems they have forgotten the words of the Prophet, who said that haste is from Satan.

– Will it happen soon?

– No, not yet.

– What are the authorities waiting for?

– They need proof and a credible indictment.

– Who told you that?

– A yuzbashi told me.

– And why do they need that?

– For the press. You see, they need to find some way to justify why there aren't any Armenians left.

– But aren't they still around?

– For the time being, yes.

– One of those Armenians is being charged as a spy, says the beggar. And he's been in prison for quite some time. But today they are releasing him.

– Has he been freed?

– No. Today he will ride through the Cannon Gate, his hands bound, escorted by twenty-five saptiehs.

– How do you know that?

– I know these Armenians, and I've been going to the prison every day for weeks now to speak with the saptiehs there who know me.

– Do you know where they are taking him?

– They are taking him to the Baghdad Railway. Then to Constantinople.

– There?

– There.

– They will only ride a part of the way along the caravan road towards Erzurum, says the blind man, but then they will take a shortcut through the mountains.

– Do you know which shortcut?

– There is only one. You know that full well, Son of the Great Bey. You Kurds call this shortcut the Al Buraq way, just like the Prophet's horse, the one who ascended to heaven.

– It's a very narrow and dangerous road.

– Yes, it is, says the blind man.

– So, there will be twenty-five saptiehs and one prisoner?

– Yes, says the blind man.

– And how many horses does that make?

– If you had enough fingers and were able to count, you would realize that that equals twenty-six horses.

– Twenty-six horses, you say?

– Yes, twenty-six.

– We could do with twenty-six good horses, says the sheikh's son. Do you know what kind of horses they are?

– They're not a bad breed, says the blind man.

– And what about these saptiehs' fur caps, and their boots?

– The fur caps aren't bad, and neither are the boots. Their weapons are also faultless, but best of all they will be wearing new uniforms. You see, each one of them was given brand new kit when the Great War broke out.

– We don't need uniforms.

– And what about the horses?

– We need horses.

– And modern rifles?

– Those, too.

– And the fur caps and the boots?

– Yes, and fur caps and boots.

– For you, picking off those cowardly saptiehs will be like shooting fish in a barrel, says the blind man, especially above the ravines when they'll be spread out and riding in single file along the mountain pass.

– It will be easy.

– Just make sure you spare the prisoner. He is a friend.

– A friend?

– Yes.

Later that day, after the Kurds had ridden away and had long disappeared beneath the feet of the hanging men's bodies and into the distance beyond the Gate of Happiness, Ali asked his grandfather, 'Will the Kurds steal their horses, and their kulahs and their boots?'

– Yes, my little lamb.

– And what will they do with the uniforms?

– They will throw them into the ravine together with the

bodies wearing them.

    – And the prisoner? What will happen to him?

    – I don't yet know.

    – Will he ever arrive in Constantinople?

    – No, my little lamb.

The mudir had overslept, and when he finally arrived at the hukumet late in the morning, the chief scribe realized that the files, which were to be given to the saptieh escort, were not yet complete. Several precious hours were lost as they worked to get everything ready so that the *Khatisian Case,* both the paperwork and the accused – for one could not go without the other – could be given the go-ahead for the march to the Baghdad Railway. Only around midday, when the papers were all present and correct, and the mudir, whose legs frantically carried him to and fro between the hukumet and the prison yard, finally gave his authorization, did the convoy move out. But first the saptiehs took the prisoner to the barracks so they could water their horses, pick up ammunition and provisions, and fill their water pouches. Afterwards they made another stop at the main post office, picked up a few important sacks of post and set off slowly, watched by the curious eyes of the crowds, along the inner city wall and towards the Cannon Gate. By the time they finally rode out of the city and disappeared onto the dusty road that lay on the other side of the city walls, the call to midday prayer had long fallen silent. They rode neither quickly nor slowly. They rode as they always did when the journey was long and unpleasant. But they knew the way. And they rode with confidence. Following the planned route, and the mudir's instructions to the letter, they would take the caravan road to Erzurum, and then turn off and take the shorter route along the narrow passes through the Taurus Mountains."

4

"At the beginning of May, the vali of Bakir called several important men into his office.

– Efendiler, how long does it take a troop of experienced saptiehs to reach the Baghdad Railway?

– Three days at most, Vali Bey.

– And what about if they take a shortcut?

– No more than two.

– But they have been travelling now for over two weeks, and we still haven't had any news. All we know is that the troop and their prisoner – this Vardan Khatisian – never reached the Baghdad Railway's terminal station.

– And they didn't arrive in Constantinople? asked the kaimakam.

– Of course not, said the vali. How should the prisoner have made it all the way to Constantinople if he hasn't even managed to cross the Taurus Mountains ... and thus reach the Baghdad Railway's terminal station?

– The railway has many terminal stations, said the mudir. And in the middle lie the Taurus Mountains.

– But there is only one terminal station from which you can travel straight to Constantinople without having to change trains.

– Yes, true, said the mudir. And the kaimakam said, 'It

certainly is. I just don't understand why those Germans still haven't managed to build a tunnel through the Taurus Mountains.'

– It's not that they are incapable, said the vali. They're deliberately taking their time so that they can keep their engineers busy here for a few more years.

– It would seem, said the mudir, that the German Kaiser sleeps more soundly at night knowing his engineers will be keeping us on tenterhooks for many years to come.

– To hell with those engineers, said the vali …

– I have sent several telegrams to the Baghdad Railway station master, said the vali. And to all the police stations along the caravan road to Erzurum and to those responsible for the area in question, the one surrounding the narrow mountain passes along which the troops travelled. But the answer is always the same.

– And that is?

– That the convoy and the prisoner were last seen leaving the caravan road to take a shortcut through the mountains. After that they disappeared.

– Into the ravines of the Taurus Mountains?

– Precisely.

– Has a search party been sent out?

– They have.

– And what did they find?

– Nothing.

– But if they didn't find anything, maybe at least that's something?

– I don't know, efendiler.

– And who might?

– Allah might know.

– Perhaps we should just leave Allah to find them?

– Yes, why not?

– Perhaps the convoy fell, and they are all lying dead in one of those many ravines?

– It's possible.

– Or the Russians snatched them.

– That's also possible.

– No, said the mudir. The Russians cannot possibly be involved. The Russians are still much too far away. It's impossible that they fell into the hands of Russian troops.

– Perhaps they were Russians on patrol?

– But even the patrols wouldn't venture that far ahead.

– Who else could it have been then?

– Allah will know, said the mudir.

– It could also have been the Kurds, said the mudir. When they are in need of horses and weapons, they'll stop at nothing. It wouldn't be the first time they ambushed a group of saptiehs.

– Yes, that is true.

– And they make sure no one survives to tell the tale.

– That is also true.

– If any of them had survived, they would have made an appearance by now. But there hasn't been a single trace of them since.

– What do you mean, Vali Bey? Not even of their horses?

– Not even of their horses, Mudir Bey.

– And the prisoner?

– No sign of him either.

– And what will become of the trial?

– What trial?

– You know, the whole business with the Khatisian case …
I mean the business with the murder of the Austrian heir to the
throne and his wife, and the whole business with the Armenian
global conspiracy?

– Yes, that.

– To be quite frank with you, Mudir Bey. I never really
believed in it. After careful consideration, I have come to the
realization that if we had gone ahead with it, we would only have
made a mockery of ourselves in front of the whole world.

– Then perhaps it is better that the prisoner is now dead and
the whole case has resolved itself?

– Yes. Precisely.

– And we can be absolutely certain that the prisoner is dead?

– Yes, said the vali. If there has been no sign of any of the
troops in almost two weeks, then all of them are dead.

– When the Kurds do a job, they make sure it's done properly.

– True, said the vali.

– Let's forget about the Khatisian case, said the vali. There are
more important matters to attend to.

– Such as? said the kaimakam.

– Such as the whole business with the uprising in Van.

– Have you heard anything specific yet?

– Yes, said the vali.

And the vali said, 'Efendiler. Now we finally have a credible reason to indict those Armenian vermin.'

– And that would be?

– A few days ago Armenian bandits began shooting at Turkish troops. Until now we have had no exact information, but yesterday we received detailed reports from the vali of Van. It is all true. An uprising has broken out in Van's Armenian quarter! And behind the front, too!

– Unbelievable.

– It has been proven, efendiler. The whole world will know. And let's not forget, there are Armenian volunteer battalions fighting on the Russian side of the border and there are plenty of soldiers who aren't Russian citizens. They come from all over the world and are lining up to join the ranks of the Russians.

– Just to fight against us?

– Precisely.

– Are there Turkish citizens among them?

– A few. Armenian deserters.

– Good heavens!

– And now this uprising in Van, said the vali. The Dashnaks are behind it. And they have people everywhere; in every town and in every village. All across the land, plans for an uprising are being made.

– Do they have proof that the uprising in Van is not an isolated case … and that the uprisings are spreading? Is there a master plan behind it all?

– Efendiler, said the vali. Nothing has been proven, but proof will be found.

First, there was frost and cholera," said the storyteller. "And with the arrival of the warmer weather and spring came typhus and dysentery. Herds of beaten Turkish troops from the Caucasus began flocking back to Anatolia, followed by the Kurdish regiments who had fought alongside them. As they retreated, the Turkish and Kurdish soldiers raided Armenian villages, massacring the inhabitants. Djevdet Bey, Enver Pasha's brother-in-law, who after Enver Pasha's hasty retreat to Constantinople was made commander of the Third Army – the army that had been deployed in the Caucasus – made no secret of the fact that he would annihilate all the Armenians in the Vilayet of Van. You see, Djevdet Bey was not only an army commander, he was also the vali and provincial governor of the Vilayet of Van. You see, Djevdet Bey was not only an army commander, he was also the vali and provincial governor of the Vilayet of Van. The Armenians in Van, allegedly the largest and most beautiful Armenian city, knew what lay in store for them. And as Djevdet's troops arrived at the city's gates and the local gendarmes began arresting Armenian notables, and even executing some of them; as word got out that women were being raped and men beaten in broad daylight, the Armenians retreated to the center of the city, shut themselves away and reached for their guns.

They didn't have many guns," said the storyteller. "Most of their weapons came from the Young Turks' armories, and a substantial number of arms were smuggled into the city from Persia by the Dashnaks during the Armenians' persecution under Abdul Hamid. The Armenians in Van had neither planned an uprising nor did they have any affiliation with the steadily approaching Russian army or the Armenian volunteer battalions on the

Russian side of the border. All they did was prevent the local saptiehs and Djevdet Bey's troops from entering their residential quarters. It was a defensive maneuver, nothing more ... the only option they had to prevent a massacre from taking place or their people being deported.

But nothing better suited the extermination plan that the Committee of Union and Progress had concocted than the fact that Armenians were now shooting at Turkish troops. It meant they finally had their proof of high treason which would justify the impending, definitive measures to be taken against the Armenians in the eyes of the global press. What was in fact an act of self-defense could now be declared an act of high treason by the country's own press, as well as drummers and criers in villages and cities across the land: 'An Armenian uprising behind the Turkish front'. All they needed to prove now was that an uprising was being planned across the entire country.

And so in my mind," said the storyteller, "I picture all the heads of the Committee of Union and Progress merging to form one enormous head, and this giant head sits on the shoulders of a uniformed figure in an office in one of Constantinople's government buildings. This uniformed man is not alone for I, the storyteller, am also there. But he cannot see me because I am sitting inside his ear. And as he is devoid of imagination, he doesn't sense that he is being watched, and he doesn't believe in the voices of our thoughts.

– The Armenians still don't know what we have in store for them, says the man in uniform ... I mean they still have no idea about our definitive measures or our final solution to the Armenian problem.

– But surely they must know, I say.

– We began expelling them from the army back in winter, and made them work as laborers behind the front.

– Inshaat taburi?

– Yes, inshaat taburi. Later we had them all shot.

– I know, I say.

– Of course, we weren't able to shoot them all as many of those cowardly dogs deserted and went to hide in the mountains, and also in villages and cities with friends and relatives.

– Yes, I say.

– We had everyone living in the small town of Zeytun and the surrounding villages deported. They all witnessed the death marches and yet still they refuse to see.

– Yes, I say.

– Those deportations in Zeytun were only meant as a warning, nothing more.

– I understand, I say.

– We had many of them hanged and arrested thousands of their notables. And yet they still don't get it.

– They don't believe that you are capable of exterminating an entire people, I say.

– No, says the uniformed figure. These stubborn fools believe it won't go any further: beyond these insignificant and harmless incidents, I mean. And they don't realize that this is just a taste of what really lies in store.

– Do you mean the final solution?

– I do.

– What do you make of the uprising in Van?

– Not much, says the uniformed figure. The world's press will play it down. Those son-of-a-bitch newspaper hacks will claim it was self-defense.

– And the Armenian volunteer battalions on the Russian side of the border?

– The world's press will play those down, too.

Those newspaper hacks will want to deceive the world into believing that it's all just an internal Russian matter that has nothing to do with the Turkish-Armenians.

– But that would all work in your favor?

– Of course it would, said the uniformed figure. And we're already trying to exploit these events to the fullest – for propaganda purposes, you understand. But it's not enough.

– What do you mean?

– We need very different evidence for the ultimate indictment, the one that will lead us to initiate definitive measures.

– And what evidence will that be?

– We have a plan.

– What form will this definitive solution take?

– It will be very easy, says the uniformed figure. Once the Van uprising spreads and all the Armenians in Turkey revolt against us, that's when we'll attack.

– But there isn't a country-wide uprising.

– We will provoke one.

– And how do you intend to do that?

– Well, we have a plan.

– What form will the final solution take?

– We're not even entirely sure ourselves, says the uniformed figure. But some have made suggestions. Like I said, we don't have a precise idea just yet.

– It's all very straightforward, says the uniformed figure. This growing uprising, that doesn't actually exist and couldn't possibly exist because the Armenians have neither the weapons nor a sufficient number of men and are neither well organized nor coordinated enough – we will crush this very uprising before it begins. Then we will have all suspicious men shot. And as everyone capable of bearing arms is suspicious, we will have them all shot as a precautionary measure.

– And what will you do with the women, children and elders?
– We will deport them.
– Where to?
– Nowhere.

And the uniformed figure, who didn't seem quite so satisfied with the word *nowhere,* says to me, 'We mustn't forget our allies, and the world's press. That's why we'll say the deportations have a purpose. We will announce that these vermin need to be moved to Mesopotamia for reasons of safety, or simply resettled in the Syrian Desert.'

– Resettled?
– Yes, says the uniformed figure.

– I don't believe that human beings are naturally designed to stay in one place, says the uniformed figure. Man can basically live anywhere as long as the climate is agreeable and there is enough food and water.

– Yes, I say.

– And plants can grow everywhere, too, as long as they have sun, soil and water.

– It has to be the right type of soil, I say, and the right type of sun and water.

– Absolutely, says the uniformed figure.

– And when these basic needs aren't met?

– Well … says the uniformed figure … then they suffer a terrible, untimely death.

– These deportees will be hounded along difficult passes through the Taurus Mountains, says the uniformed figure, and through the Pontic Mountains and other mountain ranges, of which there are plenty in this land … others will be forced to walk in circles or taken a certain distance with the Baghdad Railway and then left somewhere and forced onwards. They will be made to walk until they have no feet left or just remnants of feet, and the saptiehs on horseback will hurry them forward with their whips until they fall down dead. The rest … or those who refuse to lay down and die and who still cling on doggedly to their lives, even though they have lost all worth … we will dump them in the desert with no transport, no food and no water. And some of them will even make it that far, the most tenacious ones I mean. And there we will set up spacious camps so that the world's press doesn't think that we neglected to provide for them or, perhaps, that the whole maneuver isn't a proper resettlement at all, for the aim of a proper resettlement is to help people build a new home and start a new life, right? Isn't that how it works? This bunch of lowlifes will be resettled alright, but far away from the front – for strategic reasons. But there, in those camps, there will be nothing for them to eat because we are at war and don't have

much ourselves. Those people in the press will understand …
and the consulates, those of our allies as well as those of neutral
countries, will also understand. But once the war is over, there
will be none of those vermin left.

– So that will be the end of Anatolia's Armenian issue?

– That's right.

– Because that will be the end of the Armenians.

– Correct.

– When will the Armenian issue be resolved?

– By the end of September at the latest.

– The end of September?

– Yes.

– And how will you justify your actions to the world's press?

– That will be easy. Look, we'll just ask our Minister of the
Interior, Talaat Bey, to face the world's press and give an official statement. And he will do so with a clean conscience for
even at this very moment he could quite happily say to them,
'Gentlemen, I have no idea what you want from us. In Turkey's
disputed Anatolian provinces there is neither a problem with
Armenian nationality, nor is there an Armenian issue or even
an Armenian majority. For you see, gentlemen … as far as I am
aware, there are no longer any Armenians left there at all.' "

And in one gigantic leap, I jumped down from the ear of the
uniformed figure and flew to the Last Thought, who was hovering
over the Gate of Happiness waiting for me. I told him about the
conversation I had just had and said, "My little lamb. As you can
see, none of it is really that complicated. Essentially, it is nothing
more than a question of willingness: willingness to be good or
to be evil, and the fact that certain people see evil deeds as good

makes the whole thing even easier. The priests and pious church-going women blame large-scale, man-made catastrophes on the Lord God. They just say, 'It was the will of God'. Those planning to implement changes on the maps and in the country, however, pound their chests and speak of national necessity, of conscience as an obstacle that needs to be overcome, and they speak with an air of self-aggrandizement of the triumph of the will, of the solutions that are bad because of their lack of resolution and finality, and of the good, final solutions, carried out with determination.

And so soon the machine of Turkish bureaucracy would pull out all the stops it had at its disposal to turn the plans hatched in the brains of the country's leading figures into reality. The Turkish people were not consulted. All orders came from above and were passed down the chain. I, the storyteller, was astonished when I saw how the corrupt, poorly oiled machinery of the Turkish bureaucratic system was able to carry out every single one of the measures commanded by the Committee of Union and Progress with an almost Prussian level of efficiency and precision. A plan such as this, with finality its ultimate aim, is comparable to a work of art. Or could I be mistaken? Perhaps it is life that is a work of art, not the act that leads to its destruction … for life is more complicated than death and isn't it much more challenging and wonderful to bring life into this world than to take it away? Surely any fool can do that? I could feel the whole business getting under my skin, but why should I, the storyteller, lose any sleep over it?

The fact of the matter was that the organizers meant business. The Special Organization, called *Teshkilat Mahsuse,* originally founded for the purpose of carrying out political warfare on the other side of the border – as an organ for agitating and generating counter-propaganda that aimed to incite hatred of the enemy among Turkish citizens and other Muslims and minorities living in enemy territory – this Special Organization was now tasked with hunting down the Armenians. Just as the first heat wave and the first early summer storms of 1915 descended upon the land, representatives of the Special Organization, eminent gray figures dressed in Stambul suits and each with a red fez, travelled to the provinces. Their message was unequivocal and the men wouldn't tolerate a single objection to the orders they proclaimed on behalf of the Committee. It was all crystal clear. The valis were each responsible for carrying out the measures in their own vilayets. And the valis had to pass the orders on to the commanders of the individual sanjaks, the kazas and the local gendarmeries ... to the mutasarrifs, the kaimakams, the mudirs and all the other lower ranks, whose duty it was to receive and execute commands. It was crucial that the Armenians were found to be in possession of guns, and they had to be concealed guns; secret stockpiles containing huge numbers of weapons which the government knew nothing about and which could serve as evidence of a planned uprising. However they did it, they needed to make sure the execution of all able-bodied men was carried out swiftly. The bigger the surprise, the easier it would be for the government to remain in control of the situation. The deporta-tion of women, children and elders also had to happen according to schedule. Everything had to be over by fall, even sooner in the vilayets close to the front: they had to be cleared in a matter of weeks. The gentlemen from the Special Organization made it clear to the valis that not all of those deported could be allowed to reach their final destination. They explained that the Kurdish clans in the mountains were to be warned of the arrival of the women, children and elders, and ordered to slaughter them as they passed through the Kurds' territory – with impunity, of course. The Kurds were to be encouraged and assured valuables, clothes, shoes and other spoils. The gentlemen also promised help. The regional saptiehs would be given support to assist them in their difficult and solemn task. They said entire regiments of gendarmes were already on the move; some would help with the executions, others would oversee the deportations. *Chetes* were also making their way over, each one of them criminals that Enver had personally enlisted from the workhouses to help rid the Turkish people of their Armenian plague. Chete task forces were stationed wherever they were needed: at every crossroad along the caravan roads, in the mountain passes and along the banks of the rivers. Their mission would be, so the travelling gentlemen from the Special Organization claimed, to massacre the women, children and elders, either with axes or shovels, bayonets, knives or any other instrument of death, or with their guns, providing they had enough ammunition. You see, the government planned to give the chetes very little ammunition as these were difficult times, and ammunition had to be used sparingly. Although the chetes were thieves and murderers, so the gentlemen from the Special Organization said, they would be given the opportunity to right their wrongs by doing their duty for the Fatherland. The government, so the gentlemen said, wouldn't pay the chetes wages, but had ordered them to take their payment from their victims, to help themselves to whatever they wanted, so to speak, which was entirely justified under the circumstances. Thus a blind eye would be turned to any of the chetes' pillaging. Otherwise the government expected the chetes to be treated with respect by those representing the official gendarmerie, as well as the army, for the chetes would be wearing the uniform of Enver Pasha, the Minister of War, and were soldiers just like all the others, even though they were essentially nothing but irregulars, just like the Hamidiye and bashi-bazouks of days gone by."

5

"During the early days of summer a stream of coded telegrams arrived at the vali of Bakir's office whose astonishing contents were painstakingly decrypted and then the letters burned for – so went the order from Constantinople – no documented evidence could be left behind. When the first gentlemen from the Special Organization arrived in Bakir to communicate the Committee's orders in person, even those who had claimed to have not quite understood the telegrams' contents were finally persuaded and prepared for the inevitable.

– It's a good thing, said the mudir to one of the gentlemen from the Special Organization. The fact that we'll finally be doing away with these rats, I mean.

– Yes, that's what they are. Rats, said the vali.

– Well, said one of the gentlemen from the Special Organization. That's just how it is.

– I just don't understand, said the mudir, why we're supposed to have the old women deported as well. Those old women won't make a fuss.

– When you exterminate rats, you have to get rid of them all, said the vali. The old women will die during the deportations, and that is precisely what we want.

– Let's be realistic, said the gentleman from the Special

Organization. Rats or no rats … those old women are dangerous because they talk too much. If they survive, they might talk about us, spread lies and stories that will give us a bad name.

– And the dead can't speak?

– That's right, Mudir Bey. A dead mouth cannot unleash its venom.

– And what about the small children?

– They are the most dangerous of all, said the gentleman from the Special Organization. You see, they will grow up and avenge their fathers.

– And their mothers, said the mudir.

– And their sisters and brothers, said the vali.

– They are the most dangerous of all, said the man from the Special Organization.

– And what about the consulates? asked the mudir. Especially the consulates of our allies?

– You've no need to worry on that score, said the man from the Special Organization. If they ask any pesky questions, we'll have a good excuse. You see, everything that the government decides to do is legal.

– And what about the execution of the men?

– It's common practice to shoot insurgents. After all, we are at war. Other nations with similar internal problems would do exactly the same.

– And the deportations?

– Which deportations?

– You know, the deportations.

– Oh, those deportations?

– Yes, precisely.

– Well, Mudir Bey. What we are doing here is carrying out an evacuation of sorts: removing our internal enemies from a war zone.

– Not all the provinces lie in a warzone.

– It's all a warzone, Mudir Bey. Do not forget: the enemy within can be found everywhere.

– And how are we supposed to explain to the consulates why most of the deportations have no specific destination?

– Tell them the truth, Mudir Bey. Tell them that the chetes and the Kurds are to blame for the slaughter. And even the consulates know that no one can keep control of the chetes and the Kurds. Tell them that we've deployed the chetes as auxiliaries because our men are on the front. And tell them – just to reassure them, of course – that we had no idea that the chetes would overstep the mark.

– And as for the Kurds, well, I've already explained: they are impossible to rein in. And we certainly don't want to stir up trouble with them now that we are at war. What are we supposed to do if they decide to come down from the mountains and massacre women and children? Should our saptiehs, who are more often than not just a small group of escorts, take aim at the Kurds when they have hundreds of riders and guns at their disposal? That would be pure suicide. So you see, none of it is our responsibility.

– But the saptiehs will also have a hand in killing the deportees.

– The saptiehs will simply be doing their duty and kill only when absolutely necessary.

The gentlemen spoke for a time about this, that and the other. They smoked many rounds of chibouk and drank plenty of strong, sweet coffee, which was served in small bowls.

– Do you know what, efendiler? said the gentleman from the Special Organization. That Abdul Hamid fellow was a pathetic, incompetent fool. Back in his day he had a couple of Armenians bumped off, in '94, '95 and '96, but the Armenians that survived multiplied so quickly afterwards that they made up their losses several times over. Just take a look around. The Armenians are clogging up the land like weeds on our fine fields.

– I realized something similar only recently, said the vali. It's true. There really are more and more of them.

– Let's get down to business, gentlemen.
    – Yes, let's get down to business.
    – What's the situation with the weapons?
    – The Armenians have handed them in, said the vali.
    – When?
    – Back in winter.

– Immediately after the first wave of measures were taken against the Armenians, said the mudir, around the time that the Armenian soldiers were expelled from the army and the law banning Armenians from bearing arms came back into force, we sent the munadis into the Armenian mahalles. And we had them announce all the new decrees and put up posters on the houses.
    – Saying what?
    – Telling them to hand in their weapons.
    – What weapons?
    – They were legal weapons, said the mudir. Weapons that

were distributed to the people by the Committee the year they took power. Armenians included.

– Yes, I know, said the gentleman from the Special Organization.

– We ordered the Armenians to hand those weapons back in.

– And did they follow the order?

– But of course, said the mudir.

– We threatened them with the death penalty if they didn't return the weapons, said the vali.

– That's right, said the mudir.

And the vali said, 'It's true. With Allah as my witness.'

– It's possible that some of those Armenians held on to their weapons, said the mudir, but we shouldn't let that trouble us; it couldn't have been many. We counted the weapons that were returned and we have more or less the same number as was handed out back then.

– And what about the Dashnaks' secret arms caches?

– They are difficult to find, efendiler.

– Indeed, they are, said the vali. Very difficult to find.

– We have already searched through all the Armenian houses, said the mudir.

– As well as their courtyards, barns and cemeteries?

– Yes, those too.

– Especially the cemeteries, said the mudir. We lifted up the gravestones. But we didn't find their secret stashes.

– They have hidden those weapons with the help of Satan, said the gentleman from the Special Organization.

– Indeed, they have, said the vali. How right you are, efendi.

– Well, said the gentleman from the Special Organization. We are fully aware of it all. And do not think for a second that the Committee is stupid. We are not stupid.

– With Allah as my witness, said the vali, I swear that I have never thought the Committee to be stupid.

– Well, there you go, said the gentleman from the Special Organization.

– The Committee has decided, said the gentleman from the Special Organization, that the weapons, as proof of the planned uprising supported by the Dashnaks and the Russians, will be found within the next three weeks. And the Committee, in its wisdom and prudence, has also decided to help you find the weapons.

– Why?

– Well, said the gentleman from the Special Organization.

– It's all very simple, efendiler. In the coming days you will send your munadis back out onto the streets. And wherever there are Armenians living, they will put up posters instructing them to hand over their weapons.

– But these secret arms caches might not even exist?

– But they have to, efendiler.

– Yes, they absolutely must exist, said the vali. And with Allah as my witness, we will find them.

The gentleman from the Special Organization said, 'Vali Bey. Those weapons exist. And may Allah have mercy upon you if they don't.'

The gentleman from the Special Organization said, 'Of course, the Armenians won't return the hidden weapons, the ones that perhaps don't even exist. But the Committee, in its prudence, wisdom and sense of justice, has found a solution.'

– A solution?

– Yes, sir. A solution.

– A solution to a problem as difficult as this?

– For the Committee, there are no unsolvable problems, efendiler. Indeed, Allah knows it to be true.

And the gentleman from the Special Organization said, 'Have the Armenian notables arrested and hold them as hostages. Tell the communities that the hostages will be executed if the weapons are not handed over.'

– And if the weapons don't exist?

– I'm sure some guns will turn up.

– Is that all?

– No, there is more.

– Then you will arrest a few hundred men and have them tortured, together with the notables, of course. Do whatever you feel appropriate.

– A standard foot whipping?

– You can whip their feet if you like.

– We could also tickle their balls. Maybe scratch them open a little?

– Use your imagination.

– We once tried to pull out their beards. But it's not an effective method.

– True, it's not particularly effective.

– We chopped some of their hands and feet off. We made them drink their own piss and gouged their eyes out, but that didn't do much either. An Armenian won't talk if he doesn't want to.

– We even tore out a few tongues, said the mudir, but then they said even less.

– Use your imagination, said the gentleman from the Special Organization. Keep torturing the prisoners until they tell you where they've stashed their weapons.

– Their weapons that perhaps don't even exist?

– Precisely.

– And then what?

– Then you will find the hiding places and you will realize that there are indeed no weapons.

– And then?

– Then you will make the prisoners a proposal.

And the gentleman from the Special Organization said, 'In its wisdom and justness and prudence, the Committee has decided to sell four thousand guns to those stubborn Armenians in Bakir, which they will then use to fill up their empty arms caches.'

– But, efendiler. Surely the Armenians wouldn't agree to such a rotten deal.

– You are mistaken, Vali Bey. They will agree to it.

– Look here, Vali Bey. The torture will have worn the prisoners down. And you, Vali Bey, will say to them, 'Efendiler. The Committee of Union and Progress has decided to deliver you from the agonies of torture for nothing could be further from what we stand for as a party than this beastly and archaic practice. Therefore, the Committee, in its wisdom, justness and prudence, has decided to simply sell you the weapons that you are supposed to hand over upon the Committee's orders. We will thus sell you four thousand guns at a very reasonable price. You will go and place them inside your arms caches, the caches we tell you to use so that we can then find them again. Then you will reveal the names of your leaders to us. And we, the authorities of the city of Bakir, will tell the Committee in Constantinople that the uprising was uncovered just in time, the weapons were found and the leaders arrested. And you, efendiler, can return home reassured.'

– But the Armenians would never agree to such a rotten deal.

– Of course they wouldn't, efendiler, said the gentleman from the Special Organization.

And he said, 'The Armenians are a people of traders and speculators. They, in turn, will make you a proposal. You will consider their offer and then make another proposal of your own.'

– Makes sense, said the mudir.

– Indeed, said the vali. And what kind of counterproposal to the counterproposal made by the Armenian should we make?

– Well, let me tell you, said the gentleman from the Special Organization. You will say to the Armenians, 'Efendiler. We won't find any hidden weapons at all: You will hand them in. Look here, efendiler. Let me explain. We will sell you four thousand good-quality guns made in Russia; captured arms, obviously. And, of course, live ammunition as well. You will collect it all under the cover of darkness so that no one else sees. You will take the arms and ammo back to your hiding places and then we will give you three days. During these three days our munadis will order you to hand over the weapons given to you by the Russians. For three whole days the munadis will scream their lungs out. And they will also promise a general amnesty if you hand over your weapons freely. We will also stick up posters outlining the same requests and the same promises. After the three days have expired, you will retrieve the weapons from their hiding places and bring them to the barracks where we will be waiting for you. We will count and register the weapons and we will tell the Committee what we must, i. e. that the uprising has been uncovered, the Armenians have delivered their weapons freely and thus amnesty has been granted. All that will then be left to do is arrest the leaders. But don't worry. We will give you the names of the leaders in question and they will have enough time to disappear. Well, what do you say, efendiler?'

– That is a brilliant proposal, said the vali.

   – It's unprecedented, said the mudir.

   – The minds of the Committee came up with it, said the man from the Special Organization.

– But if we do that, won't we have to let all the prisoners go?

   – Of course, said the man from the Special Organization, but only so that we can catch them again a few days later.

   – And what about the promise of amnesty?

   – There will be no amnesty, said the man from the Special Organization.

– The Armenians won't have time to return the weapons you sell them because the very next day, the day after you've sold them the weapons, all the saptiehs in the Vilayet will fan out and search through all the houses, as well as the arms caches we are already aware of. You will find the weapons, confiscate them and arrest all the able-bodied Armenian men. The next day you will announce that weapons have been found, stating just how many there were and where they were made, and at the same time you will begin the mass executions.

The man from the Special Organization smiled, and I, the story-teller, saw him smile and could read his thoughts: 'Four thousand guns and the ammunition to go with it at a reasonable price still to be fixed. The vali will have to hand the money over to the state, but this vali is more cunning than he looks. Surely he will sell the Armenians six thousand guns, but only deliver four thousand of them … and the surplus money will vanish into his pockets. But what can you do? Anyway, it is pointless trying to teach the Committee's ethics to these backward people who still live in the age of Abdul Hamid and his corrupt regime. What do they understand of the ideals of the new leadership: their fight against corruption, their sense of neatness and order, their open-mindedness and westward-looking attitudes, their aim of establishing a New Order and national unity? No, it is pointless. These irredeemable fools will carry on betraying the state and continue to fill their pockets at the government's expense. But we need their cooperation, so it's best not to ask any questions.'

– If everything goes to plan, said the vali, the Committee can expect the executions to take place before the start of the holidays. It will be Ramadan in a few weeks. By the time the faithful start their fast, the whole thing should be over.

– Strictly speaking, said the man from the Special Organization, it all has to be long over and done with by then.

– And when are we to begin deporting the women, children and elders?

– After the executions, but before the holidays begin. By the time Ramadan starts, all the Armenian quarters must be empty.

– And how should we deport them? On foot?

– You will go part of the way on foot, part using ox-drawn carts.

– But where are we supposed to get hold of so many ox-drawn carts?

– You'll think of something.

– Why can't we just chase the whole lot of them out of the city on foot?

– Because of the press and the consulates. Remember that we're only supposed to be evacuating, or rather resettling, them. It should all be done decently, humanely.

– And what about provisions?

– As long as it remains uncertain whether the press and the consulates are watching, bread and water will be distributed.

– And then later, when the transports vanish into the ravines of the Taurus Mountains?

– Then there will be no more provisions.

– And what about the Armenians' houses? The furnishings inside? And their clothes and other possessions? And what about their gold and their money and their jewelry?

– Valuables have to be turned in, said the man from the Special Organization, and this will be under penalty of death. In terms of luggage, the Armenians may take whatever they can carry either on their backs or on the ox-drawn carts. We will announce that all immovable property will be returned once the deportations and the war are over.

– Will any of these people ever return?

– We will make sure that not one of them does.

– Then none of it will be given back? I mean, none of their immoveable property?

– That's right."

And I, the storyteller, say, "Regardless of whether they return, their houses will still stand. But others will be living inside. Turks and Kurds, but mainly Turkmen and muhajirs; yes, mainly the muhajirs, Muslims who have fled from the Caucasus and European provinces lost during the Balkan Wars.

– Some day, when the time is right, the gentleman from the Special Organization said later to the vali over a glass of raki. Some day we will manage to turn the Kurds into real Turks. But that will never happen with the Armenians. The Armenian is like an alien creature living in our skin, a cynical thorn that can be neither trained nor absorbed nor reshaped; the perpetual other, staring blankly back at the Turks, or perhaps it's not so much that it stares at us, rather it digs tenaciously into our skin, its sole aim being to poison the body from which it feeds.

– The mudir said something along those lines not that long ago, said the vali, and I too have thought something similar.

The gentleman from the Special Organization nodded, and at

the same time smiled sympathetically. Abdul Hamid still believed that turning the Armenians into Muslims would be enough to solve the problem. But we Young Turks have learnt from the Europeans that it is not just the religion of our citizens that we need to be wary of, but their national identity, their race and their blood. Enver Pasha has promised to unite all the Turkish people of this world, and he promised to turn all those he can into Turks.

– Yes, said the vali.

– Abdul Hamid knew nothing of these new ideas, and so he could never have known that trying to convert the Armenians was pointless.

– Pointless, said the vali.

– The Armenians abroad have already turned the unbiased press against us, said the gentleman from the Special Organization, most of all the American newspapers, and as soon as we commence our definitive measures, their fury will grow even louder. That won't come as a surprise. But we did warn them. And we already said months ago that should the Armenian people throughout the globe one day manage to turn the rest of the world against us, it would mean the extermination of their entire race.

– Within our sphere of influence, efendi?

– Quite right, Vali Bey."

6

"A few weeks before the Muslim holidays began, passers-by who enjoyed going for a stroll along the prison wall right next to the hukumet could distinctly hear the screams of the prisoners as they were tortured. It wasn't the first time as torture had been carried out in Turkish prisons for as far back as anyone could remember. But this time the screams were unlike any they had heard before, or at least that was how it seemed. The screams shook them to the very core. Sometimes the sound called to mind a singer stretched out on a rack trying to crudely sing an unknown scale in time with a tone-deaf jailer. There were different types of scream: The gurgling, prolonged screams could only come from prisoners who had had something stuffed into their mouths, but the scream wasn't muffled completely; perhaps some saptieh was just holding the tip of the prisoner's tongue between his fingers, giving it a bit of a tug, but nothing too forceful. After all, the prisoner would still require his tongue until he had given all the confessions they needed. Other screams came in steady intervals, during lashings, say, and so people knew that this particular prisoner was being whipped on his bare flesh, most likely on the soles of his feet. An Armenian's feet were widely considered to be particularly sensitive. You see, these people – a people that considers itself to be a master race; that wished to bring their

Wirtsvolk, their host people, under control – didn't walk bare-foot, at least not in the city. And passers-by could also tell that the owner of these particular feet had sensitive skin. These were not the hardened, calloused feet protected by a layer of thick skin that one found in the lower classes of Bakir, such as those of the Turks and Kurds. These feet were used to being in fine footwear, perhaps even silk stockings which, to add to the luxury, might even be regularly washed and changed. These were prim feet, and the screams of their owner were prim, too. Of course, there were also other kinds of scream, and one didn't need a degree from Constantinople University to know exactly what was happening behind those cell walls. Screams that were elicited using sharp objects were particularly easy to discern. There were screams in every pitch of a perverse musical scale which seemed to come from another world, perhaps from the bowels of hell .... dull, sharp, shrill and other sounds came from the depths of those tortured bodies; others just came from their wretched, fleshless souls. Some passers-by made bets, claiming to know exactly what type of scream it was or what the saptieh in charge was doing at that very moment, or what he had planned.

Then, suddenly, the prison fell silent, and nothing more could be heard.

The gentleman from the Special Organization was proven right. After a few days of torture, the Armenian notables and all the community representatives were willing to do anything, even to accept the rotten deal that involved buying weapons. They realized that the vali of Bakir needed to show proof of the planned uprising to satisfy the Committee in Constantinople. The vali had promised an end to the torture and a general amnesty, provided they handed in the weapons – weapons that they did not but might possess – freely.

And how could the community representatives refuse such a generous offer, particularly as these arms were being provided at such a reasonable price?

The biggest part of the mission was carried out overnight. Only once the majority of residents of the city – a city people said was home to a thousand and one mosques – had blown out their oil lamps, did Bakir's armories come alive with activity. Long lines of ox-drawn carts stood ready at the barracks. They were loaded with guns and cases of ammunition and then they set off towards the Armenian mahalle. Fatigued saptiehs escorted the transport, and even the drowsy, fat vali rode some of the way with them. Even the mudir and the mutasarrif and the kaimakam and, of course, the gentlemen from the Special Organization were there. In the Armenian quarter only those who had been briefed knew about this whole comedic spectacle that was to close a chapter of Armenian history so that a new one could begin. Although those who were aware of the deal blew out their oil lamps, they didn't lie down to sleep: In spite of the curfew they went out onto the street, which clearly didn't bother the vali or the other gentlemen ... they received the weapons, took them to their hiding places under the watchful eyes of the saptiehs, and later on they met in the house of the former Armenian mukhtar and went to the *Hayastan* restaurant which, although closed for weeks, had been ordered to reopen its doors at this unusual hour upon the request of the vali. Those notables who still had hands and legs, who had had nothing chopped off and who hadn't been too severely beaten or injured: those who could still walk or at least limp, entered the *Hayastan* alongside the government's representatives after the weapons had been securely stashed away, and they drank a glass of raki together, swore their loyalty to the government in Constantinople, listened as the representatives explained to them yet again the complex reasoning behind the rotten deal with the weapons and the general amnesty, were understanding, allowed the vali to proclaim reassurance after reassurance, closely inspecting the faces of the other gentlemen as he did so, showed their relief and then spoke no more of the arrangement, only briefly mentioning a short while afterwards that they would ensure their lips stayed sealed and that they would return the weapons three days later as agreed.

But the whole show was already over by the next morning. Or perhaps I should say it had only just begun. You see, the very next morning as, for the first time in a long time, the notables woke up without a feeling of dread in their stomachs and stroked their wives and said, 'Now everything will be fine. The situation has calmed down, we've reached an agreement with the authorities,' the saptiehs were already waiting at their doors. They didn't wait long: as soon as it was announced that weapons had been found, that Armenian arms caches had suddenly been discovered; as soon as word got out that the weapons were being loaded up, weapons that these traitors hadn't handed in, that they had been given by the Russians and their instigators for the long-planned uprising, which was due to break out once the Russians were at the city's gates ... as soon as that was announced, the saptiehs forced their way into their homes.

Yes, it all happened very quickly. According to plan. On that exact same day, the day on which the weapons were found, a wave of arrests took place unlike any the city had ever seen. It was June 20, 1915, just under two weeks before Ramadan, a month of fasting and spiritual purification that was due to begin on July 2. In fact, they had plenty of time to carry out the executions, which weren't supposed to disturb the faithful during their month of fasting; the first cannon blast from the citadel that would signal the start of the fast, in accordance with tradition, was still days away. Nevertheless, the vali ordered the executions to begin the very next day at the break of dawn. Not that the vali was in a hurry, of course. He wasn't. It was just that the gentlemen from the Special Organization wanted to be on their way, and they claimed that they couldn't leave without seeing the whole mission completed. The vali gave the mudir the order. And he appealed to the mudir's conscience and made it clear to him that all the able-bodied men had to be shot. And able-bodied meant anyone who could hold a long stick in their hand without help from their mother, and anyone who still had teeth that weren't still milk teeth, or a tinkler that he didn't just use for tinkling: Anyone who looked dangerous or who could become dangerous in the near future was considered a threat.

For three whole days, able-bodied men were lined up in rows of four, tied to each other with rope and led out of the city in the early hours of the morning. At the same time the public criers screamed their lungs out, announcing the news of the uprising in Van, the Armenian volunteer battalions on the Russian side of the border and how the Armenians in Bakir were working together with these scoundrels. Now everything had been resolved, and the Turkish Fatherland had been saved by Allah in its hour of need. Even the imams in their mosques proclaimed something similar, and the hodjas spoke to the children in their Qur'anic schools and warned them to be wary of the Devil, the Djinns and the Armenians. Alarming posters put up along the city walls, the city gates and the walls of its houses denounced the Armenians, and the newspapers tried to outdo one another with increasingly damning reports of the Armenians' betrayal. Turkish and German officers stood sheepishly alongside one another in the streets of Bakir, and the consulates of neutral nations closed their windows in embarrassment.

In most Anatolian cities the Armenian men were shot in front of the city gates, but in Bakir the authorities were more tactful. As the high mountains were not far from the city, the men were led on a little walk, no more and no less than forty smokes. There, where the ravines were so deep that even the saptiehs were afraid to look over the edge, where the Djinns bellowed into the wind and even a strong man couldn't pee down into the abyss without feeling his heart race; where men feared to tread and held on tightly to their horses' reins ... that is where the men were shot. Of course, not all of them were shot; the external gendarme regiments, who had been assigned here to offer their support to the saptiehs of Bakir, said they needed to save ammunition as the bullets had been allotted sparingly and, of course, times were hard – a fact mentioned by many who had gone before them – and so, these external saptiehs simply hacked the men down. And then there were the chete task forces, who arrived just in time. And these chetes had a great many axes in their saddlebags.

The slow-witted, sluggish saptiehs from Bakir were amazed

when they saw the skill with which the chetes smashed in the skulls of the Armenian men with their axes. It was as though it was all they had ever done for as long as they had lived. They were also lucky that they had no need to find somewhere to bury the bodies: The ravines provided the perfect graves. And as they had so many bodies to throw down into the ravines – for not all of the corpses tumbled down neatly all the way to the bottom; some of them decided to be difficult and landed on the mountain paths below – they decided to leave those dead dogs to be dealt with by their living counterparts. After all, there were plenty of those in this country, even if they were dogs of the four-legged variety. That is why so many Franks called Turkey the land of the masterless dog. Nowhere else in the world, so the Franks said, were there as many masterless dogs as here. They outnumbered the vultures of the land and ate every dead creature they found lying in the alleyways of the villages and cities, the country roads and the mountain passes. The whole country was their hunting ground and even if they weren't as fast as the birds of death that flew through the air, they did a much more thorough job as they could tear off larger pieces of flesh and rarely left anything behind.

The gentlemen from the Special Organization were surprised that the Kurdish mountain clans hadn't participated in the massacre.

The Kurds were usually the first to appear whenever such events took place and there were boots and clothing to be had.

– The Kurds are biding their time, said the vali. Perhaps they don't want to risk a run-in with the chetes and all the many troops of saptiehs from the Erzurum Vilayet.

– We have already warned the mountain clans, said the

gentleman from the Special Organization, and we also told them that the transports of women, children and elders would soon be passing through their territory.

– That will be it then, said the vali. The Kurds are waiting for the families of these executed men to pass through their territory because they assume they will only be accompanied by a handful of saptiehs.

– Yes, that will be why, said the man from the Special Organization.

– And because they expect to gain a bigger haul from the women, children and elders than from the able-bodied men who, of course, don't have any luggage with them.

– That's right, Vali Bey.

– Still, we should keep the Kurds in check.

– Quite the opposite, said the man from the Special Organization. If we chase the women, children and elders over the mountains, where's the harm in the Kurds finishing the job? It's better for the foreign press and the consulates' reports, you see.

– What about them?

– Well, I've explained it all to you already. The other gentlemen have heard it, too: The insurgents were shot because of the war. We can answer to that charge. But we should leave the massacre of the women, children and elders to the Kurds. Then the government can say that it had nothing to do with it.

– Yes, you did explain that to us earlier.

– Well, there you go.

– And the saptiehs' brutality … and, most of all, the chetes?

– I also explained that to you and your people not that long ago. The Committee knows what it is doing, and it knows just how great its responsibility is. The saptiehs are only doing their duty, and when they occasionally have to make use of their guns in order to maintain order, I'm sure people abroad will understand. And the chetes? Well, as we've already said, they are quite simply a group of vagabonds and murderers. We have to deploy them because of our lack of manpower. What are we supposed to do? Is it our fault if the chetes break the law? Lest we forget, they come from the workhouses. Should we assign each one of them a jurist? The eyes of the law cannot be everywhere at once. Times are hard, Vali Bey. And we simply had no choice but to deploy the chetes.

– And the deportations?

– There are no deportations. Do I have to explain that all to you, too? Look here: People are being resettled for strategic reasons because of the war. These Armenian women with their children and unsteady elderly relatives are just being sent on a journey. Why else would we provide them with decent ox-drawn carts and allow them to take luggage? So you see, it's just a short journey. Nothing more, nothing less."

7

"Here in Bakir the days running up to the month of fasting referred to as Ramadan became known as the days of the munadis, for never before had the drummers and criers been so busy shouting the authority's decrees against the Armenians' closed windows and doors. The majority of the criers knew the owners of the ears for whom their message was intended, and they knew that an Armenian was always awake, from the moment he was born to the moment he died, and that even in his sleep he could hear the ominous gospels that were conceived for him in the name of Allah. But Armenians were naturally stubborn and pretended to take little notice of their kismet, or in fact anything that was preordained and written in the Book of Fate, a book whose predictions no one on earth could escape. Initially, the Armenians acted as though they had misheard; as though the deportation date was not one written in Allah's calendar. The munadis could hear the relatives of the executed men as they wailed and moaned behind their closed windows and doors, and so they shouted louder than ever before in order to ensure that the mourners would hear. Some of the munadis were kind and would have gladly helped the Armenians if they could, for throughout all the years that Allah had blessed them with until this day, they had done business with the Armenians: They had traded with them, bought from them, had their clothing and shoes made by them, as well as their leather moneybags, their kulahs and kelims, their copper tableware, their iron house keys … even their large drums and drumsticks came courtesy of talented Armenian hands. And so it was that after having made the important announcement in the name of Enver Pasha, Djemal Pasha and Talaat Bey – and in the name of the Committee of Union and Progress as a whole – some of the munadis would seek out their recipients' ears to speak with them in private: sometimes they spoke with young children, sometimes the elderly, but mostly they spoke to the women. And so some of them would say, 'There is no use lamenting over your men and pretending you didn't hear what I said. You need to give all of your valuables and money to the state. But the state is generous and will allow you to take 300 piaster with you. So pack up your things and take your 300 piaster. And if you still have gold or jewelry that you haven't handed over or that you don't want to hand over, don't hide it in your clothes, or your hair or in your pussies or even up your backsides as they will find everything and take it off you. Bury it in a place where you will be able to find it again.' – And many of the Armenian women took heed of the munadis' words and buried whatever they didn't want to give to the state, but there were many who didn't for they believed that no one should ever embark on a journey without their nugget of gold.

Before the eyes of the consulate officials, a peculiar spectacle played out during those final days before Ramadan. It started as early as daybreak and lasted until nightfall. Thousands of women and children and elders walked in long lines, escorted by mounted bands of soldiers, though the gates of the city.

Those who hadn't managed to find space on the back of one of the ox-drawn carts walked. And similar transports came from the surrounding villages and smaller towns, all of them passing through Bakir. 'Hundreds and thousands are on the move,' the gentlemen working at the consulates wrote to their governments. 'They are all being resettled. The government claims they are being moved to Syria. The details are vague. No one knows the true destination.'

Understandably, a few craftsmen and certain individuals whose services were irreplaceable were spared execution and deportation. Their families were also spared for how could these duty-bound folk be expected to do their jobs properly if their families were taken away and they were left all alone? And given that the artisan trades in this part of the world were almost exclusively in Armenian hands, it happened – or it came to pass – that the most important workers, or those who were the most indispensable to the state, were allowed to stay. A few rich Armenians were allowed to stay, too, as the vali had something in mind for them which the gentlemen from the Special Organization didn't need to know about.

At the end of June 1915, exactly two days before Ramadan, the vali summoned the owner of the *Hayastan* restaurant into his office.

– Hajgaz Efendi, said the vali. I have eaten in your restaurant many times, and the mudir has eaten in your restaurant many times, as has the kaimakam and the mutasarrif. The lower-ranked officers have, too ... yes, even the saptiehs and the munadis have eaten in the Hayastan. Your cuisine is exquisite. The finest there is.

– Yes, said Hajgaz. My wife is a good cook, and I have always done my level best to ensure the satisfaction of our guests.

– Precisely, said the vali. I couldn't agree with you more. And you never took a single piaster from anyone in a government uniform.

– Why should I? said Hajgaz.

– And we have always offered you protection.

– Yes, said Hajgaz.

– You cannot deny it.

– No, said Hajgaz.

– I have spared your house, Hajgaz Efendi, said the vali. But do you seriously think for one second that I did it simply because I enjoy your food?

– No, said Hajgaz.

– I had my reasons.

– Yes, said Hajgaz.

– The government, said the vali, has given me permission to spare fifty craftsmen and their families.

– Yes, said Hajgaz.

– But I have written to the Committee, telling them that I need one hundred tradesmen in order to prevent the city from grinding to a halt. Do you understand?

– Yes, said Hajgaz.

– But I don't actually need that many, said the vali. Do you understand?

– No, said Hajgaz.

– Well, said the vali. Let me explain. I will list fifty of the richest Armenians in my books as additional craftsmen. And do you know what that means?

– No, said Hajgaz.

– It means that these people will be allowed to live, even though they aren't really craftsmen at all. Do you understand?

– Yes, said Hajgaz.

– I have entered you on the list as a carpenter, Hajgaz Efendi. So, from now on, you are a carpenter.

– Yes, said Hajgaz.

– Do you know anything about carpentry?

– No, said Hajgaz.

– Well, that doesn't matter, said the vali. All that matters is that we understand one another.

– Why are you doing this? asked Hajgaz.

– Well, why shouldn't I do it?

And the vali said, 'You have buried a great deal of money and jewels, efendi, away from the clutches of the state, so to speak. But we don't know where.'

– I have hidden nothing, Vali Bey.

– Oh yes you have, said the vali. And we're not just talking about a few coins either.

And the vali said, 'Every Armenian has four hiding places. If I have him tortured, he will reveal the location of the first to me in order to make the torture stop. But this first hiding place doesn't contain the real treasure. Do you understand?'

– Yes, said Hajgaz.

– And if I have him tortured a second time, perhaps he will reveal the location of his second hiding place. But the real treasure isn't hidden there either.

– Yes, said Hajgaz.

– And perhaps he will also reveal the third to me, said the vali. But even there you will find but a meagre portion of his wealth.

– Possibly, said Hajgaz.

– The real treasure is in the fourth hiding place, said the vali. But he will never reveal its location to me.

– Yes, said Hajgaz.

– Whatever I do, said the vali. He will never tell me.

And the vali said, 'That is why there is no point in having you tortured, efendi. Truthfully, there isn't.'

– Yes, said Hajgaz.

– I have thus come up with another solution: something more effective; something that would be better for both of us.

– What is it, Vali Bey? asked Hajgaz.

– You will bring your treasure to me voluntarily, efendi, said the vali. You will even ask me to take it from you. Every day you will come to me on your knees, here to the hukumet, and you will plead with me to take your treasure.

– Why, Vali Bey? asked Hajgaz.

– Well, for this and that reason, said the vali.

And the vali said, 'Our German allies mock us for having a customary military exemption tax, which currently stands at forty-four Turkish lira. We call it bedel and at one point every Armenian that had been dropped by its mother had to pay this tax. Why then should an Armenian like you, efendi, not pay bedel in exchange for exemption from the deportations? Don't get me wrong. This isn't an official bedel. Where would we be if every Armenian that we intend to have shot or cast out into the desert could buy their freedom for the paltry price of bedel? No, that would never do.'

– It wouldn't?

– If you keep this to yourself – and I would suggest that you do – then we might be able to do something about it.

– So something can be done?

– Yes, efendi. With Allah as my witness, there is indeed something that can be done.

And the vali said, 'Every day you will pay me forty-four lira – as a bedel – in gold and silver coins. If you pay in jewelry, we shall have to calculate the actual value of the piece and then add it up to forty-four liras worth every day.'

– What about paper money?

– No paper money, said the vali. Because of currency devaluation.

– I see, said Hajgaz.

– As long as no one else knows – just the two of us, you understand? – then you, and of course your immediate family, will be spared deportation.

– I understand, Vali Bey.

– You are now a craftsman, efendi; a carpenter whose skills are needed. Isn't that right?

– Yes, Vali Bey.

– It is regrettable that we have to confiscate all the Armenian houses, but you, as a craftsman, may stay in your house for as long as you are needed by the state.

– Yes, Vali Bey.

– Every day, you, efendi, will open up your vault to fetch all the gold and silver and jewelry you need. As time goes on, you will revisit all those hiding places you dug out in order to deceive the state. Gradually, you will bring forth all of it without me ever having to have you tortured or subjected to some other cruel treatment. I won't have you lashed or anything like that. We won't pull out any of your teeth, hack off your greedy fingers, or even your cock, which spawns that breed commonly known as the Armenians. We won't even tickle your balls. We won't need to. Every day you will fetch your money or your jewelry, for you see, these valuables mean one more day of reprieve and another day spared from deportation. And you will give it all to me of your own free will.

– Yes, Vali Bey.

– If the war continues for quite some time, sooner or later you will also find your fourth hiding place, the one where the biggest treasure of all is hidden, and you will dig it out and bring it to me.

– Yes, Vali Bey.

– That's what will happen, said the vali.

And Hajgaz said, 'Thank you, Vali Bey.'

– It's just a shame, said the vali, that we had to have your brother, Dikran, hanged some time ago.

– Yes, Vali Bey.

– He was a good cobbler. And we need good cobblers nowadays. The boots of all those dead Turkish soldiers need to be urgently repaired so that they can be worn by those still alive. And even the boots of the living – particularly after those long marches – are more often than not in a poor and sorry state. You see, efendi, materials are scarce. And a good cobbler can work wonders. But most of the crafts- and tradesmen were Armenians. Where are we supposed to get hold of all these cobblers we so desperately need now?

– Almost all of the cobblers were Armenian.

– You're quite right there, efendi.

– Yes, said, Hajgaz.

– It's such a shame, said the vali.

– Those Armenian lowlifes had the golden touch, said the vali. Everything they laid their hands upon was crowned with success. The Devil must have helped them along; how else can you explain their ability to do everything so flawlessly? Go on, tell me. You see, efendi. Even I, the vali of Bakir, had my boots made by an Armenian. My civilian suits, too. Even my uniform. Armenians make clothes with flair. I would even say they deliver a striking and suspiciously high level of quality. But what difference does it make? I enjoyed wearing my Armenian boots, as well as my suits and my uniform. That man, the one who made my uniform for me, was a true artist. And that uniform, which I still wear to this day, makes me look ten years younger and ten okes thinner.

– Yes, Vali Bey.

– And yet I still had him shot because it turned out that there were already too many tailors on the list of protected craftsmen.

– I see, Vali Bey.

– It's such a shame, said the vali.

– What about your brother Sarkis. Wasn't he a goldsmith?

– Yes, he was, said Hajgaz.

– I will check to see if he's on the list of craftsmen, said the vali.

– He's not, said Hajgaz.

– And how do you know?

– He was shot along with the others, said Hajgaz.

– Such a shame, said the vali. He was such a skilled goldsmith.

– Yes, said Hajgaz.

– It would have been a different story had he been a blacksmith, said the vali. Goldsmiths aren't needed during war, at least not by the cavalry. They need blacksmiths.

– Yes, Vali Bey.

– The best blacksmiths were Armenians, said the vali. And now there are so few of them left. It's such a shame.

The vali offered Hajgaz an *Amroian* cigarette. 'These are the last *Amroians*,' he said. 'An inexpensive but exquisite cigarette: genuine Armenian quality. You know, efendi, I made sure to stock up because the cigarette factory run by that Armenian Amroian no longer exists.'

– It's a fine cigarette, said Hajgaz.

– Have you any news of my brother Vardan? asked Hajgaz. Vardan Khatisian?

– No, said the vali. We believe him to be dead, and we've already given up all hope of finding him.

– So there won't be any trial?

– No, there won't be any trial. And the vali said, 'The Vardan Khatisian case was the brainchild of the mudir. He was obsessed with it. And I'm happy that the case is over and done with. And do you know what, efendi? If those tattlers from the press ask me any questions about what type of case it was, I will say to them: Efendiler, I don't know the case of which you speak? Do you mean the Khatisian case? And I will laugh into their faces and say: Efendiler, this case was like one of those Turkish stories, those people say begin with the words: Once there was one, once there were none. – This case, efendiler, doesn't exist. And it never did: not once, not ever.'

The Vardan Khatisian affair, more succinctly known as the *Khatisian Case,* no longer exists, my little lamb." And I, the storyteller, repeat those words to my shadow. "And later, after the war is over – in better times that are perhaps not really any better – anyone searching for it in the history books will find nothing. No mention of the Khatisian case I mean, or of a certain Vardan Khatisian, who was once accused by a falsifier of history – I'm of course talking about that obsessed mudir – of having shot dead the Austrian heir to the throne and his wife back on that day in Sarajevo. And I wager with you, my little lamb, that those who like to stick their curious noses in the pages of history will occasionally shake their weighty heads, particularly whenever I, the storyteller, happen to be sitting in their ear. They will say to me, 'No, we've never heard anything about this Khatisian case. The Turks pinned the blame on the Armenians for so much. What more could there possibly be to add? An Armenian is supposed to have assassinated the Archduke as well? And, by firing those deadly shots, started the Great War? We don't buy it. That's nothing but complete and utter nonsense!'

But I will say to them, 'Of course it's nonsense. But listen here, ladies and gentlemen. What difference will it make if we add one more false accusation to the one thousand false accusations that have already been made against the Armenians … so that we can say: Once upon a time there were a thousand and one accusations …'

An awkward silence descends. The voices of all the prospective historians' thoughts chatter away excitedly to one another. One of the thoughts speaks to me, 'Look here, Meddah. Everything written here in my books – these history books – is essentially nothing more than a succession.'

– What do you mean a succession?

– You know, Meddah. A succession of mass murders – some big, some small – since the beginning of time. And they are all justified. There was a pretext for every single one. And for each pretext there was an accusation. I see now, Meddah, why the accusation itself is of no real importance.

– Right, I say.

– So, did the Khatisian case exist or not?

– It doesn't matter, I say.

– And what about the global conspiracy and the Devil, the one who is to blame for everything?

– I don't know, I say.

– There's nothing written about it in my textbooks.

– Well, I say. That doesn't matter.

And I turn to all the ladies and gentlemen present.

– Ladies and gentlemen, I say. You will find nothing of Satan or a global conspiracy in your textbooks, but look inside your minds. And give it some thought! Or better yet: Don't give it any thought at all."

8

"Do you see that queer German, the one who is still prowling the men's toilets in the hukumet and showing the saptiehs his backside – do you see him, my little lamb? And do you also see the other German, the one with the glasses? And do you see their gray military uniforms?"

"I can see the two," says my shadow.

"The one with the glasses has just written something down," I say. "Can you see how he's grinning? Now he's saying to the queer fellow, 'According to our calendar, in 1915 our allies' Ramadan is supposed to fall on July 2. And it will be over by August 1.'

– That's a long fast, says the queer German.

– It's only half as bad as it sounds, says the bespectacled one. The fast begins and ends with a blast of the cannon. It's the same procedure every single day. Whilst the sun is up, the Muslims pull their belts tighter and after sunset they loosen them entirely. Then they gorge themselves on food and drink like their horses.

– And what about love?

– The Qur'an says, 'Your women are your fields, go into your fields whichever way you like.'

– Even during the fasting period?

– No, not really.

– Then love during Ramadan is forbidden?

– It is only forbidden during the day, but it's allowed at night.

– Between sunset and sunrise?

– Yes.

– Is it written in the Qur'an?

– The Qur'an says, 'You are permitted to lie with your wives during the night of the fast.'

– Is that all?

– No. The Prophet also said, 'Now you can lie with them – seek what Allah has ordained for you.'

– And what about practicing the other sort of love during Ramadan?

– What other sort of love?

– I just mean … how does it work with the love from which women are excluded? Is a faithful Muslim, who just happens to be bent, also allowed to mount a man during Ramadan?

– You'll have to ask the imam, said the bespectacled German.

– Or one of the hodjas?

– Yes, or one of them. They'll also have the answer.

The authorities had never gone about their tasks as quickly or as thoroughly as they did in the last few days before Ramadan. It was as though the ubiquitous presence of the German Kaiser's soldiers had blown a little gust of Prussian wind through the chaotic offices of their Turkish allies. And so it came to pass that as early as one week before the fasting period was due to begin, the city of Bakir had already been cleared of all its Armenians. Only a few craftsmen remained, as well as the few rich Armenians that the vali had been able to save from execution or deportation. The German officers were cursing the fact that there was now nothing they could buy for their wives as the Armenian jewelers were closed. The tailors' workshops were closed, as were the fabric and silk traders' stands, the spice stalls and all the other Armenian shops that offered mystical delights for curious eyes from the occident. Everything in the city seemed different since the Armenians had gone. The bazaars were almost empty; the streets and alleyways quieter. They also smelt different. The magical scent that the Germans so enjoyed in moments when they were overcome by feelings of romance, even though the air wasn't just filled with sweet and foreign and delicious fragrances, but also the stench of waste and decay, was suddenly missing. The city had become somber, and somber too was the yellow sun which shone down on the caps of the foreign soldiers.

– It's just strange, said the queer German to his companion. Since the Armenians vanished, no one else has been hanged from the Gate of Happiness.

– Yes, that is strange, said his companion.

And as there isn't anyone at present who could be hanged," say I, the storyteller, to my shadow, "I propose that you hang yourself beneath the gate's archway."

"But I don't have a neck," says my shadow.

"I know that," I say. "I don't intend to actually hang you just because the black hook beneath the Gate of Happiness happens to be empty. I just want you to wait for me here so that I can find you again."

"You want to fly away without me?"

"Yes. I'm going to fly away for quite some time.

And so I flew after the transports of women and children and elders to see why the ox-drawn carts, on which they and their luggage had so calmly left the city, had all come back empty.

I soon found out that the women and their relatives had not been shot immediately. Not even the old men. All that had happened was that the arabadjis, who were responsible for the ox-drawn carts, had taken their customers as far as the caravan crossroads where the turn towards the marshlands of Konya lay and then stopped. I also heard one of the arabadjis, an old, city-dwelling Kurd, saying to one of the saptiehs: 'We won't go any farther. The mudir told us to only go as far as the Konya crossroad.'

– Fucking crossroad, said the saptieh.

– But we won't go to Konya, the old, Kurdish arabadji said. You see, we have to take the empty carts back to Bakir so we can reload them.

And then the commander of the saptiehs came over and said, 'Yes, I know. Just throw these lowlifes onto the road. These Armenian vermin can walk the rest of the way.'

– Are you really going to Konya? asked the arabadji.

– I don't know, said the saptieh commander. We're going somewhere. To Mesopotamia, I think.

– But then you should be taking a different road.

– I've been ordered to first take these people to Konya, said the saptieh commander. That's where I'm supposed to hand them over. And then they'll probably keep walking.

– To Mesopotamia?

– Perhaps, said the commander of the saptiehs. Or perhaps not. The Devil is supposed to come and fetch these vermin and they shall be taken somewhere, although we don't quite know where that somewhere is. And the saptieh commander spat his chewing tobacco in a high arc whilst simultaneously signaling to the other saptiehs with his riding crop.

Everything was dealt with humanely. Even the saptiehs, who had been present just a few days before as the husbands of these women were shot or beaten to death, were amazed that the chiaus leading the troop didn't order them to simply do away with the women and their spawn, or even the old men, who everyone said were basically women for they certainly weren't real men with excitable cocks anymore. Yes, it would have been more practical to make short work of these infidels; what was the point of chasing this pack of lowlifes onward by foot, along with all their luggage and all the hidden valuables that these leeches had scavenged and squirreled away even, though they rightfully belonged to no one else but the Turks? Konya? Why bother going to Konya when the shortest route to Mesopotamia would be through Malatya and across the Euphrates?

As the saptiehs began to force the people down from the ox-drawn carts with their leather whips and to throw their luggage onto the road, the Turkish and Kurdish arabadjis started to laugh. But after a while their smiles faded.

Everything was dealt with humanely. And Allah bore witness to the fact that it was not the fault of the saptiehs that the Armenians had so much luggage: more than they could carry. Most of it was left on the road after the saptiehs had begun moving people on by cursing and swearing at them: they also tickled them a little with their riding crops. As many of the Armenians, particularly those who were very old, couldn't walk fast enough, the whips were sometimes required to do more than just tickle; they lashed out with force. But it was entirely justified for how else were they supposed to show what the order to 'march forward' meant? And even later on, when the very old and the weak began to collapse and had to be shot as no one could be left behind – at least, not living – the saptiehs knew that essentially they were handling their deportees humanely.

It was on a hot day in June when I, the storyteller, flew after the first ever transport of five thousand Armenians. I wasn't thirsty for I had no body, but I could hear the howls of the victims who, after just a few hours of walking, started screaming out for water as the afternoon set in. The longer I followed the transport, the more I noticed how the rows began to dwindle. An increasing number of old and frail, sick and crippled, exhausted and weak-spirited deportees fell behind and were shot by the saptiehs. I mentioned that it was a hot June day, didn't I? The temperature certainly was high. And the dead shouldn't be left to lie on the roads for too long. But Allah, in His wisdom and prudence, provided; he instructed the vultures in the air and the masterless dogs of the land to follow closely behind the transport. And they suddenly appeared to rip open the dead bodies' clothes and to gnaw the flesh from the bone before they began to decompose, for the heat truly was intense. That's how it is in this country. Winter is ruled by a beastly cold whilst the summer is always hot. And behind the snarling, spitting, ravenous dogs and the cawing, morsel-devouring vultures lurked the rabble from the city of Bakir and the surrounding villages. They kept their distance for they didn't want to cause trouble with the saptiehs. But they found the luggage on the road, and they found the remains of the dead Armenians' clothes, particularly head scarves and other items that hadn't been pecked or nibbled at, as well as boots and shoes. Even this rabble didn't have it easy as they were almost all on foot, and some of them also had difficulty walking, and they had to fight each other off when it came to deciding who would take the best spoils. They had to tussle around with others who had their eye on the exact same prize, and some of them also wound up injured or dead. Yes, that truly is what took place. The poorest of the Muslims had been lured out of their homes so that they could take from the Armenians all that Allah had deprived them of for centuries in the state of the Sultan and his corrupt officials … but they arrived too late, for the saptiehs had already rifled through the luggage and taken any hidden treasures for themselves. The rabble were furious and they ripped the partially-eaten clothes of the dead even further open so that they could find the nuggets of gold which people said the Armenians sewed into their garments. They also tore off the heels of their boots and sometimes they found something, sometimes they didn't.

The Armenians' houses remained surrounded until the transports had left the city. Then the pillaging commenced. The authorities proclaimed that the houses and furnishings of the infidels would be returned to them after the war, and for some time they acted as though they would secure most of the goods. In reality nothing was registered, and the authorities kept whatever the rabble didn't haul away. Anything that appeared to be of value vanished out of sight of the Committee.

The pillagers were confused. The odd one would say, 'They've buried their gold,' and others said, 'No. They took it with them. We should go after them along the country road. They have sewn it into their clothes and hidden it in their shoes.' But there were others who said, 'No, the Armenian is shrewd. I bet you they swallowed it. We should cut open their bellies.'

No, not all of the Muslims ransacked the houses. The genteel among them had already made their move as the drummers passed through the city and everybody knew whose hour had come. They bought whatever they could for as little as they could pay. Many Armenians gave these genteel Muslims the odd item for free and asked them to keep it safe until they returned. Among the genteel Muslims were also a few infidels that I accidently counted as Muslims for behind their empty words of sympathy lay eyes filled with the exact same greed. A few Greeks were among them, as well as a few Jews. One Greek bought a piano for seven piaster: a ridiculously low price. And a Jew, who was standing next to the Greek and enviously watched as the transaction took place, asked the now former owner of the piano whether he had another one for sale and said that he was even willing to pay eight piaster, but the man didn't have a second piano. The Greek tinkled around on the keys, which annoyed the Jew as he knew more about tinkling a piano's keys than the Greek for he was more musical. 'There once was a time,' the Jew said to the Armenian, 'when they were after us Jews, but those times are over, thank God.' And he told the Armenian about the Pogroms that happened under the Russian Tsar and about the crusaders' massacre and the flames of the Spanish Inquisition.

For a few weeks, I, the storyteller, flew around Anatolia before returning to Bakir. I unhooked my shadow from the hangman's hook – the one beneath the Gate of Happiness – and I stroked him and took him on my lap.

I am the storyteller," I said. "Call me Meddah." And I said, "The stories that I tell are not made up. They are real stories."

And then I told my shadow what I had seen.

"So a great many lay dead on the country road?" my shadow asked. "And those who could still walk carried on living?"

"For two whole days," I said, "they walked along the caravan road towards Konya. Their numbers grew fewer and fewer. Or, to put it another way, the country road became more and more colorful, strewn with the dead bodies that had been left along the side of the road … in their clothing of many colors and their yellow, brown, red, black and blue shoes. We also shouldn't forget the dead women's headscarves and veils, mostly of the finest quality, and of course the brimless hats of the old dead men and the protective head coverings worn by the small children. The dead were like milestones and signposts along the road, and in fact that's what they became: The regiments of saptiehs and chetes who came after the line of deportees needed to know which way to go, where the deportation was being led and on exactly what type of road.

Many reserve troops followed the trail of corpses mounted on their Anatolian horses. But most of them were already waiting in the ravines of the Taurus Mountains; after two days spent closely following the caravan road, the escorting saptiehs decided to take a shorter route through the mountains. Along the mountain passes, and also in the valleys, the chete task forces were already lying in wait.

Yes, it's true. The chetes are known for getting straight down to business without much ado. But they wanted to mount the young women first … and what would have been the point of killing the women only to climb on top and penetrate them when they were no longer thrashing around and screaming? That is why they only killed the old women. And they also killed the young children and the old men. They then tore the clothes off the bodies of the young women and threw them down onto the furrowed, summer ground that wasn't dry despite the sun and the wind and the lack of rain, but moist and sticky from the terrified women who had befouled themselves. But the chetes weren't put off by a bit of piss and shit. They thrust their hands inside and enjoyed every second. And they showed the women their gristly manhoods that were crowned with bulging red lesions and flayed and circumcised and looked mighty and threatening. Sometimes the chetes employed the help of their bayonets when the manly growth between their legs couldn't find the opening between their victim's thighs or if fear had caused the opening to clamp tightly shut. The saptiehs also felt like joining in the fun and took off their military trousers, and as they didn't want any trouble with the chetes, they shared out what the chetes had left behind equally, like brothers.

You wouldn't believe the things I could tell you about the juices of the saptiehs and the chetes. Even the older ones amongst them became young again. It was as though the women's screams and their terror was just what their attackers needed to really get their blood flowing. Yes, it was hot and humid in the ravines of the Taurus Mountains, even though the yellow sun could not always be seen.

Where were the Kurdish mountain clans? Well, that I don't know. The authorities had warned them about the transports long ago because, as we know, they wanted to pin the blame on them for the massacre. They showed up eventually as what was left of the five thousand moved deeper into Kurdish territory. All of a sudden there they were. They had free rein for the authorities had promised them a generous haul, and the guards were aware of this. They came out of their mountain hideouts in their hundreds – both on horseback and on foot – jeering and roaring. They shot their old rifles into the air as if hoping to scare not only their victims but the guards as well. And indeed they were afraid. None of them wanted to get into a fight with the Kurds. The Kurds only ever showed up during the day, before the sun had to be hauled back into its large, black tent. They mounted the women who were still left. And they rode them like the waves of the sea thrashing against the sandbanks. Some of them carried the women away; some of them left the women where they lay and slit their throats because they were either already dead or because they looked so old, they were ashamed at having done the deed with them.

The Kurds had taken all the clothes and shoes of the victims, which didn't bother the guards; they thought that, as it was summer, surely their victims wouldn't catch a cold if they were made to walk on naked and barefoot. And they had to continue on, for they had to be handed over in Konya so that the saptiehs in Konya could march them even farther, all the way to Mesopotamia. And some of them, so they said, needed to even make it as far as Mesopotamia for this was just a resettlement after all. And what sort of a resettlement would it be if none of the people being resettled actually reached their final destination?

Eventually," said I, the storyteller who also goes by the name of Meddah, to the shadow sat on my lap, "eventually, my little lamb, the commander of the saptiehs realized that the naked deportees could perhaps still have gold and other valuables hidden about their person. But where could the victims be hiding them if they were naked?

And so it was," said I, the storyteller, "that first of all the saptiehs searched through the hair of their victims, most of all the women's thick buns. And as they only found a few pieces of gold there, they tore open their victims' mouths and tried to push their fingers right down to their stomachs because they believed that the purpose of an Armenian's stomach was to hide gold from the state. They also slit open their victims' bellies and rummaged around in their guts. The openings where excrement comes out as well as the holes through which babies are born were also searched, and the saptiehs and the chetes stuck their hands inside. Sometimes they even found gold.

The commander of the saptiehs, who held the rank of chiaus, said to one of the chetes, 'The Armenian mothers in particular have a terrible habit of hiding good, Turkish gold so that they can use it to buy bread for their bastards: someday, somewhere, when they can shit the gold out without anyone noticing.'
– But where could they buy bread out here, Chiaus Agah? said the chete. And how are they supposed to shit it out without us noticing if we check their shit each time they go? And what would be the point of buying bread for their bastards when all the bastards are already dead?
– Not all of them, said the chiaus. A couple are still alive.

The chiaus was still suspicious. 'You don't know the Armenians,' he said to the chete. 'They are shrewd. Not even their own shit can tell us where the real treasure is hidden.'

— True, said the chete. Even when they're dead, they still have secrets.

— True, said the chiaus. And it's also true that the vultures and dogs know more than we do.

— What do you mean, Chiaus Agah? said the chete.

— I bet you, said the chiaus, that the vultures and dogs have not only eaten the bellies of the dead, but also everything that was contained within … including the nuggets of gold.

— Do you really believe that, Chiaus Agah?

— Yes, said the chiaus.

— Then we would have to shoot down all the vultures and dogs and investigate, said the chete.

— True, we would, said the chiaus."

I spoke with my shadow for quite some time, and I told him about the hundreds of thousands who were on the move, travelling in the transports from Kayseri and Moush, Trebizond and Erzincan and elsewhere.

"A whole people is on the move," I said. "They are simply being led away by the saptiehs. Some won't need to travel far as they will be shot at the outskirts of the city or slaughtered with axes and bayonets; others will have to go farther."

"So they are coming from all directions?"

"From all directions," I said, "although I'm not entirely sure how many directions there are in this world."

"And in which direction are they being driven?"

"Nowhere," I said. "You see, that's the point. Somewhere the roads stop, the destination becomes blurry: You are nowhere.

And yet there has to be a final destination for I was up in the air for quite some time and my eyes can see farther than those of the golden eagle. And I saw that there were survivors crossing the Euphrates. And they were stumbling under the lashes of the saptiehs' whips through the flat wilderness that was as bare as the head of the mukhtar of Yedi Su. The land appeared to have swallowed up everything that the Lord God had allowed to grow; it had even engulfed the mountains and hidden them beneath the flat sands. There were camps of tents and huts there. The few who reached this place were packed tightly together and left without food or water."

I said, "I heard the screams of the thirsty and hungry. And I heard the yellow sun laughing as it hung mercilessly over the land in the middle of a clear, blue sky. And I heard them scream. And I saw dead infants sucking on the dried up breasts of their mothers."

"But how can dead children still be sucking at their mothers' breasts?"

"It only looked as though they were," I said. And I said, "I saw mothers whose eyes were ablaze with madness. And I saw how some of them ate their dead children in order to still their hunger, and how they drank their blood in order to quench their thirst."

And while I was telling all this to my shadow, I felt something flinch between us and I thought, 'It's just the Last Thought of Thovma Khatisian. Something must be troubling him.'

9

"I see a saptieh in Bakir," said the Last Thought, "a saptieh who looks different from the rest. His eyes are different."

"I see him, too," I said. "He has the eyes of an Armenian, and any Turk who looks him in the eye will recognize him instantly."

"He's walking through the Armenian quarter," said the Last Thought, "past the deserted houses and the boarded-up shops. His eyes are half-closed, but occasionally he opens them up wide. He's trying to walk inconspicuously: slowly, as though just going for a walk."

"If you try to be inconspicuous, you're more likely to be noticed," I said, "and there is something artificial about the way this peculiar saptieh is moving. He shouldn't try too hard not to attract people's attention. That will arouse their suspicions."

"Who is that man?"

"We will find out in a moment for he is now approaching the Gate of Happiness. Soon he will be here."

The saptieh with Armenian eyes walks ever more slowly. He seems tired, and looks as though he wishes to sit down somewhere so that he can rest. But he doesn't stop anywhere for it is Ramadan, and the coffeehouses only open after the cannon has been fired from the citadel to signal the breaking of the fast. One of the kahvedjis is sitting on a cushion before the coffeehouse's door. And he calls the saptieh over, 'Hey, Saptieh Agah. Allah has blessed me with fresh, green coffee beans, and I have already roasted them. They are now brown and fragrant, and are sitting smiling inside my sack like the eyes of a bride behind her veil. But it is Ramadan, Saptieh Agah. Come back when the sun has disappeared and I'll make you a coffee that will perk up even a tired man's head.' But the saptieh just smiles and says nothing.

In the meantime the muezzins have begun calling the faithful to their mosques. According to the Franks' calendar, today is July 27. The fast is now in its final days and, as is usually the case during the last days of Ramadan, more Muslims than ever are flocking to prayer. The muezzins' calls are more forceful, even though everyone has heard their message many times before: *Allahu Akbar. God is the greatest, I testify that there is no God other than Allah. I testify that Muhammad is His servant and messenger. Hasten to worship! Hasten to success! Allahu Akbar. La Ilah illa 'llah. God is the greatest. There is no God but Allah.* – And as this day is a public holiday, and on top of that Ramadan, I, the story-teller, hear the muezzin continue his singsong call. I hear him cry, 'Feed, oh ye faithful, the orphans, the needy, those who wander and those who are dependent, feed them for His sake, and say: We feed you for it is the will of Allah, and we demand no word of thanks or reward from you.'

The saptieh with Armenian eyes has reached the Gate of Happiness. There is also a crowd beneath the gate's archway, but not because people have come to delight in the spectacle of the three bodies that the authorities have had hanged – a sight now once again familiar – but because the poor have come out of their huts and caves, which lie beyond the city walls, to conduct their evening prayers in the city. The saptieh comes to a halt next to the blind beggar who is sitting there like a statue, one hand in his lap, the other open over his collection cloth. The saptieh stands silently in front of the beggar for a long time. He stands there until the beggar notices and begins to anxiously inspect the boots of the saptieh, moving his hands up to the trousers of his uniform as if to make sure he has the right man.

– It's me, says the saptieh. Vardan Khatisian.
– Vardan Khatisian?
– Yes, says the saptieh.
– Vardan Efendi, says the blind man. Thank Allah, you are alive.

It's almost dark. I, the storyteller, see the beggar give the saptieh a sign, and I hear the two whisper, and so I too whisper something into the ear of the Last Thought. "Watch out," I say quietly. "Your father must be wary for beneath the Gate of Happiness are informers and cutthroats and denouncers, and anyway it isn't advisable to stand around here for long, particularly when you have the eyes of an Armenian." And so we three, my shadow and I and the Last Thought of Thovma Khatisian – we watch as this peculiar saptieh turns his back on the beggar and allows himself to be carried away by the crowds of worshippers.

"He's following them into one of the mosques," I say, "because there, at this hour, he will be least conspicuous; as you can see, my little lamb, your father is not the only man in uniform."

"That I can see," says the Last Thought. "My father isn't the only one. There are many saptiehs and uniformed men amongst the worshippers."

"I assume," I say, "that your father has arranged to meet the beggar later. I'm sure they plan to meet soon in the prayer room or outside in the courtyard where the followers wash.

The three of us observe your father, the fake saptieh in the courtyard of the Mosque of the Holy Mantel, and we watch as he carries out the prescribed washing ritual as though he had done it all his life, and we assume that he learned it from Gog-Gog and the other Turks in Yedi Su. He blends right in. Even later on as he prays inside the mosque. Your father drones out the ritual prayer recited every evening just like the others, and like them he kneels and shouts to Allah, even though I'm sure he's thinking of Christ. And, just like the others, he occasionally fixes his gaze, as if spellbound, on the back of the imam who stands before the kiblah, emitting sharp cries and calling out the name of Allah. The imam presses his thumbs behind his earlobes whilst spreading out the remaining four fingers, and he sobs and calls out to his god and falls to his knees and places his hands over his stomach, and later he places them on his knees and twists his body, and during the whole procedure he often casts a glance sideways as if he might at any moment catch a glimpse of the Holy Khidr or the Mahdi, who will perhaps reveal some of the secrets of paradise to him.

After prayers, your father stands in the courtyard of the mosque looking lost. A few pious Turks speak to him for they think he is a man without a family who is looking to escape a night in the barracks; perhaps they think he is one of those saptiehs from another town of which there are many in the city. One of the Turks, who is very old, says, 'My son, no one should be alone during Ramadan. My house is open for every believer.' But your father shakes his head. He says, 'I know that I will offend you if I refuse to take you up on your offer. But I have already been invited by another. And I mustn't offend him either.'

Then … your father suddenly spots the beggar.

All three of our gazes follow your father, who slowly heads into the evening alongside the blind man. The blind man leads the way with his stick to the Gate of Happiness, and then farther, out of the city and to the huts and the caves of the poor.

The beggar's dwelling consisted of one single, windowless room. A powerful fire was burning in the tonir, which the Turks call the tandir. There were a few women and children in the room who were part of the beggar's family and all of whom he fed. Even his grandson Ali was there.

– This man has come back from the dead, said the beggar. He is my guest.

With each bite the Turks take after a long day of fasting, they say *Bismillah.* It was no different with the beggar and his family. And your father also said *Bismillah,* even though he thought of Christ as he did so. Your father enjoyed his food and ate a little too hastily for much time had passed since he had had any food in his stomach. He was particularly drawn to the many spicy starters. The beggar kept refilling his wooden plate. One of the women passed the sofras around and your father didn't shy away from taking a generous helping. Later on that evening they sat on the even earth next to the tandir, the beggar had blown out the small oil lamp and they could only see each other's faces in the reflection of the tandir's flames. Even the blind man could see their faces even though he had lost his sight, but to your father it seemed as though his blind eyes saw more than the rest.

– It was unexpected, said your father. We were riding one after the other over the mountain pass. Suddenly the Kurds opened fire.
   – Did you know that they were Kurds?
   – No, I didn't.
   – I was the one who sent them, said the blind man.
   – I know, said your father. I was told afterwards.
   – By the son of the sheikh?
   – Yes, said your father.

– It all happened very quickly. The saptiehs were dead before they could even reach for their weapons. Yes, it all happened very quickly indeed.

– The Kurds then took me to the next village, a village where there was one other Armenian: a blacksmith who the saptiehs had let live because he was needed. The Kurds also killed the saptiehs in the village – there were only a few – and then they took hold of the Armenian blacksmith and ordered him to cut through my chains.
   – Your chains?
   – Yes.
   – Did the farmers see you?
   – No, said your father. It was the middle of the night.

– And the Armenian? He definitely saw you.

– The Armenian won't give me away, said your father.

– Afterwards I walked around the area surrounding the village. The Kurds gave me the uniform of one of the dead saptiehs along with a pair of boots and a cap. The only thing they didn't give me were the dead saptieh's papers.

– That was a mistake.

– Yes, said your father. But they did it because the son of the sheikh has a particular hatred of anything that resembles paper and stamps. The son of the sheikh had all the papers burnt.

– Even the papers of the saptieh in the village?

– Those, too.

– That's a shame, said the blind man.

– Yes, your father said.

– What did the Kurds do with the bodies?

– They undressed them and threw the naked corpses into the ravine.

– Was it a deep ravine?

– It was very deep.

– And the bodies of the saptiehs in the village?

– The Armenian had to bury them.

– The blacksmith?

– Yes, that's the one.

– And how do you plan to continue onwards without any papers?

– I'm not entirely sure.

– You'll have to get hold of some new papers.

– Yes, I will.

– There is an Armenian in Bakir who can make false documents, said the beggar. His name is Kevork Hacobian and he is a master of his trade. I even know where he lives. His house is in the feltmaker's alleyway, just behind the hamam. But I very much doubt that you'll find him; you see, they shot all the men, and only a couple of craftsmen and a couple of the vali's minions were spared. Some have also gone into hiding.

– Perhaps he's still around, said your father. Perhaps he's one of the craftsmen or minions on the list.

– He was a printer, said the blind man. And printers are sometimes needed. Yes, perhaps he is still around.

– Did you go to Yedi Su?

– No, said your father. If the authorities are looking for me anywhere, then that will be the place. I assume they will be waiting for me there.

– No one is looking for you, said the blind man.

– How do you know?

– I just do, said the blind man.

– Your name is on a list of dead men, said the blind man. They are no longer looking for you.

– Was it written in the newspapers?

– The newspapers don't mention things they don't want people to know. But the saptiehs in the hukumet and the prison can't keep their mouths shut.

– Did you speak with them?

– I did, Vardan Efendi.

– And that's what they told you?

– They told me many things.

– I actually came to Bakir to free my wife from the women's prison, said your father. I don't quite know how I'm going to do it, but I thought to myself, 'Perhaps Mechmed Efendi will have an idea.'

– Indeed, I have had an idea, said the blind man. And as he uttered those words, he looked straight into your father's face as though his darkened eyes could actually see the tense breathing of the man sat opposite and the light flickering in this fake saptieh's Armenian eyes.

– I knew that your wife was in the women's prison, said Mechmed Efendi. The saptiehs told me. They said that they were keeping your wife hostage.

– Yes, said your father. My wife and the unborn child she was carrying.

– That's right, said the blind man.

– Yes, said your father.

– But you have come to Bakir for nothing, said the blind man, for in the eyes of them all, you are dead. Even the mudir believes it. And the mudir cannot pressure a dead man by keeping someone hostage, even when that hostage is the wife of the dead man who is carrying his child in her womb.

– What do you mean?

– The prisons are overcrowded, said the blind man, and so they have sent most of them home, including your wife, whose services as a hostage are no longer needed. It's more practical for them, you see, given that the Armenians are going to be deported anyway. Why shouldn't they send them back to their villages and cities where they can be rounded up together, instead of keeping them in prison and feeding them at the government's expense?

– So my wife isn't here anymore?

– They let her go, said the blind man. I was standing next to the saptiehs in front of the gate of the women's prison. And as I am but a blind, old man, they even spoke to me. Especially when Ramadan started and the saptiehs' consciences began to weigh heavy and they suddenly started giving alms to the poor as a symbol of Allah's mercy: that's when their tongues began to loosen. And when I asked about your wife, they told me.

– Then she must be back in Yedi Su, said your father.

And the blind man said, 'Yes. She has returned to Yedi Su. And if the village hasn't been cleared already, she must still be there.'

– You know the village, said your father. It is far and isolated, and it was already overlooked once before, when Abdul Hamid's Hamidiye began carrying out their massacres.

– I know, said the blind man. And if it is the will of Allah, they will overlook it again. Someday you will return to Yedi Su a free man, and you will find your wife and your son, who might already have been born by then.

– It's a wonderful thought, said your father, and he sighed and closed his eyes. For a moment, his face appeared happy, and only I, the storyteller, knew that he didn't believe it.

They spoke about many things as the evening wore on, even the *Hayastan* restaurant that had been closed for months. Your father tentatively asked the old man questions to try and find out who of his family members in Bakir was still alive and who was still in the city, but this time the blind man, who otherwise always seemed to have all the answers, had nothing to tell him. All he said was: 'If some of them are still in the city, they won't show their faces. But I'm sure they'll turn up again eventually.'

They all slept crammed in together on the floor. Your father had nightmares and often woke during the night. At one point he noticed that the blind man was kneeling next to him.

– You're having bad dreams, said the blind man.

– I was dreaming of the bodies hanging beneath the Gate of Happiness.

– There are three of them, said the blind man.

– Are they Armenians?

– No, two of them are Turks and one is a Kurdish hamal.

– What crime have they committed?

– They hid Armenians in their homes.

– Is that forbidden?

– Of course it's forbidden. Don't you know that the munadis proclaimed in the name of the government that any Muslim who hides an Armenian will be treated like one?

– No, I hadn't heard, said your father.

– I also dreamed about my brother, said your father. I only found out on my last morning in prison, just before the saptiehs came to take me away, that he had been hanged.

– Dikran, the cobbler?

– Yes, that's the one.

And the blind man told him the story of the boots.

– I didn't know that they were your brother's boots, he said. I only realized when I felt them with my hands.

– Did you sell them?

– No, said the blind man. I opened up the heels, but there was no gold inside. And the boots' goatskin leather was worn out and had seen better days. And yet people say they were once the most beautiful boots in all of Bakir.

– Yes, said your father.

– I saved the boots for you, said the blind man. You can put them on tomorrow morning.

– Keep them, said your father.

Your father couldn't go back to sleep straight away. In the darkness he continued to see the faces of the three men who were last hanged: not Armenians, but two Turks and a Kurd. And later, in the silence of this Ramadan night, he wondered whether they were the only ones or whether there were other Turks and Kurds who were helping the Armenians. And with this thought, he fell asleep.

Early in the morning – before daybreak – he was awakened by the drums of the hodjas as they called the faithful to breakfast. One of the hodjas knocked against the door to the hut four times with his staff. And your father, still half asleep and somewhat confused, heard the hodja, who was responsible for all his sheep here in this slum, proclaim his blessings. The hodja standing before the door seemed to know the beggar for he cried out several times, 'Oh Mechmed, oh Mechmed. What a glorious night it was. Get up, Mechmed. The time for fasting is nigh. Allah is the greatest, and Mohammed is his prophet. Blessed is He who created the world.'"

10

"Never before in his life had your father eaten such a generous breakfast before dawn. You see, during Ramadan Muslims would eat a sumptuous breakfast that would keep their bellies full during the day while they were fasting. And so they ate plenty, and they ate fast for once the sun came up and the cannon of the towering citadel gave the signal that the fast had recommenced, the feast had to be cut short and followers could do nothing more than rinse out their mouths.

Before your father started on his way, he told the blind man about the question he had been pondering in the middle of the night as the faces of those three hanging men appeared before him in the darkness: three dead faces who had never had Armenian eyes.

– Many Muslims are now helping the Armenians, said the blind man. It's just that nobody sees them.

– You see them on the gallows.

– Yes, you see them there, said the blind man.

– Will there be more?

– Many have been arrested. And many will be hanged.

– Are any of them well-known Muslims?

– A few. Even the chief scribe of the mudir of Bakir is among them. Just imagine!

– The chief scribe? – Did he hide Armenians in his house?

– No, he just provided a few false papers.

– That's a dangerous thing to do.

– Quite right, Vardan Efendi.

– It's a shame that he's been arrested, said your father. I could do with a set of papers right now.

As he walked, your father thought about the chief scribe, and he remembered how the man would occasionally give him strange looks back when they were sitting in the mudir's office. 'You will be out of this city by the time that man is hanged,' he thought to himself.

Your father cautiously made enquiries about the Armenian who might be able to provide him with false papers. But the authorities had long taken him away. People at the bazaars gave him other addresses – addresses of counterfeiters, or middlemen who knew someone who could do the job – but as he knocked on each of their doors, he realized that none of them was home. And so eventually he decided to take the only route left open to him: He went to the American consulate.

The American Consul! A small, inconspicuous and aged man. Even my shadow could tell from the way he gestured and his overall manner of speaking that this man was not what the Turks would consider a stereotypical American. Even the Last Thought, who danced his way between us both and hovered behind your father as he made his way from the hallway, past the secretary and into the Consul's office, noticed that this American was rather peculiar. But then wasn't Vardan Khatisian a peculiar sort of

American, too?

He's a Greek fellow, that American Consul," I said quietly to the Last Thought. I repeat the same thing to my shadow. "He's a Greek man from Smyrna. One who ended up leaving at some point. He speaks many languages, including Turkish. And, most importantly of all, he knows how to handle the Turkish authorities."

"And what about the Khatisian case?"

"It's not filed away in one of his cabinets: He has it ready on his desk."

"So he knows?"

"Of course he knows. For months he's been trying to do something to help. But as we know, it was all to no avail."

"And the American press?"

"They got wind of this unusual case. And, as a matter of fact, they reported on the Khatisian case for weeks until everything was once more eclipsed by the war."

"So everyone forgot about the Khatisian case?"

"It was forgotten along with everything else. The daily newspapers have no memory."

"And the Consul?" asked the Last Thought, "Did he know my father?"

"He met him twice: both times in the *Hayastan,* where he was a regular guest and had his own reserved table. He was also friends with the owner."

"With my father's brother?"

"Yes, with Hajgaz.

And so it was that the Consul was not in the least bit surprised to see a man that everyone took for dead standing in front of his desk, and wearing a Turkish saptieh's uniform to boot.

– Did anyone recognize you as you walked in here? he asked.
– No, said your father.

– You've been forgotten, said the Consul. You don't exist anymore.
– Yes, said your father.
– Even the world's press has forgotten about you. You have become as irrelevant as everyone else who is no longer needed.
– It's good, said your father. They're not looking for me anymore.

– We can smuggle you out of the country, said the Consul. It won't be easy.
– And my family … mainly my wife and child?
– We can't help them, said the Consul.
– My son hasn't yet been born, said your father.
– I see, said the Consul.
– I cannot abandon my wife and son, said your father. I must do something to help them, although I don't quite know what.
– Yes, said the Consul.

– I could have a new passport made for you, said the Consul, but that will take a few weeks as I don't have any at the moment. I'll have to order them first. These things take time. Can you wait that long?
– No, said your father.
– You will also need a photo.

– A proper photo?
– Of course a proper photo.

– That won't be possible, said your father. And I cannot wait either. I have to get to my wife. And my son. We plan to call him Thovma.
    – Thovma?
    – Thovma.

– Where are they both now?
    – They were in prison.
    – I know, said the Consul.
    – Now they are back home.
    – In their village, you mean … what is it called again?
    – Yedi Su.
    – Yedi Su … the village of the seven waters?
    – Or the village of the seven wells, said your father.
    The Consul made an attempt at a smile. If they haven't cleared the village already, he said, you might have a chance of seeing the two alive again … your wife and your son.
    – We plan to name him Thovma, said your father.
    – Yes, I know, said the Consul.

– The village is some distance from the caravan road, said your father. It was overlooked once before, back during the massacres that took place under Abdul Hamid.
    – And you think that they might overlook it again?
    – I don't know what I should think, said your father.

– All right, said the Consul. You want to go back to the village. Listen very closely. I'm sure you're aware of what took place in Van?

– An uprising?

– It wasn't an uprising, said the Consul. All the Armenians did was refuse to allow their men to be shot and their families to be dragged away. They fought back, and they even managed to successfully defend their quarter for a time. They were completely surrounded of course. But then, in May of this year, the Russians came. And with the Russians came the Armenian volunteer battalions. They even got there first.

– So the city was liberated?

– Yes, said the Consul. That was in the middle of May. But then the Turks pushed forward again and recaptured Van. Most of the Armenians fled with the Russians, and the few who remained were slaughtered.

– Van, said your father.

– Van, said the Consul.

– And what about Van?

– The Russians have just retaken it. But that's not all. The Russians are now gaining ground. It's said to be a major offensive. If my calculations are correct, they will have overrun this entire region by early fall.

– Does that mean that the Russians might take Bakir?

– Yes, said the Consul.

And the Consul said, 'Allow me to make a suggestion. You go and fetch your wife and your son before the saptiehs kill all the men in the village and before they deport the women, children and elders. But you'll have to hurry. Bring your wife and your unborn son to this consulate. You may stay here as well. Nobody can arrest or deport you here. Nobody would dare drag you away from here as this consulate stands under diplomatic protection: We are on American soil.'

   – And what will we do here?

   – Wait until the Russians come.

   – Until the Russians come?

   – Yes.

   – And then?

   – Then we will take you, your wife and your son to one of the liberated ports on the Black Sea, perhaps Trebizond. The city will have been freed from Turkish control by then. Or farther, to one of the old Russian ports. And there we'll put you on an American ship.

– Yes, said your father.

   And the Consul nodded and said, 'Yes. You shall have to hurry though. I'll make sure you have a fast horse, and couple of blankets and provisions. Will you hurry?'

   – Yes, said your father.

And yet they continued to sit together for quite some time as the Consul wanted to wait until sundown before leaving to fetch the horse and the blankets and the provisions. And he also didn't want your father to go out onto the streets before night had fallen.

– Morgenthau has done everything he can to try and appeal to Enver Pasha's conscience, said the Consul. And here Morgenthau is the voice of America.

   – I have heard of Morgenthau, said your father.

– A German pastor who goes by the name of Lepsius also spoke with Enver and pleaded on behalf of the Armenians.

– Lepsius?

– Yes, said the Consul. This Lepsius man is a Teutonic saint. The German Consul in Bakir told me that he was the true voice of Germany.

– And what about the voice of the Kaiser?

– His is the other voice of Germany.

– The Germans are the only ones left who can still help you Armenians, said the Consul. They are the Turks' most important allies. Just one serious threat from the Kaiser to the Committee would be enough to stop the massacre. But the Kaiser is keeping quiet. And the German press is, too.

– So does that mean that the Germans aren't doing anything?

– Not quite, said the Consul. There are people such as Lepsius. And an endless stream of reports being sent by the German consulates and the imperial embassies to the Ministry in Berlin … reports about the massacre. Petitions have been presented to the Committee of Union and Progress and gentle admonitions made on behalf of the Kaiser and the high-ranking military officers. The Committee has a good laugh over them for up in Constantinople they know full well that the Germans wouldn't dare take any drastic measures, and that they have decided not to directly intervene in internal Turkish affairs.

– So there's no real support coming from the German Kaiser?

– No, no support at all.

– Those Germans call themselves civilized, but they are a strange bunch, said the Consul. Sometimes it seems as though the conscience of their poets and thinkers has tucked itself away behind their generals' monocles, only to someday vanish inside their soldiers' bootlegs where it will be carelessly trampled underfoot.

    – They won't offer any support, said your father.

    – No, they won't, said the Consul.

– The American government, said the Consul, has indicated to the Turks that if they continue with this massacre, their actions will not be without consequence. In terms of our country's neutrality, I mean. The Turks know that the massacres have already made headlines in the American press, even ousting the war reports from the front pages. They also know that President Wilson is indignant and that our military officers are pressuring the President to take concrete steps to put a stop to the Turks. But believe me, none of it had any effect. The extermination of the Armenians seems to be the Committee's absolute priority. Sometimes you could even think it was more important to them than events on the frontlines, America's neutrality or the progress of the war.

    – I just don't understand, said your father.

    – No one does, said the Consul.

The Consul then said, 'The reports on the massacres are on my desk.'

– The last report, said the Consul, mentioned something about 25,000 massacred Armenians in the Kemach ravine. It's along the Euphrates River. 25,000! We have no idea if these numbers are true. Allegedly the massacre was mainly carried out by Kurds. But saptiehs and chetes also had a hand in the bloodletting. And the report says that cavalier units of the regular Turkish army were involved. My report states that the young children were simply flung into the Euphrates. And the women jumped in after them. Many women also flung their children in themselves for they feared that the Kurds would slash them open if they got there first. The report states that there were so many bodies floating in the Euphrates that the Turkish cavalry regiments, who were on their way to the southern front, could no longer ride across the river because the horses were so startled and the soldiers had vomit spewing out of their mouths. The report states that the waters of the Euphrates and its tributaries ran as red as the rivers of blood that flow through one of the larger cities' abattoirs. Have you ever laid eyes on such an abattoir?

– Not one as large as that, said your father. In our village we would slaughter the animals one at a time. Mostly behind the house.

And so it was," said I, the storyteller. "The Consul procured a fast horse, as well as blankets, provisions, full wine and water pouches, quinine tablets and everything else required for a journey. And so it was that your father, fully equipped, left the city after night had fallen. In fact, he had everything with him that a normal saptieh would need. All he was missing was a gun and valid papers.

Your father knew that it was conspicuous to travel into the mountains without a gun. The fact that he was alone would also arouse suspicions as saptiehs rarely rode on their own; even the saptieh from Yedi Su wouldn't dare leave the village unless he was accompanied by the saptiehs from neighboring villages. But your father was careful. The Consul had given him a couple of pieces of cloth and an old flour sack, along with a large knife so he could cut them up. And so your father cut up the old sack and wrapped bits of it around the horse's hooves. He rode all night long. During the day he slept in one of the concealed ravines. Your father was just like the Armenian *fedayee* of old, those legendary freedom fighters whom the Kurds feared more than the Dashnaks. There was much talk of them at the turn of the century: the fedayee, men who used secret routes to cross over the Persian border and take their revenge on the Kurdish bandits – and they always appeared whenever the Kurds had raided another village and shot the men and kidnapped the women. The fedayee also only rode at night and slept in their hideouts during the day, which meant they were constantly vanishing into the mountains without a trace.

Your father didn't advance as fast as he had hoped. The mountain paths in the Kurdish territory wound between bare cliffs at dizzying heights. His horse often stumbled and panted fearfully as it looked down into the pitch black precipices below. Your father gripped on tightly to the reins and spoke softly to the animal in a reassuring and gentle voice. The journey lasted two days and two nights. The Consul had given your father cigarettes but he didn't dare light one up for fear that the Kurds would spot him. He slept restlessly during the day, mostly just dozing lightly. And then he would ride the whole night through.

At the end of the second night he found himself close to the village. As he was impatient and afraid that something might have already happened to his family, he hurried the horse along in the hope that he would reach the village before daybreak. But the day was faster than the horse's faltering steps along those winding, stony paths. Dawn was already coming into view on the other side of the village; around them the birds naturally began to stir, sounding their first calls of the day, and the unfettered sun sleepily poked its fiery red head just above the horizon. But your father didn't seem to care. And as the sun finally lifted its bright, circular body above the village of Yedi Su, he continued to ride into the new day. He threw all caution to the wind for he was sure he could hear his pregnant wife calling. Even his unborn son seemed to be calling to him. He rode brimming with fear and anxiety, and as he was blinded by the dazzling sunlight, he saw neither the wisps of smoke behind the hills that lay just before Yedi Su nor the many saptiehs and chetes who were waiting for him at the entrance to the village.

The chetes knew that a saptieh would never ride through the mountains without his gun. This saptieh, however, who rode towards them on his tired, sweaty horse, had no weapon. The saptiehs, too, who were standing around the entrance to the village with the chetes, thought the same, even though they generally weren't the kind of the men to give much thought to anything. But most of all the chetes recognized your father on account of his eyes for an Armenian's eyes tell a completely different story to those of a Turk. The chetes were specialists, and they knew how to recognize the prey they had been sent to dispose of.

Everything that then took place happened within a matter of minutes, beneath a silent sky which, on that morning, contained not a trace of cloud. The chetes grabbed hold of your father and yanked down his trousers. And they laughed when they saw he wasn't circumcised. They took hold of his member and one of them brandished a knife so as to chop it off. But it didn't come to that as one of the saptiehs standing close by had already drawn a bead on your father. And he shot him in the head. The others shot, too, and the chetes pounced upon him with their knives."

11

"When Bulbul the Kurd, who although rather old was still very sprightly, rode into the village on her nameless donkey late in the afternoon, what she laid her eyes upon was so horrific that she saw the Armenian tea, which was spiced and fragrant, and the Armenian lavash bread that she had eaten with a spread of mulberry syrup – basically everything that people here in this country would call a decent breakfast – come back out of her body. It simply spewed out of her old stomach and onto the neck of her nameless donkey. And she was so terrified and appalled that she pissed herself on the blanket on which she sat. For a time she searched among the hacked bodies, many of which were missing heads, to see if she could find anyone she knew, until she eventually gave up and rode to the hut at the edge of the village where the only Turkish family lived. Surely they had been spared, she thought. And indeed she was right, but the Turks were behind locked doors and windows, and no matter how hard she knocked, no one opened. She then happened upon the village policeman Yuksel Efendi, who had been serving here in Yedi Su since the year 1902, in other words, since the pockmarked saptieh Shekir Efendi had taken his retirement. It seemed that saptieh Yuksel Efendi had hidden himself away somewhere, but now that the coast was clear, he had come back out and suddenly appeared next to Bulbul.

– Hey, Yuksel Efendi, said Bulbul. When did this all happen?

– Yesterday afternoon, said the saptieh.

– And why did they burn down the Armenian church as well?

– Because they had locked the women and children inside, said the saptieh.

– And you were there?

– I was there, Bulbul. But I wasn't involved. What was I supposed to do? Those thugs would have killed me if I'd have said anything. Afterwards I went and hid.

– And who did all of this?

– Those out-of-town saptiehs did it. And the chetes. Saptieh Yuksel Efendi pointed to the burnt out church and then towards the mountain path at the entrance to the village. There's another one lying up there. It's Vardan Khatisian. He came back first thing this morning. They killed him.

– Vardan Khatisian?

– Yes.

– And he's lying up there?

– Yes. Up there.

Vardan Khatisian was naked. And he was bleeding from many wounds. But he wasn't dead. As soon as Bulbul realized this, she suddenly felt a sense of urgency.

Do you know, my little lamb," I, the storyteller, say to the Last Thought, "no one knows why the Lord God sometimes delays a person's death and defers their passing, if you will, to another day or another time."

"Don't you know why, Meddah?"

"No."

"Couldn't God banish death away forever?"

"No, He couldn't. Death is more cunning than God; it always finds a way back."

"So it can only be deferred?"

"Yes."

"And why didn't the Lord God want my father to die up there on that mountain path?"

"I don't know, my little lamb. It could well be that He still has a few things in store for your father."

"Yes. You're right. It could well be the case."

"Yes," say I, the storyteller. "It must be the case in fact. Why else should it be any different? Of course the Lord God still has a few things in store for your father. But we shouldn't worry our heads about that. And we also shouldn't wonder whether what happened on that day was a miracle or just sheer coincidence. The fact of the matter was that your father was still alive ... in spite of it all. And it was also true that Bulbul was suddenly in a hurry, and the saptieh, too, for your father urgently needed help.

The out-of-town saptiehs and the chetes had moved on. By the time Bulbul, together with saptieh Yuksel Efendi and their severely injured patient, arrived back down in the village, the terrified Turks had opened their front door, fetched their spades and were just getting ready to bury the dead. The old family patriarch Suleyman, whom the Armenians used to call Tashak – on account of his groin hernia or, to put it another way, his large, dangling sack – was standing before the front door giving orders. But when the old man spotted the nameless donkey with the severely injured man on its back, as well as Bulbul's withered face as she led the animal by the reins, and saptieh Yuksel Efendi, who was holding the motionless body on the donkey's back, he appeared to forget the corpses that littered the village. He grabbed hold of his stick and limped towards them.

– It's Vardan Khatisian, Bulbul said to him. And saptieh Yuksel Efendi also said, 'It really is him. It's Vardan Khatisian!'

They brought your father into the Turkish family's home.

– He's going to die, said the patriarch's wife.

– He's not going to die, said Bulbul.

– But he urgently needs a doctor.

– What he needs most is strength, said Bulbul. And he also needs the help of that strange saint he believes in … the one who died on the cross because he knew too much and refused to keep quiet … the one that Priest Kapriel Hamadian once referred to as Allah's son on earth.

– And what else does he need? asked the patriarch's wife.

– A strong stomach, said Bulbul, a couple of hearty belches and a loud fart so that I can be sure that his spirit has not yet flown away. I'll see to it that he has everything else he needs.

– And what do you plan to do, Bulbul?

– Whatever it takes, said Bulbul. This one here won't be the first to have a few bullets pulled out of his flesh and bone by my good hand. And I treat stab wounds, too. I just need to fetch my herbs. They are up in my hut.

Can you see how dark it is in old Tashak's hut?" I, the storyteller, say to the Last Thought. "You see, they still haven't got around to building any windows. And it's also very noisy and chaotic. And yet this place is home to only the elderly couple and the wife and children of their youngest son. All the others have long moved out, and some of their sons are at war, including Gog-Gog, your father's childhood friend. Gog-Gog, who was named after the call he used to entice the hens over to feed.

They all nursed your father back to health, as the saying goes. When he reopened his eyes for the first time, the corpses that lay on the streets of the village had long been buried, the wisps of smoke had dispersed and the smoldering ashes had faded.

– His eyes are open, said saptieh Yuksel Efendi, who came by several times a day to look after your father. Hey, Bulbul. He's actually got them open. With Allah as my witness. But as Bulbul had nodded off where she was sitting next to your father's bed, she didn't respond.

– You can breathe easy now, efendi, the saptieh said to your father. The air is clean. It truly is, for those out-of-town saptiehs and chetes were as unclean as the filthiest pork munchers alive. And the saptieh gulped and belched and let loose a fart as though he himself has eaten something unclean.

– They just burned down the church, he then said to your father, because they thought that women and children would burn better in a church than on a pyre in an open field. For you see, in an open field it might rain and then they wouldn't burn as well.

– What women and children? asked your father.

– You know, the women and children, said saptieh Yuksel Efendi. They locked them in the church.

– In which church? asked your father.

– In your church, said the saptieh. Have you forgotten about it already? The saptieh shook his head in amazement.

– Not all the women and children were burned, he then said.

You see, they set fire to it at night. That meant a few women and children were able to jump out of the window unnoticed, even though the church has no windows.

– How did it happen, efendi?

– Well, the church had a sort of air vent. I presume that the smaller children and the thinner women would have been able to crawl through it.

– And they ran away?

– Yes. The nights are dark, as are the mountains after sunset, even though the fire burned brightly. And then they simply ran off into the mountains.

Your father didn't ask after his family, not even his wife or his unborn son, for he couldn't remember anything. The saptieh carried on talking for quite some time, trying to convince your father that the story was true, and he spoke of Allah's miracles that sometimes allowed even pregnant women to crawl through narrow air vents with their unborn babies, and said that even a large, swollen belly couldn't stand in the way when it was the will of Allah. Bulbul also said something similar. Then your father fell asleep and neither said nor heard anything more.

– He's lost his mind, said Bulbul. He knows nothing. He was no memory.

– But he's a poet, said saptieh Yuksel Efendi. Didn't his priest, Kapriel Hamadian, once tell us that poets are our memory?

– Yes, that's what the priest said.

– So he can't have lost his memory?

– I don't know, said Bulbul.

– Well … they did give him a good knock on the head, said the saptieh. And the bullets that you pulled out weren't made of cow shit.

– They weren't made of cow shit, it's true, said Bulbul.

Every now and again one of the saptiehs from the seven villages would come by. They hadn't taken part in the massacres for they had served in the villages of the Armenian millets for many years and were friendly with the Armenians. But as there were no longer any Armenians left in the seven villages, they now found themselves bored. One of them said to Bulbul, 'Soon the muhajirs will be here to take over the Armenians' houses. This time it will probably be immigrants from the eastern borders who have fled together with our troops. Before the muhajirs came from Macedonia and other countries which I've never heard of. The government supports them because they are Muslims like us.' Then the saptieh said, 'My village is as dead as the Armenians who used to live there. The Djinns even speak to me during the day. But no one can see them. I am the only person in my village and I'm bored.'

– Yes, said Bulbul. I can imagine.

– It will stop being boring when the muhajirs come.

– Yes, said Bulbul.

– It's terrible when you're all by yourself, said the saptieh.

– It is, said Bulbul. And she said, 'What do you do all day long now that you're the only person in a dead village?'

– I wait for the boredom to end, said the saptieh.

– Do you think that the muhajirs will also be able to play cards and tavla just like the Armenians in the coffeehouse who you often used to play with?

– I don't know, said the saptieh. And I also don't know whether they'll give me my usual baksheesh as the Armenians always did.

– Neither do I, said Bulbul.

– Life was good with the Armenians, said the saptieh. Those people knew what baksheesh was, and they knew what was good and proper.

And when another one of these saptiehs came by the village some weeks later, one who had gotten on well with the Armenians, he said to Bulbul, 'People say the muhajirs are coming this week. They are coming and they are bringing everything with them, as well as their wives and children and parents and grandparents and their parents and grandparents and who knows who else. And many other saptiehs will ride with them as their escort, assigning them the Armenians' land and houses. When those other saptiehs see this injured man and find out that he is Armenian, they will kill him. And they will kill you, too, and the Turks who are nursing him and hiding him, because it's forbidden.'

– What should we do? asked Bulbul.

– You need to get him away from here, said the saptieh.

– We'd best take him to my hut, said Bulbul, who knew the saptieh from before. What do you think? Surely those lazy dogs wouldn't ride so high up into the mountains?

– I'm sure they wouldn't, said the saptieh.

And so, with the help of old Tashak, Bulbul strapped your father onto the back of the nameless donkey. And Tashak's wife gave Bulbul a sack of provisions and a few blankets for your father. The way to Bulbul's hut was strewn with stones, and the path was narrow and dangerous because it led over the devil's ravine from which there was no return for anyone unlucky enough to fall in. But Bulbul wasn't concerned and neither was her nameless donkey, who knew the way. This donkey looked just like the other donkey that Bulbul had owned when your father was born. And it was just as smart: proof that donkeys with brains were no exception.

As they set out, a few broken rays of sunlight skipped over the ravines; they danced before them like a will-o'-the-wisp in all its enticing, colorful glory. The clouds burst along the cliffs of the devil's ravine, and the Djinns competed with the wind to see who could whistle the loudest. The donkey walked at a leisurely pace. And Bulbul walked behind. She waddled as she always had done, with her bowed legs, and crooked back, her long stick in her old hand. Sometimes when she stumbled she stopped herself from falling by grabbing hold of the donkey's tail. Bulbul cursed under her breath the whole way there, and as the Committee in Constantinople couldn't hear her, she told them all to go to hell: Enver and Talaat and Djemal, the whole triumvirate. And the new Sultan, too, who was nothing but a puppet in the Committee's hands. She cursed those out-of-town saptiehs and the chete task forces and those marauding Kurds who, although they weren't involved in the Yedi Su massacres, had a hand in the killings in neighboring villages. She cursed the German Kaiser and his associates. And she cursed the drummers and all the public criers who gave proclamations that should never be made in the name of Allah. At the grotto, which had long been known as the Kurds' Grotto and which lay close to Bulbul's hut, the donkey stopped out of habit. From here the mountain path wound its way more steeply upwards, towards the clouds and the heavens.

'Mount Ararat is somewhere around here,' she said to your father, pointing her wrinkled hand in a vague direction. 'Somewhere, my son, stands your holy mountain. They say an eagle could spot it from here.' Then she smiled to herself for a time before giving the donkey a powerful kick and a tug of the tail. As the donkey started to move forward again, panting as it went, she said, 'It's really not much farther to the hut, my son. You've been here many times before, even back when you were small. Do you remember? You rode on my knee and played with my titties.'

But your father couldn't remember anything.

As the nameless donkey finally panted its way to the hut's entrance, where it came to a halt, Bulbul noticed that your father had lost consciousness. His head lolled almost lifelessly along the donkey's sweaty side, his eyes closed, his mouth gaping wide. 'It was to be expected,' Bulbul said to her donkey. 'It's nothing serious. I'll wake him up again later.' She spat and wiped her mouth, and she stroked the donkey whose tail she had tugged and whose side she had kicked a few moments earlier. 'It's just a shame,' she said to the donkey, 'that he can't see the hut as that might have jogged his memory.'

She pulled the unconscious body down from the donkey and cursed as the body slumped heavily to the floor, and she swore as she dragged Vardan over the threshold. Then she prepared a soft bed for her patient, and in spite of the summer heat she covered him with thick lambskins and blankets that Tashak had given her as she believed that he couldn't possibly fall victim to wound fever, or to the Djinns that dwelled within that dreaded illness, as long as he was kept properly wrapped up.

When your father woke up early in the afternoon, he could hear a cacophony of voices, and as he opened his eyes and looked around, he was terrified by what he saw: Around the tonir sat three Turkish soldiers who were chatting away to Bulbul. Their uniforms were so dirty it looked as though they had just crawled out of their own graves. But Bulbul came over to his bed and spoke to him reassuringly.

– You needn't be afraid of these men, she said. They are Armenians. They were soldiers in the Turkish army. They were executed in the spring.

– And how can they still be alive? whispered your terrified father.

– Because the Turks are a poor shot, said Bulbul. Especially when they try to gun down too many men at once. The three crawled out of a mass grave and dragged themselves here so that I could patch them up again.

Bulbul laughed and lit her chibouk. 'They are living in the mountains,' she said, 'but they sometimes come by to pay me a visit.'

The men didn't care about your father. They drank liquor from their water pouches, grunted with each gulp, spoke more softly as if they had something important to discuss, passed the hookah around, then stood up and left the hut, leaving nothing but their stench and a room filled with tobacco smoke.

After the men left, Bulbul had thrown some fresh tezek into the fire. She now stood in front of the open hearth and busied herself roasting pumpkin seeds in a soot-covered, dented frying pan. Dressed in generously-sized shalvar trousers, a gray wrap made of sackcloth and a colorful belt that was slightly askew, Bulbul resembled one of Yedi Su's scarecrows that superstitious farmers used to say would come to life during the dark days. She stood slightly hunched over the frying pan, sniffing away. Her face was slightly red from the reflection of the flames; it seemed to have sunken into her black headscarf and looked as shriveled as Armenian soil in the dry season.

Your father lay silently on the floor, a few steps away from the old woman. His eyes had already grown accustomed to the darkened, smoke-filled room, and it didn't take long before he was able to distinguish the individual objects inside the hut from one another: dirty straw mats on the floor; instead of a divan, a couple of large, rounded pillows with protruding chicken feathers; a roughly constructed dresser; two floor cushions covered in goat skins; a sideboard which had no door and poplar branch shelves that held all manner of rags, as well as tobacco leaves and food; brass pots and earthenware jugs, woven bags, wall hangings and donkey harnesses hung on the walls. He also noticed the small oil lamp on the floor next to the tonir and the still smoldering hookah alongside it, whose long hose stretched out like a snake towards the fire in the tonir.

Every now and again his gaze fell upon the open doorway beyond which he could make out the outlines of the mountains, faint in the cloudy haze ... black and gray lines. Outside in front of the hut he could see hens running around, romping about in the sparse grass. A large, speckled rooster sat silently on the wheel of an overturned cart. He also spotted two black goats, who were peacefully grazing at the entrance to the hut, as was the nameless donkey that Bulbul hadn't tied up.

A moment earlier, Bulbul had said to the men, 'I once knew a rooster whose name was Abdul Hamid. He belonged to the Khatisian family down in the village. Yes, sir, Abdul Hamid. But mine has a different name. He's called Enver Pasha.'

The men laughed. One of them asked, 'I don't suppose you plan to chop his head off, do you?'

– Oh, yes, I certainly do, said Bulbul. In fact, I shall do it today.

– But why?

– Because he is old and no longer up to much.

– What's wrong with him?

– He can't crow properly anymore, and his chicks croak prematurely.

– Prematurely?

– Yes, prematurely.

The men laughed, but they didn't utter another word.

A gnawed bone of uncertain origin hung on the skewer above the open hearth. Bulbul pulled it off the skewer and threw it outside into the courtyard. She then fetched two round flat breads from the sideboard, dipped them in sesame oil, sprinkled salt and some green spices over them and gave them to your father.

– Later I will slaughter Enver Pasha, she said. When those men return, they will be hungry. She fetched the frying pan that contained the roasted pumpkin seeds and placed it next to your father's bed where he lay on the floor. And she squatted down next to the pan and grinned at your father.

– Tell me, why did you come back from America? she asked. How on earth could anyone be so stupid? Over there you were safe. She giggled. Then she said, 'And that trial! And all that time spent in prison in Bakir! You could have spared yourself all of it!' But then she saw that your father couldn't remember anything and hadn't a clue that he had even been to America. And he knew nothing of a trial or an interrogation or a prison in Bakir.

As evening fell, it began to rain. The animals sought shelter inside the hut for there was nowhere for them to take refuge outside in the open. First, it was the nameless donkey that came stamping through the open door, sniffing like an oversized mouse. He was followed by the two black goats. The hens gradually also scurried over the open threshold. The large, speckled rooster was the last in.

Bulbul stoked the fire and, as she was doing so, cast furtive glances across to Enver Pasha the rooster whom she planned to slaughter because of his old age. The rooster had flown up onto the top of the sideboard and was watching Bulbul with its twitching head, as if it knew what she had in mind.

Your father helped himself to a few pumpkin seeds from the frying pan, began cracking them open with his teeth and spitting the shell out in a high arc just as people in this region had always done. He noticed that Bulbul had put the fire striker away and was now standing in front of the open tonir with her arms folded. The fact that Bulbul was standing still seemed to calm the rooster. His attention had now shifted to a certain hen who was larger and whiter than the rest. This hen was prowling around the sideboard looking for grain. The rooster raised his head, stretched it out slyly and then suddenly … in a single, fluttering leap … he pounced onto the hen.

Your father smiled and thought to himself, 'That's one good rooster. Why does she want to kill it?' He watched as the large, white hen willingly spread out her wings, lowered herself down towards the earth and clucked as the rooster made scratching motions as if it wanted to tear the hen to pieces. That's when Bulbul made her move. She caught the rooster by the wings and lifted him up. The rooster emitted a sharp cry. Bulbul took hold of the wood axe that lay on the floor, threw the rooster over the sideboard so that its neck fell across the hard, wooden edge. Then she lifted the wood axe and chopped the rooster's head off with one swift blow.

Your father stopped chewing. The rooster's head had fallen onto the floor and rolled over to his bed. The beak was wide open as if he still had one more crow left. Disgusted, your father kicked the head away and returned his gaze to Bulbul. He saw the rooster's headless body flapping wildly and hopping around on the sideboard. A great deal of blood was spurting out of its neck and a few spots had even hit Bulbul. The bird slipped on the sharp edge of the sideboard and fell down onto the large, white hen who was sitting, crouched down and paralyzed in terror, on the floor next to the sideboard, her beak in the dust. The hen's white wings turned red. Both rooster and hen twitched. It looked like a final act of passion.

Bulbul had hung Enver Pasha the rooster out on the long washing line to allow the blood to drain. She had placed a large washing trough underneath, and the dripping blood made a sound like rain falling on the hut's roof.

– That's how they chopped the heads off the Armenian men of Yedi Su, Bulbul said to your father. Just like that.

– I thought they were shot.

– Not all of them, said Bulbul. Some were beaten to death, and most of them were beheaded.

– Were you there?

– I wasn't, said Bulbul. The village saptieh, the one who didn't take part in the massacres but who witnessed them, he told me.

– And what did you see?

– Not much, said Bulbul. When I came down into the village the next day, I saw the headless bodies on the street. And I also saw a few heads that had rolled away, and most of them were unrecognisable.

– Have they all been buried?

– Every single one.

– The heads, too?

– The heads, too.

– And is it true what they say about the women and children?

– Yes, it's true. They were burned alive in the church. She then added, 'But not all. Some of them managed to escape.'

As the rain began to ease off, Bulbul cursed and kicked the animals back out of the hut. The three Armenian soldiers came back later, long after Bulbul had plucked, gutted and hung the rooster over the fire. The men were hungry and gazed longingly at the sizzling rooster."

12

"Your father's health returned. Bulbul nursed and fed him as the weeks passed by. Whilst summer was still in the air, they hardly felt the tepid wind that blew down from the mountains, fanning the hut's roof, sometimes feebly shaking the creaking wooden sheds that had been withered by age, and barely advancing past the threshold and into the large, soot-covered rooms. But in early fall the wind became more ferocious. Chubby-faced Djinns blew cool air over the ravines. The wind no longer whispered: It howled around the huts, and the Djinns, who rode along inside the wind's currents, told stories of wilting foliage and the changing color of the leaves. By the time fall was preparing to take its leave, your father had already started walking unaided. His wounds had healed and he was no longer in any pain. But something was still not right with his head.

Your father had forgotten everything that had happened to him … before he was shot in the head and beaten; in fact, he didn't even know his own name anymore for he had become like a child: a child that asks questions to which he may or may not get an answer, and so old Bulbul started speaking more about the past than she normally would. She told him everything: about the Khatisians, the family, the villagers, describing each individual one and telling him the names of his parents and grandparents and everyone else who had belonged to the clan. She even told him the names of the animals that he had played with as a child. Most of all she made sure to drum his own name into him, which she did every day until she was sure he knew what he was called and would never forget it. Bulbul was clearly trying her hardest, even though she was often irritated by the fact that he had lost so much of his mind and memory. Many visitors came by as the fall weeks passed: Armenians who had escaped death, soldiers and others, even women and children. It was as though they had all crawled out of those ravines of death. They lived in the mountains and furtively made their way to the hut when they were sick or in need of anything. Or they simply came to prove to Bulbul that they were still alive. And as secretly as they had come, they would disappear again.

– They're all waiting for the Russians, Bulbul said to your father. They are on the advance and will get here eventually.

Once an Armenian priest came to visit. He was the only person from the seven villages to survive. When he laid eyes on your father and realized that he had forgotten everything, he told old Bulbul the story of Sodom and Gomorrah and of Lot's wife, who turned into a pillar of salt.

– Why, of all things, did the Lord God turn her into a pillar of salt? old Bulbul wanted to know.

– Because He felt sorry for her, said the priest, for she had seen something terrible, and the Lord God knew that any human who had witnessed such horrors couldn't carrying on living with those memories.

But Bulbul didn't believe the priest's words. 'These Christians are all talk,' she thought. 'They exaggerate and lie, just like they did with that whole story about the Blessed Virgin, whose slit was never opened or penetrated and yet somehow she still gave birth to a child. These Christians are nothing but storytellers. And although this Vardan is a Christian, he's certainly no pillar of salt. He's just had a knock to his head. That's all.'

– What do you think? she asked the priest. Could it be that Vardan Khatisian has banished his memory away to some corner of his mind? Perhaps behind those holes that those cursed saptiehs and chetes bored into his head? Could it be that he's deliberately keeping it locked away just to annoy me?

– If anyone has hidden his memory away behind the holes in his head, said the priest, then it must be the will of God.

– Well, said Bulbul. That might well be. And she grinned pensively for a while before saying to the priest, 'We have the same God, Father. Perhaps we should both pray together for this forgetful soul?'

And then the time came. During winter the Russians made their push. A large-scale offensive was well underway and the only thing holding it back was the rainy weather and the muddy roads. By 1916 the Tsar's troops had captured a large area of Anatolia.

Trebizond had fallen along with Erzurum and Bakir. One morning Bulbul rode down into the village. And when she returned on her nameless donkey, she said to your father, 'The Russians are here.'

Different people now lived in the village of Yedi Su. Many were in fact muhajirs – Muslim emigrants – who had been promised the Armenians' houses by Enver Pasha's government, but Kurds and Turks had also come, as well as landless farmers and some of the rabble from larger cities. The Russians couldn't converse with the people, but they drank vodka with them and when they were under the influence they sang strange, melancholy songs which expressed more than words ever could. The wives of the new settlers were raped immediately after the foreign soldiers invaded; people said they were no different than the chetes and the saptiehs and the Kurdish bandits, who had had their way with the Armenian women without asking for permission. And yet it wasn't true for the foreign soldiers neither dragged the women away nor did they kill them. And they were kind to the children and didn't lay a finger upon them. The wives of the new settlers said that the Tsar's soldiers had large, pale ceps between their legs that penetrated any patch of moss whether the women cried out to Allah or not. Some women said that they weren't ceps at all but stiff keys made of bone and skin that opened every hidden lock; others said they were ugly worms that had found their way inside the women's stables. The women's husbands were furious and swore revenge.

The Russian invasion also meant the arrival of the Armenian volunteer battalions. They wore Russian uniforms. Many of the Armenian volunteers had lost their entire families during the massacres. And so it was that some of them took revenge and murdered Turks wherever they found them. The majority, however, did no such thing and told their fellow men that it was wrong to take an eye for an eye."

13

"In the spring, the Turk Tashak harnessed his mule, Osman, up to his old araba which had stood in his shed for years. And he said to Bulbul and Vardan, 'This mule is strong and I've sprinkled some flour on the axle. Now you can go out and find Vardan's wife.'

– And his son, said Bulbul, who must have been born by now.

– Weren't they going to name him Thovma?

– They were. Thovma, said Bulbul.

– I'm sure my wife didn't burn to death in the church, said Vardan. They say some women jumped free of the flames. They fled into the mountains. Bulbul told me so.

– Yes, said Tashak. That's what they're saying.

– If she didn't burn to death in the church with all the others, said Bulbul, then perhaps she's still alive.

– And perhaps his son is still alive, too, said Tashak.

– But she was pregnant, said Bulbul. She was eight or perhaps even nine months along. I saw her shortly before. She had a big, swollen belly: too big to have allowed her to crawl through such a narrow air vent.

– If it is Allah's will, said Tashak, even a camel can crawl through the eye of a needle.

– True, said Bulbul.

– She was big and strong, said Vardan. Bulbul described her to me. I've forgotten everything, you see. And if she was big and strong, then surely she was able to fight her way out. And I bet you both that she was one of the first to crawl through the air vent just in time to make it out alive.

– It's possible, said Bulbul.

– We will find her, said Vardan. And we'll find my son, too. And I will recognize them both when I see them.

– Yes, said Bulbul.

And so off they went, the old woman and the younger man with no memory, who had lost every image and recollection that had ever meant anything to him.

– We will find them, said Bulbul. Now I am sure of it, too. We will ride through every city and village. And we will ride along all the deportation routes. And we will ask the farmers.

– Yes, said Vardan.

– Anyone who has seen your wife could never forget her, said Bulbul, for she was very big. And she had no face, only eyes.

– Yes, said Vardan. That's how you always describe her.

– The farmers will remember her. I will say to them, 'You must have seen her. She was very big. Her face was burnt. In fact, she had no face at all. But she did have large, Armenian eyes, the largest and most beautiful that you have ever seen.'

But first they journeyed to Bakir in search of her family for if Anahit had survived, she would most likely have fled to Bakir to go into hiding with her relatives. And even if she wasn't able to go there straight away, she would almost certainly have contacted them soon after the liberation. Surely they would know where she was. Bulbul knew the *Hayastan,* and she knew Vardan's eldest brother, Hajgaz.

Once in Bakir they were told that shortly before the Russians invaded, the chetes and the saptiehs had liquidated all of the Armenians that were left in the city, including the craftsmen, whose skills were needed right until the very end, and the vali's minions. It happened on the last day before the city was handed over. The Russians were already at the city gates – people said they couldn't just hear the Russians' cannons and their machine guns, which had been audible for several days: When the wind blew the right way, they could even hear the Russians farting and bellowing. In fact, they were on the verge of breaching the city when the last Armenians were shot. But their victory hadn't quite been sealed even though the regular Turkish troops had already withdrawn and the only fighters left in the city were the rear guard, the chetes and the saptiehs who were under the control of the mudir, who himself was answerable to the vali and the mutasarrif and the kaimakam. By the time the last Armenian was killed on the city wall, the authorities had already packed their bags; their sprung yaylis and arabas, with their filled, bulletproof sandbags, were already standing in front of the hukumet, ready to go.

Whilst the executions were being carried out in front of the eastern city gate, so people on the streets of Bakir said, a group of armed Armenians suddenly appeared. They came from the mountains and were wearing Turkish uniforms. No one knew who they were and where they had gotten their weapons from. There weren't many, perhaps seven or eight. They had tried to halt the executions and had managed to shoot some of the saptiehs and chetes dead. But as I said, they were only few, and the many saptiehs and chetes ultimately finished them off.

Indeed, it is true. Those armed Armenians did not die in vain. You see, the brief shoot-out that took place in front of the eastern city gate allowed some of the victims to escape, and they fled back to the city and hid with Turkish or Kurdish friends. They were not many, but at least there were some who would live to tell the tale.

Not one of Vardan's relatives in Bakir had survived. All the Armenians who had survived and who gradually began to crawl out of their hiding places were not Khatisians. One of them did, however, know Hajgaz from the *Hayastan* and he knew Vardan for he had once seen him there.

– I recognized you instantly, the Armenian said to Vardan. Do you remember me? We once sat in the *Hayastan* together at the same table. In the summer of 1914. You married young, at least that's what they said. You were with your wife.

– My wife? said Vardan, who could remember nothing.

– Your wife, said the Armenian.

– Have you seen her since? asked Bulbul. Her name was Anahit, and she had a burnt face and large eyes.

– I remember her name, said the Armenian, and I remember what she looked like.

– Have you seen his wife … at any point since?

– No, said the Armenian. I haven't seen her since.

Afterwards Bulbul and Vardan rode with their mule and their araba through the villages and cities of the liberated country. They rode along on squeaky wheels which, despite the flour, still made the usual racket that accompanies any two-wheeled cart whose wheels don't turn around an axle. They weren't particularly conspicuous, but they didn't go entirely unnoticed either. Many were travelling in similar arabas; some were on foot or riding some animal. Most were looking for someone. The farmers gave as much information as they could. Even in the cities, both large and small, people tried to answer their questions for now was the time for questioning and for searching. But nobody could remember Anahit. No one had seen her.

One day, in a small village on the bank of the Tigris, a female farmer said that she had seen a woman who matched Bulbul's description of Anahit. Yes. She had seen a line of women and children and elders being marched through the village. A saptieh had told her that there were some women in the transport who had tried to hide in the mountains, but that they had recaptured them, she explained. One of the women in the line had particularly caught her eye. She was larger than the other women and she was pregnant, probably nine months along. The woman also had a burnt face similar to the woman Bulbul described … and large, black eyes. She wasn't wearing a veil. She'd probably lost it along the way.

The woman pointed towards the Tigris. She said that's where they were taken.

Along the banks of the Euphrates they heard similar accounts. Where before their enquiries were met with shaking heads, now they were suddenly finding nods. Wherever they went there was someone who claimed to know something. Many had seen pregnant women on death marches, even women who were larger than the others and who had burnt, scarred faces that often weren't really faces at all, just masses of flesh and bone with large eyes.

– Here the Euphrates ran red, said one farmer, probably from the blood of the small children thrown from the cliffs by their mothers, and she added, 'So that the chetes and the saptiehs and the Kurds didn't get them. You see, they would kill the children in front of their mothers.' – Another farmer laughed. She said, 'Nonsense. The Euphrates wasn't red from the blood of the children but from the bellies of the mothers that had been slit open before they plunged down from the cliffs. The children,' the farmer said, 'were thrown alive into the water by their mothers and so drowned without losing any blood.' – Others said that that wasn't entirely true for even the guards had stepped in and thrown the children in the river first when the mothers weren't quick enough, and they even slit their little throats beforehand, too.

– And this woman with the burnt face? Did anyone see if she drowned in the Euphrates? – But no one had. A Turkish farmer said, 'We didn't see any of it. We just know that it happened.'

One time they met a Turkmen farmer who said that an Armenian woman had hidden in his house during the massacre. She was pregnant and had given birth shortly after the massacre. He said she was still in his house, slept in his bed and had a burnt face. As a matter of fact, he said, she had no face at all, but that didn't bother him as she was good in bed and always obedient. They went to see the woman in the Turkmen's house. Vardan's heart was racing. Even Bulbul's old face was beaming with excitement.

But it wasn't her. No, said Bulbul. This woman is not Anahit. It's someone else.

In the semi-nomadic Kurdish villages and even in the black tents of the wild mountain clans they met Armenians who had survived the massacre, and they were amazed to discover that there had indeed been Kurdish clans who had hidden Armenians. One of the Kurdish beys said to them, 'My clan is peaceful and we did not take part in the massacres; I told my men that we would stay out of it.'

– But many of the Kurdish clan were involved, said Bulbul. Sometimes they were even more merciless than the chetes.

– That could be, said the bey. But the Turkish officials were the ones who sent their messengers into the mountains to tell the Kurds that there were rich pickings to be had. And the officials said there would be no punishment. The government would guarantee it. And the officials' messengers told the beys and their people, as well as the herdsmen on the mountain pastures, about the Armenians' fine clothing and the women's jewelry, and they said the women had holes that were filled with honey.

As they made their way back to Bakir, they encountered a Turk without any legs. He was unshaven and wore a tatty uniform.

– I knew nothing of it, said the cripple, even back when I rode over the Euphrates with the cavalry of the Fourth Army. They told us we were going to Syria. The English and the French were said to be stationed somewhere, but they were still far away.

And as we began to force our horses into the water so that they could swim across the river, they turned away and refused to follow our commands. You see, the Euphrates was full of corpses. Mostly women and children. And the water was as red as a tandir's flames. And at that time I still had both legs as I only lost them later, on the front. And so, as I still had both my legs, I swam across the river without my horse. Others herded the reluctant animal behind me and it whinnied like an old horse at the slaughterhouse. And believe me, my friends, I saw it all and yet I knew nothing. Nobody will admit to knowing anything about it.

One night, as they were riding back to Bakir, Vardan climbed down from the araba and said to Bulbul, 'I'm just going to take a leak. I'll be right back.' – And he never returned."

14

"People in the village were surprised to see Bulbul return alone. As old Tashak unhitched the mule, Bulbul said, 'Vardan simply climbed down and never came back.'

– Strange, said Tashak.

– But as he left, Vardan said he just needed to take a leak.

– I don't understand, said Tashak, how someone could take such a long leak.

The farmers who had moved to the village barely knew who Vardan was, and so it didn't take long before they forgot about him. Tashak's family were the only ones who occasionally mentioned his name, as well as Bulbul. It was another hot summer, food was scarce in the village and the farmers were concerned about the drought and plagues of locusts that were sweeping through the land. Returning soldiers had brought cholera and typhoid with them. Despite everything, traders continued to come from the cities to sell their wares. In the past the traders spoke Armenian, but these new traders were Turks and Kurds, and there were also a few Jews and Greeks among them. Only once did an Armenian trader come to the village and when he did, the muhajirs laughed and said, 'Those Armenian traders, you just can't get rid of them. Look, now they're back!'

And the summer drought eventually passed and with it the plagues of locusts. A few farmers died of cholera and typhoid. The farmers hung the clothes of the dead from the branches of the village's holy tree and were convinced that the evil spirits in the dead person's clothes would no longer haunt the homes of those still living. And the furnaces of the Armenian tonirs, that the Muslims now referred to as tandirs, would also remain spirit-free, along with everything that was cooked and fried over the flames and eaten by the dead person's relatives. Winter descended quickly and was as cold as it always was, and spring returned without any surprises. The fresh grass and the nascent flowers, and the buds growing on the trees didn't seem bothered by the war. Towards the end of 1917 the traders told of a Russian revolution over on the other side of the Caucasus, and they told of mutinying soldiers in the great army of the Russian Tsar, and a few other things as well.

– But that can't possibly be true, said the farmers. Such a thing doesn't exist: simple-minded soldiers beating their own officers to death? How can it be possible? Who has ever heard of a servant beating his master to death?

– Soon the Russian army will be no more, said the traders. And when that happens, the Turks will return.

In a way the traders were right. And yet things didn't quite happen as they had predicted. The Turks wouldn't return just yet. Although the Tsar's army had been weakened, they still retained enough cohesion in this part of their territory to hold their entrenched positions a little while longer. And after yet another winter and summer came and went, the English and the French arrived from Syria.

As word of the Turkish capitulation reached the village in 1918, the news filled the farmers with more dread than cholera and typhoid, drought and plagues of locusts. You see, they had heard that the Russians had retreated, and that the French and the English would retreat, too. The country, so the traders said, was now occupied by Armenians.

– But all the Armenians are dead, said the farmers.

– Not all of them, said the traders. The Russian-Armenians are still alive. And so are the Turkish-Armenians who fled across the border just in time. And there are also Armenians showing up here in this region, too. Like Djinns they are crawling out of caves and ravines and other hiding places. They are mainly members of the Armenian volunteer battalions who joined the Tsar's army. Afterwards the Russians took their weapons away because they too grew fearful of them, but they've managed to procure more guns. Now they are everywhere. They want to establish a new state here that they will call Hayastan.

– Hayastan? said the farmers. We've never heard that word before in our lives.

Many Armenians, who had fled to the Caucasus or had hidden in the homes of Turks or other people, came back to reclaim their property. But that didn't happen in Yedi Su. There was no one left who could lay claim to ever having lived in the village – no one other than Vardan Khatisian, but he demanded nothing and remained missing.

– If the Armenians seize power here, said the Muslim farmers, that means their officials will also come to Yedi Su and they will order us to return the houses to the dead.

– You'll have to give the animals back to the dead, too, said the traders, and everything else that belonged to them.

But yet again these predictions didn't come to pass. After the collapse of the Russian Empire, the Muslims from Azerbaijan joined forces with the Georgians. And the Armenians from the Russian side of the border also joined their alliance, and within the vacuum that was left on the redrawn map of the region they founded a temporary state which they called the *Transcaucasian Federation.* However, given that the Muslims could tolerate neither the Christian Armenians nor the Georgians, and because relations between the groups were so strained, with all three refusing to accept the other's differences, for this reason – or for this and other reasons – the alliance was soon dissolved. The Georgians decided to become independent and founded their own state. The Muslims and the Armenians followed suit.

When, for the first time in many centuries, the Armenians proclaimed the creation of their own state on May 28 of the year 1918 – the free and independent state of Armenia, which was actually supposed to be called Hayastan, even though it wasn't – the only ones celebrating in Yedi Su were the dead who had died a natural death before the great massacre. News of the founding of an Armenian state on the other side of the old Russian border only reached the village the following year, and the farmers weren't told any of the details until 1920 when journeying Greek traders arriving from the Caucasus enlightened them. The traders explained that the American president, President Wilson, who people said was the most powerful padishah in the entire world, even more powerful than the Kaiser, the Tsar, Abdul Hamid or Enver Pasha ever were ... well, this great padishah from America had promised to include the Armenians in the post-war peace negotiations because no other people on this earth had suffered as much during the war. The traders said that Padishah Wilson had promised the Armenians that their tiny but free state on the wrong side of the border would include all the land that once belonged to Hayastan, above all the land that lay on the right side of the border, in other words, the Turkish side. Wilson also promised the Armenians Mount Ararat, said the traders, even the cities of Erzurum and Trebizond along the Black Sea coastline, and Bakir and the majority of the mountain region all the way down to the Mediterranean, including parts of the country where there were still Turks and Kurds living, as well as gypsies, devil worshippers and other groups. But this promise, so the traders said, existed only in writing for, so people claimed, two large armies were already on the advance with the aim of crushing this small, temporary Armenian state before the cartographers even had time to painstakingly map out its actual borders.

And that is precisely what happened. Eventually the beaten Turkish army reorganized itself and drove the foreign troops out of the Anatolian land. It now had a new leader and his name was Mustafa Kemal Pasha. The traders said that this Kemal was not only the father and liberator of all Turks, he was also a conqueror whose troops had already crossed the old Russian border with the objective of freeing the people of the Caucasus: all the tiny, new states in the region, including the Armenian one. The traders said, 'And on other side of the Caucasus, marching from the opposite direction, other troops with the exact same mission are approaching.' This other army, so the traders said, was also advancing towards the Armenian border, they were just coming from the other direction: they were from the new Workers' and Peasants' Red Army and carried red flags, with a hammer and scythe visible on their old Russian hats. These two large armies – the Turks approaching from one side, the Red Army from the other – were simply going to crush this feeble Armenian state. And as the farmers didn't want to believe it for they had little imagination and were unable to picture in their minds just how a state could be crushed, one of the traders took the fresh egg of a young hen in his large and greedy hands and delighted in slowly crushing it between his fingers. 'Like that,' said the trader. 'Just like that.'

– What a waste of an egg, said the farmers. They now understood what the trader had meant, but they were annoyed for he had taken a good, precious egg from a hen that was still young and deliberately wasted it before the eyes of Allah.

A few months later, when the short-lived Armenian state and its independence were already history, a miniature re-enactment of the Great War, a minor episode in the game of chess that were the peace negotiations and the redrawing of borders – for such matters take time, that was just how it was – new traders came from the Caucasus and they told the farmers the story of the tired legs.

– You see, the soldiers had tired legs, said the traders, both Kemal Pasha's soldiers and those of the Workers' and Peasants' Army, for the Great War had been long and they had marched almost the entire time. But the tired legs of the Workers' and Peasants' Army were quicker than those tired legs of the Turks. And so it was that the small, independent Armenian state was swallowed up by the Reds before Kemal Pasha could invade.

– That's tough luck for the Armenians, said the farmers.

– No, it was a stroke of fortune, said the traders. You see, Kemal Pasha would have carried out a great massacre had he got there first. He would have annihilated everyone who had survived: the remnants of the Armenian people.

– And how can you be so sure that all this is true?

– An Armenian mother told me.

– What did she say?

– Well, what do you think she said? Her words were, 'It is better to cradle a living child under the Russians than a dead one under the Turks.'

– Did she really say that?

– She really did."

15

"Bulbul didn't hear of Vardan again until 1921 when a few relatives of the dead Armenians from Yedi Su began to make their pilgrimage to the village to pray for the souls of the dead before the mass graves at the Armenian cemetery. One of them was already very old. He had met Bulbul before. And he knew the Khatisians for he was the uncle of the red-haired blacksmith who had been Vardan's godfather. The old man used to visit the village often, and he was present at both Vardan's first and second wedding. And so not only did he know who Anahit was, he also knew that her son, of whom Vardan often spoke, was to be called Thovma.

Even Bulbul herself was now showing signs of her advanced age, and had become very old and frail in recent years. She had started to live more in the past than the present, and couldn't always cope with the reality in which see existed. She followed the old man to the cemetery, waited until he had said a prayer for the dead and sat down next to him on the soil of the cemetery, which was mute and absent of the Djinns' usual whispers, and they both chatted away endlessly as the place was so silent. They chatted as old folks do and neither of them knew whether what they were saying was actually real or whether it was a dream, or memories and fantasies that were woven out of dreams and memories.

– I would love to know whether Anahit nursed little Thovma, said Bulbul, for who else would have nursed him whenever and wherever she was when she gave birth to him.

– But I heard that back then she burned to death with the others in the church, said the old man who tried to imagine the church burning down with everyone locked inside it – where should she have given birth to her child? You think the flames gave birth to him?

– But Vardan is convinced that she didn't burn to death, said Bulbul.

– She fled into the mountains, said Bulbul. It's just that nobody saw her. She leapt through the flames and she forced her fat body through that narrow vent and out into the open, together with her unborn child. And she extinguished her burning clothes with sand. And then later, after she had wandered around the mountains for days, she was caught. And she was deported towards Syria and Mesopotamia. She was sent on a death march. And on some country road she gave birth to her little Thovma. And I bet you that little Thovma is still alive, even if his mother didn't survive. That little Thovma must be a tenacious, little fellow, just like his forefathers who lived very long lives and reached a grand old age.

– And Vardan?
    – No idea.
    – I've heard a few things from people who knew him.
    – What have you heard? asked Bulbul.

– They say he signed up with the Armenian volunteer fighters, said the old man. But then later, when the Russians grew distrustful of the Armenians because they decided they did want to found their own state after all, and they wanted to do it in Russian-controlled territory that the Russians had no intention of giving up, they disbanded the volunteer battalions. A few Armenian officers, who ordered their soldiers not to surrender their arms, were arrested. Vardan, too, was an officer for he was a poet and could read and write, and he could also draw up plans and read maps. They arrested Vardan as well and put him in chains. He was taken to Siberia along with the other officers.

And he remained there in Siberia for quite some time, said the old man, until the revolution erupted and the Reds came and freed all of the prisoners. Then he fought for the Reds. And then later he suddenly showed up in Yerevan, the new Armenian capital where the Russians had now hoisted their red flag, and he wandered around there for a time. People say he also went to Syria to find the camps where the deportations arrived because he had wanted to find something out about his wife and his son, Thovma, who must surely have been born long since.

And then he returned to Yerevan, said the old man. In the spring of that year the Armenians staged a coup against the Reds after they had withdrawn their troops to Georgia in order to bring the Georgians to their senses. They say Vardan was one of the leaders of the coup, but its success was short-lived for the Russians soon returned. People say they plan to stay there permanently.

– What do you mean permanently? said Bulbul. Have you ever seen anything in this life that was permanent?

– No, I haven't, said the old man.

– We don't even know whether death itself is permanent, said Bulbul, for the faithful believe that one day the resurrection will come.

– And who told you all of that then? asked Bulbul.
  – People who knew Vardan.
  – Did he know them?
  – No, said the old man. People say he knew no one.

– And where is Vardan said to be now? asked Bulbul.
  – Somewhere, said the old man."

16

"Somewhere along the way even I, the one who goes by the name of Meddah, lost track of Vardan Khatisian," say I, the storyteller, to my shadow. "And so I had no other choice but to track down another: The man who would one day claim to be his son."

And I, the one who goes by the name of Meddah, say to my shadow, "Soon after the World War was over – just after it had finished – plans started being made for a new war. You see, historians wanted to give the *Great War,* which they simply referred to as a *World War,* a number so that it wouldn't be lost in the drawer containing all the wars the world had seen. But in order to be able to call the *Great War,* which was a numberless world war, the *first* war, there would have to be a *second.* And that was no difficult feat. It wouldn't even need to be invented; like most inventions, war had already been around for a long time. Historians merely needed a pretext or a trigger so they could state that this *Second World War* did indeed exist, and allow them to confidently place the word *First* before one and *Second* before the other. The numbers *1* and *2* would also be possible, of course succeeded by *st* and *nd* respectively; after all, everything must be ordered properly, and the spelling had to be correct, too.

But I don't want to digress," say I, the storyteller. "I just want to tell you about the trace left by Vardan Khatisian, who had vanished into the passing wind and time, and who suddenly reappeared in the shape of his son, Thovma. You see, this Thovma existed. He really did. Nobody knows whether he was just a storyteller or a mad man who simply imagined things he claimed to actually know. But just ask the priests and the clerics and the rabbis and the mullahs, and all the others of their kind who still exist; ask the saints and the preachers on the mountains and in the valleys. They all claim that belief is knowledge. And this Thovma was a true believer. He believed that he was the son of this Vardan Khatisian from the village of Yedi Su, whose inhabitants had disappeared and whose names had been erased. And so this man, who called himself Thovma – Thovma Khatisian – after the Second World War this Thovma sat around the coffeehouses of Vienna telling peculiar stories to the pompous and well-heeled citizens of the city. Of course, not all of them were pompous and well-heeled. Many of them weren't. And there were Armenians there, too. Survivors of the massacre, people with memories and people who claimed to have none – and they happily listened to what this Thovma had to say. For almost sixty long years, so this Thovma Khatisian claimed, he had gone in search of traces of the past. And he said he would carry on searching until he had pieced together a new story for he, so he said, was an orphan, one that was born on a country road during the massacres of 1915. He would never stop searching.

And that's exactly how it was," said the storyteller. "This man never grew tired of searching. And even as he, too, grew old and was merely months short of his seventy-third birthday, he was still searching.

He wasn't far away from a heart attack. He could feel it; death had often knocked at his door in his dreams. He was sitting in a coffeehouse. And just as he had done so many times before, he told the man sitting opposite him his story, a story which grew with each passing day, often changing but always following the same main thread. But this time the man sitting at his table was Armenian.

– I once met a man whose name was Vardan Khatisian, said the Armenian. It was a long time ago. This man could never find peace. After the First World War he lived in many countries and had changed his citizenship several times. Last I heard he had a Swiss passport.

– A Swiss passport?

– Yes. Although it was under a different name. You see, the Turks once suspected him of being a spy and he was afraid the Swiss wouldn't trust him for that very reason.

– Why wouldn't they trust him?

– Well, people aren't particularly fond of spies here.

– So he went by a different name?

– Yes. The name Vardan Khatisian wasn't written anywhere. But that was what he was called. And he also came from Yedi Su. And he told me of his wife who had a burnt face – in fact, she had no face at all – just eyes: very large, dark eyes. This Vardan Khatisian said her eyes had a strange glow, as if they had seen Christ.

– That man is my father, said the man who called himself Thovma. And the woman with the burnt face and the sacred glow in her eyes is my mother. He was given an address which he went to that same day. But there was nobody there who was called Vardan Khatisian. An older woman opened the door. When he mentioned his father's name and explained to her who he was, she simply replied, 'An Armenian once lived here. It's true. It was a very long time ago. It must be more than forty years ago now. One of them moved in here. 1942 it was.'

– So it was during the war?

– Yes, during the war ... you know, the one we Swiss were spared, thank God ... back then one of those people was renting a room from my parents ... here in this apartment. In those days I was young, very young. Yes, I remember. His Armenian friends called him Vardan Khatisian, a name that he had had changed.

And the woman said, 'This lodger, this Vardan Khatisian, who of course went by a different name, he disappeared a few months later without a trace. It was in spring ... the spring of 1943.'

And the woman said, 'This bearded Jew came to him and knocked on his door. It was one of those unpleasant ones, you know what I mean, an orthodox, with sidelocks and a beard and a fur cap and garlic breath ... I didn't smell it myself, of course ... but I know that those people eat garlic. So he arrived and he knocked on his door. And then the two of them left.'

'Vardan Khatisian,' said the woman. 'He returned once more. And he told me that he was travelling to Poland. I don't know why.'

– Did he travel to Poland?

– I don't know. All I know is that he packed an enormous

suitcase and said that a car was coming to collect him.

And so we can only imagine what happened," say I, the storyteller, to my shadow. "Because sometimes you have no other choice but to find the ultimate truth in the realm of your imagination."

"What was it like?" asked my shadow.

And I say, "Well, it was like this and it was like that."

17

And so I tell my shadow a story for I do not know the ultimate truth that I seek.

No. It's not a Turkish story. And it doesn't begin as all Turkish stories do … *bir varmish, bir yokmush, bir varmish* – once there was one, once there were none, once upon a time … This story has a very different beginning; it begins as Jewish stories do, or like other, similar kinds of story. This is how the tale begins:

"Once upon a time there was an old Polish Jew. He knocked at Vardan Khatisian's door, a man he knew from a local coffeehouse where the two had often chatted.

– I have a business proposition for you, said the Jew.

– I am a poet, said Vardan Khatisian. I don't deal in business.

– Even poets sometimes lend their hand to business, said the Jew. And the proposition I am about to make you is an honest one.

– There's no such thing as honest deal, said Vardan Khatisian.

– Oh, but there is, said the Jew.

– Listen, said the Jew. My entire family is in Poland. The majority of Polish Jews are poor. But my family is an exception.

They are very rich.

– Rich? asked Vardan Khatisian.

– Yes, said the Jew. They own gold and jewels and large suit-cases filled with money. Eventually my family will be taken away. And they won't be able to take either their gold or their jewels or their suitcases of money with them.

– Yes, said Vardan Khatisian. I understand.

– You have a Swiss passport, said the Jew. I don't. That's why I can't travel over there to fetch their valuables.

– You want me to go there and fetch them?

– Yes, said the Jew. That's exactly why I'm here.

And the Jew said, 'I know the Swiss Consul in Warsaw. You will be taken across the border in an embassy car. With your Swiss passport, you shouldn't be given any trouble, not with your visa or with anything else. You will fetch the jewels and the gold and the suitcases full of money, and then the embassy car will bring you back over the border. Have no fear. There won't be any checks. Nothing will happen to you.'

And the Jew said. 'You will do it all for free. Out of the pure goodness of your heart. We won't give you anything: no cut, no commission – not even an advance. Nothing at all.'

– Yes, said Vardan Khatisian. I understand.

– You can't even begin to understand, said the Jew.

And the Jew said, 'You will hold onto the bags of money and the gold and the jewels. Should my relatives survive, you will return it to them after the war. And by that I mean all of it; this deal is an honest one and there will be no commission.'

– And if they don't survive?

– Then it all belongs to you. All of it.

– What are their chances?

– It's difficult to say, said the Jew. Nobody knows for certain where the Jews in Poland are being sent off to and whether or not they will return.

– My relatives have nothing to lose in this deal, said the Jew. How else are they going to smuggle their valuables out of Poland?

– I will return everything to them, said Vardan Khatisian. And should only one of them survive, then I will give that sole survivor everything that the rest owned.

– I see you've understood, said the Jew.

– But if they all die, said Vardan Khatisian, if not a single one of them survives, I will keep the valuables and the money. All of it.

– That's right, said the Jew. You are a poet. I can see that you've understood how all this will work.

– No one stands to lose anything in this deal, said the Jew. You included.

– I don't have anything to lose anyway, said Vardan Khatisian.

– Look …

– And what do you stand to gain?

– Don't worry about me, said the Jew. If just one member of my family survives, he or she surely wouldn't let me starve. After all, I thought the whole thing up.

– And if none of them survive?

– Then you will provide for me, Vardan Khatisian. The Jew smiled for the first time. I know the Armenians, said the Jew.

And I know the Jews. Neither of us ever forgets those who have caused us suffering. But we also never forget those who have shown us kindness.

– That is the truth, said Vardan Khatisian.

And the Jew said, 'That is the truth.'

And so, in the year 1943, Vardan Khatisian travelled to Poland in an embassy car and with a Swiss passport. He arrived in a small town where the Jews had not yet been taken away. They were living in a segregated part of town, but they were all still together. Word quickly spread amongst the Jews about the purpose of Vardan's visit. And as he had a letter of recommendation and kind eyes, the Jews trusted him. It wasn't just the family of the Polish Jew living in Zurich who gave him money and all their valuables, others also came forward and gave him what they had. And the news of Vardan Khatisian's mission spread throughout the land, and messengers came from Jews living all over the country who brought him money and valuables. The Jews hugged and kissed him for this was a type of business deal that met their approval. They knew that this Armenian was an honest man for if the Jew back in Zurich, who was considered a saint by the pious, had sent him, there was no need to doubt the man's scruples.

– If we survive, they said, then you will return everything to us. And if we don't, well, then you won't. In that case we wouldn't need it anyway. They gave Vardan liquor and clinked glasses with him. And they cried tears of joy over this good man and his honest mission.

The embassy car arrived right on time to pick Vardan Khatisian up again. He packed the suitcases and the bundles marked with the name tags of each owner – all of the money and the valuables – into the embassy car and told the driver that he needed to drive to Warsaw to take the luggage to the consulate.

– The Consul will be travelling to Switzerland the day after tomorrow, he told the driver. We'll have to pack it all away again then.

– And then you'll be driving back to Switzerland, too? the driver asked.

And Vardan laughed and said, 'But of course.'

They unpacked the luggage once they reached the consulate. Only once Vardan had made sure that all of it was carefully stored and tucked away inside locked cupboards and doors within the consulate building did he make his way to his hotel.

Vardan Khatisian couldn't remember the last time he slept so well. When he woke up the next morning, he realized that his papers were missing. He rummaged through everything – his coat, his suit, his small suitcase – but, alas, with no luck. He called the guard down at the entrance, complained to the hotel managers, but no one knew who could have taken them.

He called the consulate.

– Do you sleep with the window open? asked the Consul.

– Yes, said Vardan Khatisian.

– And were you in your room the entire time?

– I only left once in the night to go to the toilet. It's outside in the corridor.

– Someone must have done it, said the Consul. Someone was in your room. Perhaps a cleaner or someone else. Who knows?

There are many Poles living underground nowadays. They've gone to ground, you see, and they are in urgent need of new papers.

– What should I do now?

– Nothing, said the Consul. Don't worry. We'll provide you with a temporary passport for now. It's best if you come to the office straightaway.

And so Vardan Khatisian left his hotel to make his way to the consulate. He just happened to leave as a raid was taking place in the same area as his hotel. It was nothing special; just some followers of the New Order and their aides trying to track down a few Jews: stateless lowlifes, so they claimed, that often held false papers, or even none at all, and that sometimes ventured outside of their allocated quarters. Vardan was also arrested as he had dark features and no papers about his person. The New Order's aides took him and a few others to an ordinary-looking train station which stood right next to the hotel. Everything that took place seemed unremarkable to the eyes of passers-by, who showed little concern for they held valid papers. Most of them didn't even look over; others smiled and many grinned maliciously. Even at the station, where large crowds of people stood under guard waiting to be taken away, everything ran smoothly, without much of a stir and no wailing or screaming whatsoever, for the travelers knew that there was no point disrupting the New Order or antagonizing their followers.

The overcrowded, barred freight trains left the station without incident. It was stiflingly hot in Vardan's wagon even though it wasn't yet summer, but that could be explained by the fact that the people inside were so tightly packed together: They were warming up the wagon with their body heat. The people were quiet, including the children. Even the infants didn't dare whine and instead sucked silently on their mothers' breasts. The farther the train travelled from the city, the quieter the people became for they had realized that they could do nothing to change their fate. This was not the time for complaining. Even Vardan knew that. And so he said to himself, 'You could complain to the Swiss consulate, but it's far away. And there isn't a telephone or a post office anywhere near. And it's impossible to speak to the escorts on this train.'

Vardan saw the Polish landscape through his barred window and he recognized it as the same landscape that he had seen from the window of his car just a few days before. The fresh scent of the early months of the year and the bright sky were the same. Among the few clouds, and travelling with the biting wind, flocks of birds passed by. They came from far away, and he knew that they were the first to return to Poland with the arrival of spring – but that they would be the last that they would lay eyes upon in this life.

For days the train continued in a straight line. At least, that's how it seemed to him. A few elderly passengers died of hunger and thirst and exhaustion. And they lay where they expired. As there were no toilets and as the doors were never opened, people relieved themselves there and then. There was nowhere to sit or lie, and so the travelers simply pissed or shat themselves where they stood. Nobody seemed to mind.

Eventually the train came to a halt. Here the landscape was different. Here there was barbed wire. And behind the barbed wire stood large ovens that pumped out endless plumes of smoke. As the people in the wagon were hungry and thirsty and had begun hallucinating, they thought the ovens were part of one large bakery. And where there was bread, there would surely be water, too.

One of the Jews said, 'They're taking us to a bakery.'

Another said, 'They promised us work. They probably want us to bake bread.'

– Are you all bakers? asked Vardan.

– No, said one of the Jews. But there's nothing that can't be learned. Even baking. They will retrain us.

The train stood on the empty platform for a long time. All the jolting and jerking had stopped. The locomotive's hissing had also ceased. As the doors still remained closed, some of the Jews poked their noses through the small barred window, and one of them had a very keen nose.

'It smells strange,' he said to the others. 'It doesn't smell of bread.' Now the others seemed to have noticed the smell, too. One of the Jews suddenly screamed, 'It smells like human flesh.'

Some of the Jews began to cry, others screamed. But Vardan tried to reassure them. 'Calm down,' he said. 'There's no need to get upset. Listen to me. I'm going to tell you a story.'

And Vardan told them the story of Max and Moritz, two mischievous boys who tried to steal from a baker and ended up in his oven. When the tale was over, the Jews were calm. Some of them even laughed. One of them said, 'It really is just a story;

such a tale can't possibly be true.'

– Max and Moritz were turned into bread, said Vardan. The master baker simply turned them both into dough and put them in the oven.

– A story, said the Jews. Nothing but a story.

– Of course it's only a story, said Vardan.

– And who wrote it?

– A German by the name of Wilhelm Busch.

– A German story, said the Jews.

– One day we should erect a statue to this Wilhelm Busch fellow, said one of the Jews, for he has reassured us that Germans would only do such things in fairytales.

– Indeed, said one of the others, who looked like a rabbi. This Wilhelm Busch character should be proclaimed the Jews' favorite German writer for he has taken away our fear of the Germans.

Vardan had to tell them the story of Max and Moritz again and what happened when the two boys were baked. And the Jews listened to his words and as he finished the story, they began to laugh heartily. They were no longer afraid. They felt reassured. It was then that the doors were yanked open."

18

"Among all the souls of the gassed and burnt bodies of the Jews who were also sitting on the chimney of the incinerator that day, sat the souls of a Turk and an Armenian, whose name was Vardan Khatisian.

— What brings you here? Vardan asked the Turk.

— And what brings you here? asked the Turk.

— I was in Warsaw on business, said Vardan.

— Are you a businessman?

— No, said Vardan. I'm a poet.

— I was in Warsaw on business, too, said the Turk. And I'm also a poet.

— Did you lose your papers?

— Yes, said the Turk. I lost them and then they simply took me away during a raid.

— What are we actually waiting for? asked the Turk.

— For the signal to depart, said Vardan.

— And where are we flying to?

— I don't know, said Vardan.

– You know, a Turk shouldn't actually fly up to heaven alongside an Armenian, said the Turk.

– And why not?

– Because of a story a Meddah on one of the great bazaars once told me.

– What kind of story? asked Vardan.

– Just a story, said the Turk

And the Turk said, 'Once there was one. Once there were none. Once upon a time … Once upon a time there was a dead Turk whose soul was flying off to heaven alongside the soul of a dead Armenian.

– What are you so jolly about? asked the Armenian.

– I'm going to heaven, said the Turk. All faithful Muslims are assured a place in heaven, you see. In paradise, no less.

– And the infidels?

– They go to hell.

– But you won't be able to truly appreciate the wonders of paradise, said the Armenian, for only one who has known evil can appreciate the good.

– What do you mean?

– Well, let me tell you, said the Armenian. Anyone who has seen the depths of hell for just one second will savor paradise twice or even three times as much, for he has seen the other side.

– You're right, said the Turk. Makes perfect sense.

– I feel sorry for you, said the Armenian, for you will never fully appreciate the joys of paradise because you have never seen hell.

– So what should I do? asked the Turk.

– I don't know, said the Armenian. But have a think. I'm sure you'll come up with something.

And so the Turk thought for a moment and said: How about if the two of us swap clothes? I'll put on your black cloak and visit hell for just a fraction of a second so that later I can say that I've seen it. And you, Armenian … you put on my white cloak so that you can take a look at paradise for a fraction of a second.

– Sounds like a good idea, said the Armenian.

And that is exactly what the two men did. When the pair arrived at Allah's gate, the Archangel Gabriel was away. His replacement, a young, inexperienced angel, wasn't entirely sure how the job worked.

– We swapped cloaks, said the Turk to the angel. You see, I want to take a look at hell for a fraction of a second and the Armenian wishes to see paradise. It will do me good. I'll be much happier afterwards when I'm in paradise. And it will do this infidel good, too: he should see what he's missing.

The angel didn't care either way. And so he led the Turk down to hell and took the Armenian to paradise. And as there is no return from either of these destinations, the Turk rots in hell for all eternity while the Armenian basks in paradise.'

– That's a nice story, said Vardan. But why are you telling me that now?

– Because a Turk cannot trust an Armenian, said the Turk. Not even in death.

– Are you really afraid to fly up to heaven with me?

– Yes, said the Turk. I am.

The Jews had overheard the story and didn't know what to make of it. One of them said, 'Did you all see that? Even dead men's souls have prejudices. What on earth should we expect if even souls have no faith in one another?'

The Jews cursed to themselves for a while. But then they calmed down for the Lord God gave them all the signal to fly away.

And then all the souls rose up and flew off together to heaven. All that was left were the last thoughts of their mortal bodies for they were immortal and destined to wander the earth, together with all the dreams and hopes that ever touch a human in the course of their life, for all eternity.

Vardan's Last Thought was also sitting on the chimney of the incinerator. After all the thoughts had cleaned their wings, they too took flight. Many of the Jews flew back to the land where the Final Solution had been created because that was their home; others flew to other countries. But most of them flew to Jerusalem.

Vardan had lost sight of the Turk. He soared high up into the air and flew after the Jews who were heading towards Jerusalem. He flew very fast, faster and faster, until eventually he caught up with the Jews.
  – Where are you flying to?
  – Jerusalem.
  – Jerusalem?

– Yes.

– Are you passing over Turkey?

– Of course. It's on the way. Haven't you ever seen a map?

– I've forgotten many things.

– What are you looking for in Turkey?

– The land of Hayastan.

– Hayastan?

– Yes.

As they flew over Mount Ararat, Vardan heard a voice. It came from outer space. 'I will send you an eagle,' said the voice. 'And you will climb down onto its wings.'

– And what if it isn't an eagle? said Vardan. What if it's just a mosquito that I'm supposed to climb down onto? What will I do then? The flies will eat the mosquito and then I'll never reach Hayastan.

– You Armenians are so distrusting, said the voice. You're like the Jews. No faith in the world!

– How can you expect us to still have any faith left? asked Vardan.

– You make a fair point there.

– Will you really send me an eagle?

– Yes, I'll send you an eagle.

And Vardan flew on the wings of an eagle to Mount Ararat. And then farther down into the vast Armenian land known as *Hayastan*. Vardan saw that he wasn't the only thought who would be living down there: the Armenians' thoughts were everywhere. They were in every flower, on every blade of grass, on the buds of the trees.

And the day drew to a close. And night fell. A whisper of voices rose up from the heads of the flowers and from the buds of the trees. And the whisper emanated from the grass and from across the entire landscape.

– The Turks have nightmares when they hear the Armenians of the night whisper, said the voice. In fact, it terrifies everyone in this region.

– Where are my parents? asked Vardan. Where are my brothers and sisters? Where are all the people that I loved? And where is my wife?

– They are here, said the voice.

And Vardan suddenly saw his family. And he saw his wife, who was perched on top of a flower.

– Have you come back to me? asked Anahit.

– I have come back to you, said Vardan.

Vardan greeted all those he had ever cared for in his life and then returned to Anahit.

– It's a shame that our son Thovma isn't here, he said to Anahit.

– It is a shame, Anahit echoed. How I wish he could be by my side.

– I wish I had been able to see him, said Vardan.

– For years I have dreamt of him, said Anahit, and I have tried to imagine how he might look.

– So have I, said Vardan.

– In fact, our son isn't called Thovma at all, said Anahit, for you see, back then when they set fire to me in the church, I had a dream.

– What kind of dream?

– I dreamed that I climbed through the flames to save Thovma, little Thovma in my belly. The flames didn't touch me for I was carrying something holy inside my body. There was a huge crowd in front of the only air vent because everyone wanted to be the first through, but people stepped aside when they saw that I was pregnant. And after I had safely made it through the flames and effortlessly crawled through the narrow air vent, despite my large belly, I fled under the cover of darkness. For some time I wandered around the mountains until one day those henchmen came and caught me. And every day the sun rose and set. And I dreamed of a death march on a country road along the bank of the Euphrates. There I saw myself, right in the middle of the saptiehs and all the many sorrowful people. I dreamed the contractions had already started for I was nine months pregnant and had to find a place to deliver my child. When the time came, I simply lay down on the road. And one of the saptiehs slit my belly open with his bayonet. – And look, can you see? Little Thovma crawled out. He looked so sweet: so small and mucky and innocent. Then I heard a voice and that voice said, 'This one shouldn't be called Thovma: His name is Hayk.'

– Hayk? asked Vardan. Just like the first Armenian?

– Exactly, said Anahit.

– It wasn't a dream, said Vardan. It's the truth.

– What truth? asked Anahit.

– The other truth that couldn't be destroyed by the flames.

- So I really was on that country road?
- Of course you were.
- And that's where I gave birth.
- Yes, Anahit.
- And I bore you a son?
- You gave birth to my son.

Many years would pass before Thovma, who was now called Hayk, would find his way back to his parents. But as thoughts have no sense of time, Vardan and Anahit didn't even notice just how many years came and went as they waited. They often spoke of their son. And one day they both raised their eyes to heaven. And look, there it came: the Last Thought of Thovma Khatisian flying down from the sky. His name was now Hayk. That really was his name. The two beckoned to him, and Thovma, who was now called Hayk, just like the first ever Armenian, recognized them instantly.

Hayk kissed and hugged his father. Then he fluttered towards his mother and perched atop her large milk-filled breasts.

- I never breastfed you, did I? said his mother. Why don't you shrink down until you are very small so that I can finally give you my breast?

- I'm already tiny again, said Hayk. Can't you see? And I'm drinking your sweet milk.

On a neighboring flower sat a former Armenian priest. He watched as Anahit, the mother of Armenia, found her lost son. 'Hayk will become fertile and have many offspring,' he thought. 'And Hayk's children and their children's children will populate the land that was always destined for them.'

And he held this thought for a long time. And all the other thoughts heard the voice of his thought and thought exactly the same."

Epilogue

"You opened your eyes again," said the voice of the storyteller inside Thovma Khatisian's head.

"Will it be the last time?"

"It will be the last time."

"Where is my Last Thought?"

"It's still inside your head."

"And the story?"

"Perhaps it wasn't a story."

"What do you mean?"

"I simply told you how it could be and what might happen when the Last Thought finally takes its leave."

"When will it go?"

"Soon."

And the voice of the storyteller inside my head becomes softer. Soon it will vanish completely and I won't hear anything. It will all become very quiet.

I know that my Last Thought will fly back into the gaps in the Turkish history books. And with this knowledge, I shall die more peacefully than those who have gone before me without it.

– Minister, I'm flying back!

– Where to, Mr. Khatisian?

– Into the gaps in your history books.

– But Mr. Khatisian, I cannot allow you to do that!

– And why?

– Because I might find it unsettling.

– I'm sure it will unsettle quite a few people, I say, when the last thoughts of the dead Armenians in the land of Hayastan whisper.

– Do you believe that, Mr. Khatisian?

– I do, Minister.

– But whispers are contagious, said the minister. The whispers of those dead Armenians could force their way over the borders and be heard by ears everywhere.

– Possibly.

– Other voices might start to whisper, even those who have never dared raise their whispering voices before. There would be a huge cacophony of whispers if all the victims that ever walked this earth suddenly began voicing their whispered lamentations. The whole world would drown in a sea of whispers. And where would we end up then? No, no, I won't allow it, Mr. Khatisian. Some of us will come down with stomachache as the whispers of those victims upset our digestion. We might start contemplating and all that contemplation would give us a headache. And have you given a thought to the nightmares that will rob us of our sleep? Who would want that? And what would be the point?

– Not everything has to have a point, Minister, said Thovma Khatisian. And with that, he breathed his last breath.

Glossary

The Turkish and Armenian words used in this book have not been written in accordance with the reformed Turkish script as these language reforms only took place after the First World War. Instead, I have mostly used standard Ottoman spelling as seen in translations[1] published prior to World War One. Some Ottoman words, notably Persian and Arabic loanwords, were discouraged from use during Turkey's language reforms, which began in 1928, and can no longer be found in any modern dictionary.

The plot and all characters that appear in this novel are fictitious; the story is based on true historical events.

Alk (Arm.)	Ghost/spirit
Araba (Turk.)	Carriage
Arabadji (Turk.)	Coachman

---

1   Translator's note: German translations were referenced in the author's original work. English translations from the period were used in this translation.

Atschket louis (Arm.)	Light in your eyes (expression of congratulation)
Bairam (Turk.)	Religious festival
Baklava (Turk.)	Sweet pastry, dessert
Bashi-bazouk (Turk.)	Irregular soldier of the Ottoman army
Bash-Khatib Agah (Turk.)	Chief Scribe (form of address)
Bedel (Turk.)	Tax paid for exemption from the military
Bismillah (Turk.)	In the name of God
Chiaus (Turk.)	Sergeant in the Ottoman Army
Chibouk (Turk.)	Turkish tobacco pipe
Dede (Turk.)	Grandfather
Doshek (Turk.)	Mattress
Efendi (Turk.)	Sir
Efendiler (Turk.)	Gentlemen
Ekmek (Turk.)	Bread
Fedayee (Turk.)	Self-sacrificers
Frank (Turk.)	Colloquial term for a European
Frankistan (Turk.)	Colloquial term for Europe

Gatnachpjur (Arm.)	Well of milk, also a traditional milk-based dish
Gelin (Turk.)	Bride
Giaour (Turk.)	Infidel
Ginka mair (arm.)	Godmother
Hadig (Arm.)	Sweet jelly dish, blancmange
Hafiz (Turk.)	Someone who has memorized the Qur'an
Hamal (Turk.)	Laborer
Hamam (Turk.)	Steam bath
Harissa (Arm.)	Meat and barley stew, Armenian national dish
Hars (Arm.)	Bride
Hayastan (Arm.)	Armenia
Hodja (Turk.)	Teacher
Hukumet (Turk.)	Government building
Inshallah (Turk.)	God willing
Jorgan (Turk.)	Blanket
Kahvedji (Turk.)	Coffee seller
Kahvehane (Turk.)	Coffeehouse
Kaimakam (Turk.)	District governor
Karagoz (Turk.)	Turkish shadow puppetry
Kaza (Turk.)	Borough

Kelim (Turk.)	Decorative wall-hanging, carpet
Kiblah (Turk.)	Direction Muslims face during prayer
Kismet (Turk.)	Fate
Konak (Turk.)	Building
Kulah (Turk.)	Conical lambskin hat
Kutan (Arm.)	Large plow
Lavash (Arm.)	Bread
Madsun (Arm.)	Yogurt
Magus (pl. magi) (Pers.)	Priest
Mahalle (Turk.)	District which is home to a particular ethnic group
Mahdi (Turk.)	Holy figure in Islam
Meddah (Turk.)	Storyteller
Meron (Arm.)	Holy oil
Mirza Selim (Turk.)	The honorable Selim (form of address)
Mobed (Pers.)	Priest
Moonch (Arm.)	A vow of silence taken by a young bride
Mudir (Turk.)	Governor, chief of police and head of the gendarmerie
Muezzin (Turk.)	Person who recites the call to prayer
Muhajir(s) (Turk.)	Emigrant(s)

Mukhtar (Turk.)	Mayor
Mullah (Turk.)	Honorary religious title
Mustahfiz (Turk.)	Second-class/last reservists
Mutasarrif (Turk.)	District administrator
Namaz (Turk.)	A ritualistic prayer
Nargileh (Turk.)	Hookah pipe
Nazar (Turk.)	Eye/eyesight, also: charm to ward off the evil eye
Oda (Turk.)	Living room
Oghi (Arm.)	Armenian spirit
Oke (Turk.)	Unit of weight
Padishah (Turk.)	Highest-ranking territorial lord
Para (Turk.)	Smallest monetary unit in the Ottoman Empire
Patat (Arm.)	Grape leaves stuffed with rice and meat
Pativ (Arm.)	Honor
Pokhint (Arm.)	Sweet dessert
Rayah (Turk.)	Nonbeliever, also: subject or flock
Rayah tax	Tax payable by rayah
Sanjak (Turk.)	Large administrative area
Saptieh (Turk.)	Ottoman military police officer

Sebil (Turk.)	Public water fountain built outside a mosque, also: a kiosk distributing free water
Selamlik (Turk.)	Large living space, reception room, living room
Shalvar (Turk.)	Loose-fitting trousers gathered at the ankle
Shapkali (Turk.)	Hat wearer
Shekerli (Turk.)	Sugar-sweet
Shekerli celebration	Celebration of sweetness, also: a celebration to mark a child's first steps
Sinek kagidi (Turk.)	Flycatcher
Sofra (Turk.)	Tray
Stambul	District of Constantinople
Tavla (Turk.)	Dice game, similar to backgammon
Tebk (Arm.)	A key event, also: massacre
Teskere (Turk.)	Passport
Tezek (Turk.)	Dried cow dung burnt to produce heat
Tonir (Arm.)	Fireplace, oven
Vali (Turk.)	Governor of the province
Vartabed (Arm.)	Priest
Vilayet (Turk.)	Province

Yayli (Turk.)	More sophisticated (horse-drawn) carriage
Yedi Su (Turk.)	Seven Waters